A Nazareth Manifesto

A Nazareth Manifesto

Being With God

Samuel Wells

WILEY Blackwell

Library of Congress Cataloging-in-Publication Data is available for this title
Hardback ISBN: 9780470673256
Paperback ISBN: 9780470673263

A catalogue record for this book is available from the British Library.

Cover image: Fraser Ayres and Will Adamsdale in Stuart: A Life Backwards, by
Alexander Masters, Edinburgh 2013. Photo © Robbie Jack

Set in 10.5/13 pt Minion Pro by Aptara
Printed and bound in Malaysia by Vivar Printing Sdn Bhd

1   2015

For Stanley

Contents

Part IV: Explorations   **229**

Part V: Implications   **269**

Prologue

The Most Important Word

This sermon, on the text John 1:1–14, was preached in Duke University Chapel, Durham, North Carolina, on December 24, 2010.

I want to describe to you three scenes that I'm guessing will be familiar to everyone here. And then I want to think with you about what these three scenes have in common.

The first is your relationship with the most difficult member of your family. Let's say it's your father. You spend some time in the stores after Thanksgiving and you find presents for most of your friends and colleagues and family. But somehow you have no idea what to give your father. It bothers you because deep down it feels like your inability to know what present will make your father happy is symbolic of your lifelong confusion about what might truly make your father happy – especially where you're concerned. So in the end you spend more than you meant to on something you don't really believe he wants, pathetically trying to throw money at the problem but inwardly cursing yourself because you know that what you're buying isn't the answer. When Christmas Day comes and your father opens the present, you see in his forced smile and his half-hearted hug of thanks that you've failed yet again to do something for him that might overcome the chasm between you.

Here's a second scene. You have family or friends from out of town coming for Christmas. You want everything to be perfect for them and you exchange a flurry of emails about who's going to sleep where, and whether it's all right for them to bring the dog. You get into a frenzy of shopping and baking, and you're actually a little anxious that you'll forget something or burn something, so the kitchen becomes your empire, and you can't bear for someone to interrupt you, and even at Christmas dinner you're mostly checking the gravy or reheating the carrots, and as you say goodbye to them you hug and say, "It's such a shame we never really talked while you were

A Nazareth Manifesto, Samuel Wells © 2015 John Wiley & Sons, Ltd. Published 2015 by John Wiley & Sons, Ltd.

here," and, when they've finally left, you collapse in a heap, maybe in tears of exhaustion.

Here's a third scene. You feel there's something empty or lacking in the cosy Christmas with family and friends, and your heart is breaking for people having a tough time in the cold, in isolation, in poverty, or in grief. So you gather together presents for children of prisoners or turn all your Christmas gifts into vouchers representing your support of a house or a cow or two buffaloes for people who need the resources more than you and your friends do.

What do all these scenes have in common? I want to suggest to you that they're all based on one tiny word: it's the word for. When we care about those for whom Christmas is a tough time, we want to do something for them. When we want our houseguests to enjoy their Christmas visit, our impulse is to spend our whole time doing things for them, whether cooking dinner or constantly clearing the house or arranging activities to keep them busy. When we feel our relationship with our father is faltering, our instinct is to do something for him that somehow melts his heart and makes everything all right.

And those gestures of for matter because they sum up a whole life in which we try to make relationships better, try to make the world better, try to be better people ourselves by doing things for people. We praise the self-lessness of those who spend their lives doing things for people. People still sign letters "Your obedient servant," because they want to tell each other "I'm eager to do things for you." When we feel noble we hum Art Garfunkel singing, "Like a bridge over troubled water, I will lay me down ..." – presumably for you to walk over me without getting your dainty feet wet. When we feel romantic we put on the husky voice and turn into Bryan Adams singing "Everything I do – I do it for you."

It seems that the word that epitomizes being an admirable person, the word that sums up the spirit of Christmas, is for. We cook for, we buy presents for, we offer charity for, all to say we lay ourselves down for. But there's a problem here. All these gestures are generous, and kind, and in some cases sacrificial and noble. They're good gestures, warm-hearted, admirable gestures. But somehow they don't go to the heart of the problem. You give your father the gift, and the chasm still lies between you. You wear yourself out in showing hospitality, but you've never actually had the conversation with your loved ones. You make fine gestures of charity, but the poor are still strangers to you. For is a fine word, but it doesn't dismantle resentment, it doesn't overcome misunderstanding, it doesn't deal with alienation, it doesn't overcome isolation.

Most of all, for isn't the way God celebrates Christmas. God doesn't set the world right at Christmas. God doesn't shower us with good things at Christmas. God doesn't mount up blessings upon us and then get miserable and stroppy when we open them all up and fail to be sufficiently excited or surprised or grateful. For isn't what God shows us at Christmas.

In some ways we wish it was. We'd love God to make everything happy and surround us with perfect things. When we get cross with God, it's easy to feel God isn't keeping the divine side of the bargain – to do things for us now and forever.

But God shows us something else at Christmas. God speaks a rather different word. The angel says to Joseph, "Behold, the virgin shall conceive and bear a son, and they shall name him Emmanuel, which means, 'God is with us.'" (Matt. 1:23) And then in John's gospel, we get the summary statement of what Christmas means: "The Word became flesh and lived among [with] us" (John 1:14). It's an unprepossessing little word, but this is the word that lies at the heart of Christmas and at the heart of the Christian faith. The word is with.

Think back to the very beginning of all things. John's gospel says, "The Word was with God. He was in the beginning with God ... Without him not one thing came into being" (John 1:1–3). In other words, before anything else, there was a with. The with between God and the Word, or as Christians came to call it, between the Father and the Son. With is the most fundamental thing about God. And then think about how Jesus concludes his ministry. His very last words in Matthew's gospel are, "Behold, I am with you always" (28:20). In other words, "There will never be a time when I am not with." And at the very end of the Bible, when the book of Revelation describes the final disclosure of God's everlasting destiny, this is what the voice from heaven says: "See, the home of God is among mortals. He will dwell with them as their God; they will be his peoples, and God himself will be with them" (Rev. 21:3).

We've stumbled upon the most important word in the Bible – the word that describes the heart of God and the nature of God's purpose and destiny for us. And that word is with. That's what God was in the very beginning, that's what God sought to instil in the creation of all things, that's what God was looking for in making the covenant with Israel, that's what God coming among us in Jesus was all about, that's what the sending of the Holy Spirit meant, that's what our destiny in the company of God will look like. It's all in that little word with. God's whole life and action and purpose are shaped to be with us.

In a lot of ways, with is harder than for. You can do for without a conversation, without a real relationship, without a genuine shaping of your life to accommodate and incorporate the other. The reason your Christmas present for your father is doomed is not because for is wrong, not because there's anything bad about generosity; it's because the only solution is for you and your father to be with each other long enough to hear each other's stories and tease out the countless misunderstandings and hurts that have led your relationship beyond the point of being rescued by the right Christmas present. The reason why you collapse in tears when your guests have gone home is because the hard work is finding out how you can share the different responsibilities and genuinely be with one another in the kitchen and elsewhere that make a stay of several nights a joy of with rather than a burden of for. What makes attempts at Christmas charity seem a little hollow is not that they're not genuine and helpful and kind but that what isolated and grieving and impoverished people usually need is not gifts or money but the faithful presence with them of someone who really cares about them as a person. It's the "with" they desperately want, and the "for" on its own (whether it's food, presents, or money) can't make up for the lack of that "with."

But we all fear the with, because the with seems to ask more of us than we can give. We'd all prefer to keep charity on the level of for, where it can't hurt us. We all know that more families struggle over Christmas than any other time. Maybe that's because you can spend the whole year being busy and doing things for your family, but when there's nothing else to do but be with one another you realize that being with is harder than doing for – and sometimes it's just too hard. Sometimes New Year comes as a relief as we can go back to doing for and leave aside being with for another year.

And that's why it's glorious, almost incredible, good news that God didn't settle on for. At Christmas God said unambiguously, "I am with. Behold, my dwelling is among you. I've moved into the neighborhood. I will be with you always. My name is Emmanuel, God with us." Sure, there was an element of for in Jesus' life. He was for us when he healed and taught, he was for us when he died on the cross, he was for us when he rose from the grave and ascended to heaven. These are things that only God can do and we can't do. But the power of these things God did for us lies in that they were based on his being with us. God has not abolished for. But God, this night, in becoming flesh in Jesus, has said there will never again be a for that's not based on a fundamental, unalterable, everlasting, and utterly unswerving with. That's the good news of Christmas.

And how do we celebrate this good news? By being with people in poverty and distress even when there's nothing we can do for them. By being with people in grief and sadness and loss even when there's nothing to say. By being with and listening to and walking with those we find most difficult rather than trying to fob them off with a gift or a face-saving gesture. By being still with God in silent prayer rather than rushing in our anxiety to do yet more things for God. By taking an appraisal of all our relationships and asking ourselves, "Does my doing for arise out of a fundamental commitment to be with, or is my doing for driven by my profound desire to avoid the discomfort, the challenge, the patience, the loss of control involved in being with?"

No one could be more tempted to retreat into doing for than God. God, above all, knows how exasperating, ungrateful, thoughtless and self-destructive company we can be. Most of the time we just want God to fix it, and spare us the relationship. But that's not God's way. God could have done it all alone. But God chose not to. God chose to do it with us. Even though it cost the cross. That's the wonder of Christmas. That's the amazing good news of the word with.

Introduction

God Is With Us

God is with us. These four words express the character of God, the identity of Jesus, the work of the Spirit. They are the Christian testimony about the past, witness in the present, and hope for the future. Each word offers itself as the heart of the gospel.

Thus the gospel is first and last about "God." God's nature and purpose are expressed by the three words that follow ("is with us"). No words can define God, if definition means to limit, to circumscribe, or to prescribe. God is the root, the rhyme, and the reason for all things. God is goodness, truth, and beauty. God is before all things and after all things. Without God, is not anything that is. Yet without the three words that follow, this central statement of Christian heritage, conviction, and destiny has no context, no theatre in which to reverberate, no relationship in which to matter. God does not *need* context; indeed the interrelationship of the persons of the Trinity indicates that the Godhead has an inner context of its own: all other context is secondary and dependent on God. Context is a fruit of grace.

The second word declares that the gospel is about now. God "is." In that brief statement lies faith that God is always present. For sure, God has acted and will fulfill: but most of all, God *is* – is here, is present, is now. "Is" means the incarnation, the passion, and the coming of the Spirit have abiding, not just fleeting, significance: they are past events but have permanent dynamics. Meanwhile Jesus' resurrection constitutes the "is" event par excellence: it guarantees that not even death can dismantle God's "is." Without the resurrection, the incarnation might be simply a past event – a "was" ("God was in Christ"). Without Pentecost, the Ascension might mark the conclusion of the human encounter with the living Lord. But resurrection and Pentecost ensure the definitive action of God in Christ remains a present event – an "is." God exists, and perhaps alone truly exists: all other existence is by analogy with, and by the gift of, the true being, which is God.

A Nazareth Manifesto, Samuel Wells © 2015 John Wiley & Sons, Ltd. Published 2015 by John Wiley & Sons, Ltd.

This is the simplicity of truth: there is no frenzy of activity – there is simply abiding existence. God is. This is the faith of Israel, the name of the God of Moses, the unflinching underpinning of reality.

These are claims long held, from the beginning, to be central to Christianity. But the third word has not always been held in such high regard as the first two – or dwelt upon quite so acutely. This book seeks imagine what theology and ethics would be like if it were. My argument abides in the "with" of God. God is with. God's whole being is shaped to be with. Being with is about presence, about participation, about partnership. It is not about eliding difference, or denying separation, or neglecting otherness. On the contrary, it is about being present in such a way that such contrasts and tensions are made visible, recognized, named, and embraced, rather than ignored, suppressed, or exploited. Being present is above all a Trinitarian condition. God is three persons in one substance. In other words, God isn't a thing, an achievement, an edifice, a piece of technology, an impressive vision, even a dazzling light, or a blazing fire. God is a relationship. God is a relationship of three persons, so wonderfully shaped toward one another, so wondrously *with* one another, that they are one, but so exquisitely diverse and distinct within that unity that they are three. With is the key to the identity of the God who is.

These three words together become focused on the fourth word: "us." This is the wonder of grace. Us – humanity, set amidst the good creation – is the object of God's attention, made subject in the miraculous word "with." This is not an exclusive choice, with losers and outsiders; it is an inclusive covenant, held with fierce intensity, as if each one were the only one. And this relationship, at the same time personal and corporate, is made permanent in the abiding affirmation of "is." This, then, is the axis of Christian faith: that God, whose being is "with" – the inner interrelationship of the three persons of the Trinity – is not just "with" within, but determines to be with externally: to be with *us*. God's whole life is shaped by the permanent resolve never to be except to *be with us*. Here is the direction, the fixed purpose, the orienting goal of the ordering of God's life: *being with us*. This, indeed, is henceforth the name of God: if we are asked who God is, what God is called, what is God's nature, what we most fundamentally answer is that God is "with us."

Each moment of salvation history bears the character of God being with us. *Creation* is God making a context in which to be with us, and a theater in which we may discover how to be with one another and with God. Humanity's *fall* distorts that creation. It interrupts God's being with us, and ours with God and with one another, such that our lives become grievous to God, to one another and to ourselves, and God's life becomes grievous to us. The *covenant* – liberation, law, and land – crystallizes God's resolve to be with Israel, and thus to be with all peoples and the whole creation, through sustained and personal encounter. The *exile* is the season par excellence when Israel discovers that even sin, even estrangement, even loss of tangible signs of land, king, and temple, cannot break, but only refine God's resolve to be with. The *incarnation* is the disclosure of God's utter commitment to be with us, and of the grace that such an orientation is at the heart of God's identity. *Salvation* is God isolating the process by which being with became a constraint, a curse, and a threat, God finding ways to dismantle such distortions, and God restoring our being with ourselves, with one another, and with God so that it becomes an abiding blessing and an abundant joy. *Church* is being with God, one another, and ourselves, and celebrating and embodying the ways such restoration takes place. *Kingdom* names the ways God brings about this restoration sometimes regardless of, sometimes in spite of, sometimes alongside, and sometimes through the church. And *eschaton* names the final existence of God and the whole creation being with one another with all curses and threats having passed away. Thus every dimension of theology finds its telos in God being with us.

These, then, are the two dynamics that lie at the center of all things: God's perfect inner relationship, which we have just considered; and God's very life shaped to be in relationship with us through Jesus in the power of the Holy Spirit. Both are characterized by the preposition "with." The task of theology, I suggest, is to describe that "with." The task of theological ethics is to inhabit and imitate it. Such is the purpose of this book.

1

Being With

Argument

My argument is as follows. I maintain that the word with is the most important word in theology. Hence the Prologue, which articulates that conviction as best and as succinctly as I am able. This is not an Anglican theology that sacralizes the created order by claiming divine participation in it through Christ. It is an enquiry into whether with is the pervading theme that runs through Trinity, creation, incarnation, atonement, the sending of the Spirit, ecclesiology, and eschatology.

In Part I, I come from two angles to the same arrival point. In Chapter 3 I argue that the human project in the West has been to secure life against limitation in general and mortality in particular, but that such efforts have only deepened the true predicament, which is isolation. In Chapter 4 I suggest that efforts at reconciliation fail because Christians invariably approach the situation with exasperation and impatience, whereas it turns out that there is no gospel that is not reconciliation – and restored relationship is the epicenter of God's mission.

In Part II, I continue this introductory survey of the significance of with by first exploring, in Chapter 5, how with is the central theme, not just of Jesus' ministry, but of the whole scriptural narrative. I then in Chapter 6 narrow down on what I judge to be the single most important story in the Bible for grasping my argument – the parable of the Good Samaritan – and show how the way the story is read reveals people's commitments and assumptions about social engagement and their status before God. Then in Chapter 7 I offer a critique of the other three modes of engagement – working for, working with, and being for – to explain why I make the bold claims for being with that are to be found in Chapter 2.

A Nazareth Manifesto, Samuel Wells © 2015 John Wiley & Sons, Ltd. Published 2015 by John Wiley & Sons, Ltd.

Part III is the center of the book. Those who have perhaps read *Living Without Enemies*, and are convinced of the centrality of being with, and wish to know more what it involves and implies, might want simply to start here. Chapter 8 is the numerical and thematic heart of the argument. Here I outline eight dimensions of being with in philosophical and pastoral perspective. In the following chapter I suggest what it means to see Jesus as the embodiment of the phrase "God with us." Then in Chapter 10, Chapter 11, and Chapter 12 I explore and illustrate the ways being with has been played out in a carefully chosen range of contexts.

In Part IV, I make a start on what could well be a much larger project – to imagine the implications of being with for theology and ethics. Chapter 13 offers some pointers within some of the conventional theological loci, and Chapter 14 looks in detail at one particular approach to social engagement that I judge to have promising resonances with my argument.

In Part V, by way of summary and review, I anticipate what I expect to be the two most consistent criticisms of my argument. In Chapter 15 I set out what being with means in relation to more conventional working-for and working-with notions of justice and in the process offer a model by which one may set these different approaches side-by-side as complementary forms of engagement. Then in Chapter 16 I look at suffering and consider ways in which being with clarifies what is at stake in Christian witness in the face of suffering. In the end, being with rests on a renewed notion and practice of prayer.

The book concludes in the Epilogue as it began in the Prologue, with a sermon: this time with a simple, tangible encounter that seeks to epitomize the hopefulness and humble spirit of the book, and affirms that being with one another and with God are not, ultimately, two different things.

I should add a note on style, assumptions, and forebears.

Style

I have published conventional academic monographs and works in a more homiletic vein, introductory works to ethics and other subjects, and more provocative and exploratory works in new areas. This book includes elements of all of these. I am a scholar and a practitioner, a writer and a speaker, a pastor and a broadcaster, a theologian and a priest, a preacher and an academic. It became clear in the writing that this book was going to find it difficult to settle in one genre alone. I trust this comes across as an asset rather than a defect.

The reason the style varies is that I am trying to do several things in the same book. The early chapters are seeking to persuade the reader that there really is a practical and theological problem with the way social engagement is conventionally carried out. They make this argument in a direct and somewhat popular style. I am not seeking to amass data to compel agreement; I am setting out to capture the reader's imagination to see the world a whole different way. The theological and practical arguments cannot, in the end, be disentangled from one another, so for example in Chapter 3 and Chapter 4 they are intermingled. Likewise I see the move to being with fundamentally as a conversion, and so I begin and end the book with a prologue and epilogue that suggest a whole outlook on life that I do not finally know how to communicate other than in a homiletic genre.

The surveys of biblical and theological themes are similarly not intended to offer comprehensive analysis of a century of scholarly writing on the subjects they cover. Instead they seek to paint broad brushstrokes that locate anomalies, highlight key questions, and point to fertile areas of development. Almost any chapter in the book could have developed into a book in its own right, so the challenge has been to avoid digging down into exhaustive detail but instead to keep the perspective broad and general. When it comes to the central chapters in the book in Part III, the method changes somewhat. The most significant chapter is Chapter 8, because there I do my best to articulate precisely what being with involves – and here I draw on a significant tradition including such figures as Gabriel Marcel, Iris Murdoch, Martin Heidegger, Emmanuel Lévinas, Giorgio Agamben, and Martin Buber. This is perhaps the only chapter in the book where I am seeking to be definitive rather than polemical or suggestive, and in order to be definitive I need to establish roots among those who have sought to be definitive before me. The other chapters in Part III are largely illustrative: the broad principles of being with are fairly easily grasped, and my sense in the main task is then to show how deeply being with is grounded in scripture and to illustrate what its commitments imply in particular contexts.

Readers will already have noticed that the language of with and for, and the categories of working for, being for, working with and being with, pervade the book. I do not put such terms within speech marks, nor do I italicize them. This may take a bit of getting used to, but it is in keeping with my aspiration to make such terms part of regular theological and ethical vocabulary. When I use a term such as working for adjectivally I hyphenate it to avoid misunderstanding – hence "a working-for solution." They are not watertight categories, and the book is not designed to chase everything but being with out of town; but I hope the reader will quickly find they offer a helpful lens to assess ethical and theological questions.

Is therefore the whole argument of the book an exaggeration? Does healthy social engagement involve a sober balance of all the four approaches rather than a heavy steer toward one of them? I have three ways of answering this question. First, no: a request to bear in mind that this is a book primarily concerned with the plight of those who by any conventional social assessment are in a lot of trouble. Thus the three illustrative chapters are concerned not with suburban docility but with chaotic homelessness, chronic and often acute ill-health, and subjection to political tyranny, respectively. These are invariably contexts in which working-for approaches have failed or at least proved inadequate. To say it is time to consider an alternative approach is not so very radical or reckless.

Second, yes: sometimes one does need to exaggerate to get a point across, and if I offer vivid examples I am doing so to draw the reader in to what is in the end a subtler argument. In particular I stress the differences between being with and working with, even though I am well aware that there are often significant and appropriate crossovers between the two, and that working with is often the only way to gain trust in order to attempt to be with. I stress the differences in order not to confuse the necessary and the tactical with the eschatological and the teleological. Being with is, fundamentally, a teleological claim about the ultimate purpose and character of God.

Third, yes – but in a different vein: I would suggest the whole of the gospel is an exaggeration – the whole call to discipleship and nature of the church is an exaggeration; attempts by scholars and pastors to bring the message under control and make it digestible are often distortions of the character of God. God's original decision never to be except to be with us in Christ is an absurd exaggeration of what many would prefer to deal with: a more benevolent and understated divine orientation toward our well-being. If this argument is an attempt to imitate and ponder the exaggerated character of God, then so be it. That is what theological ethics is for.

Some Assumptions

This book makes a number of working assumptions, and is most easily read alongside other works that make similar assumptions.

One is that there is no impermeable divide between doctrine and ethics. I understand doctrine as an understanding of the action of God, and ethics, particularly theological ethics, as an understanding of the most appropriate response of humankind to the action of God. It will already be clear that this book is designed to be a prime example of theological ethics – that is, a study in how human beings may best respond to the nature of God's action in creation, the purpose of God's action in making the covenant with Israel, the manner of God's action in Christ, the pattern of God's action in calling the church, and the destiny of God's action in the final consummation of the eschaton. Being with is, I believe, a succinct term that summarizes the nature and destiny of humankind and the creation before God. Being with is the dynamic of the inner relations of the Trinity – God being with God; it is the essence of God being with us in Christ; and it is the fulfilment of the Spirit's work in our being with one another. The last of these is the sphere generally known as ethics; but it is a sphere whose content is shaped by the previous two.

A corresponding assumption is that there is no impermeable divide between Jesus and ethics. In the terms of this study, one can regard the longstanding divide – between those who see Jesus as a model for Christian ethics and those who do not – as a tussle between working with and working for. We may perceive the Jesus-as-a-model view as a working-with approach, in that it tends to see a significant part of Jesus' ministry and mission as establishing a template for human flourishing. The reaction against this approach, often based on a judgment about its naïvety in the face of human sin, tends toward a working-for model, since it sees Jesus' cross (and sometimes his resurrection) as delivering humankind from the slavery of sin and death, thus achieving something to which humankind could not have aspired on its own. Being with introduces a new element into this longstanding debate. In some ways being with is an extreme version of working with, and subject to many of the same criticisms; but it also has its own criticisms of working with – and of course vice versa.

Another similar assumption that may be noted more briefly is that the inner life of the Trinity may be drawn upon as a source for ethics. Some theologians regard this move as speculative or implausible. However, in view of my contention that being with represents the nature of God as well as the origin and destiny of God's purposes, it is a necessary and essential move.

We could call these three claims assumptions about God, about Jesus, and about the Trinity, respectively. My final assumption is about the church. This is a study in ecclesial ethics, a term I have identified and described in detail elsewhere.[1] By ecclesial ethics, I mean not ethics for everyone, as the field of ethics is widely understood; I believe such ethics is flawed because it is often insufficiently mindful of its social location, because it concentrates overmuch on moments of decision rather than the development of character, and because it makes assumptions about what "everyone" thinks that are empirically and philosophically unsustainable. Neither do I mean ethics for the excluded, as I characterize an approach that foregrounds social location and seeks to prioritize the reassertion of hidden and suppressed voices. While I have much common ground with this approach, and for all its language of solidarity, I fear it can be as inclined to a working-for mentality as what it sets out to supplant. Instead I seek to do ethics with the church – with the body of people that sees itself as occupying a time between the full revelation of God's purpose in Christ and the fulfillment of that purpose in the eschaton, aspiring to imitate the former and anticipate the latter.

My work on being with attracts two principal lines of (consequential) ethical criticism. One is that it is too soft – that it does not stand up to evil, expose power relations, or make the world a better place. The other is that it is too hard – it asks too much of people, it is too difficult, it requires sacrifice, it is too uncompromising. It strikes me that these are the two principal (consequential) criticisms of Jesus. And, on a good day, the two principal criticisms of the church.

Forebears

An attempt to survey the historical field would be a major project, so here in a spirit of humility I simply seek to register my awareness and/or indebtedness to many from different traditions who have taken up these questions in their own discipleship. I believe the place to start is the New Testament and specifically the gospels; and in Chapter 5 suggest that the main contours are already set in shape by the Old Testament and especially the themes of Sabbath, covenant, and exile. But during the period before the division of the churches perhaps the key figures are the Cappadocian theologians of the fourth century who articulated what I would call God being with God as Trinity – what has sometimes been called the social doctrine of the Trinity. It is hard to imagine what I describe as the dimensions of a Trinitarian being with outside the work done by Basil, Macrina, and the two Gregorys in Cappadocia.

The next place to turn is the lively medieval debates on voluntary poverty and mendicancy.[2] Here, for example, we see Thomas Aquinas basing his economic teachings on the virtues of humility, patient receptivity, and hopeful trust.[3] We see also the way Francis of Assisi renounced property and thus became immune from disputes over property rights, offering a living alternative to the growth of the market economy, and an embodiment of reciprocal charity in a world becoming dominated by the contract.[4]

Since the Reformation different strands of the church have developed their own characteristic forms of encounter. My own tradition, the Church of England and the Anglican Communion, has sought to make the language of incarnation its own. The document that epitomizes this more than any other is *Lux Mundi*.[5] In this volume eleven Oxford theologians sought to affirm the incarnation as the central doctrine of Anglican theology. While this became associated with the negative aspects of incarnational theology (reducing the significance of the cross and investing the status quo, particularly the establishment of the Church of England, with almost revelatory authority) it gave the efforts of Anglo-Catholic priests in slum parishes an articulation of the theological aspirations of their social commitments. Thus Anglicanism, particularly in England, where the parish system is so significant, has continued to be closely identified with incarnational understandings of mission. While other traditions stemming from the magisterial Reformation have issued in forms of incarnational mission, it is most associated with Anglicanism because Anglicanism, particularly since *Lux Mundi*, has stressed the theological, as well as missional, significance of the incarnation.

Two twentieth-century figures may be taken to represent Roman Catholic practice in this tradition. Dorothy Day and the Catholic Worker movement, founded in 1933, are most associated with radical hospitality and the daily practice of the works of mercy. This movement is a wide-ranging attempt to renarrate theology and social engagement. It believes, for example, that "True prayer does not consist in asking favors from a king-God, but in giving alms to a beggar-God." God is, in short, a beggar. "The game of freedom then is not how to maximize use of the resources God has entrusted to us to prove ourselves good stewards, but how to give ourselves in love to the One who grasps at nothing."[6] Mother Teresa of Calcutta is an iconic figure who may still be regarded as part of the same Catholic encounter with Christ in the face of the poor. Her Missionaries of Charity have, since 1950, sought to encounter the hungry, naked, homeless, crippled, blind, lepers, all who feel unwanted, unloved, or uncared for throughout society, those who have become a burden to the society and are shunned by everyone; in particular it has sought from the beginning to help those "who have lived like animals die like angels – loved and wanted."[7]

Among the resurgence of evangelical interest in what is often now called incarnational ministry, a particular contemporary movement, particularly involving young adults, is known as New Monasticism. Like Catholic Worker houses there is much emphasis on face-to-face engagement with disadvantaged people, hospitality, and communal life. There is also in many cases a commitment to shared prayer and contemplation. Other features include relocation to society's margins, lament for racial divisions and active pursuit of a just reconciliation, and support for celibate singles alongside monogamous married couples.[8]

These are among the ecclesial strands that inform this study. But just as significant in understanding the context of the argument are the professional culture that I describe in Chapter 3 and Chapter 14 and the growth and development of international humanitarian aid that I discuss in Chapter 7.[9] I regard the theological assumptions listed earlier as prior to the ecclesial and humanitarian forebears cited here in comprehending my project; but I do not for a moment pretend I am the first to discuss these subjects, still less live courageously in the light of them, and so this section has named some of those with whom I anticipate many of the readers of this book will already be in conversation.

Notes

1. Samuel Wells and Ben Quash, *Introducing Christian Ethics* (Oxford: Wiley-Blackwell, 2010): especially 180–206. A caricature of this aspect of contemporary theology sees it as absorbed in the inner workings of the church, and unaware or uninterested in justice, poverty, or social exclusion. I have never seen why that is assumed to be so. It may be that some who have read deeply in Aristotle, Karl Barth, Alasdair MacIntyre, John Howard Yoder, and Stanley Hauerwas, let alone Thomas Aquinas, Ludwig Wittgenstein, or John Milbank have remained in a somewhat select academic culture. I started reading such people because they seemed to address better than anyone else the questions that were arising for me in seeking to address poverty and disadvantage in a largely post-Christian context; I find, all these years later, that they still do. I see this book as a humble contribution to the field of ecclesial ethics which may in some small way correct the wrongful assumption that the field has nothing to say about poverty or justice.
2. In these debates I have been guided by Christopher A. Franks, *He Became Poor: The Poverty of Christ and Aquinas' Economic Teachings* (Grand Rapids, MI: Eerdmans, 2009); Kelly Johnson, *The Fear of Beggars: Stewardship and Poverty in*

Christian Ethics (Grand Rapids, MI: Eerdmans, 2007); and Oliver O'Donovan and Joan Lockwood O'Donovan, *Bonds of Imperfection: Christian Politics, Past and Present* (Grand Rapids, MI: Eerdmans, 2004).

3. Christopher A. Franks, *He Became Poor*: 2.

4. Kelly Johnson, *The Fear of Beggars*: 13–69. Johnson also points out the problem that arose when Francis' approach became too popular. The question "What if everybody did it?" is one I have been posed many times when I have spoken around the USA, Canada, and Britain about being with; my answer has always been, "If I thought there was the remotest chance of my proposals being widely adopted I might speak slightly differently."

5. *Lux Mundi: A Series of Studies in the Religion of the Incarnation*, edited by Charles Gore (London: John Murray, 1902).

6. Kelly Johnson, *The Fear of Beggars*: 198. The first quotation comes from the co-founder of the Catholic Worker movement, Peter Maurin.

7. Kathryn Spink, *Mother Teresa: A Complete Authorized Biography* (New York: HarperCollins, 1997): 55.

8. Rutba House, *Schools for Conversion: Twelve Marks of a New Monasticism* (Eugene, OR: Cascade Books, 2005): xii–xiii.

9. This last is explored in a large number of studies, of which I have found the following the most helpful: William Easterly, *The White Man's Burden: Why the West's Efforts to Aid the Rest Have Done So Much Ill and So Little Good* (New York: The Penguin Press, 2006); David Rieff, *A Bed for the Night: Humanitarianism in Crisis* (New York: Simon and Schuster, 2003); Alex de Waal, *Famine Crimes: Politics and the Disaster Relief Industry in Africa* (Bloomington and Indianapolis: Indiana University Press, 1997); Dean Karlan and Jacob Appel, *More Than Good Intentions: How a New Economics is Helping to Solve Global Poverty* (New York: Dutton Penguin, 2011); Paul Collier, *The Bottom Billion: Why the Poorest Countries are Failing and What Can Be Done About It* (New York: Oxford University Press, 2008).

2

A Nazareth Manifesto

Being With and its Alternatives

The following treatment takes for granted that the reader is willing to *see* poverty, in this case in the form of people who sleep outside, and believes such poverty requires of them a personal response.[1] (It assumes that homelessness epitomizes poverty because it is a particular kind of distress that brings together hardship in the past, powerlessness in the present, and poor prospects for the future.) A quick survey of perceptions might illustrate why such is not always the case.[2]

Many people see a person who is homeless, and see before them (1) a personal tragedy. Here is someone who is more than likely struggling with addiction, who may be dealing with various kinds of mental illness, who may have relied on having a structure for their life through being in the armed forces or perhaps having had a period in prison; somehow, at this moment in their lives, the trapdoor between them and the abyss has given way and they find themselves on the streets. (2) A related but slightly different point of view sees a person who is homeless, and thinks, "It appears I've come late onto the scene of a crime." Here, it seems, is someone who's most likely been the victim of abuse. They may as a child have been a tool in a grown-up's game, or at the very least have been subject to neglect. As an adult they may have been assaulted, been thrown out of the house, and been made to live in such fear that sleeping outside was significantly preferable to the threat that lurked at home.

But there are contrary views. The opposite of personal tragedy is (3) public policy failure. For many people, to focus on individuals and their poignant stories is to overlook the larger structural and systemic issues, which include unemployment, the quantity of available low-cost housing, the closure of mental institutions, and the eradication of the safety net around vulnerable people. This requires not individual transformation or healing but a reallocation of public-sector resources and the realignment of private-sector initiative. The opposite of crime is a fourth view that completes the circle. It's the assumption of (4) choice. Choice can have a romantic guise, as the free spirit who can't be constrained by conventional lifestyle limitations; or it can have a more pejorative guise, as the perception of lurching from one bad life decision to the next, from dangerous companions to feckless patterns of consumption. Either way it maintains a simple argument: people are homeless because they have chosen to be – or have, at least, made unwise choices that led to their losing their home.

Somewhere within this fourfold compass of personal tragedy, victimhood, public policy failure, and choice, lie individual stories of homeless people themselves. We are each inclined to zoom in on the story that fits our view of the world; but most homeless people's stories are a mixture of all four. In my own experience of spending time with people who sleep outside, I have heard stories that covered all of these points on the compass. We can't pretend that one is right and the others are prejudiced or naïve. They all have an element of truth in them. These perceptions color the way people respond to homelessness.[3]

Before moving to responses it is worth acknowledging reasons why people may not feel moved to respond to poverty, in general, and homelessness, in particular. One might be because they believe the person themselves is to blame, and that until they see the error and fruitlessness of their ways there is no one that can help them. Another might suppose that it is the state's responsibility to care for those who fall into poverty, and that taxes are paid so that the safety net will be there. Another might be concerned that their own well-being is in jeopardy, and that there are no material or emotional resources to spare to address the well-being of anyone else. A fourth might believe that poverty is primarily a spiritual issue, and that material conditions are secondary compared to one's status before God.

Allowing for such perceptions and possible reasons for non-engagement, let us turn now to four broad ways in which a person might be moved to engage with poverty. These forms of engagement govern most of the arguments of this book.

Imagine you are walking through Trafalgar Square and you see a homeless person. I suggest you have four options. The first is to say, "We need to get people off the streets into housing, employment, and profitable use of time." You may be energized to join the board of a night shelter or a day center assisting homeless people; you may be more direct and immediate and bring the homeless person in question a drink or a sandwich or an item of clothing or a leaflet advertising various services. If you are a person with professional skills, you may seek ways to bring your talents and facilities to their advantage – as a medical practitioner for their health, as an educationalist for their learning, as a lawyer for their legal situation. You may be motivated to advocate for this person and many people in similar circumstances, lobbying your political representative or bringing together a meeting to address homelessness in Central London.

The second option is to speak to the homeless person, to explore with them the reasons why they are homeless, to ensure they know what options are available for them – the local drug and alcohol rehabilitation schemes, the places where free healthcare is available, the drop-in centers where there is training and career advice, the places where there are art and singing and football groups to help build confidence and make connections, and to offer to take them to these places, now or later. One could also explore whether they know other homeless people, whether they together have common concerns, how they can work together on those questions, and whether they have a good sense of where those issues might find a hearing.

The third option is simply to sit down beside the homeless person and pass the time of day with them – share first names, talk about where they are from, ask what it is like to spend a day or a night outside, wonder what they think of people like yourself scurrying by, enquire if they feel frightened or lonely, drink a cup of coffee with them, discuss the latest developments in politics or the arts or sports or celebrity culture, and gradually locate the questions they really want to ask and the wisdom they deeply have to share. In this approach the physical posture is as significant as what is actually said. No longer does the person with the "problem" sit while the person with the "solution" stands: now the two sit together, and what they are talking about is not the deficit in the one and the surfeit in the other, but matters of common concern to both.

The fourth option is to feel rising anger about the fact that there are so many homeless people in Central London, to denounce this situation on your blog site, to get very exercised about the use of the term "the homeless" instead of "homeless people," to give money to appeals for organizations that work with homeless issues, and to make every effort to ensure that no one who meets a homeless person makes any assumptions about mental health or a history of being abused or substance addiction or poor choices. One may be quick to see homelessness as a symptom of a society ill at ease, and to find further symptoms that indicate barriers to human flourishing, in government, the market, and the wider culture – barriers that may have a hidden, perhaps sinister, root cause.

We may call the first option *working for*, because when you go on boards and lobby politicians you're working for the homeless person. Both words are significant: you are clearly *working*, because you are directly engaging obstacles that stand in the homeless person's path; and you are working *for* the person, in that the person has not been the instigator of the work nor an active participant in it – it is being done on their behalf, to enhance their well-being.

And the second approach is *working with*. It shares the energy of the first option, identifying and addressing barriers, and in this case building coalitions of people with common issues, and thus it is *working*; but this time the work is in partnership alongside the homeless person, actually engaging them in their own redemption, rather than deciding and operating for them, so it is not for but *with*.

The third approach, where you simply sit beside the homeless person for a coffee and a chat, is *being with*. Like the second option, it is a genuine encounter: the two parties are equally involved, and the engagement only proceeds if they both continue to be so; hence it is *with*. But it is not, in the same way, working; it focuses much more on stillness, on disposition, on letting the homeless person take the decisive steps and identify the significant issues; this is not working, but *being*.

And the fourth option is being for. You don't actually encounter the homeless person at all – your every judgment is based on information received at a distance or wisdom gained second- or third-hand: thus it is not with but *for*. Meanwhile there is not an active pursuit of the homeless person's interests, which would be working; instead there is an orientation of one's life for their well-being, and the well-being of many others who are as you perceive it casualties of the economic, political, or social system: thus it is *being*.

Nazareth as a Theological Claim

My argument in this book is that, while there is a place for working for, working with, and being for, it is being with that is the most faithful form of Christian witness and mission, because being with is both incarnationally faithful to the manifestation of God in Christ and eschatologically anticipatory of the destiny of all things in God. Whereas working-for models tend to treat the world as a problem to be solved, being-with approaches are more inclined to perceive creation as a gift to be enjoyed. A working-for model is likely to assume Christ became incarnate because there is a job of redemption to be done and only he can do it. A being-with approach generally assumes the whole point of creation was that God would dwell with us terrestrially in Jesus and eternally in heaven.

Consider the shape of Jesus' life. The incarnation presupposes that it was not enough for God simply to be for us. God is always for us, but that is an inadequate way of understanding God's purpose in making us and the world. God's purpose is to be with us. For a week in Jerusalem, for moments in Galilee that we call miracles, in teaching and in challenging religious authority Jesus was working for us. There is a difference between creator and creatures: there are some things – most obviously creation, resurrection, and inaugurating and fulfilling the kingdom – that only God can do. But the gospels do not show us a God who in Christ is merely for us. They show us a Christ who is fundamentally with us. Jesus works with the disciples in Galilee – he shows them, employs them, trains them, empowers them, sends them, chastises them. However frail and foolish they turn out to be, there is no question of him going to Jerusalem on his own. We are so familiar with the notion of Jesus teaching his disciples, we seldom reflect that if delivering us from our sins was all Jesus came to do, calling disciples was superfluous. There is a job for the disciples to do, but that job is distinctively collaborative – it is, by definition, working with Jesus.

But the ministerial period of calling, training, and sending disciples, the working with part, and the atoning process of passion, death and resurrection, the working for part, together only make up perhaps 10 percent of Jesus' life among us. What is the theological significance of the hidden 90 percent – the 30-odd years Jesus spent in Nazareth? Those Nazareth years demonstrate, in their obscurity as much as their sheer duration, in their simplicity as much as their large majority, God's fundamental purpose to be with us – not primarily to rescue us, or even empower us, but simply to be with us, to share our existence, to enjoy our hopes and fears, our delights and griefs, our triumphs and disasters. This is the way incarnation echoes creation and anticipates heaven: Jesus simply relishes life with us, and bewilders and disarms us with his patience, his gentleness, his presence, and his attention. All the other actions of God – in being for us, working with us, and working for us – are all ways of preparing and redeeming the ground for the fundamental purpose of creation, salvation, and final redemption: God being with us. That is what was ever in God's heart, and what ever shall be.

Let us consider this proposal negatively and positively. What it says negatively is that Nazareth is not simply a training ground – not simply a ladder that is kicked away when the public ministry begins. Jerusalem is not the whole of Jesus' ministry and purpose. Jesus did not "come to die," in the sense that there is no validity to his life and ministry other than as a prelude to the cross. Jesus fulfilled what God had proclaimed through the Sinai covenant: God's commitment to be with us. The "us" was altered, through the incorporation of the Gentiles. The "with" was altered, because of the incarnate presence of God in the earthly form of the human Jesus. But the being of God, shaped to be with us, had not changed. Being with us is the nature of God – the grain of the universe; Jesus' coming made that manifest, and clarified how integral and costly it was to God; but did not otherwise say something new.

What is being proposed is that we read the gospel story backwards. The working for, epitomized in Jerusalem, takes place in order to restore the with. To the extent that Jesus' death and resurrection dismantled sin, made a path through death, and fatally undermined evil, Jesus was addressing the factors that jeopardize our covenant with God; thus the nature of redemption is that Jesus restores the with between God and us. There is no for that is not designed to bring about with. That is what it means to say being with is an eschatological conviction: being with is the telos of all God's action, and thus should be of ours.

Meanwhile when Jesus was in Galilee, proclaiming the kingdom, performing miracles, teaching, training, debating, and dialoguing, he was working with – in order to open paths to be with. For example when he debates with the Samaritan woman in John 4, or heals the woman with hemorrhages in Mark 5, or heals the paralyzed man in Mark 2, he is seeking to restore each of them to community with their neighbors and with God. What is being made possible is what Jesus had already practiced in Nazareth: God being with us, in the ordinary, in the everyday, in the stuff of life, in birth, growth, nurture, work, play, community, and rest. It is not that Nazareth, and to a lesser extent Galilee, are a means to bring about Jerusalem; it is that Jerusalem, and to a significant extent Galilee, are a process of making possible for everyone at all times what had already been embodied by Jesus in Nazareth.

What being with says positively is that Nazareth is an apt name for what has been neglected in exegesis, theology, and ethics. What the incarnation means doctrinally, in the conjoining of humanity and divinity, Nazareth embodies socially, in the face-to-face and shoulder-to-shoulder embedding of God's divinity in human community. The world was not created as a plaything, to be tossed away when it became troublesome, tedious, or tired. Yet neither was it made as a project, a focus for constant upgrading, relentless improving, or perpetual tinkering. It was made as a theater of relationship – fundamentally relationship between God and humanity, and by extension human relationship with one another and the wider creation. Nazareth is important, not because it is a stage on the way to something more significant, but precisely because it is an extended window into heaven: God and humanity in peaceable interaction, perhaps with good work, perhaps with good food, perhaps with learning and growing and nurturing and celebrating, but fundamentally just being, because there is no better place to be and no better company to keep and no better thing to be doing. This is Sabbath – the crown of creation; simply being with God.

If Nazareth is so important, how do we account for the relative silence of the gospels, and the New Testament in general, on the subject? The New Testament is not a straightforward handbook for Christian theology or ethics. It is preoccupied with portraying the cross, not simply as defeat and shame, but as necessary, purposed, transformative, and glorious, and of identifying the character of the one who went to the cross and the life of those who share in his resurrection. There is no detailed account of Nazareth – but that does not mean it carries no symbolic role. There are many similar questions one could ask; such as, if Jesus came to open the gate of heaven, why is there no detailed and explicit account of the life of heaven in the New Testament? The absence of such an account is by no means a suggestion that heaven is not central to the imagination of salvation. Likewise, the absence of an account of Nazareth need not be regarded as an in-principle reason to dismiss its theological and ethical significance.

Indeed, it is not hard to put together traces of Nazareth from moments recorded across the gospels. The story of Mary and Martha in Luke 10 invites immediate correspondence with the practice of working for (Martha) and being with (Mary). Such moments may be taken as emblematic of what I am calling Nazareth. Again, when Jesus says "'Who is my mother, and who are my brothers?' And pointing to his disciples, he said, 'Here are my mother and my brothers!'" (Matt. 12:48–49), we may see that being with in Nazareth transcends traditional family ties and models a more diverse, dynamic form of community. Most of the healings and many of the controversies in the gospels take place against a backdrop of Jesus enjoying people's company, receiving their hospitality, sharing their days: he seldom seeks people out to heal them or call them to follow – the relationships are cherished for their own sake, and the calls for healing or wisdom come as interruptions to the abiding presence of Jesus among the common people and the disciples. In this sense Nazareth abides in Galilee.

Attention in reading the New Testament has understandably focused on, "What does this document say is wrong?" and "How does this document see Jesus putting that wrong right?" The same is true of engagement with disadvantaged people today. The conversation is dominated by the question, "What is wrong? (And why is it wrong?)," and, "What can be done to put it right?" But just as important – and perhaps in the long run, more important – are the questions, "What might 'right' look like?" and "How can we model in the way we address the wrong, not just the route out, but the destination?" Or, transferred to the New Testament, "What features of Jesus' life depict, not just his ability and preparedness to save us, but also his portrayal and embodiment of the life he makes possible?" These are the questions that take us to being with: and this is why, even though they get only a handful of references in the gospels, it is nonetheless valid to see the heart of social engagement in those 30 years in Nazareth.

Such is the exegetical claim advanced in this book.

A Nazareth Manifesto

At the risk of oversimplification, and by way of summary, here are what I regard as the ten principles of being with.

1. *Our calling is to imitate the way God is.*
   The Christian faith is that God originally made, and has endlessly re-iterated, a decision never to be except to be with us. And our way of embodying that faith is constantly to look for ways to be with God, with one another, and with the creation. Being with us is the purpose of creation; and is the purpose of salvation. It is the continuous thread running through the nature and actions of God. There was no purpose for which humanity was created other than to be with God as God's companions; there is no job that humanity has to do beyond accepting the invitation to that restored relationship with God and one another. This is how we shall spend eternity, and so there is no better way to spend our temporal existence.

2. *Our clue to how to imitate God is to follow the way God is with us in Christ.*

   Just as Christ's ministry had (1) a season of abiding in Nazareth, (2) a season of healing, teaching, training, and debating in Galilee, and (3) a season of sacrifice in Jerusalem, so may we expect our own experience of being with to include (3) pain and suffering, to include (2) solidarity, exchange of experience, and controversy, and to include (1) abiding, enjoying, and sharing existence with one another. If our lives are oriented toward the disadvantaged we may expect all three kinds of encounters, but we may take the percentages of Jesus' ministry – with the preponderance in Nazareth – as normative.

3. *Our first awareness is the abundance of God and our own scarcity – together with our gratitude that we have been given so many ways to transform our scarcity with God's abundance.*

   In the face of God we are deeply aware of our own scarcity. Through story, sacrament, prayer, and practices God has given us an abundance of gifts to graft us into the companionship and fellowship of the Holy Spirit. Our encounter with disadvantage begins therefore with a sense of our own neediness; but also a confidence that God is in the habit of giving us more than we need. What matters therefore is that we adopt appropriate ways to receive it.

4. *It is a miracle of grace that God meets our scarcity through the abundance we discover in those apparently more exposed to scarcity than ourselves.*

   This is the lesson of Matthew 25:31–46. "When did we see you naked?" is a question that echoes through our imaginations and our consciences. Jesus was naked on the day of his crucifixion. He was hungry and thirsty on that day too. Hence his cry, "I thirst" (John 19:28). Jesus was also a stranger: hence the words, "He came to what was his own, and his own people did not accept him" (John 1:11). He was sick: in Gethsemane his sweat became like great drops of blood falling down on the ground (Luke 22:44). And he was led away to prison after Judas' kiss. And on each occasion his people failed to be with him. And so the irony of the six acts of mercy is their simplicity. Give food; give a drink; welcome; clothe; care; visit. Not end famine, heal disease, reduce recidivism; just the simplest encounter, that requires face-to-face meeting without a solution or cure or even panacea to hand. Here is the promise: that if we can have the courage and humility to open up this encounter, we will meet Jesus. Whoever bemoans scarcity has been told where to find abundance.

5. *A community seeking regeneration has already within it most of what it needs for its own transformation.*

We do not go into situations assuming we have the solutions. No individual has everything they need: the wonder of being with is for the relationship to elicit surprising surpluses to meet its more obvious deficits. We are not Good Samaritans: we do not have about our person or our donkey all the answers, all the resources, all the wisdom, all the knowledge. We are the one in the ditch, and the wonder of the encounter is that the despised one, the one from whom we might imagine nothing good could come, turns out to have abundant resources that abound for our salvation.

6. *We do not configure situations as problems needing solutions.*

Being with does not start with a problem – or, if it does, the problem lies with ourselves, rather than with the person in whom we perceive scarcity. We do not sit and have a coffee with a homeless person because we are trying to solve their problem – we do so because we want to receive the wealth of wisdom, humanity, and grace that God has to give us through them. We are not the source of their salvation: they are the source of ours. If we talk about their problems, we make sure we are attending to the ones they name and identify, rather than the ones we perceive or imagine. Our every effort is to enjoy their being, and share our own, rather than change their reality assuming a script we have imposed from elsewhere.

7. *We cannot understand, listen to, be taught by, or receive grace from people unless we inhabit their world which we see as valuable for its own sake.*

The goal of all our working for and working with is not independent, free-standing individuals, released from all setbacks and problems and challenges; but an interactive and permeable community of interdependent beings, who discover gifts where others might only see needs, and unearth treasure where others might only see trouble. Being with means letting go of unsustainable and mistaken notions of altruism – which portrays a perpetual holding-of-the-nose in the face of unpleasant responsibilities and settings – and replacing it with a genuine relish for circumstances and challenges that open up the imagination, the mind, and the heart. Being with evinces a genuine sense of expectation about what new thing God will disclose from the most outwardly unpromising of beginnings.

8. *There is no goal beyond restored relationship: reconciliation is the gospel.* Being with is not a means to an end: it is an end in itself. It is not a strategy designed to win trust so that collaborative prospects may prosper: it is an anticipation and a glimpse of the kind of interactions that may arise if the collaborative projects were to succeed.

9. *The center of ministry is worship (being with God); and the center of mission is being with the disadvantaged, and receiving abundance from them.*
   Just as at the center of the church's common life is worship, the simple being with God for no purpose than the glory and goodness of being so, so at the center of its mission should be being with the stranger, with the expectation of meeting and learning from and wondering at and enjoying the Christ made known in them. This is how worship and mission are demonstrated to be two sides of the same coin: they are both about being with, and the incarnation means that the truest encounter with God is also a revelation of the nature and purpose of humanity, while the truest human encounter also discloses something of the nature and purpose of God.

10. *Being with is both the method and the goal of social engagement.*
   There is an honored place for working for and working with – and even, in the right circumstances, for being for – provided that each recognize they depend on, must almost always to some degree be preceded by, and always aim to issue in, being with. Being with is the heart of mission, because it imitates the primary way God interacts with humanity and the creation; and so being with is always the default of any initiative, which may then be modified as circumstances and opportunities dictate.

Notes

1. Thomas Malthus long ago set the terms of the debate. "Even in the relief of common beggars we ... are more frequently influences by the desire of getting rid of the importunities of a disgusting object than by the pleasure of relieving it." Thomas Robert Malthus, *An Essay on the Principle of Population*, edited by Donald Winch (Cambridge: Cambridge University Press, 1992), quoted in Kelly Johnson *The Fear of Beggars: Stewardship and Poverty in Christian Ethics* (Grand Rapids, MI: Eerdmans, 2007): 1.

2. These four causes of homelessness were articulated in dialogue with the work of Laura Stivers. See her *Disrupting Homelessness: Alternative Christian Approaches* (Minneapolis, MN: Fortress Press, 2011). While I differ from her judgments in various places, I find her work provocative in helpful ways, particularly for pushing me to make clear what the categories I discuss shortly mean in practice. For other works that have informed these ideas see Warren R. Copeland, *And the Poor Get Welfare: The Ethics of Poverty in the United States* (Nashville, TN: Abingdon, 1993); Daryl Collins, Jonathan Morduch, Stuart Rutherford, Orlanda Ruthven, *Portfolios of the Poor: How the World's Poor Live on $2 a Day* (Princeton, NJ, and Oxford: Princeton University Press, 2009); and Duncan B. Forrester, *On Human Worth: A Christian Vindication of Equality* (London: SCM, 2001).

3. Kelly Johnson highlights the way people fear beggars. Among these sentiments are "fears that the beggar might turn violent; that neither giving nor refusing will be morally satisfactory; that behind one beggar stand a thousand others, whose needs will overwhelm any generosity; that the beggar sees an alarming truth about humanity, about *me*; that had things gone differently, that beggar could have been any one of us" (Kelly Johnson, *The Fear of Beggars*: 4, italics in the original).

Part I

Realignment

My argument suggests the focus of theology and the priorities of ethics have long and often been misdirected. Not everywhere, and not always; but often, and repeatedly. My main interest lies not in highlighting, diagnosing, or narrating the error but in suggesting a focus and proposing where the priorities should be.

In this first part of the book I set about showing where the issue lies. In Chapter 3, I suggest that there is a widespread consensus across the Christian and secular imagination regarding the predicament in which humanity is placed. That way of configuring the predicament justifies, and perhaps determines, the way most educated people in the West set about "doing good." But, I argue, that way of configuring the predicament is wrong. And thus the conventional way of "doing good" is based on a false premise. I suggest an alternative description of what constitutes the human predicament – which leads to an alternative notion of the good to be sought, and the methods of seeking it.

The second chapter reaches the same conclusion but by a different route. I consider the widespread interest in reconciliation as a Christian practice. I suggest that most people involved in reconciliation experience a significant degree of exasperation and impatience – exasperation that the warring parties find themselves so locked in division when good sense or good nature would have avoided such tension; and impatience that this battle is such a drain and a delay and a distraction from the real matter in hand, the real mission to be pursued. By contrast I argue that reconciliation is not a process of preparation in order that people may be in a position to practice and spread the gospel – reconciliation *is* the gospel. There is no gospel other than the one that requires and makes possible restored relationships with God, one another, and the creation. God has no ambitions and seeks

A Nazareth Manifesto, Samuel Wells © 2015 John Wiley & Sons, Ltd. Published 2015 by John Wiley & Sons, Ltd.

no final goal beyond restored relationship. That relationship is the telos of creation.

Together these two chapters are intended to break up the ground of widespread assumptions so that the larger arguments advocating the pattern and practice of being with may gain a hearing.

3

Reassessing the Human Predicament

Introduction

The 1992 novel, also a 1996 film, *The English Patient* is set in Egypt during the Second World War.[1] A married Englishwoman, Katherine, finds herself often alone in Cairo as her husband pursues a cartographical expedition. She falls in love with an impossibly exotic Hungarian nobleman, Laszlo. Count Laszlo, another cartographer, discovers a wondrous cave, decorated with prehistoric paintings, deep in the Sahara Desert. Laszlo and Katherine fall into a passionate affair.

Katherine's husband, sensing the affair, plans a murderous revenge. He puts Katherine in the back seat of his biplane and flies toward Count Laszlo's excavation camp near the famous cave. As the plane draws near to the camp and Laszlo comes out to the landing strip to meet it, it becomes clear Katherine's husband is intent on landing the plane right on Laszlo himself, whatever collateral damage may ensue. But the bloodthirsty plan catastrophically backfires. It turns out it is Katherine's husband himself who dies in the crash. Laszlo, the intended target, sustains only minor injuries; but Katherine, the woman at the center of two men's passionate rivalry, is badly hurt. We witness Laszlo carrying Katherine slowly and tenderly to the prehistoric cave.

Now Laszlo and Katherine face an unspeakable predicament. Katherine's injuries are, without question, life-threatening. If Katherine is going to live, Laszlo is going to need to set out to find medical help. But finding medical help means going to Cairo – and Cairo is three days' walk away. It is a dangerous journey. Even if Laszlo gets there unscathed, there may be no one he can persuade to bring help. And even if all these ifs meet happy whens, there has got to be only a small chance Katherine will still be alive when Laszlo gets back. What are they to do?

A Nazareth Manifesto, Samuel Wells © 2015 John Wiley & Sons, Ltd. Published 2015 by John Wiley & Sons, Ltd.

I begin with this question because I take it to be the defining question of contemporary Western life. I regard it as the point of most significance in the presence of the word of Christian faith in the world. I see it as the window through which we may articulate a whole philosophy and ethic of Christian being-in-the-world.

The great tide of assumptions in Western culture orients people toward solutions, toward answers, toward ways to *fix* things – whether those things are the human body, the human mind, the world's economy, the inside of a laptop, the woes of Washington, the Arab–Israeli conflict, the poverty of Somalia. Are we ready for a problem that doesn't have a solution? That is the question that discloses our true subject.

Mortality

Here is a more conventional candidate for a defining question. What is the essential problem of human existence? I want to dig inside this question to identify the answer most educated Western people would probably offer to such a question. I want not just to name that answer, but to explore it in such a way that we can see how that answer shapes a number of things we do.

Here is my hypothesis. The operational assumption of late modernity has long been that the central problem of human existence is mortality. From the moment we come into the world, our fundamental crisis is that we are going to die. In the words of Samuel Beckett, we "give birth astride of a grave, the light gleams an instant, then it's night once more."[2] Given that eternity is rather extensive by anyone's measure, any limited life span that falls short of eternity is bound to be unsatisfactory; and three score years and ten are not inherently less adequate than a million or two: as Isaac Watts, recalling the words of 2 Peter, reminds us, "A thousand ages, in thy sight, are like an evening gone; short as the watch that ends the night, before the rising sun."[3] But the issue is not simply that life is limited in terms of duration. Human flourishing is circumscribed by a host of other limitations. If we simply invoke nine, we might note disability, chronic ill health, and terminal illness; poverty, hardship, and malnutrition; adverse weather, famine, and limited natural resources. It is a formidable list. We are hemmed in on all sides not just by death but by a host of other constraints.

What has changed in perhaps the last 50 or 60 years is that, at least in the West, humanity no longer feels such limitations are integral to its existence. There was a time when death and taxes named the unshiftable givens of human experience, and that life was a largely Stoic matter of learning to live within the boundaries of limited human potential. Death took place in the home, most illnesses had little or no chance of a cure, and it was best to prepare oneself for a fragile existence or face hubristic disappointment or humiliation. The world's resources of course held enormous potential; but the technology and techniques for tapping that potential were still in their infancy.

But those days have gone. A cascade of technological advance, in fields such as medicine, transport, and information transfer, has made constraints seem absurd, rather than necessary. The human project is no longer about coming to terms with limitations and flourishing within them. It is now, almost without question, about overcoming and transcending limitations. Human contingency is to be swept aside like racist legislation during the civil rights movement. It is not something one learns to live with: it is something one expects to conquer. Doing so is part of human self-assertion, human full expression – the spreading of humanity's wings. It has more or less become the defining project of the human race.

It seems all are agreed that the key project of our species is the alleviation, overcoming, and transcendence of mortality. We achieve this by inventing medicines, discovering new dimensions of experience, reducing or reversing limitations such as blindness, breaking athletic records, and circumventing such tragedies as famine or muscular dystrophy. That is what we strive for. That is what gains outstanding individuals rewards and acclaim. That is what our culture prizes most highly.

Our society celebrates nothing more than the overcoming of limitation – in sport, in science, in communications, in health. Every invention, every new world record, every new gadget is a sacrament of the deepest human desire of our age – to become free by transcending limitation, and thus, for a moment, believing we can withstand even death. One example is the Paralympics. When the Paralympics took place in London in 2012 they enriched the human project, as I have defined it. For many people the Paralympics are redefining sport. No longer is sport simply about excellence and making sacrifices and being better than others; now sport is primarily a celebration of overcoming obstacles and adversity and thus opening a door to independence and freedom. In other words sport has ceased to be an enjoyable diversion from the central quest of humankind. It has instead become the definitive embodiment of that central human project.

In the middle ages the most celebrated cultural moments were the discovery of precious documents from the classical period. Each one represented a reclaiming of a piece of and an avenue into a lost golden era. Today the golden moments are the transcending of another dimension of human limitation. When we advertise our organizations we seldom still say, "Making lead pencils the same way for 150 years." Instead we say, "Testing and stretching the boundaries of knowledge: making the impossible, possible." The single notion that sums up this sense of throwing off limitations is freedom, and the term we employ to commodify freedom and give it retail value is choice. So the basic line in promoting what we do is to say our product or service overcomes one or more of the real or perceived constraints of our daily or lifelong existence and thus gives us more choice.

Poverty

Wealth has thus come to be perceived as depth and breadth of choice. Poverty, by contrast, comes to mean the dearth of choice. This is not a book about poverty, as such; but poverty is perhaps the most significant motif in understanding and illustrating what this book is about. It is instructive to consider the powerful metaphors that govern perceptions of poverty. For the sake of simplicity, I shall divide those metaphors into two kinds: metaphors of deficit, and metaphors of dislocation.

(1) Starting with metaphors of deficit, let us consider first of all the notion of (a) poverty as desert. The desert metaphor assumes people are poor because they do not have enough. They do not have enough money, food, good relationships, skills, education. This is not really anyone's fault. It is more a problem of scarcity of resources or poor distribution. The solution is to give people more – in the short term more money, or, in a material economy, more nutritious food and clean water; in the long term more education, more training in healthy work and family patterns, more stable institutions, more access to credit and outlets for their skills.

There are two things to note at the outset about the desert metaphor. The first is that it is the most widely held. It is the most widely held because it is the most easily grasped conceptually (people do not have enough); because it most easily plays into the agreeable notion that poverty can be "fixed" (by transferring resources from those who have enough and to spare, perhaps even too much); and because it does not require a narrative of blame or a diagnosis of structural injustice. The second thing to note about it is that it is seriously flawed, both descriptively and in terms of the outworking of policies for which it becomes the basis.

The desert metaphor doubtless motivates many non-poor to active involvement in relief and development, but it invariably encourages a quasi-colonial attitude that misses people's humanity. It is inclined to assume an "us-and-them" where "we" are defined by what we have and "they" are defined by what they lack. The reality is that, on a global scale, food aid can have a destructive effect on the economy of the recipient nation and contribute to more hunger and poverty in the long term. Free, subsidized, or cheap food tends to undercut local farmers, who cannot compete and are driven out of jobs and into poverty, further enhancing the market-share of the larger global producers. Many poor nations are dependent on farming, and so such food aid amounts to food dumping. Suspicions abound that more powerful nations have increasingly used this as a foreign policy tool for dominance rather than for real aid. What seems to be going on is that rich nations simply use aid as a lever to open poor-country markets to their products. The goodwill that appears to be embodied in aid is undermined by the way protectionism simultaneously denies market access for poor-country products. The result is that aid enhances dependence, while routes to economic stability are blocked. The desert metaphor ends up underwriting a system that benefits the donor economically while increasing the donor's reputation for benevolence. Thus does ill-informed compassion quickly translate into withering cynicism.

Another metaphor of deficit is that of (b) poverty as defeat. Life is a competition, so the argument goes: some win and some lose. The poor are simply those who lose. They were perhaps dealt a tough hand, from bad luck, bad genes, a bad background, or a bad environment; they maybe lived in the wrong country, faced the wrong climate, or found themselves in the wrong place at the wrong time. Or, some would say, they did not make the most of their opportunities: everyone, it is sometimes maintained, has the same chance – it is tough, and those with skill and application make it. This view tends to come with a strong emphasis on personal responsibility. It is often pointed out that if everyone were given an average person's annual salary at the start of a week, patterns of trade, barter, saving and profligacy – leaving aside criminality – would mean that a significant number would be destitute by the weekend.

In this view tax and welfare increases poverty by taking away incentives for effort while punishing those who succeed. A certain almost punitive streak is necessary in response to national and international poverty, because the best way to perceive poverty is as a backs-to-the-wall stimulus to initiative, courage, energy, and imagination in finding sources of income, particularly entrepreneurial commercial ones. (Needless to say this assumes a global movement of labor that is seldom in fashion in wealthier economies.) But it is worth noting a philosophical assumption that lies inside the defeat metaphor: the notion that all may avoid defeat. Can all succeed? The way to preserve an affirmative answer to this question is to infer that poverty indicates moral failure: if people had kept their marriages, families, jobs, and local network together, all would be well. To illustrate this point, one need only reflect on the associations in North Atlantic culture of the word "loser." The term blends moral, social, and circumstantial failure. Perhaps a deeper dimension of the defeat metaphor, particularly in this moral guise, is the impulse to find an explanation for all ills in the stars or in ourselves. There seems to be no such thing as an ill that doesn't have a culprit.

A third metaphor of deficit, but this time with less of an odor of judgment, is that of (c) poverty as dragnet. The picture here is of a trapdoor, like a cat flap. It is easy to fall into; but escape is impossible. In a dragnet, fish are pressed so tightly against the net and each other that they cannot wriggle free. Jeffrey Sachs, in his book *The End of Poverty*, speaks of the inability of very poor countries to reach the "bottom rung" of the ladder of economic development, and the trap that closes in when the population is growing faster than capital is being accumulated.[4] He cites six major kinds of capital that the extreme poor lack: human capital (health, nutrition, and skills needed for each person to be economically productive); business capital (the machinery, facilities, motorized transport used in agriculture, industry, and services); infrastructure (roads, power, water and sanitation, airports and seaports, and telecommunications systems, that are critical inputs into business productivity); natural capital (arable land, healthy soils, biodiversity, and well-functioning ecosystems that provide the environmental services needed by human society); public institutional capital (the commercial law, judicial systems, government services and policing that underpin the peaceful and prosperous division of labor); and knowledge capital (the scientific and technological know-how that raises productivity in business output and the promotion of physical and natural capital).[5] He defines the poverty trap like this: "The poor start with a very low level of capital per person, and then find themselves trapped in poverty because the ratio of capital per person actually falls from generation to generation. The amount of capital per person declines when the population is growing faster than capital is being accumulated."[6] He goes on to say, "Capital is diminished, or depreciated, as the result of the passage of time, or wear and tear, or the death of skilled workers .... The question for growth in per capita income is whether the net capital accumulation is large enough to keep up with population growth."[7]

Sachs's solution is "clinical economics." The phrase is extraordinarily telling. This is intervention with medical degrees of precision. In Sachs' view, sufficient foreign aid (around 0.7%) can make up for the lack of capital in poor countries, raising the stock of capital up to lift families above mere survival.[8] This is the philosophy of the eight Millennium Development Goals, the implementation group of which Sachs chaired for three years to 2005.[9]

(2) Turning to metaphors of dislocation, one is that of (a) the dungeon. The dungeon metaphor sees the problem as about not scarcity but sin. Poverty is a kind of incarceration. The poor are kept in poverty by a widening circle of exploiters: by the local non-poor who siphon off resources and benefits that were intended for the disadvantaged, by local authorities who use blackmail and violence to rob the poor, and by local employers and traders who use their strong bargaining position to force economically vulnerable people to sell their goods and labor below market value. Conversely some see poverty as a prison in which people put themselves, either by passive characteristics such as laziness or lack of ambition or by more active destructive tendencies such as reckless behavior or substance addiction.

The dungeon is in many ways a reaction to the desert metaphor. It tends to be favored by those who are disillusioned or angry about the naïvety of the imagery of desert. It shifts the emphasis from resources to relationships. It undoubtedly motivates many social justice and evangelistic responses, generally of a more sophisticated kind than "desert" approaches. However, it shares something significant with the desert metaphor: it is still dominated by the external application of a solution. Thus it can get so caught up in social theory or theological paternalism that it can miss people's specific humanity just as much as the desert metaphor does. It can easily overlook the extraordinary ingenuity required to live in poverty and demonstrated by those poor people who survive.

A second metaphor of dislocation is that of (b) disease. A disease is a condition with a non-human root cause and physical, mental, social, and spiritual symptoms, which nonetheless requires a very human response in every dimension.

This metaphor regards poverty as a kind of sickness. Sickness is usually not something a person is born with, but something they can quickly pick up from those around them. Sickness lies fundamentally in relationships, communities, and societies rather than in individuals. Like any other disease, that response is sometimes aimed at identifying and facilitating a cure, and sometimes focused on continuing to care when a cure is not perceivable. Either way it's about balancing the general characteristics of the disease with its particular manifestation in each person and community and realizing that physical change is only part of an ecology of relational, spiritual, and communal dimensions of healing.

Sickness is a compromise between the metaphors of desert and dungeon. Unlike the dungeon metaphor the language of disease isn't about blame; but unlike the desert language it takes the complexity of poverty seriously. Thus disease language hints that poverty, in some of its dimensions, can afflict even the circumstantially rich.

A third metaphor of dislocation is that of (c) desolation. This picture is less preoccupied with causes and more with symptoms. It perceives geographical, social, and economic isolation. It recognizes that women perform two-thirds of the world's work, earn one-tenth of the world's income, are two-thirds of the world's illiterate, and own less than a hundredth of the world's property. It identifies with people who live in substandard housing with inadequate sanitation, who lack the regular means to feed themselves, with little or no land, livestock, or spare cash, who do not get enough nutritious food to give them energy and help them fight off infections, who often do not live near places where goods are bought and sold, or places where capital or credit are available, who find what money they are able to save is likely to be blown away by obligatory cultural rites of passage, and who live so close to the edge that a natural disaster could force them to sell what few assets they have simply to secure short-term survival.

These are often people who have no relationships in which they can trust, and experience the fraying of domestic, extended family and community ties, resulting in vulnerability to the forces of exploitation – the moneylender, the protection racketeer, the merciless landlord, the bogus holy man, the drug dealer. (Many or most of these conditions can apply to disadvantaged people in the West too.) In such a situation it is hard for anyone to identify what has gone wrong, and it is hard for anyone to identify exactly what a willing person could do to help.[10]

I have offered six metaphors that grip the imagination of debates about poverty. But what I want to highlight is the broad distinction between two kinds of metaphors. On the one hand there are metaphors of deficit, which see the problem as lack of resource, of wisdom, application, skill, or education. On the other hand there are metaphors of dislocation, which see the issues as more about a breakdown in or strain on relationships, health, or community. These two strands name different anthropologies, different notions of aid and development, different notions of sin and redemption, different understandings of public policy, and different perceptions of the church's mission. It is time to explore the dimensions of these differences.

Isolation

These six metaphors of poverty are significant because they all presuppose a view on the fundamental predicament of human existence. Each of the first three metaphors largely assumes that the fundamental human problem is mortality; and thus directs the great majority of our endeavor toward creating opportunities for people to overcome the world's limitations and their own. I am suggesting that educated people in Western culture generally assume the fundamental human problem is mortality, specifically, and human limitation, more generally. Poverty is taken to be an extreme case of the limitations inherent in the human condition, an extreme constraint of freedom.

But this brings us to the heart of the issue. What if it turned out that the fundamental human predicament wasn't mortality after all? What if it turned out that poverty wasn't basically about limitation? What if it turned out that all along the fundamental human problem, and the central factor in poverty, was isolation? What if the answer, for Laszlo, doesn't lie in walking to Cairo?

What do I mean by this? If the fundamental human problem is isolation, then the responses we are looking for don't lie in the laboratory or the hospital or the frontiers of human knowledge or experience. Instead the responses lie in things we already have – most of all, in one another. Let me explain this by asking a basic theological question. Why do Christians, to use conventional and familiar language, want people to be saved? An obvious answer might be, "Because those people are going to die, and maybe they'll go to hell, or oblivion, or nothingness," or whatever the latest term for downstairs happens to be. But if one says, "And what is so great about going to heaven, then?" what kind of an answer do you get? Heaven is the state of being with God and being with one another and being with the renewed creation. That's to say, heaven is not simply a matter of continued being: what matters is that that continued being is *being with*. In other words, a heaven that is simply and only about overcoming mortality is an eternal life that is not worth having. It is not worth having because it leaves one alone forever. And being alone forever is not a description of heaven. It is a description of hell.

There is no value in being unless it is being *with*. There is no value in existence unless it is existence in relationship – with God, one another, and the creation. The heaven that is worth aspiring to is a rejoining of such relationship, a restoration of community, a discovery of partnership, a sense of being in the presence of another in which there is neither a folding of identities that loses their difference nor a sharpening of difference that leads to hostility, but an enjoyment of the other that evokes cherishing and relishing. The theological word for this is communion.

If we look at that second set of metaphors of poverty – the ones I called metaphors of dislocation – we find dungeon, disease, and desolation. These are all fundamentally about the breakdown of relationship. They are not about limitation and mortality – they are about underusing and misusing the gift of one another. They do not presuppose scarcity, competition, and conflict: they open the imagination to limitless possibility in restored connection.

Why Alleviating Mortality Heightens Isolation

I have argued that Western culture assumes the fundamental human problem is mortality; that the fundamental human problem isn't mortality, but is, instead, isolation; and that, in the case of poverty, the metaphors that dominate the discourse can be broadly separated into those that presuppose mortality and those that presuppose isolation. Now I want to show why this distinction between mortality and isolation is so important to the church's mission.

It is not difficult to see how a philosophy based on overcoming mortality and a philosophy based on overcoming isolation can come into tension with one another. As humanity's quest to overcome mortality has gathered pace, the degree of human isolation has increased with it. For sure, enhanced transportation, telecommunications, and information technology have made it possible to communicate in ever more extensive and complex ways. But they have also facilitated lifestyles where people are in touch with conversation partners on the other side of the planet, but not with next-door neighbors; where insurance lies in investments and pensions, rather than in friendships and extended families; and where face-to-face human interaction is ceasing to become the encounter of choice for a generation who are used to having plentiful alternative ways to make themselves known to one another. The flipside of making ourselves more independent and self-sufficient is that we are simultaneously becoming more isolated and more alone.

And this brings me to the crucial point. If you see the central quest of life as overcoming isolation, rather overcoming mortality, your notion of mission will change accordingly. Mission that seeks to overcome isolation does not look to technology to solve problems and reduce limitations. It does not assume that its own knowledge and skill are the crucial element required to change the game. Of course, if you are in the business of overcoming mortality, you are going to need plenty of knowledge and skill. But if you are in the business of overcoming isolation, then you begin to appreciate that concentrating on enhancing and promoting your own knowledge and skill may be as likely to be counterproductive as productive.

In Ephesians, Paul cites one compelling metaphor for what Christ has done in bringing salvation. Paul says, "In his flesh he has made both groups into one and has broken down the dividing wall, that is, the hostility between us" (2:14). Paul is referring to the hostility between Jew and Gentile, but the point goes for any such degree of antagonism and alienation. Indeed, the greater the degree of isolation or antagonism, the more profound the significance of overcoming it. Thus mission becomes recognizing those from whom one is alienated and antagonized and seeking and finding ways to be present to them. Mission is not primarily using one's skills in conflict resolution to bring peace between warring parties, but instead perceiving contexts in which one is one of the warring parties and submitting oneself to a process of making peace.

The approach that sees overcoming mortality as the goal tends to approach mission like this. We, as outsiders to disadvantage and distress, and thus not, in any significant way, part of the problem, nonetheless have expert eyes to see what the problem is, and ready-made solutions to hand. We will appear in the local context, deliver our solution, and then withdraw, quickly to resume our regular activities, which are not considered to have any material bearing, positive or negative, on the problem we have identified and resolved. If we have listened and learned from repeated interventions of this kind, we will have gathered that it is good to form relationships on the ground, good to involve local participants in some way, else local wisdom be neglected and local goodwill be needlessly undermined. But the point is that this local participation is never more than a means to an end. The end is never in question. The end always comes in the form of overcoming the limitations of the local environment or skill-base, and the provision of technology or the enhancement of the capacity to use it.

Contrast this with the kind of mission that emerges from a conviction that the goal is to overcome isolation. We are not exactly sure what the problem is, but we take for granted that we are a part of it. We do not assume that the solution is to make other people more like us by ensuring that they have what we have and live as we live. We take it for granted that we have a deficiency, and we presume that deficiency is due to the poverty or absence of our relationship with those who have important and invigorating things to share with us, if only we could open up channels to receive those things. We may well embark on projects that seek to alleviate distress or transfer resources or develop skills. But the point of these projects is not to achieve a specific material goal: these endeavors are simply means of forming relationships from a safe common starting point. These programs are ladders that will fall away once the relationships are in place and genuine dialogue is happening. What we might call the "mortality model" insists that what is required is the introduction of new information, new technique, and new technology. The "isolation model" asserts that in most cases a people or a neighborhood already has almost everything it needs for its own redemption: what inhibits such redemption is the energy lost in isolation and wasted in antagonism.

One can tell the story of modernity as the tussle between two key principles: liberty and equality. They broadly name the two major party political options, at least in a British and perhaps in an American context. But when one returns to the motto of the French Revolution, as adopted by the Third Republic, fraternity may appear to be the neglected one of the three. Of course each term has many definitions, and fraternity is too masculine a term to be fit for wholehearted commendation. But the general point stands – that liberty and equality are noble aims but finally only means to an end. And it is fraternity that should be regarded as the proper goal of its two more celebrated predecessors.[11]

The identification of isolation as an alternative to mortality, and the distinction between metaphors of deficit and metaphors of dislocation, together yield an irony that this chapter has been designed to highlight. And that irony is this: those initiatives in mission that generally begin with a deficit notion of poverty, and assume the human predicament is mortality and limitation, have a tendency of actually increasing isolation. In all the haste to provide technology and enhance technique and alleviate the limitations of climate or scarcity or skill, mortality-motivated service can often underline and even enhance the kinds of social alienation that, from the isolation perspective, constitute the problem in the first place.

To return to poverty: in the understanding I am following, poverty is not fundamentally about the absence of money, or about the lack of conventional forms of power. It is about the impoverishment, the instrumentalization, the manipulation, the breakdown, or the perversion of relationship. For sure, poverty diminishes human dignity – and human dignity is often taken to be a fundamental matter whose upholding needs no advocacy. But notice, again, that the quest to assert and affirm human dignity may have the unanticipated side-effect or the less explicit implication of leaving people alone, and reinforcing their isolation. There is something more fundamental than detached dignity, and that is the enrichment of genuine and enhancing relationships. There is no way of simply providing those relationships *for* people. A notion of mission predicated on mortality and limitation risks becoming a form of technology that seeks to make a better world without us needing to become better people, a kind of device that seeks to rescue people without the bothersome business of relationships. All that such initiatives can do is to facilitate circumstances and conditions in which crucial relationships can begin, take root, grow, and thrive. Such initiatives can address mortality and limitation, but they cannot overcome isolation.

Conclusion

Let us return to *The English Patient*. We began this chapter with Laszlo's choice of whether to stay beside Katherine and be her companion in her last hours, or walk to Cairo in search of assistance. In the story, Laszlo scarcely thinks twice before he sets off on his three-day journey to find help. He has all sorts of adventures before he finally makes it back to the encampment and the ancient cave. And when he does, Katherine is very, very dead. Laszlo is so committed to believing that there is a solution to Katherine's agonizing plight, and that he has the solution, that he overlooks the one thing needful. And that is, being with Katherine. He is so concerned to solve the problem that he leaves her alone in her hour of greatest need.

Could it possibly be that the real reason Laszlo went to Cairo was because he couldn't bear to watch Katherine die? Is not Western late modernity a culture in which we fill our lives with activity and creativity and productivity because we fear if we sat still we'd go to pieces? What Katherine needed was the man she loved to be with her as she faced the near-certainty of her own impending death. But Laszlo did not, or maybe could not, give her what she needed. We are turning our world into a Laszlo society, full of products, full of gadgets, full of devices, full of techniques, full of energy, all of which make the world go round very effectively. The result is that we have all become Laszlo.

Yet the irony of the film is that when Laszlo, returning to Cairo with Katherine's body, crashes another plane, and is himself horribly injured, he is found in the desert, and carefully extracted from the wreckage, and tenderly accompanied by strangers – who then care for him until the point of his death. He receives from strangers at the end of *his* life the patient love he was unable to give to Katherine at the end of hers.

Can we, in the face of every pressure of our culture and our day, learn from his parable, and come to be wiser than him? That is the subject of this book.

Notes

1. Michael Ondaatje, *The English Patient* (Toronto: McClelland and Stewart, 1992); Anthony Minghella, director, *The English Patient* (Miramax, 1996).
2. Samuel Beckett, *Waiting for Godot* (London: Faber and Faber, 1956): Act II.
3. Isaac Watts, "O God, Our Help in Ages Past," first published in his *The Psalms of David Imitated in the Language of the New Testament* (1719).
4. Jeffrey Sachs, *The End of Poverty* (New York: Penguin, 2005).
5. Jeffrey Sachs, *The End of Poverty*: 244–245.
6. Jeffrey Sachs, *The End of Poverty*: 245.
7. Jeffrey Sachs, *The End of Poverty*: 245.
8. Jeffrey Sachs, *The End of Poverty*: 288.
9. The eight Millennium Development Goals are: (1) to eradicate extreme poverty and hunger; (2) to achieve universal primary education; (3) to promote gender equality and empower women; (4) to reduce infant mortality; (5) to improve maternal health; (6) to combat HIV/AIDS, malaria, and other diseases; (7) to ensure environmental sustainability; and (8) to develop a global partnership for development. See www.un.org/millenniumgoals (accessed December 6, 2014).
10. The most helpful and informative study of global poverty of which I am aware is Anirudh Krishna, *One Illness Away: Why People Become Poor and How They Escape Poverty* (Oxford and New York: Oxford University Press, 2010). Krishna offers four main reasons why people become poor – health (illness, disability, healthcare expenses), household characteristics (the gender of the head of the household, social and ceremonial expenses such as weddings and funerals), land-related events (land division, crop disease, rainfall failures, land exhaustion), and high interest private debt (which is linked to all the previous factors). He points out that many people move into and out of poverty frequently throughout their lives.

11. "Civil enterprise is not satisfied activating only the first two principles of modernity – liberty and equality – it also aims for fraternity, a principle that turns liberty and equality into humanizing and civilizing experiences." Luigino Bruni and Stefano Zamagni, *Civil Economy: Efficiency, Equity, Public Happiness* (Berne, Switzerland: Peter Lang, 2007): 185. I am grateful to Luke Bretherton for bringing this book (and the notion of civil economy) to my attention.

4

Reconceiving the Divine Purpose

Chapter 3 relocated the human predicament from mortality to isolation. This chapter seeks to advance a parallel argument in relation to God's purpose for humanity and consequently humanity's notion of its own mission and well-being.

My focus is on the notion of reconciliation. I point out that reconciliation usually takes place against a backdrop of exasperation and impatience. What all parties generally assume is that healthy coexistence – which we could call "peace," often taken to be the permitting of one another to flourish in their own chosen way without undue interference from others – is normal and achievable: and thus that if such coexistence has been interrupted, damaged, or destroyed, it must be because the other party is irrational or evil. Time taken up in reconciliation, though possibly necessary and unavoidable, is nonetheless time wasted, because there are urgent and important tasks to be attended to elsewhere, tasks from which this conflict has been a tiresome distraction.

However, from the perspective being developed in this book, there simply is nothing more important than reestablishing relationship. Reconciliation is not a tiresome distraction: it really is the center of divine purpose and human mission. It is what God shapes the life of the Trinity around; it is what Jesus calls his followers to practice. Discovering this is as significant as realizing isolation is the central human predicament. The two insights complement each other and set up the constructive argument of the book.

A Congregation in Conflict

There is no such thing as silence. What we call silence is a selection of which noises we choose to hear. One of the joys of silent meditation is that we become aware of sounds that would usually be drowned or ignored.

A Nazareth Manifesto, Samuel Wells © 2015 John Wiley & Sons, Ltd. Published 2015 by John Wiley & Sons, Ltd.

In the same way there is no such thing as peace, if peace is taken to mean the absence of conflict. There is only the selection of which kinds of tensions, differences, and disputes we choose to regard as significant, and the degree to which they are harmonious, constructive, or suppressed. The cessation, resolution, or, more likely, translation of one conflict simply creates time and space to become aware of others. When we regard a conflict as a waste of time or energy, it is not because conflict itself is pointless; it is because we believe this conflict in question is distracting us from conflicts elsewhere that are more urgent, significant, rewarding, or otherwise worthy of our attention. Reconciliation is not about replacing conflict with peace. It is about the transfiguration of conflict into glory. True peace is not the absence of conflict, but the transformation of destructive tension into dynamic creativity, the turning of the competition that presupposes scarcity into the complementarity that assumes abundance, the emergence of thankfulness in place of resentment, and the retelling of a story that ceases to believe stray elements can or should be written out of the script.

I once had a role that included overseeing a couple of dozen churches. I got a call from a vicar in distress asking me to come and chair an extraordinary congregational meeting in a church that was torn apart by strife in many ways but had finally chosen to have it out and shed blood over the stained-glass windows. There were five arches at the east end of the sanctuary. Four contained Victorian stained glass that had been covered up during the 1930s. The central, larger, arch was different. It had had an abstract colored glass design installed in the 1950s. A few months before this crisis meeting, a couple of powerful characters had taken it upon themselves to uncover the four Victorian windows. The resulting five panels went together about as well as ice cream served with tomato ketchup. Civil war broke out among the congregation, and a special meeting was called.

The vicar was prepared to let the meeting run for only one hour. Perhaps he thought that would keep the level of emotion under control. If so, he was wrong. Influential protagonists gave opening seven-minute arguments for and against. It turned out the issue of non-matching stained-glass windows had a bearing on everything from global poverty to world evangelism to climate change to arts opportunities in major cities. Leaving time for summing up, I had 30 minutes left for contributions from the floor. I asked how many people wished to speak. Fifteen hands were raised. I did the arithmetic and said it was therefore going to be two minutes each, no more, and we would start with the person nearest the front and work our way back.

A 35-year-old woman began the debate. She had a sheaf of maybe 20 pages of handwritten text in her hands and there was no way two minutes was going to be enough for her. After a minute and three-quarters I told her she had 15 seconds left. She took no notice. She just spoke faster and crashed through the time barrier. I said "It's time to stop." She continued, with a little laugh. I said in a louder voice "I'm just going to talk over you so people can't hear what you're saying until you stop talking and sit down." After 10 seconds of unequal struggle, she gave up.

Up stepped the second speaker. He spent his first minute and three-quarters telling us he'd been chair of this and major-general of the other. I said "You've got 15 seconds left." He said "I'm not going to be told I can't make my point by somebody who ..." I said "It's time to stop ... and I'm going to talk over you as well until you let someone else speak." After that people got the message. I formed an impression that no one had stood up to these people for a generation or more. This was a group of parishioners so locked into a cycle of bullying and manipulation that the whole church was being held to ransom. Here was a community where conflict had simmered for decades. The fight presented itself as being about worship and the beauty of holiness but it was really more about taste and power and having no confidence in the leadership and therefore bypassing due procedure, and people coming to terms with having less influence in a congregation than they had at work or at home.

This story isn't about Syria or Rwanda or Northern Ireland or South Africa. I offer it in all its bourgeois provinciality because it presents precisely the exasperation and impatience that conflict, particularly in the church circles, tends to evoke. It is those responses that I suggest may disclose a reconception of the divine purpose.

My argument comes in four parts. I want first to note the mood of conflict in the church and among Christians. The word I discern to identify that mood is exasperation. I then want to deepen the diagnosis of that mood. The word on which I focus that diagnosis is impatience. In the third part of the chapter I explore the theological issues behind that word, "exasperation." Finally I dig away at the theological questions that lie inside that term, "impatience."

Exasperation

And so to the word "exasperation." There are two kinds of exasperation.

The first is a notion of progress. Of course Cain and Abel had their difficulties, but we have moved on since then. We have abundant economic resources; Cain and Abel had to choose between livestock and soil – but we can have both. We have breathtaking communications devices: there is no need to be in any doubt about what was said, here or on the other side of the world; it can all be recorded and transmitted and proved and received within seconds. We have long-established political and legal procedures: if we are not sure how to handle a new question, there are oceans of people happily employed to help us and advise us and show us and prepare us.

The one thing we do not seem to have improved is other people. We ourselves are much improved, of course; we have read self-help books, we have recognized our tendency to be conflict-averse, we know all about assertiveness, we were brought up by parents who were much more in touch with their feelings than their own parents were, and we've had plenty of chance to tell therapists how cross we are with our parents despite their much-improved handling of our childhood. But other people seem to be just as exasperating as they ever were. All the fruits and momentum of human progress have gained compelling force in every other place: but in this person I am in conflict with right now they seem to be entirely absent. This really is absurd. At that debate about the stained-glass windows it was very difficult for anyone to maintain eye contact with their opponent for even a moment. Each speaker seemed to agree that it was simply too bad that people as dumb-headed as the other crowd even existed on the planet, let alone in the same congregation. That is the first kind of exasperation.

The second kind of exasperation is a notion of salvation. Jesus has broken down the dividing wall of hostility. How very good and pleasant it is when kindred live together in unity! It is like the precious oil on the head, running down upon the beard. When two or three are gathered, Jesus is in the midst of them. We are one body with many members. In other words, for Christian believers, Christ's redemption has ended conflict with God and with one another. The war is over. To carry on fighting is as ridiculous and quaint as one of those Japanese soldiers found in the forests of Sumatra in the sixties who never got the message about Nagasaki and thought the Second World War was still going on. Christ's salvation is secured, and the only tasks remaining are to spread the good news and deal with the sticky problem of oil on the beard.

Thus, if all were faithful and simply accepted the good news of Christ's salvation, there would be no conflict. Again, conflict is exasperating. Either my opponent must be stupid, and not grasp the good news, failing to realize that I am its messenger; or my adversary must be perverse, as if the Japanese soldier knew the war was over but just decided to keep on fighting anyway.

And this latter moment, the point at which I assume my adversary to be perverse, is a point of great danger, because it legitimizes demonization and induces an atmosphere in which quickly the only way to limit the damage my adversary can do seems to be the use of force. Christ's achievement of peace suddenly becomes a pretext for compulsion, because the opponent is either too ignorant or stupid to understand peace or too perverse or evil to accede to it.[1] When the first speaker in the windows debate assumed her prepared statement entitled her to extra time, and when the major-general listed all his previous triumphs, I took it that in different ways both were expressing dismay that they had to put their argument into words, because surely it should go without saying.

For these reasons Christians face conflict inside and outside the church in a mood of exasperation. It is something that simply should not be. There is a story about a Russian train that ground to a halt on a snowy night in a forest. All the famous leaders of the twentieth century were on board. Lenin went forward to the cabin to re-educate the driver. The train remained stationary. Stalin went forward and shot the driver. Still the train did not move. Finally Brezhnev went through the train closing all the curtains and telling the passengers the train was moving. It is not a bad parable of how Christians deal with conflict. Some concentrate on education and persuasion; others use force; others again resort to denial. What they all share is fury that the train is not moving – a fury that I am calling exasperation – and an assumption that the problem is not really down to the train, but to the other people on it.

Impatience

And so to impatience. If exasperation comes from thinking the conflict is ridiculous, impatience arises from inferring the conflict is wasteful. The kingdom may not have definitively come in wind and fire with Christ's return on the clouds of heaven in quite the way many members of the early church anticipated, but one thing that has not changed since the first century is the sense of urgency held by Jesus' followers. People may disagree about the rights and wrongs of issues and questions; they may have different understandings of points of principle and points of no return; they may have varied perceptions of shame and humiliation and disgrace and abhorrence; but what they can all agree on is that their opponent has dragged them into a fight that has brought an unconscionable dissipation of time and resources, has distracted them from the certain course they were pre-viously on, and has left an ever-mounting agenda of items that will perhaps now never receive the attention they deserve.

This form of impatience creates a vicious circle: the more wasteful you sense the conflict is becoming, the less energy you have to take any serious time over it; the less serious time you give it, the more likely you are to make moves that inflame the conflict or miss opportunities to downscale it; and thus the more intense the conflict becomes, with an attendant consumption of time and resources. In the great stained-glass debate, everyone without exception took this view: the people on the other side were grossly wasteful, either by neglecting the glories of Victoriana, or by dissipating the insight of the postwar vision. The sentiment that the money wasted on the debate should go to address the causes and alleviate the symptoms of global pover-ty drew applause from both sides.

This mindset of impatience makes two fundamental assumptions. One is that resources and time are in short supply. This is certainly the language of the market. The market depends on creating the notion of scarcity, so that consumers will commit to an ever-higher price for goods that seem quicker, better, finer, stronger, slicker, safer. But the kingdom of God is not the mar-ket. In the kingdom of God, God gives disciples everything they need to do the work God calls them to do. Happiness in the kingdom of God is about learning to love the things that are not in short supply – like the fruits of the Spirit. What are these things that are so needy and so urgent that we are so impatient to get to them, and have neither the time nor the resources to be delayed by tiresome and distracting conflicts? Are we not really saying, "I am fed up of this conflict that I unaccountably do not seem to be winning and I want to release more time to focus on conflicts where I have more confidence that I do seem to be winning"?

A second assumption is that God's work of redemption is somehow in-complete – that there was something God was either too busy, or too for-getful, or in too much of a hurry to do, or in some other way constrained from getting done in Jesus. This would mean we really would be in a hurry, because God would be relying on us to complete the work of salvation, and there would not be a moment to lose. Or is the issue that we alone have the knowledge and ability to fulfill the vocation of bearing Christ's mission, and this paltry conflict is an insult to our agenda because there is work that only we can do and now we may never do it, or have time to do it properly?

In other words, lurking behind this sense of impatience, is there either rather too little faith in God, and the comprehensiveness and completeness of God's work of salvation, or rather too much faith in ourselves, and our indispensability to the fulfillment of God's mission? Could it possibly be that when we examine this impatience closely, what we find is that this impatience isn't impatience with sin, but impatience with God and the world for not being conformed to our desires?

Leaving aside for a moment the precise diagnoses, I trust I have made the case that our experience of conflict is invariably one of exasperation and impatience: exasperation, because the parties to the conflict, along with reconcilers, tend to be of the view that if all were faithful, there would be no conflict; thus the enemy must be either stupid or perverse; and impatience, because all sides, and observers, lament that this conflict is taking up huge amounts of energy and delaying the work of the kingdom that is the true call of discipleship. Now I would like to explore further the truth of those judgments.

Difference

What I am going to do in this part of my argument is to ground what I am saying in perhaps the three most decisive parts of the Christian story: creation, salvation, and eternal life. I want to emphasize that reconciliation is at the heart of all things, and impossible to disentangle from God's way of being with the world, yesterday, today, and forever.

I'm going to start with the notion of difference. Here let me make three very simple, yet easily neglected, claims. First, creation is, by its very nature, the inception of difference. God is pure essence; but when that essence is translated, by a process we call creation, into time-bound and contingent existence, then out of nothing comes diversity. And at once we have the dynamic that underwrites everything that follows: will that diversity be harmonious – will that difference of creatures from God and one another issue in joy – or will there be tension, conflict, disharmony, and discord?

There are two rival answers to that question. One is that tension and conflict inevitably arise from difference; and because difference obviously cannot be eradicated, authority emerges to limit the dominance of the weak by the strong, to arbitrate between rival claims, and to police rules of fairness and equality. The other answer is that creation is a symphony, and even though more than one instrument is likely to be playing at any one time, and by no means always playing the same notes, that is how symphonies work, and the point of creation is to enjoy the different instruments and melodies enhancing and augmenting and bringing the best out of each other.

Notice the way these answers assume alternative views of flourishing. For the first answer, other beings are fundamentally an obstacle and a threat to our own flourishing, and order is required to ensure they don't inhibit our well-being inordinately. There is no explicit understanding of what constitutes flourishing, but a perpetual anxiety about being constrained and limited. For the second answer, flourishing means the harmonious development of beauty in interactive partnership with the complementary gifts of other beings; far from being always potential inhibitors of our well-being, other creatures are inherent to its expression, and there's no flourishing without them.

Notice also that for the first model there is every hope and reasonable expectation that humanity should be able to arrive at a set of rational and sustainable laws and guidelines that should govern and ensure just interaction in this and every age. For the second model, by contrast, there will never be a set of sustainable laws; all one can aspire to is a set of skills by which all parties seek to improvise in ever-new circumstances as creation takes on ever-new configurations. What this means is that those who uphold the first model will constantly be exasperated by failures in the system that lead to one party seeming to undertake an unfair action or maintain an unreasonable position, and the recourse will almost inevitably be to law as an even-handed mechanism for resolving disputes and reasserting a balance of power, followed by force to back up that law. By contrast for those who assume the second model, there is no impartial equilibrium, and there is no aspiration to restore a past moment of balance and stillness: all is flux, and the skill is to take the energy generated by difference and seek to make that energy as constructive and its clashes as positive as possible.

One way to illuminate this distinction is to distinguish between construction and horticulture. That which is built begins immediately to decay; the effort is to keep it as much as possible like it was on the day it was completed, and other buildings are more likely to be a threat than an asset. This resembles the first model. By contrast, that which is planted begins immediately to grow; the effort is to prune and steer in such a way that maximizes growth and interaction with the rest of the garden. To imagine returning to the moment before it was planted is out of the question; meanwhile it needs other vegetation to flourish. An understanding of difference sits much more easily with the horticultural metaphor; coping with conflict is much more like tending a garden than like restoring a set of buildings to their pristine condition.

Let me move to my second fundamental, but easily overlooked, claim. Heaven is the perfection of difference. Let us tease out the significance of this apparently innocent assertion. Heaven is not a freeze-frame of ecstatic or euphoric stillness: it is a dynamic interaction of God, redeemed creatures, and the renewed creation, in which there is partnership without pain and expression without envy. It is not the absorption of all difference into the infinite, or the reversal of creation by the assertion of God alone, or essence without existence. In heaven, God, humanity, and the renewed creation continue to interact with one another, but this interaction issues in continuous iterations of ceaselessly new fruits. There is change, but no death; growth, but no loss; creativity, but no suffering.

See how this claim highlights the assertions we have already made. Heaven is a place of abundance and not scarcity. There is no hurry, because it is eternity. There is no necessity for any individual to get anything done against any kind of deadline or in response to any kind of need – only benefit for everyone from each person fulfilling their God-given role in the orchestra. And note most significantly, heaven is not a set of roles carried out within timeless rules, but an ever-growing, never-repeating, constantly improvising, emerging relationship in which every gesture changes the template and every intervention creates new and unlimited possibilities and configurations. In other words, reconciliation is not the restoration of an untroubled condition before a conflict; it is the creation of something that might never have been without that conflict.

And so to my third claim, which arises from the first two. Between creation and eschaton, or heaven as I am calling it, lies the story of God. And the story of God is, from beginning to end, and at every moment along the way, a story of tension and conflict. In Genesis 3:9 God says to Adam and Eve, "Where are you?" In Genesis 4:9 God says to Cain, "Where is your brother?" And God keeps asking Israel these same two questions throughout the Old Testament; and has been asking the church the same two questions ever since. "Where are you?" and "Where is your brother?" – questions that name the conflict between humanity and God and between humans and one another.[2] In Egypt Israel discovers what it means to be at enmity with an oppressor, and to find itself in slavery; in Babylon Israel appreciates what it is like to have wandered far from God, and to redefine itself in exile. In the exodus we see God's liberating will and power in parting the Red Sea;

on Sinai we see God's covenanting purpose in shaping ways for Israel to keep its freedom.

At every stage there is conflict. One can portray Israel – and Jesus' disciples, correspondingly – as fragile, foolish, and faithless; but that would be to miss the point. The point is that at every stage salvation is contested, and emerges out of setback, suffering, and fierce debate. God's way of salvation is not to obliterate controversy and replace it with simple accord; it is to take failure and turn it into the opportunity for discovery, transformation, intimacy, and hope. There would be no Old Testament without Egypt and Babylon; there would be no New Testament without the cross. If you see conflict and tension as a source largely of exasperation and impatience, you are missing out on the Bible, the gospel, and the church. There is not much left.

Gospel

Even those who are committed to practices of reconciliation often assume that the central concerns of the Christian faith are the gospel and the kingdom of God, and that it is worth whatever it takes to get to the place where they and others can wholeheartedly share the gospel and dwell in the kingdom of God, and all their work in reconciliation is a humble and self-denying precursor to that wondrous ministry and mission. But the truth is, far from being an essential, tiresome, and time-consuming precursor to the gospel, reconciliation *is* the gospel. There is not anything more important to which reconciliation is but the prologue.

It gets back to one of the most fundamental theological questions of them all, which is this. Did Jesus come in response to the fall, as an agent to do the work of restoring human relationship with God – and thus was his saving work, his passion, death, and resurrection a device to rectify that relationship and secure forgiveness and eternal life? Or was the coming of God written into the DNA of creation, because of God's primordial and eternal decision never to be except to be with us in Christ? If one takes the first view, then Christ's saving work is a ladder both humanity and God ultimately kick away because the whole point is the restored relationship; for both parties the moment will eventually come when the historical events of the gospels are all a very long time ago and, profoundly grateful for them as we will always be, they will be displaced by happier, more blissful, and more seamless joys.

But if one takes the second view, that the coming of God was always going to happen, regardless of whether or not there was a fall, because of God's
decision never to be except to be with us in Christ, then Jesus' passion,
death, and resurrection are not a means to an end: they are the revelation of
the truth about us and the truth about God – and the truth about what happens when we and God get as close as God always destined for us to be. In
other words the tension and conflict we see in the passion, death, and resurrection of Jesus are not a mechanism to bring about the kingdom of God:
they *are* the kingdom of God. There is no God lurking beyond Christ's passion to which Christ's passion is but an entry ticket. This is God – constantly
vulnerable to human rejection, embodying agonizing love, and yet never
letting that suffering have the last word. And there is no sublime pacific
ocean of repose beyond the glory of resurrection: there is only the breaking
through of wondrous love amid the scars and hurts of painful conflict.

Most of all, there is no gospel to which Christ's passion, death, and resurrection are the precursor: Christ's passion, death, and resurrection *are*
the gospel. Christians don't believe in the God of Jesus Christ because they
want forgiveness and eternal life and adjudge Jesus as the best route to both.
Christians believe because they are drawn into the mystery of Christ's passion, death, and resurrection, and find in that story all the truth they can
imagine about who God is and who they are. It is not a stepping-stone: it is
all there is.

When Mary Magdalene clings to Jesus in the garden outside the empty
tomb, she wants to believe the resurrection is now the whole of reality, that
pain and grief and death and suffering and loss and anger and misery are
over and she can be in the arms of the risen Lord forever. Who can blame
her? But it is not so. What has happened has confirmed how things will finally be – sin and death will not have the last word. But tension and conflict
will be around a long while yet, and the kingdom of God will appear *amid*
this tension and conflict, not after they have been resolved or when they've
been averted. The irony and paradox of the Old Testament, on which the
New Testament is founded, is that the people of God were as close to God in
the wilderness as they were in the Promised Land and that they saw God's
heart more truly in exile than they did on their return. Faith is not the solution of a problem but the entering of a mystery.

The work of reconciliation is not about offering techniques and best
practice and facilitation and listening skills and procedures to take people
out of the wilderness and exile and bringing them to the Promised Land
and the rebuilt Jerusalem. Neither is it about both parties coming to realize

that the conflict is ridiculous and the issue is not worth fighting over and they would be much better off getting on with their regular lives and forgetting about it. The work of reconciliation is about recognizing that when God and humanity came face to face, the cross was the result, and about believing that, just as God brought glory out of the cross, God will bring transfiguration when energies that are arrayed against one another are gradually, often painfully, and always wondrously realigned to create dynamism and new life.

If for a moment we set aside our exasperation and impatience, what do we see? Think again about the infuriating story about the stained-glass windows. What was really going on? The people obsessed about a 1950s glass design saw it as a symbol of the fresh air that came into the whole church in the fifties, of social justice, global awareness, and the beginnings of a post-imperial post-pietist sense of holiness. They had great hopes for the new vicar but those hopes disintegrated in petty administrative failures and relational fragilities. The people fixated on the Victorian windows were pining for a stable, ordered society that has gone away, for church and nation in harmony, for arts and faith to sing together once more, for a common life that was not dominated by invasive transport and interfering technology. Only if you hear out these stories do you get to the point of repentance where people can acknowledge their demeaning remarks and underhand stitch-ups and small-minded accusations.

And only now, with truth in one hand and repentance in the other, can we begin to see that Christ died for this, for this mundane congregation with its bourgeois battle about windows, because this battle about windows is really a struggle for faith and relevance and meaning and impact and hope and trust and discipleship and grief and mission and beauty and longing. This is the moment when we need to ask both parties for some gesture of penance, some sign that acknowledges one another's wounds and integrity. Only at this point – and it requires us to set aside impatience and exasperation and exercise all our time and courage and wisdom and perseverance to get to this point – only at this point can we hope to glimpse some forgiveness, and inch toward something like reconciliation; and only when the dust has begun to settle on reconciliation can we start looking for healing.

And yet we moan to our wise counselor that this windows story is ridiculous and exasperating and wasting way too much of our time. But our wise counselor gently says to us, "Tell me what it is about." And we say "It is about 1950s art snobs and Victorian antiquarians." And our wise counselor says, "Tell me what it is really about." And we say, "It is about faith and relevance and meaning and impact and hope and trust." And our counselor leaves a silence, and says, "Anything else?" And we say, "It's about discipleship and grief and mission and beauty and longing." And our counselor leaves an even longer silence, and says, "And you are telling me that you have got more important things to worry about than those."

And we say, "But this church is crucifying me." And our counselor tenderly says, "No, it may feel like that. But really, this church is crucifying Jesus. All churches do. Your choice is whether you are going to impose or pretend a false peace because you think you have got more important things to do, which really means more winnable battles to fight elsewhere, or if you are going to get stuck into the hassle and hustle of truth-telling, repentance, penance, forgiveness, reconciliation, and healing. Which one do you think looks more like the cross?" And at this juncture we mutter a short, Germanic, guttural word – which is exasperated code for saying, "I get it, you are telling me it's all about Jesus' passion, death, and resurrection. You are telling me we never get bigger than the cross. I somehow got into thinking I was beyond that."

Conclusion

In Chapter 3 I argued that the postponing of mortality and the diminishment of limitation (that we so earnestly seek) are no good to us if they are acquired without the restoration and enjoyment of relationship; and that the clear-sighted attempt to delay mortality and reduce limitation often has the consequence of actually increasing isolation and militating against the flourishing of relationship.

Here I have made a parallel argument. I have explored ways in which those devoted to Christian mission see reconciliation as a tiresome, albeit necessary, distraction from the true purpose of their ministry; while in fact reconciliation is the essence of God's mission in Christ and thus of all Christian mission. There is no gospel to which Christ's passion, death, and resurrection are the precursor; there is no mission from which the work of reconciliation is a distraction.

The argument of these two chapters has been designed to "loosen the soil" – to question assumptions and undermine certainties in the whole area of human well-being and care for others. Time with others – time that is not inherently purposeful, goal-oriented, and solution-seeking – is not wasteful, indulgent, neglectful or worthless: it is, on the contrary, the goal of creation, the telos of humanity, and the vision of God.

Notes

1. People "seek a universal standard of human good. After painful effort they define it. The painfulness of their effort convinces them that they have discovered a genuinely universal value. To their sorrow, some of their fellow men refuse to accept the standard. Since they know the standard to be universal the recalcitrance of their fellows is a proof, in their minds, of some defect in the humanity of the non-conformists. Thus a rationalistic age creates a new fanaticism. The non-conformists are figuratively expelled from the human community." Reinhold Niebuhr, *Beyond Tragedy* (New York: Scribners, 1965): 237.
2. For more on these two questions, see Samuel Wells, *Learning to Dream Again: Rediscovering the Heart of God* (Grand Rapids, MI: Eerdmans, 2013): 130–135; (UK edition, with substantial alterations, Norwich, UK: Canterbury, 2013): 117–123.

Part II

God is With Us

Thus far we have explored two routes to the same goal. The first argument is that the human predicament is not so much about mortality as it is about isolation – yet that the majority of humanitarian endeavor proceeds as if the opposite were the case. The second argument is that the mission of God is always about reconciliation and relationship – there is no further goal beyond that to which God is urging us, however impatient and exasperated we might become in accepting that.

In this second part of the book we consider the skeleton of the scriptural story – in liberation, covenant, exile, baptism, cross, and resurrection – in order to identify and highlight the ways the narrative portrays God being with Israel and with all humanity in Jesus. While we shall return to the centrality of Jesus in Chapter 9, the argument here is that the Bible offers a consistent message, of which Jesus' incarnation and crucifixion are the most explicit embodiments; and Chapter 5 seeks to trace that message as one of God being with us.

The sixth chapter remains with Jesus but turns attention back to poverty by considering at length what is sometimes seen as the definitive Christian statement about poverty – the parable of the Good Samaritan. Here we see that Christians are called to a change of heart: far from simply seeing the needy as their responsibility, they are asked to see ways in which they, individually and collectively, are needy, and ways in which God sends those they like to call the "needy" to disturb, surprise, and ultimately convert them. The Christian relationship to poverty is thus not fundamentally working on behalf of the poor but developing reciprocal relationships and expecting to receive from the poor.

Chapter 7 returns to the four notions of engaging disadvantage outlined in Chapter 2. The book as a whole is designed to be an articulation of the principle and practices of being with. But some treatment of the other three notions is called for, and in this chapter I discuss at some length the strengths, but especially the weaknesses, of these other approaches. It does not occur to me that being with displaces the other approaches altogether: to do so is not possible, nor necessary, nor even desirable. There is a time and a place for all four. However I need to articulate more precisely why being with is invariably bypassed in the eagerness to practice the other three approaches, and this chapter is the place to do so.

If Part I of the book was designed to whet the appetite for being with, Part II argues that being with has always been God's way with the world, that despite familiar readings of emblematic themes and stories it is the heart of Jesus' message, and that other approaches to social engagement, while when practiced alongside being with are complementary to it, when practiced in isolation from it are profoundly flawed.

5

The Story of Jesus

In this chapter we consider five closely related arguments about the God revealed in the Bible. The first is that Jesus is our-being-with-God, prefigured in the Old Testament notion of the Sabbath. The second is that the Old Testament hinges on the dynamic between Egypt and Babylon – between the God who delivers the Israelites from slavery and the God who brings comfort to people in exile; and that, as we found in Chapter 4 in relation to reconciliation, God's underlying purpose is toward relationship – that if God acts for Israel, it is to serve the ultimate purpose of being with Israel. At this point the next logical step would be the incarnation, but here I refer the reader to the sermon that forms the prologue to this book. Thus the third stage in the argument suggests that the moment in Jesus' story that brings Egypt and Babylon most explicitly together is Jesus' baptism, and that Jesus' baptism is an embodiment of the logic of the incarnation in Old Testament perspective. Fourth, looking to the cross, what looks like the definitive action of God on our behalf turns out to be a further demonstration of God's commitment to be with us. And fifth, the resurrection heals the "without" – that which inhibited the with between humanity and God – and at the same time makes the with permanent forever.

Sabbath

The Sabbath is God's way of enabling Israel to make friends with time. Abraham Heschel recognizes how deeply contemporary civilization fears, resents, distrusts, even hates time. "Time to us is sarcasm, a slick treacherous monster with a jaw like a furnace incinerating every moment of our lives" (5).[1] From this starting-point, Heschel makes two claims. One is that there is a fundamental tension between time and space, and that humans invest in material things because of their fear of and antipathy to time. The other is that Judaism has a particular relationship to time, mediated definitively by its practice of Sabbath, and this relationship affirms the triumph of time over space.

To start with the tension between time and space, Heschel puts it this way. "Technical civilization is [our] conquest of space. ... In technical civilization, we expend time to gain space. ... yet to have more is not to be more. The power we attain in the world of space terminates abruptly at the borderline of time. But time is the heart of existence" (3). Technical civilization, Heschel goes on, begins when we engage in a struggle with nature, with the twin aim of enhancing our safety and increasing our comfort. Heschel notes how proud we are of the instruments we have created and the commodities we have produced; but he strongly suspects that "the forces we had conquered have conquered us" (27). Heschel maintains, "Space is exposed to our will ... Time is beyond our reach. ... We share time, we own space" (99). The constant mistake we make is to think we can conquer time through space. Time can only be encountered through time. Our obsession with space blinds us to the true dynamics of time. "Time, that which is beyond and independent of space, is everlasting; it is the world of space which is perishing. Things perish within time; time itself does not change. ... It is not time that dies; it is the human body which dies in time" (97).

In this context the Sabbath is not a way out, but is instead "the day on which we learn the art of *surpassing* civilization" (27, italics in original). How is this done? Here we come to the particular relationship of Jews to time, embodied in the practice of Sabbath. The following words highlight the proximity of Heschel's concern to my own argument: he looks to a challenge

> To set apart one day a week for freedom, a day on which we would not use the instruments which have been so easily turned into weapons of destruction, a day for *being with ourselves*, a day of detachment from the vulgar, of independence of external obligations, a day on which we use no money, a day of armistice in the economic struggle with our fellow men and the forces of nature. (28, my italics)

Just as the legitimate Sabbath activities are those that were necessary for constructing the sanctuary in the desert, such a Sabbath becomes "a sanctuary in time" (29). Thus "The Sabbaths are our great cathedrals; and our Holy of Holies is ... the Day of Atonement" (8). Heschel notes that God blessed the seventh day – but there is no parallel reference to making any object holy (9). The Sabbath celebrates time rather than space.

This claim is based on a wider understanding of time and the Jews. Heschel states,

> To Israel the unique events of historic time were spiritually more significant than the repetitive processes in the cycle of nature, even though physical sustenance depended on the latter. While the deities of other peoples were associated with places or things, the God of Israel was the God of events: the Redeemer from slavery, the Revealer of the Torah, manifesting Himself in events of history rather than in things or places. (8)

The most significant dimension of Sabbath is its teleological character – and this is where I would differ slightly but importantly from Heschel. Heschel explains the teleological quality of Sabbath in these terms: "To the biblical mind ... labor is a means toward an end, and the Sabbath as a day of rest, as a day of abstaining from toil, is not for the purpose of recovering one's lost strength and becoming fit for the forthcoming labor. The Sabbath is a day for the sake of life" (14). It is the telos of heaven and earth. "It is not an interlude but the climax of living" (14). This telos is in the territory that, for Christians, would be Christological. "The likeness of God can be found in time, which is eternity in disguise. ... The love of the Sabbath is the love of man for what he and God have in common" (16). It has a hint of an Aristotelian mean – Heschel observes that "Labor without dignity is the cause of misery; rest without spirit the cause of depravity" (18). Sabbath is the mean between the two. It preceded and completed creation – it is "all of the spirit that the world can bear" (21). It is an intimation of the world to come.

Heschel's eloquent argument is similar in some respects to the case I make in Chapter 3 above that the human predicament is not limitation but isolation. Many of his targets – technology, technique, commodification, instrumentalization – correspond to the targets I identify there. And there are significant correspondences with his description of Sabbath and the notion of being with I identified in Chapter 2 and will explore in detail in Part III. He even uses the term "being with ourselves" (28). In his vivid portrayal of Sabbath there is a deep sense of the enjoyment I explore at length in Chapter 6 below. But what is missing – no doubt implied, but nonetheless not explicit – is a rich notion of Sabbath as being with God, one another, and the renewed creation. In the argument of this book, being with is a teleological pattern of life that anticipates eternity in its practice of divine and human relationship. There is nothing in Heschel's account that excludes this, and thus I regard his treatment of Sabbath as highly illuminating and enriching of my teleological notion of being with; it is just that he does not give any details of what this form of relating might involve. The idea of Sabbath connotes renunciation and inactivity in ways that are not necessarily helpful or essential to my notion of being with; but the emphasis on Sabbath as pivotal to a healthy balance between rest and activity offers a more constructive picture.

Thus Sabbath offers a suitable template on which to begin a scriptural survey of the key themes of being with. It is a notion arising from creation; we now turn to notions more connected to salvation.

Egypt and Babylon

Incarnation and cross do not represent a change in God's character or purpose: all that the New Testament reveals lies within the texture of the Old Testament.

The Old Testament tells a story with two main events. The first event we could call Egypt. In Egypt the people of God found themselves in slavery through no fault of their own. The defining narrative of the Old Testament is the way God brought Israel out of slavery and made with Israel a covenant by which it could keep its freedom. The second main event we could call Babylon. Babylon is the place the people of God found themselves when they had got the covenant wrong. They were not in exile through no fault of their own: they looked back and realized the wrong turns they had made that had led to their demise.

But the crucial discovery, on which arguably the whole Bible rests, is this: in Babylon the people of God did not find that God had deserted them. On the contrary, they found that God was close to them – closer, even, than in the Promised Land; and they saw new sides to God's character: they saw not just that *they* would suffer because of their faithlessness, but that *God* suffered because of their having gone astray – and that this suffering was in some way redemptive. They wrote down their story to record their discovery that God was with them in their suffering and to affirm their faith that the God who had once delivered them from slavery in Egypt would deliver them again now that they were in exile in Babylon. And that is what they came to understand was happening in the return from exile in the Persian era.

And the New Testament is shaped by this story. When Jesus died and rose again, the early disciples reflected back on the story of slavery and exile, of Egypt and Babylon. In the resurrection they saw a re-enactment of the exodus, in which God brought liberation from all the powers that oppress us, most of all death. But in the cross the early church saw a re-enactment of exile, of the way God identifies with our suffering and is present to us in some ways even more closely in our suffering than in our flourishing. And these two discoveries, liberation (Egypt) and solidarity (Babylon), are the foundation of the Christian faith.

The story of the Old Testament is, in the broadest terms, a journey from for to with.[2] Of course it is more complicated than that – but the point is that that journey takes place *within* the Old Testament, not after it. The Old Testament is interlaced with testimony and counter-testimony, is not all narrative, and is by no means a narrative entirely from one perspective or in one linear trajectory. Nonetheless, if we are prepared to identify Egypt and Babylon as the twin pillars of the story, we can see the outline of the journey I am describing.

Perhaps the most explicit portrayal of this journey is the relation between the Red Sea and Mount Sinai. The deliverance at the Red Sea – the parting of the waves, the safe passage of the Israelites, the destruction of the pursuing Egyptians – is not an end in itself. The climax of the exodus is the covenant. The covenant is the *raison d'être* of the Old Testament. The whole purpose of God calling Abraham, sending Jacob and family to Egypt, meeting Moses, and rescuing the Israelites is to make the everlasting covenant at Sinai. The whole purpose of God thereafter is to uphold or restore that covenant. And the heart of that covenant is that God and Israel will be one another's companions forever. Not equal partners; but partners that bring one another joy.

In the story of God's appearance to Moses in the burning bush, the bush burns, but is not consumed: here is an indication that God is holy, but need not inherently burn up all that comes near. God's name is "I am who I am": here is a God who needs no one. But God has resolved not to be alone; God has resolved to be with. "I have observed the misery of my people who are in Egypt; I have heard their cry on account of their taskmasters. Indeed, I know their sufferings" (Exod. 3:7). It turns out God has been with Israel for a long time. This story of the burning bush is conventionally read as the beginning of a story – a story of for, punctuated by God's mighty acts; but it turns out to be the continuation of a story, a story whose telos was fundamentally always with. Thus when Moses wonders who he is, to take on such a daunting task, God's promise to Moses is sealed with these words: "I will be with you" (Exod. 3:12). That is the whole story – the purpose of redemption, the direction of exodus. Later, as if to confirm the promise made at the burning bush, we are told "The Lord descended in the cloud and stood with [Moses] there, and proclaimed the name, 'The Lord.'" (Exod. 34:5)

Thus Babylon names the time when it began to dawn on Israel that God's fundamental purpose had always been with. Israel always longed for for – that God's mighty acts would once again bring deliverance and well-being in the Promised Land. But in exile Israel could look back and see that the for was never the whole nature of God's encounter. The larger purpose of God was always to dwell with Israel, and, through Israel, to dwell, as a blessing, with "all the families of the earth" (Gen. 12:3). This larger purpose is embodied in the pillar of cloud, the ark of the covenant, the tent of meeting, the temple – in the ways God's presence is celebrated and enshrined. The pillar of cloud is about presence at least as much as direction: it is an assurance that God will not leave Israel alone. The ark of the covenant is the epitome of with: it is the tangible form of the covenant which is the heart of Israel's existence and the essence of God's commitment never to be except to be with Israel. The tent of meeting is exactly that – a place of God being with Israel. Atonement is less a process God enacts in order to secure Israel's righteousness than it is a reaffirmation that, despite Israel's sin, God's will to be with Israel will never be thwarted for long. Most complex is the temple, which may appear to be straightforwardly the place of working for – where the priests work for Israel by making sacrifices and God works for Israel by removing its sin. But the temple is best thought of as the ark of the covenant on a grand scale – in other words as the embodiment of the covenant, the setting-up of the epicenter of Israel's heritage and destiny at the heart of its national life. Of course there is a strong element of working for in the temple; but it is a working for that is grounded in and designed to restore the more fundamental being with.

It is often remarked that liberating Israel is part of the identity of God – even a part of the holy name, as in the preface to the Ten Commandments (Exod. 20:1). But there are other places where God's being with Israel is just as much a part of God's identity. Following the controversy over the golden calf, God tells Moses that Israel will be given the promised land despite their disobedience, but declares, "I will not go with you, because you are a stiff-necked people and I might destroy you on the way" (Exod. 33:3). Moses responds, "If your Presence does not go with us, do not send us up from here. How will anyone know that you are pleased with me and with your people unless you go with us? What else will distinguish me and your people from all the other people on the face of the earth?" (Exod. 33: 15–16). God agrees to Moses' request to go with the people. Thus Israel becomes the "people-whom-this-God-is-with." Then God passes in front of Moses declaring both a name and an essential character: "The Lord, the Lord, the compassionate and gracious God, slow to anger, abounding in love and faithfulness, maintaining love to thousands, and forgiving wicked-ness, rebellion and sin" (Exod. 34:6). Thus the declaration of God's identity and the promise to be with Israel are juxtaposed. Indeed, in the words of one exegete, "There is no such thing for Israel as a nonincarnate God ... God's act in Jesus Christ is the culmination of a longstanding relationship of God with the world that is much more widespread in the Old Testament than is commonly recognized."[3]

Thus the contours of God's being with us in Jesus are already set in the Old Testament. At first glance one could perceive the Old Testament's divine–human dynamic as largely characterized by "for": God working for Israel, definitively in the exodus, but also in the entry to the Promised Land, in the raising of the kings and the miraculous victories in battle; and then per-haps the heart of the Old Testament – the wondering whether God would again work for Israel in bringing the exile to an end in a style corresponding with the exodus. One could portray the conventional reading of the Old Testament – particularly through post-Enlightenment eyes, absorbed by the question of God's "intervention" – as a tension between God's being for as against God's working for Israel. For example, the Suffering Servant of Second Isaiah is clearly suffering for Israel: but is that suffering a suffering of love, which takes and receives and accepts and never complains? Or is it a suffering that brings transformation, that atones, that relieves and recon-ciles and gives new life? Likewise prophets such as Hosea and Jeremiah por-tray both the suffering with and the suffering for of God: they embody in their own lives the life of God; their laments are often mirrors of the divine grief over the people's unfaithfulness. But all these instances still presume that working for is the core identity of "the Lord your God, who brought you out of the land of Egypt, out of the house of slavery" (Exod. 20:2).

And the assumption of God's working for is that God will work for Israel provided Israel keeps its side of the covenant. We could call this with in the service of for. In other words, the reason Israel keeps faithful to God is not for some good or value in itself, but so that God will step in at moments of crisis. Thus when the word "with" arises it is often linked to God's favor and bless-ing, together with an assurance of protection. It is sometimes synonymous to being "on Israel's side." Withdrawal of God's presence signals disfavor or anger at disobedience or injustice, which means lack of God's protection and blessing and consequent failure or defeat. Thus, "For a brief moment I abandoned you, but with great compassion I will gather you" (Isa. 54:7).

The significance of this tension between being for and working for becomes apparent in the light of post-Holocaust theology, which asks the question already to be found in diverse parts of the Old Testament: is God content with being for and not prepared to translate that into working for? Yet in post-Holocaust theology the question hardens to become, "If so, is there then any "use" for such a God?" The question is telling: a God that works for is a useful God. A God that works with is an empowering God. But a God whose purpose is primarily expressed in – or entirely limited to – being for is an inscrutable, infuriating, perhaps even pernicious God. Such a question, and such a range of answers, seems oblivious to the notion of being with. It sets up a dynamic that impoverishes the notion of God. God's inner life is beyond knowing; God's ultimate purpose is obscure; God's reasons for "inaction" are inadequate; God exists, it seems, wholly or largely to deliver us when we are in trouble, and lead us to places of safety where we may find abundant life. Any relationship seems secondary, even dispensable. Either God comes to the plate, or dithers in the shadows (while the distressed begin to wonder if God takes some perverse pleasure in their hardship).

But what if working for and being for were not the only options? What if the character and purpose of God were expressed in the word with? Then we can begin to chart a course through the Old Testament that finds its focus in Babylon but is anticipated at almost every stage. We can see this more nuanced notion appearing in the Psalms. Many of the Psalms, while they don't often use the word "with" directly, contain requests for God's presence and anticipation of the blessing of seeing God's face:

> One thing I asked of the Lord, that will I seek after: to live in the house of the Lord all the days of my life, to behold the beauty of the Lord, and to inquire in his temple. For he will hide me in his shelter in the day of trouble; he will conceal me under the cover of his tent; he will set me high on a rock. ... "Come," my heart says, "seek his face!" Your face, Lord, do I seek. Do not hide your face from me. ... I believe that I shall see the goodness of the Lord in the land of the living. (Ps. 27: 4–5, 8–9, 13)

Perhaps the signal instance of the notion of with is the repeated refrain, "Do not be afraid." Thus, "When you pass through the waters, I will be with you; and through the rivers, they shall not overwhelm you … Do not fear, for I am with you" (Isa. 43:2, 5). The story that expresses God's being with in the face of fear perhaps more vividly than any other is that of Shadrach, Meshach, and Abednego and the fiery furnace (Dan. 3:1–30). Here we find that salvation does not mean freedom from care, anxiety, fear, pain, or threat. Shadrach, Meshach, and Abednego face all these things precisely because they uphold God's name. What salvation does mean is that when Shadrach, Meshach, and Abednego are thrown, bound, in the fire, God is with them. There are not three figures walking in the flames; there are four. The destiny of Shadrach, Meshach, and Abednego is settled not before they reach the fire by some device that makes them avoid the fire; nor is there any dramatic rescue from the flames. Their salvation takes place *in* the fire, as they discover that God is with them in the flames. "Though I walk through the valley of the shadow of death, I will fear no evil; for thou art with me" (Ps. 23:4 AV). "When you walk through fire you shall not be burned, and the flame shall not consume you" (Isa. 42:2). This is what being with means.

In this story we can see the fire represents Babylon. Shadrach, Meshach, and Abednego are not spared from the fire, nor rescued from the fire; they find God is with them in the fire. Somehow the fire is a fire not just for them but for God too. The same is true for Israel in Babylon. Israel is not spared exile. Israel is not rescued from exile. Israel finds in exile that God is there too. The appearance of the fourth figure in the fire sums up the experience of exile for Israel. God is with us. That is salvation. And it anticipates the way the early church understood the cross. Jesus is not spared the cross; Jesus is not rescued from the cross; Jesus is with God on the cross.

The Jordan

The baptism of Jesus is the moment that brings together Egypt and Babylon, incarnation and cross. Let me explain how.

When Jesus emerges from the shadows of Nazareth in Galilee and appears center stage at the River Jordan, where John is baptizing, the key question everyone involved is, what kind of salvation is Jesus bringing? As we saw in Chapter 3, there are two broad notions of the human predicament. The first is mortality. Human existence is, for most people, good, but at the same time unavoidably fragile and profoundly flawed. Life is made up of good things – creativity, beauty, wisdom, and love. But many precious things break, end, change, or die. This is the fragility of life. The second notion is isolation. Most things have a dimension of disappointment, a tinge of poison, a texture of perversion that can sometimes be controlled, but never eradicated, and represent the flawed nature of existence. Even if the material conditions survive, the relationships falter.

How does humankind deal with this predicament? There are perhaps two conventional ways. One is to try to offset fragility as much as possible, and simply extend or strengthen or restore life at every opportunity. One need only think about what a massive proportion of the GDP (Gross Domestic Product) of developed nations is spent on health care in the last weeks of life. The other conventional way, more linked to dealing with the flawed nature of life, is to escape. That can mean life as a series of exciting vacations, life in a fantasy world of computer games or consciousness-altering drugs, life in a protected, sheltered community, or life in a self-contained ideology that explains and subdues all worrisome information. In an increasingly technological world, life offers ever-more sophisticated forms of escape.

And these two methods for coping with the human predicament, preservation and escape, are especially evident in the way our culture constructs religion. On the one hand is the offer of preservation: here Christianity or the church exists to hold together things that would otherwise fall apart, like values, character, family, nation, marriage, trust, community, even the economy and society itself. Life after death constitutes a long-term guarantee of the things we think we need, an infinite extension of what needs holding together. On the other hand is the offer of escape: here Christianity or the church gives us feelings or experiences that take us out of the tawdry world, save us from its cloying clutches, and keep us pure amid its muddied messes. Eternal life becomes the ultimate form of escape, a constant promise that we can walk out the room any time we choose and find ourselves in a better place.

Thus the question for Jesus at the outset of his public ministry is how he will overcome the human predicament, that life is good but fragile and flawed. Is he offering indefinite extension, as a miracle worker who can push back the boundaries of mortality? Or is he offering wholesale escape, bringing down the curtain on history and ushering in a new dawn of righteousness and justice? Is he offering the preservation of creation, or an escape from oppression? Is he chiefly concerned with overcoming death, or sin?

Both of these models have deep roots in Israel's history – roots that the account of Jesus' baptism make explicit. The idea that life is good, but fragile, is rooted in the creation story: the Spirit descending on Jesus like a dove at his baptism is a clear allusion to the creation story, which begins with the Spirit, or wind, sweeping over the face of the waters. The idea that life is flawed, but that escape is possible, is rooted in the exodus story. When we hear that Jesus went down into the River Jordan, we're reminded of the Israelites being led by God under Moses out of slavery in Egypt through the Red Sea and under Joshua across the Jordan to freedom in the Promised Land of Canaan.

Here a more contemporary illustration may be helpful. We may recall Eastern Europe in the early 1980s. The people of Poland had been living under a Soviet-dominated communist regime since 1945. They had seen uprisings in Hungary and Czechoslovakia ruthlessly suppressed by Soviet military intervention. And yet the shipyard workers of Gdansk, led by electrician Lech Walesa, found the courage to form a trade union, and go on strike, taking 17,000 workers out on the streets. The movement spread along the Baltic Coast, closing ports and drawing in mines and factories. Within a year, one in every three workers in Poland was a member of Walesa's movement, and Walesa was on his way to winning the Nobel Peace Prize. The movement was called Solidarity.

The Polish government was in crisis, and it reacted with the introduction of martial law and the arrest of the union leaders. All political protest was stifled. There was only one institution the government couldn't dismantle by forcible repression. And that was the Catholic Church. Over the next couple of years a young priest started to preach words of gospel truth and Catholic social teaching into the events taking place in Poland. His name was Jerzy Popiełuszko. His sermons were picked up by an underground radio station and he gained a nationwide following. People started to see him as the first man who had had the courage to speak the truth for 40 years. The government panicked. They fabricated evidence against him and tried to get him sent to prison. They threatened him and intimidated him. Nothing worked. He carried on preaching and speaking the truth regardless. On October 13, 1984 the authorities staged a car accident, again without success. Finally, six days later, Jerzy Popiełuszko was kidnapped, murdered, and bundled into a reservoir.

No less than a quarter of a million people attended his funeral – the funeral of a 37-year-old priest who had never had any prestigious appointment, and had been squalidly disposed of by the authorities. It was the beginning of the end for the regime. Six years later Poland was the first Eastern bloc nation to throw off Soviet domination. This was an event of great significance in twentieth-century history.

The point of the story is that single word, solidarity. Solidarity means every attempt to make concrete the intangible links between people, links based on love and trust and dignity and understanding and respect. It means all the ways people seek to stand alongside those who are in pain or sorrow, treated cruelly or unfairly, facing fear or the unknown. Solidarity is the word "with" turned into practical action, the word "understanding" turned into genuine support, the word "identification" turned into courageous acts of witness.

Solidarity is an icon of the word "church" – Christians standing alongside one another, standing alongside the oppressed, and standing alongside God in Christ. Jerzy Popiełuszko stood alongside other Christians, the oppressed people of Poland, and Jesus. For this is the salvation Jesus was bringing, when he came center stage in his baptism by John. Jesus' salvation is not primarily about preserving life. It is not primarily about escape. It is about solidarity. Solidarity between God and humanity. Solidarity that makes concrete the intangible links between God and humankind, and makes them so concrete that they can never be broken again.

In being baptized Jesus shows that salvation means solidarity. Here at the Jordan Jesus shows his solidarity with Israel, by making Israel's story of creation and liberation his own. He shows his solidarity with humanity, by making his flesh subject to the simple touch of hand and water. He shows his solidarity with sinners, by accepting the sign of the cleansing of flawed humanity. He shows his solidarity with the created world, by allowing his naked body to be clothed by water and air. He shows his solidarity with John the Baptist, by asking John to baptize him, rather than vice versa. And in return we see his solidarity with God, when the heavens are torn and the dove descends and the voice announces, "You are my son, the beloved" (Luke 3:22).

So this is how Jesus addresses the human predicament. Not through preserving life: Jerzy Popiełuszko's story shows that preserving the life of the Polish people would have simply condemned them to continued oppression. It was the same for Jesus in the context of the Roman occupation. And not through escape – again, for Fr Popiełuszko, there was nowhere that the Polish people could escape to that wouldn't leave them right back where they started. Jesus addresses the human predicament through solidarity. He is with us in our struggle, our suffering, our searching, our striving. As the Polish government so vividly discovered, such is a solidarity that sin and death can no longer break. For Jesus, our real problem as human beings is our alienation from God and one another. That is what changes in Jesus.

Jesus is the solidarity between us and God that makes those links tangible and visible and permanent and unbreakable.

The Cross

The Gospel of Matthew begins with the angel's promise that the Messiah will be called Emmanuel – God with us. It ends with Jesus' promise to his disciples, "Remember, I am with you always, to the end of the age." In between comes Jesus' promise to the church: "Where two or three are gathered in my name, I am there with them." The Gospel of Mark says Jesus "appointed twelve, whom he also named apostles, to be with him." When the scribes and Pharisees criticize Jesus, they say, "Why does he eat with tax collectors and sinners?" And when Jesus loses his patience with the disciples, he says, "You faithless generation, how much longer must I be with you?" The Gospel of Luke begins with the angel saying to Mary, "The Lord is with you;" when the father of the prodigal son is comforting the elder brother out in the field, he says, "Son, you are always with me, and all that is mine is yours." On the Emmaus road the disciples say to the risen Jesus, "Stay with us." And the Gospel of John begins with the words, "The Word was with God, and the Word was God. He was in the beginning with God." It goes on to say "The Word was made flesh and dwelt among [with] us." Later, Jesus says, "You always have the poor with you." And on the night before he dies, Jesus says at supper, "I am not alone because the Father is with me."

In other words, as we have seen, if there is one word that sums up all four gospels, that word is "with." Jesus' ministry, above all else, is about being with us, in pain and glory, in sorrow and in joy, in quiet and in conflict, in death and in life.

And that same "with" is even more evident when we turn to the relationship within the Godhead itself, the Trinity of Father, Son, and Holy Spirit. God is three, which means God is a perfect symmetry of with, three beings wholly present to one another, without envy, without misunderstanding, without irritation, without selfishness, without two ganging up against the third, without anger, without anxiety, without mistrust. So present to one another, so rapt in love, and cherishing, and mutuality, and devotion, that they seem to transcend *with* and become *in*. The Father, the Son, and the Holy Spirit are so *with* one another that it seems they are in one another. And, to the extent that they are in one another, we call God not three, but one. These three are so with that they are one, three persons in one substance, always affirming one another's difference and distinctness in person and presence, but always bearing within one another the whole being of the other two persons. The Trinity is the perfect equilibrium of three persons so with that they are *in*, but *in* in such a way that they are still *with*.

Given this perfection of being, this intersection of being *with* and being *in*, the astonishing mystery is why the Trinity's life is not simply self-contained, but becomes open to creation, to fragile existence, to life, to human beings. Surely the grasping, mistrustful, anxious, and small-minded human spirit would ruin the perfection of the Trinity. Or could it possibly be that God's grace is more infectious than human folly? Could it possibly be that the mutual indwelling love of the Trinity could outlast and ultimately transform our human fragility and perversity? That is the dynamic behind the whole of salvation history. If God's life opens up to humankind, will it destroy God – or transform humankind? And if it ultimately transforms humankind, how much will it cost God?

The gospel of revivalist piety focuses on the gruesome, vivid, and unforgettable detail of the cross. The evangelist describes what the process of crucifixion does to the heart, the lungs, the rib cage, the windpipe, the face, the eyes, the cheeks, the hips, the feet, and the hands. But the Gospel accounts tell us almost nothing about the physical details of the crucifixion. Jesus suffered terribly, no doubt; but many people suffered then, some even worse than him, and many people have suffered since, and still do, some of them no doubt even more than he did. The poignancy of the cross is not about some contest of pain in which Jesus came out the winner. It is not that Jesus physically suffered. It's that he was forsaken.

Jesus' last words, in Mark's and Matthew's gospels, are, "My God, my God, why have you forsaken me?" (Mark 15:34; Matt. 27:46). At first sight, this is simply the last in a chain of abandonments. The disciples flee, Peter denies, Judas betrays, now the Father forsakes. It's a litany of desertion. And there is something in this litany. If the crucial word in the Gospel is with, then the events leading up to Jesus' crucifixion are a heartless and wholesale dismantling of that with. Jesus is left without all those he worked so hard to be with – the disciples (at least the male ones), the authorities, the poor – and all of them have not just disappeared, but actively deserted or betrayed him. Jesus is still with us, but we, at this most precious moment of all, are not with him.

But these abandonments are nothing compared to the one that really matters. The cross is not just an extreme version of a generic human experience of being alone, in pain, unjustly punished and cruelly ridiculed. The cross is a unique event. It is not unique because of how much pain Jesus felt or how much love he had previously expended. It is unique because the Holy Trinity is the utter presence of unalloyed with, and, at the moment of Jesus' death, that with is, for a brief moment, and for the only instant in eternal history, lost.

That with is the very essence of God's being within the life of the Trinity, and the very essence of God's being toward humankind in Christ. And yet, at this unique moment, that with is obscured, jeopardized, possibly obliterated. Like the clouds coming across the sun, shrouding the earth in shadow, the essence of God, always three persons in perfect relationship, always God's life shaped to be with us – that essence is for a moment lost. This is a poignant and terrifying moment. The two things Christians think they can know for certain – that God is a Trinity of persons in perfect and eternal relationship, and that God is always present with them in Christ through the Spirit – these two certainties are, for a moment, like a missed heartbeat, absent. The universe's deepest realities have become unhinged. The Son is not with the Father, even though he desperately wants to be. The Father is not with the Son, breaking the whole notion of their eternal presence one with another. This is the most vivid picture of hell we could imagine: not just our being separated from God, but God being separated from God, God being out of God's own reach.

The cross is Jesus' ultimate demonstration of being with us – but in the cruelest of all ironies, it's the instant Jesus finds that neither we, nor the Father, are with him. Every aspect of being not-with, of being with-out, clusters together at this agonizing moment. Jesus experiences the reality of human sin, because sin is fundamentally living without God. Jesus experiences the depth of suffering, because suffering is more than anything the condition of being without comfort. Jesus experiences the horror of death, because death is the word we give to being without all things – without breath, without connectedness, without consciousness, without a body. Jesus experiences the biggest alienation of all, the state of being without the Father, and thus being not-God – being, for this moment, without the with that is the essence of God.

And Jesus' words at this most terrifying moment are these. "My God, my God, why have you forsaken me?" He's still talking to the Father, even at the moment of naming that the with has gone. He is still talking in intimate terms – calling the Father "My God." These words come out of the most profound level of trust, the most fathomless depth of with and in. It is sometimes pointed out that this is the first line of Psalm 22, and that the Psalm as a whole is one of hope. But to suggest that really this cry from the cross is an elaborate word of triumph and trust, and that Jesus' recognition of abandonment is all part of a tidy plan, is surely to shield oneself from the unique horror and wonder of this moment.

The most tantalizing thing is that Jesus' last words are a question – a question that does not receive an answer. The question shows us that Jesus has given everything that he is for the cause of being with us, for the cause of embracing us within the essence of God's being. He has given so much – even despite our determination to be without him. And yet he has given beyond our imagination, because for the sake of our being with the Father he has, for this moment, lost his own being with the Father. And the Father has longed so much to be with us that he has, for this moment, lost his being with the Son, which is the essence of his being.

These two astonishing discoveries, the Father's losing the Son for us, and the Son's losing the Father for us, make us wonder "Is all then lost?" – not just for us, but even for God. Has the Trinity lost its identity for nothing? But this deepest of fears is what finds an answer in Christ's resurrection, when it turns out that neither sin, nor suffering, nor death, nor alienation has the last word. With is restored at Easter, and, on the day of Ascension (God being with God), and Pentecost (God being with us, enabling us to be with one another), with has the last word.

At the central moment in history, Jesus, the incarnate Son of God, has to choose between being with the Father and being with us. And he chooses us. At the same time the Father has to choose between letting the Son be with us and keeping the Son to Himself. And he chooses to let the Son be with us. That is the choice on which our eternal destiny depends. That is the epicenter of the Christian faith, and our very definition of love.[4]

From this moment we can see that the word with becomes the key to the whole story. The Holy Trinity is the perfect epitome of with: God being with God. The incarnation of Jesus is the embodiment of with: God being with us, being among us. The Crucifixion, as we have seen, is the greatest test of God's being with us, because, we see that God in Christ is so committed to being with us that Jesus will even risk his being with God to keep his commitment never to be separated from us. The resurrection is the vindication of God's being both with us, and with God, and the ultimate and perpetual compatibility, and unity, of the two. And Pentecost is the embodiment of that resurrection breakthrough, because in Pentecost the Holy

Spirit becomes the guarantee and gift of our union with God in Christ and our union with one another in Christ's body.

Resurrection

In this last section of the chapter I shall return to where we began, with Sabbath, bringing in the other elements of a scriptural overview of our theme. I want to portray the resurrection as the signal moment that draws together God's fulfillment of the commitment to be with us always.

The present tense does not exist. As soon as one tries to put one's finger on the present tense, like a horsefly under a slapping hand, it is gone. One cannot sit on a train and fix one's eyes on a tree or field or hill outside. One cannot be at a birthday party or in the midst of theater or sport or music and freeze and capture the moment and never let it go. There is no such thing as the present tense.

As soon as one realizes this one becomes subject to two primal, visceral, and existential terrors. The first terror is this: one cannot stop time. It is out of control. It is an ever-rolling stream, and it rolls all its sons and daughters away. Time will gobble up us all. That is the first terror. The second terror is, what we have done cannot be undone. However much one may try to retell the story, there is no changing what has happened. And the knowledge that the past is an ogre that will finally catch up with us – that is the second terror. Together these two terrors, about past and future, constitute the prison of human existence. There is no such thing as the present tense because it is no more than the overlap between the past and the future. And there is no genuine living in the present tense because our lives are dominated by regret and bitterness and grief and humiliation about the past; and paralyzed by fear and anxiety and terror and horror about the future. The fear of what has happened that cannot be changed is called sin, and the things that are cherished but cannot be kept are called death.

The scriptural story offers two central claims. The first is about the past: it is the forgiveness of sins. Forgiveness does not change the past. But it releases us from the power of the past. Forgiveness cannot rewrite history. But it prevents our histories asphyxiating us. Fundamentally forgiveness transforms our past from an enemy to a friend, from a horror-show of shame to a storehouse of wisdom. In the absence of forgiveness we are isolated from our past, pitifully trying to bury or deny or forget or destroy the many things that haunt and overshadow and plague and torment us. Forgiveness does not change these things: but it does change their relationship to us. No longer do they imprison us or pursue us or surround us or stalk us. Now they accompany us, deepen us, teach us, train us. No longer do we hate them or curse them or resent them or begrudge them. Now we find acceptance, understanding, enrichment, even gratitude for them. That is the work of forgiveness: the transformation of the prison of the past.

The second Christian conviction is about the future: the life everlasting. Everlasting life does not take away the unknown element of the future: but it takes away the paroxysm of fear that engulfs the cloud of unknowing. Everlasting life cannot dismantle the reality of death, the crucible of suffering, the agony of bereavement: but it offers life beyond death, comfort beyond suffering, companionship beyond separation. In the absence of everlasting life we are terrified of our future, perpetually trying to secure permanence in the face of transitoriness, meaning in the face of waste, distraction in the face of despair. Everlasting life does not undermine human endeavor, but it rids it of the last word; evil is real, but it won't have the final say; death is coming, but it does not obliterate the power of God; identity is fragile, but that in us that resides in God will be changed into glory.

And the moment when forgiveness and everlasting life coincide is Jesus' resurrection. Jesus' physical resurrection gives us back our past, because it proves that our worst sin is still not enough to determine the ultimate course of history, and not enough to alter God's decision to be with us in Christ. We cannot ruin God's life, however hard we try. And that means we cannot even finally ruin our own. Meanwhile death is no longer an insuperable barrier. The resurrection is a glimpse of restoration beyond obliteration. The body is not a prison to be escaped or a ladder to be kicked away; it is the shape of our future in Christ. Thus Jesus' resurrection turns the past from dungeon into heritage and the future from fate into destiny.

Resurrection is therefore Sabbath – the redemption of time – but a Sabbath that addresses not just contingency but also failure and malevolence. In other words a Sabbath that is not simply for, in addressing death's destruction, but at least as much with, in disarming the poison of sin. The two most obviously for moments in the story – cross and resurrection, are rendered as at least as much with; and the preceding narrative may be re-read as one of solidarity, discovery, and the restoration of relationship.

There is no such thing as the present tense. In the language of this book, there is no way to be with ourselves, with one another, with the renewed creation, or with God – because of the tyranny of the past and the terror of the future. But with the restoration of the with that takes place in Jesus' resurrection, the past is restored and the future redeemed and the with is possible: we can be with, we can be present – so there can be a present tense.

Conclusion

This chapter has set out to demonstrate in vivid terms the way being with is inextricably a Christological notion, indeed the primary Christological notion, and is grounded in the Old Testament narrative and the way that narrative is inhabited by the New Testament. The pivotal doctrine of incarnation ripples back into the Old Testament and forward to the cross, and Jesus' baptism demonstrates how Jesus adopts the abiding Old Testament themes. Having identified that with is the key to Jesus' person and work, we now turn to examine whether it has a similar role in relation to his message.

Notes

1. Abraham Joshua Heschel, *The Sabbath: Its Meaning for Modern Man* (New York: Farrar, Strauss and Giroux, 1951). Page references are in the text. Heschel's book makes the same kind of argument that I make in Chapter 3 above – that humanity has misunderstood its true predicament; but as my discussion should make clear, my sense of what the predicament is and my proposed response is somewhat different from his.

2. John Howard Yoder does not use this language, but the general argument of this section is inspired by his way of reasoning in "If Abraham is our Father," *The Original Revolution: Essays on Christian Pacifism* (Scottdale, PA: Herald Press, 1972): 91–111.

3. Terence Fretheim, *The Suffering of God: An Old Testament Perspective* (Minneapolis, MN: Augsburg Fortress, 1985): 106, 166.

4. "The Crucifixion put it up to the Father: Would he stand to *this* alleged Son? To *this* candidate to be his own self-identifying Word? Would he be a God who, for example, hosts publicans and sinners, who justifies the ungodly? The Resurrection was the Father's Yes. We may say: the Resurrection settled that the Crucifixion's sort of God is indeed the one God; the Crucifixion settled what sort of God it is who establishes his deity by the Resurrection. Or: the Crucifixion settled *who and what* God is; the Resurrection settled *that* this God is." Robert Jenson, *Systematic Theology: Volume 1, The Triune God* (New York: Oxford University Press, 1997): 189.

6

The Stories of Jesus

So far we have taken two polemical angles on our theme. First, we saw that isolation is closer to the heart of the human condition than mortality, and that relationship is the telos of God. From those insights I suggested that "with" is the definitive human aspiration, rather than "for." Second, we saw that *being with* embodies a teleological pattern of engagement; far from modeling passivity or detachment, it depicts a form of incarnate presence that imitates the way God in Christ is present with the world. We pursued this consistent vision through the scriptural narrative.

What could be wrong with any of that? In this chapter we acknowledge that this is an ethic that runs contrary to a host of popular models of mission and discipleship. Perhaps the most obvious and influential example of this ethic is conventional exegesis of the parable of the Good Samaritan. Thus in this chapter we revisit this parable to identify one source of the network of assumptions that make *being with* such a countercultural model not only to the secular world but also – perhaps especially – to the church.

Popular images of Jesus depict him as a wandering minstrel, with a memorable turn of phrase. He was a charismatic speaker, a hardy traveler, with Rasputin eyes and a rich Galilean accent that resonated with the hills and the sea. The New Testament tells us none of these things, but we somehow know them – from pictures in children's storybooks through to feature films of Jesus' life, whether pious or edgy. Jesus was a pied piper spinning poems, prayers, and promises. The big piece of evidence for this is that he told a lot of stories – stories you can read over and over again and in which you can always find something new.

Every generation has had its corresponding version of Jesus. In the nineteenth century it became highly fashionable to compose biographies of Jesus, piecing together elements of his life from the gospels and filling

A Nazareth Manifesto, Samuel Wells © 2015 John Wiley & Sons, Ltd. Published 2015 by John Wiley & Sons, Ltd.

in the rest in accord with the cultural assumptions of the day. The whole industry became known as the Life of Jesus Movement. What its proponents did was to look down a deep well of many centuries of obscurity and, at the bottom, see reflected a face of Jesus that looked very much like their own.[1] The contemporary equivalent of this movement today is to be found among those who develop elaborate evaluation mechanisms for identifying Jesus' sayings and stories and working out which ones probably predated him and he at best adopted, which ones postdated him and were attributed to him by the evangelists, and which ones he might actually have said himself.[2] Such a method is working with a largely unexamined presupposed picture of Jesus just as much as the nineteenth-century quest for the historical Jesus was.

But what all these pictures have in common – the nineteenth-century one, the one compiled by contemporary critical research, and the long-haired one with the lyrical Gaelic accent – is that they avoid the crucial question. And that is, if Jesus was this anodyne wandering banjo-playing minstrel figure, why was he executed in such a public, agonizing, and humiliating way? If he was harmless, humorous, and hairy, why was he killed?

To answer this question we here explore the parable of the Good Samaritan four times. The first time we examine what it tells us about to whom Jesus was talking. The second time we consider what it tells us about who Jesus was and is. The third time we look at the ways Christians think they know this story so well that they fail to read it closely and miss what the story is really about. And finally we read the story as it asks to be read in the context of a discussion of the notion of being with.

Here is the story.

A man was going down from Jerusalem to Jericho, and fell into the hands of robbers, who stripped him, beat him, and went away, leaving him half dead. Now by chance a priest was going down that road; and when he saw him, he passed by on the other side. So likewise a Levite, when he came to the place and saw him, passed by on the other side. But a Samaritan while traveling came near him; and when he saw him, he was moved with pity. He went to him and bandaged his wounds, having poured oil and wine on them. Then he put him on his own animal, brought him to an inn, and took care of him. The next day he took out two denarii, gave them to the innkeeper, and said, "Take care of him; and when I come back, I will repay you whatever more you spend." Which of these three, do you think, was a neighbor to the man who fell into the hands of the robbers? He said, "The one who showed him mercy." Jesus said to him, "Go and do likewise." (Luke 10:30–37)

To whom was Jesus Talking?

"A man was going down from Jerusalem to Jericho, and fell into the hands of robbers, who stripped him, beat him, and went away, leaving him half dead." Who is this man? Who could be in Jesus' mind when he says the words, "stripped him, beat him, and went away, leaving him half dead"?

Here is another familiar story. Once Israel was great. David was king. The territory of the nation was expanding. It was becoming a truly great nation. David's son Solomon built a magnificent temple. Israel had never been so certain that God was on its side and all was well with the world. But after Solomon the kingdom split. The northern kingdom was invaded and destroyed in the eighth century by the Assyrians, and the southern kingdom was besieged and ransacked in the sixth century by the Chaldeans, and its ruling elite carted off to Babylon.

Consider these words again. "A man was going down from Jerusalem to Jericho, and fell into the hands of robbers, who stripped him, beat him, and went away, leaving him half dead." Who is this man? This man is Israel. Israel had fallen into the hands of robbers, and was stripped, beaten, and left half dead. Jesus is telling Israel's story back to it. But here is the crucial part. In Jesus' version, all of this happens at the beginning of the story – in the very first sentence. Jesus is saying, this tragedy, this apocalypse, this demise of God's chosen people – this is not the end of the story: *this is the beginning.*

And that is very much in the spirit of what happened to Israel in Babylon in the sixth century BC. Having sulked and grieved and lamented and wept, Israel came to understand that it had not left God behind in the rubble of Jerusalem, in the loss of temple, king, and land. It turned out God was in Babylon too. And God was not just a tribal mascot. God was the Lord of heaven and earth, of all times and all peoples. The Lord that had brought Israel out of Egypt a millennium before was the same Lord who had created the heavens and the earth. This Lord wasn't simply punishing Israel – this Lord was *suffering with* Israel, was bearing almost bodily the pain and grief of separation and longing. And this Lord was preparing to restore Israel to its land, just as under Moses this Lord had led Israel out of slavery. This people were going to rise from the dead.

Now the great ambiguity that is vital for understanding this parable in particular, and Jesus' ministry and its reception more generally, is this. Did the return of the exiles from Babylon, beginning around 500 BC, initially as a storm and eventually as a trickle, did this return genuinely constitute the end of exile, an equivalent of the exodus a thousand years before? Some said yes, look – we've inhabited the Promised Land, we have rebuilt the great temple, we are close to God and we are living under the law of Moses. Others said no – we are dominated by foreign powers, we have not had our own king for 500 years, we have to live with the Roman emperor who thinks and wants us to think he is the real god, and we have to live under puppets and scoundrels like Herod and his sons. Here again is the first line of the parable: "A man was going down from Jerusalem to Jericho, and fell into the hands of robbers, who stripped him, beat him, and went away, leaving him half dead." Here is the existential question for the people Jesus was talking to. Is this man Israel? Is Israel robbed, stripped, beaten, abandoned? Is Israel lying in the gutter? Or is Israel, like the priest and Levite, sauntering down the road, quite at peace with the world, safe in the knowledge that it has a temple, it is quite at home, and its culture is secure?

With the very first line of this story Jesus puts his finger on the great dividing line of the society of his time. Is Israel still in exile or not?[3] To put the question on a broader canvas, we might recall Genesis 3:9, when Adam and Eve have eaten the apple and are hiding as God comes "walking in the garden at the time of the evening breeze," and God says, simply, "Where are you?" "Where are you, Israel?" asks Jesus with this opening line of the story. If all is well, *why are you hiding*? It seems Jesus is subtly saying, "You are in the gutter. You are stripped, beaten, and half dead. Stop pretending."

This is the context not just of this parable but of so much of what Jesus says. Israel is in the gutter, stripped, beaten, and half dead. Jesus is pointing this out, and saying that now is the time when God is truly sending redemption, bringing the exile to an end, inaugurating the era of freedom and justice that Israel could scarcely dream of in Babylon and had never experienced since. Now is the time, says Jesus. And here comes your savior, trotting down the road toward you. But be careful, be watchful, be alert: there are a few people coming down the road; make sure you can tell them apart.

So that is our first reading of the story. That addresses the question of to whom Jesus is talking. Jesus is talking to a mixed audience of those who believe Israel is still in exile and those who do not. And he is saying "Israel, you are still in exile – and I have come to bring you home."

Who is Jesus?

Now let us turn to the later part of the parable.

A Samaritan while traveling came near him; and when he saw him, he was moved with pity. He went to him and bandaged his wounds, having poured oil and wine on them. Then he put him on his own animal, brought him to an inn, and took care of him. The next day he took out two denarii, gave them to the innkeeper, and said, "Take care of him; and when I come back, I will repay you whatever more you spend."

We have already established that Israel has more than passing resemblance to the wounded man. But it is also more than plausible to interpret the man on a more directly personal level. Like many people, then and now, the wounded man experiences unprovoked assault, battery, and robbery, leaving him in a desperate physical, psychological, and economic plight. Then he experiences both emotional and practical neglect, as the priest and the Levite withhold not only compassion and tenderness but also medication, transport, and financial help.

Now consider what the Samaritan does. The Samaritan is traveling. He is not a mountain rescue helicopter; he is not a police squad car; he is a person with a life and purpose of his own, irrespective of the goings-on on the Jericho road. But once both he and the man in the gutter realize how desperate the man's situation is, notice the precise sequence of what happens. He comes to the wounded and dying man. He has tremendous compassion. He offers him practical assistance. He offers the man healing in the present and the hope of more for the future. Then, and this is very significant, he *goes into the city at considerable risk to himself* to secure the man's wellbeing. And the story ends with him promising to return to complete the work of salvation he has begun. The Samaritan shows love and compassion that the authorities of his day had not shown, cares for the wounded man in body, mind, and spirit, and offers safe lodging and promises more to come. It seems pretty clear, indeed unmistakable, that, in offering these details, *Jesus is describing himself.* The Samaritan does all the things Jesus does, or is going to do. He comes to us; he has compassion for us; he helps us; he heals us; he carries us; he goes into the city for us; he brings us to a place of safety; he promises to return. It is a gospel in miniature.

And this is the second thing to recognize about Jesus' stories. The first is that they are about Israel. They are about the crisis of exile and all it meant about God's longing to make Israel once again a blessing to all the peoples of the earth as in Abraham it was called to be. And the second thing about Jesus' stories is that they are about Jesus. They are about God in Christ. They are about God being the one who is made known to us in the abiding of Nazareth, the transformation of Galilee, and the sacrificial love of Jerusalem.

Who is the Samaritan?

Let us now read the story a third time, and this time I want to look at the ways we think we know this story so well that we do not actually read it closely at all and maybe miss what the story is really about.

At the risk of huge generalization, there are two divergent strands in contemporary Christianity. In some traditions and some parts of the world they are harmonized and synthesized; in other traditions either one strand is excluded or the two strands are in sharp tension. The first type we might call "personal faith." The Christianity of personal faith is centrally about an internal sense of sin and forgiveness, a relationship with Jesus as savior, and the right feelings and beliefs and habits of prayer and scripture reading. For many people personal faith is fundamentally about a conviction that they have been saved by Jesus and that when they die their eternal future is safe in heaven. The second type we might call "social action." The Christianity of social action tends to be rather cynical about piety that doesn't translate into generosity. It measures faithfulness by acts of kindness, concern for justice, and sometimes campaigning on public issues. It ruefully points out that many non-believers act more like true Christians than many who call themselves believers. Sometimes it seems the two types of Christians' principal pastime is criticizing and distancing themselves from one another.

A first look at the parable of the Good Samaritan might suggest this is very much "social action" territory. Here is a story about a man who is in trouble through no fault of his own. The priest is so taken up with keeping his nose clean and avoiding ritual impurity that he shows the dying man no compassion at all. The Levite does no better. For the Christian committed to judge faith by deeds, the priest and Levite represent a caricature of head-in-the air piety, concerned only with their own well-being and eternal salvation, meanwhile remaining heartless toward the suffering of the world. When the Samaritan comes along, the "social action" Christian says, "Aha, this is me!" When Jesus says, "Go, and do likewise," the social action Christian takes it as a succinct and unambiguous manifesto.

And when it becomes clear that Jesus, in the figure of the Samaritan, is describing the story of his coming to earth and going to Jerusalem out of love and compassion for the bruised and broken, all the more reason for the social action Christian to beam and bask in the moment. Not only does Jesus say the social gospel is what we must all embody – he adds that this translation of belief into deeds of compassion is nothing less than a reflection of himself.

But there are several problems with this way of reading the parable. The first problem is that familiarity may obscure the shape of the story. Samaritans were despised, hated, and ostracized by Jews. Before we blithely assume the figure of the Samaritan in the story is an image of ourselves at our most magnanimous, we need to pause and ask whether our own experience of life is of being perpetually despised, hated, and ostracized. The story is the wrong way around for the conventional reading to work. It is important to notice that the person in the story who is despised, hated, and ostracized is *not* the one lying beaten and robbed by the side of the road. The despised, hated, and ostracized person is the one who does the *helping* – the one who brings salvation. The way the story is conventionally interpreted, one would expect the Samaritan to be the one in the gutter. Then the reader or listener could be the big-hearted passer-by, magnanimously reaching out to the one the world turns its back on. But that is not the way the story works.

The second problem is that, if readers assume they are the Samaritan, they take for granted they have all the necessary resources in their pocket, or at least on their donkey. That means the only people who qualify to identify with the story are people of means. Those who do not have medication handy and money ready to pay for accommodation do not get to do likewise.

The third problem is that it takes for granted that the ministry the reader performs is of the same kind as the salvation Jesus brings. Jesus portrays himself as the Samaritan – so we should do the same. But that too easily makes us the agents of other people's salvation. It affirms our notion that we are the natural answer to other people's needs; and the only question is whether we will be forthcoming and generous like the Samaritan or withdrawn and heartless like the priest and the Levite. But Jesus brings things we cannot bring. And he brings them not just to others, but to us.

The fourth problem is that if readers assume they are the Samaritan they may be missing the simple heart of the gospel: that when humanity was in the gutter, God lifted creation up in his son and brought it home; when God's people were down and out and humiliated and rejected and foolish and failing and scorned and despised, Jesus touched them, heard them, forgave them, restored them, reconciled them, healed them, and gave them life with him forever. The fundamental gospel is that human beings failed to save themselves and are incapable of saving others but that Jesus saves them anyway.

So Jesus is the Samaritan. Jesus is the one who is despised and rejected and condemned and crucified. Jesus is the one who sets humanity on its feet again and binds up its wounds and bears it as his burden when it cannot carry its own loads. Jesus is the one who takes creation to a place of greater safety and makes a home for it where we it had no clear right to belong and promises to return when the time for reckoning is finally come. Jesus is the Samaritan.

But the reader, particularly the "social action" reader, is not the Samaritan. This is the third thing to recognize about Jesus' stories. The first is that they are addressed to Israel. The second is that they are about what God is doing in Jesus. The third is that they are not immediately about us. Jesus is not Aesop. He is not a teller of moralistic tales. He is not a lyrical narrator of worthy lessons we already know. The parable of the Good Samaritan is not a salutary tale promoting *noblesse oblige*. That is not Christianity, but enlightened self-interest. And it does not explain why Jesus was crucified. To say the healthy and wealthy should not be so preoccupied with their own well-being but should have a bit of care for the stricken and the victim is not an astonishing new teaching. Jesus' stories are telling us more than that.

Who are We?

The conventional reader may be wondering, "we" are not the Samaritan, and we are obviously not called to imitate the priest and the Levite, then who are we?

Here it is hard to avoid being homiletic. The parable almost requires it – at least when directed at readers of comparative affluence (in global terms). We are the man by the side of the road.[4] We are the one who is stripped, we are the one who is bruised, we are the one who is half dead. This is how we begin to reflect on questions of compassion and good deeds and social justice. We are the needy ones. We long for relationship, we long for forgiveness, we long for reconciliation, we long for eternal life. And we would be happy to accept these things from the priest or the Levite. These are people who seem like ourselves, people from our own social background. They have security. They have social esteem. They have resources. But the story is telling us those people cannot help us. They cannot give us what we so desperately need.

Why do I say we're in the gutter? Perhaps I should speak for myself. I am a Westerner, and I benefit from a global system of trade that keeps the majority of the world's population in poverty. I am an educated white resident of one the world's leading economic giants, and I benefit from a social system that privileges me and my dependents in almost every conceivable way, at the expense of other cultural and ethnic groups. Until recently I was living in a country that props up numerous tyrants abroad and whose militarism costs the lives of civilians around the world every day. I am a man, and participate in a gender system that has perennially denied women full flourishing and, in most cases, still does. I am a twenty-first century citizen of the developed world, and I take for granted that my country and my generation gets to consume up the vast majority of the world's nonrenewable resources even though it is other countries and other generations that will likely bear the consequences; and I cannot imagine things any other way.[5]

By any fair account of judgment day, I am going to be in big trouble. I may not have to shoulder the blame for causing these and other circumstances, but I am certainly going to be asked what I've done to rectify them. And the answer is bound to be, "Pathetically little." And I will not be alone in that.

This litany is not designed to display or evoke guilt. This list is designed to remind readers of what the parable's (and the gospel's) starting point is. We are in desperate trouble. We are the man by the side of the road.[6] The lawyer asked Jesus, "What must I do to inherit eternal life?" That hardly sounds like the question of a man who knows he is in desperate trouble. It sounds like the question of a man who just needs to get straight where his legitimate responsibilities lie and where his sense of guilt need not linger. But Jesus tells a story that shows the lawyer and contemporary Western readers like him that they are all in desperate trouble.

And yet, this parable brings the good news. The answer to our problems is, miraculously, ambling down the road toward us. But, shocking to discover, this person is the very last person we could imagine being any help to us. This person is a stranger. This person is an enemy. This person is more offensive to us than the robbers who have just stripped us and left us half dead. This is a person we assume is out to get us. This is a person we look down upon. This is a person we have never in our lives eaten a meal with, let alone touched. This is a person we would not dream of living next to. This is a person who claims to worship the same God but whose religion we despise and whose race we regard as inferior. This is a man whose identity,

Samaritan, is one we cannot say without spitting. This is the victim of every single one of our sins.

Everything in us resists the idea that we could have anything to receive from this person. No doubt, if the roles were reversed, we could bring ourselves to see them as an object of charity, and perhaps in time they would come to be grateful for our generosity and come to see us as their benefactor. Yet we cannot bear the idea that we might find ourselves begging them for our very life. But this is our moment of conversion. For this is the form Jesus chooses to take when he comes to save us. We are the man lying in the gutter by the side of the road to Jericho, and there is a figure coming toward us, and through our bewildered, bruised, and bloodshot eyes, we see the figure draw closer, and we realize that we cannot live without Jesus. And the form in which Jesus comes to us is as this despised stranger.

We have strong resistances to realizing we are the man by the road.[7] Everything in us wants to hold on to the idea that we're the benefactor – who might get it wrong, like the priest and Levite – but can still get it right, like the Samaritan. But we need a complete change of heart to begin to realize we are as desperate and needy as the man in the gutter. Only then will we find God saves us and gives us everything we need through the person whom our society, our economy, our culture, and even some of our churches have taught us to patronize, feel guilty about, ignore, or even despise. The parable pushes its readers to imagine the person they most despise being their salvation. It asks them, "Can you imagine even wanting to be touched by such a person?"

Dividing the reading of this story between social action and personal faith – as has so often been the pattern of interpretation – makes this story baffling and incoherent. The parable of the Good Samaritan is not a moralistic tale that affirms readers as energetic and resourceful benefactors of the neglected needy in their neighborhoods and communities. Instead it shows Christians that they *themselves* are desperately needy for relationship, for healing, for forgiveness, for reconciliation, for eternal life. And Jesus comes to meet them in that need. But the form Jesus takes to meet their need is that of the person they unquestioningly despise and hate and ostracize. This is the moment of Christian conversion – not just to see one's need of Jesus, but to be willing to embrace him in the form in which he comes to us. Are we prepared to receive the healing and forgiveness and eternal life that comes through the person we couldn't believe had anything to give us?

Then, and only then, can the reader hear Jesus' words, "Go and do likewise."

Go, and continue to see the face of Jesus in the despised and rejected of the world. You are not their benefactor. You are not the answer to their prayer. They are the answer to yours. You are searching for a salvation that only they can bring. Do not assume others will see Jesus' face in you: go, and expect to see Jesus' face in them. Let your interaction with the weak and the disadvantaged and the oppressed of the earth come not from a sense of guilt or obligation or pity. Let it come from a recognition of your own desperate plight, and then from gratitude, from joy, from an overflowing delight that you have been met by Christ in the one from whom you never could believe you had anything to receive, and an expectation that you are going to spend the rest of your life looking to similar people with the firm expectation of meeting Christ in them.

Thus our four explorations of the story have come full circle. In Jesus' telling of the story, he is saying, "Israel is in the gutter. And for it to find redemption, it is going to need help from those it despises and looks down upon." Jesus goes on to identify himself, not so much with Israel, but with those despised people in whom Israel will find its salvation. This is not simply a moral tale inviting the reader to be like Jesus. This is primarily a parable about Israel in internal exile. Contemporary readers do have a role in this story, but it is one they can only discover if they are prepared to realize how needy and desperate they are, how much they, like Israel, are in the gutter, how much they are in exile from the home Jesus is calling them to, and how they can only be saved if they are prepared to receive help from those they demean and despise, because that is the form Jesus takes when he comes to save them. In short, Jesus is telling stories about Israel; but if contemporary Western readers are going to hear those stories, they are going to need to identify with the exile Israel was in when the stories were told, and hear the stories from Israel's point of view.

For many, this is a troubling rendering of the parable. Either it seems tendentious – a deliberate and unjustified misreading of a familiar story. Or it seems unnecessarily complicated – the infusion of historical context and obfuscating detail into a straightforward fable with a transparent moral. Surely this is a story about being good neighbors, even or especially to strangers, one might think. Or again it seems disillusioning – threatening to take away one's self-justification for being a volunteer, or committed to social justice, or an activist. But it is important to recall the lawyer's question: "What must I do to inherit eternal life?" A moralistic answer would not be true to the gospel as a whole. The answer is more like this: "Recognize you are desperate. Open your eyes to the form Jesus takes in coming to save you. Swallow your pride and accept that your salvation comes from the ones you have despised. And let your heart be converted and your life be newly shaped to receiving the grace that can only come from them."

In many places and in many people one might anticipate a sense of growing fury at this answer. But this fury is telling. Jesus took stories that the members of Jerusalem leadership of his time thought they already knew, stories that justified their place in the world and their relation to Rome and their compromises and self-righteousness. And he retold those stories so as to show Israel was in exile, in the gutter, but that he, Jesus, was bringing a salvation that would make Israel not the giver of blessing like Abraham but its recipient, not the bestower of benefaction but the one who so badly needed it. That is not how the leaders of Israel liked to think of themselves. That is not how those of us committed to social justice like to think of ourselves. That story makes us angry, furious, horrified, outraged, bursting to reclaim our stories and tell them our own way again. The habits of working for, and the status of skill and benefaction that buttress those habits, die hard. Jesus' stories make contemporary activists angry. It is not hard to see how angry they made the Jerusalem authorities of his day. He took their precious stories away and retold them in such a way that made them feel like they had been stripped, beaten, and left half dead.

And that, we may infer, is why he was crucified.

Notes

1. "The Christ that Harnack sees, looking back through nineteen centuries of Catholic darkness, is only the reflection of a Liberal Protestant face, seen at the bottom of a deep well." George Tyrrell quoted in Donald Baillie, *God Was in Christ: An Essay on Incarnation and Atonement*, second edition (London: Faber, 1956): 40.
2. See in particular Robert Funk, *The Five Gospels: The Search for the Authentic Words of Jesus* (San Francisco: Harper, 1993), *The Acts of Jesus: The Search for the Authentic Deeds of Jesus* (San Francisco: Harper, 1997), and *The Gospel of Jesus: According to the Jesus Seminar* (Salem, OR: Polebridge, 1999).
3. This of course is the great question which underpins N.T. Wright's magisterial *Christian Origins and the Question of God* series. See his *The New Testament and the People of God* (London: SPCK, 1992).

4. While this is a minority reading of the parable, it is by no means unique. Among those who read the parable this way was Charles Wesley. His hymn "Woe is me! what tongue can tell" is written from the point of view of the man in the gutter. "Fallen among thieves I am," says the man, "And they have robbed me of my God, Turned my glory into shame, And left me in my blood." He addresses the Samaritan and says "In thee is all my hope; Only thou canst succour man, And raise the fallen up" – this making clear the Samaritan is Jesus. Later he says, "Good Physician, speak the word, And heal my soul of sin" – suggesting that the Samaritan has come to bring spiritual, not just humanitarian, redemption. Finally he says "Thou hast brought me to thine inn," embodying the figurative reading I offer above. The hymn may be found at www.ccel.org/w/wesley/hymn/jwg01/jwg0112.html (accessed December 6, 2014).

5. This litany of lament was inspired by Jeffrey Stout, *Democracy and Tradition* (Princeton, NJ: Princeton University Press, 2004): 24.

6. In making this proposal I am of course entering into a longstanding debate on the side of the minority report. For example, Robert Funk argues that this parable is not, as is widely assumed, an example story, but a metaphor. He suggests, "The parable of the Good Samaritan is commonly understood as an example story, offering an example of what it means to be a good neighbor. But the parable does not invite the hearer to view it as an example of what it means to be a good neighbor. Rather, it invites the auditor to be the victim in the ditch, as a careful reading indicates." Robert Funk, "The Good Samaritan As Metaphor." Available at http://goodsamaritan.johnwwelchresources.com/articles/English/FunkR2.pdf (accessed December 6, 2014). Funk has distinguished allies – see John Dominic Crossan, "Parable and Example in the Teaching of Jesus" *Semeia* 1: 63–104 (1974) and "Structuralist Analysis and the Parables of Jesus" *Semeia* 1: 192–221 (1974) – and opponents – Dan O. Via, Jr., "Parable and Example Story: A Literary Structuralist Approach" *Semeia* 1: 105–133. Funk goes on, "The parable therefore forces upon its hearers the question: who among you will permit himself to be served by a Samaritan? In a general way it can be replied: only those who have nothing to lose by so doing can afford to do so. But note that the victim in the ditch is given only a passive rôle in the story. Permission to be served by the Samaritan is thus inability to resist. Put differently, all who are truly victims, truly disinherited, have no choice but to give themselves up to mercy. ... if the auditor, as Jew, understands what it means to be the victim in the ditch, in this story, he/she also understands what the kingdom is about. ... [The parable] does not suggest that one behave as a good neighbor like the Samaritan, but that one become the victim in the ditch who is helped by an enemy" (4). Funk summarizes the meaning of the parable as follows: "(i) In the Kingdom of God mercy comes only to those who have no right to expect it and who cannot resist it when it comes. (ii) Mercy always comes from the quarter from which one does not and cannot expect it" (5).

7. Martin Luther King, Jr. insisted that white America had corresponding resistances to divesting itself of its view of itself as the Samaritan and of African Americans as the ones in the gutter. In King's view, there could only be change if white people began to realize they were in the gutter. I am grateful to Rick Lischer for bringing King's reading to my attention. This was not King's only interpretation of the parable: in his last speech he identified with the dangers the priest and Levite might have anticipated walking down the Jericho road and identified with the Good Samaritan in facing danger on behalf of the afflicted. As King put it, "The first question that the priest asked – the first question that the Levite asked, was, 'If I stop to help this man, what will happen to me?' But then the Good Samaritan came by. And he reversed the question: 'If I do not stop to help this man, what will happen to him?'" Available online at www .americanrhetoric.com/speeches/mlkivebeentothemountaintop.htm (accessed December 6, 2014).

7

Embodying the Story of Jesus

In Chapter 2 I offered a simple face-to-face example to illustrate four approaches to social engagement. I described the different approaches as follows. Working for is relying on one's own resources and skills to address a person's problems on their behalf. Being for is orienting one's life toward the well-being of others, without actually making direct contact with those others or engaging in any material actions to enhance their well-being. Working with is seeking to help others address their problems by using critical awareness to activate a coalition between one's own skills and resources, the skills and resources of those in need, and the skills and resources of third parties with an interest in these issues and their outcomes. These alternatives throw being with into relief as an approach that is never in isolation from the person in question (and thus is not *for*), never defines a person or situation as a problem (and this is not immediately *working*), but seeks not only as a goal but also as a means to enjoy the particularity of the person and see that person themselves as the principal source and activator of their own well-being.

I recognize that introducing the four models with a simple face-to-face example hides the fact that each of these models has a long pedigree – which in this chapter I seek to explore. Doing so is not intended to discredit these respective approaches. It is intended, like the foregoing chapters, to create sufficient doubt and disquiet concerning conventional approaches in order to make space in which an understanding of the significance of being with may grow.

The Pathos of Working For

The simplest model of working for is a contract by which an expert is hired to perform a limited task that a person, left to themselves, could perform

A Nazareth Manifesto, Samuel Wells © 2015 John Wiley & Sons, Ltd. Published 2015 by John Wiley & Sons, Ltd.

only badly or perhaps not all. Thus a lawyer is hired to represent a client in legal proceedings; an accountant is called in to put a person's financial affairs in order; a dentist is required to address a troublesome tooth; a doctor is needed when a patient is suffering from an injury or illness; or a mechanic is approached to set right a fault or point of damage in a car. In each case the expert is involved for a given period of time, and is rewarded with money, the satisfaction of a job well done, the sense of having brought to a third party comfort, relief, pleasure, or rescue, and the social prestige of being an expert in a valued field.

There are a number of things to note about working for. The most significant is that it dominates the Western imagination in relation to social disadvantage. The "have-nots" are defined by what they lack, and this lack is made up of both materials and skills; the "haves" are defined by what they have, and again this is defined in terms of materials and skills. If there is a problem, the assumption is that the problem lies with the "have-nots," and the "haves" will solve it. The political divide is between on the one hand those who want to reward the "haves," increase their number, make it easier to become one of them, tighten the demands on the "have-nots" so they are motivated to do whatever it takes to become one of the "haves," and highlight the degree of choice involved at each stage; and on the other hand those who want to protect the "have-nots," provide a safety net for them, reduce their vulnerability to an adverse turn of events, and offer them promising routes toward becoming one of the "haves," in the meantime giving them sufficient income to avoid destitution, and highlighting the lack of choice that exists in such situations.

In this configuration the expectation is simple: become one of the "haves," and spend your life working for the "have-nots." This is the underlying ethos of professional culture: to become, through education and advanced training, extremely good at what you do, and to spend your life doing it for people. People will be drawn to your services either because your expertise is well-suited to address a part of their lives where they are vulnerable or needy, or because your expertise is so great that it is worth having for its own sake.

I have no agenda to dismantle or denigrate working for. My complaint arises when working for is applied to all situations rather than simply the ones for which it is suitable. Working for plays a vital and indispensable role in a healthy society. When all is well, a chain of interdependence arises by which every member has a skill to bring, is suitably rewarded for doing so, attains the social standing, satisfaction, appreciation, and economic stability that arises from doing something for someone that they could not do as well, or at all, for themselves, and thus in return experiences no hardship or humiliation at securing the services of others to assist them in the same way. There is nothing to denigrate in this. There is no reason to challenge, abolish, expose, and no occasion to regret or lament in this series of occasional and respectful transactions and relationships.

But two things can go wrong. The first lies in the word *for*. When the differences of social standing are very great, the dynamics can change significantly. The whole interaction presupposes that the disadvantaged person has nothing to bring to the table: they are regarded as a problem, and as a symptom of a deeper problem; the working-for approach seeks to fix that problem, with the range of resources the professional person has to hand. There is no requirement that any significant kind of conversation or interaction takes place with any disadvantaged person. The idea that a homeless person may have a role in their own redemption doesn't seriously figure. The result is that these models generate a host of solutions but they are solutions that tend to get little or no take-up from the people they are designed to help.

Why are people so ungrateful? Most likely because if almost every interaction in your life is one in which you are the client and source of distress, while the other person is the benefactor and source of salvation, you are not going to be looking for extra encounters that reinforce such humiliation. The sense of being a problem-solver is electric. The sense of being a problem to be solved is humiliating.[1] On closer inspection it becomes clear that conventional working-for relationships generally presuppose a degree of working with. For example, a lawyer cannot easily represent a client unless an understanding and sharing of information has taken place between them; a doctor cannot best serve a patient unless a conversation has taken place about symptoms and about living well after treatment to aid recovery; an accountant needs a good deal of information from a client in order to be able to address their finances appropriately. But in addressing social disadvantage this degree of with, this partnership, this sense that both parties have a role to play, can quickly disappear. To the extent that the with disappears, the relationship becomes problematic.

John McKnight asks an uncomfortable question. "In a service economy, the welfare recipient is the raw material for case workers, administrators, doctors, lawyers, mental health workers, drug counsellors, youth workers, and police officers. Do the servicers need the recipient more than she needs them?"[2] McKnight characterizes what I am calling working for as a worldview that defines our lives and societies as a series of technical problems. The services provided in this configuration are "masked by symbols of care and love that obscure the economic interests of the servicers and the disabling characteristics of their practices."[3] McKnight portrays the following template that the professionalized service systems communicate to their clients:

> You are deficient. You are the problem. You have a collection of problems. ... As *you* are the problem, the assumption is that I, the professional servicer, *am the answer. You* are not the answer. *Your peers* are not the answer. *The political, social, and economic environment* is not the answer. Nor is it possible that there is no answer. I, the professional, am the answer. ... I, the professional, produce. You, the client, consume.[4]
>
> We will have reached the apogee of the modernized service society when professionals can say to the citizen, "We are the solution to your problem. We know what problem you have. You can't understand the problem or the solution. Only we can decide whether the solution has dealt with your problem." Inverted, in terms of the needs of professionalized service systems, these propositions become, "We *need* to solve your problems. We *need* to tell you what they are. We *need* to deal with them in our own terms. We *need* to have you respect our satisfaction with our own work."[5]

McKnight concludes that the national economy rests on these professionalized systems. Yet these systems consistently fail to meet their own goals. Rather than producing services, these systems are "producing sensitive but frustrated professionals, unable to understand why their love, care, and service do not re-form society, much less help individuals to function."[6]

McKnight vividly illustrates the pathos of working for in a social service context. Vulnerable people, such as physically or developmentally disabled people, elderly people, or ex-convicts desperately need to be incorporated into local life, but a syndrome prevents this happening – a syndrome that disables citizens and associations and renders them tools of a professional culture:

> The community of citizens and associations has often been persuaded by human service advocates that vulnerable people [1] need to be surrounded by professional services to survive; [2] are therefore appropriately removed from community life in order to receive these special service programs in special places; [3] cannot be incorporated into community life because citizens don't know how to deal with these special people.

... Many good-willed citizens volunteer to assist service systems free of charge. In this simple act, citizen volunteers trade off their unique potential to bring a labeled person into their lives and the associational life of the community in exchange for the use of their time as an unpaid agent for a service system. The community group that might ask a disabled or vulnerable person to join as a member decides, instead, to raise money for wheelchairs and rehabilitation centers. The associations of community life are led to support segregated, professionally controlled athletic events rather than incorporating a labeled person into a church bowling league.[7]

Such is the impoverishment of the ideology of working for. In summary, McKnight says, "The use of human service tools places a person at risk of a reduced sense of self-worth, poverty, segregation from community life, and disempowerment as a citizen."[8]

The other thing that can go wrong lies in the word *working*. Working becomes a habit of mind. It comes to assume that everything can be configured within the same trajectory of problem and solution, and that all relationships are, by default, ones in which I have the answer and others simply have questions. If you are the one with a hammer in your pocket, everything looks like a nail. What becomes important is not so much that a person's well-being is enhanced, their suffering alleviated, their agency empowered, but that you yourself have played a crucial role. Working can be so self-absorbed that what becomes most important is that the person with the skills gets the opportunity to use them. If what the person needs falls outside one's own range of expertise or availability, it cannot be my problem – because I don't have problems, I provide solutions: it must instead be their problem, and by having an inappropriate or unsuitable problem, they thereby lose the right to have it solved. Working can become an elaborate exercise in avoiding the pathos of the world by limiting one's engagement in it to the places where one can make a positive, tangible, immediate, and financially rewarded impact. That may be good for one's self-esteem and alleviate any lurking sense of despair – but it may not be especially good for the world or serve anyone's well-being besides one's own.

These points may be illustrated with a domestic and an international example. To start close to home, parenthood may seem to be the definitive working for. A tiny baby is the epitome of dependent need, and a new parent may be overwhelmed by the degree of self-denial required in meeting such insistent and relentless needs. But the joy of parenthood is the gradual emergence of the with, from the cooperation over feeding to the assistance in walking to the sharing in reading to the delight in playing together. If parenthood is simply for it becomes either a burden or an exercise in control; if a growing child experiences childhood as simply being on the receiving end of for they can only come to resent the humiliation or adapt and seek to replicate it in subsequent relationships. In parenthood, there must be a strong degree of for, but the for is a provisional arrangement designed to lead to with; adulthood names the time when there is no more for – no need or purpose or health in a relationship based on for – or when for becomes a reciprocal gesture of generosity and hospitality and cherishing based on a more fundamental and habitual with. Meanwhile if parenthood is all working for and no being with, it is a labor, inducing guilt, rather than a gift, inviting joy. The struggle of parenthood is when to save time by doing up the shoelaces for, and when to support growth and development by sitting on the stairs and being with as the struggles over the shoelaces continue into yet another chapter. In such particulars does the journey from for to with play out.

Turning to an international context, perhaps the archetype of working for is what is sometimes called humanitarianism. Here the model comes from the developing world, and the mood is that of crisis. Working for is the simplest, perhaps the only, model for responding to great disasters or terrible shortages of food. David Rieff has provided a wide-ranging indictment of humanitarian aid along the lines of my critique of working for. As Rieff puts it, "Humanitarianism is a hope for a disenchanted time. If it claims to redeem, it does so largely in the limited sense that in a world so disfigured by cruelty and want it intervenes to save a small proportion of those at risk of dying, and to give temporary shelter to a few of the many who so desperately need it."[9] Humanitarianism builds a consensus around the principle that human beings should not suffer: in that sense, it epitomizes the assumption that we explored in Chapter 3 that mortality and limitation constitute the human predicament. It is not a utopian dream: quite the contrary.

> Despite being founded on the broad base of a very big idea – the recognition of the fundamental dignity and value of an essential humanity common to all people – the humanitarian idea is in fact a very small idea ... an interim ethic that seeks to preserve the value of essential human dignity within the very specific, extreme, and, thankfully, usually extraordinary situation of war and armed conflict.[10]

Humanitarianism gathered pace in the closing decades of the last century, with the demise of grand plans and revolutionary aspirations, and the appeal of more modest, piecemeal engagements. No longer was the bourgeois moral conscience restricted to family, neighborhood, or nation: now, through the accessibility of the media, widespread experience of jet travel, and the possibilities of rapid deployment, there was a strong sense that Western governments and agencies both could and must address the multiple crises that surface in the course of a year. The logic is literally to set the world to rights, through humanitarian, and if necessary military, intervention. Flood and famine demand international working-for responses.

It is interesting to note how working for and being for go hand-in-hand in this context. Two groups of people emerge – the one, a tiny "saving remnant," find themselves "energized rather than demoralized" by "viewing the charnel house of the poor world"; these are those who commit themselves to working for. But the much larger group are those whose moral conscience is given an alibi –

> a way of feeling better about those parts of the world without some seemingly redemptive effort, to which no decent person, once informed, could possibly be reconciled. Far from being a story of unparalleled engagement, might not the real significance of the revolution of moral concern be that the modern conscience is thereby allowed to delegate its guilt and its anxiety to the designated consciences of the world of relief, development, and human rights?[11]

This is a pithy portrayal of being for.

A caricature of being for is played out through the notion of the right to intervene in a failing or oppressive state on humanitarian grounds. This notion

> accomplishes the difficult task of making us feel better about ourselves even when we have no moral right to do so. If we say our idea is to establish a new norm in international relations where we commit ourselves to doing something – the something in question revealingly kept as vague as possible – then the fact that we have not accomplished very much over the course of the past half-century in stopping wars or mitigating humanitarian emergencies seems far less heartbreaking or shameful.[12]

Here lies the co-dependence of working for and being for.

The pathos of working for, bereft of working with, is exposed in the dilemmas of humanitarian aid. The pressure is always to make alliance with a much larger notion of justice by becoming part of the human rights movement, or to fall in with demands for military intervention. Both take for to the extreme of excluding with. As to taking on a larger agenda of justice, the reality is that "despite all the efforts expended, studies done, speeches made, commitments affirmed and reaffirmed, it is anything but clear that the world is a fairer or more peaceful place than it was at the beginning of the so-called human rights revolution." As to "arguing for military intervention on humanitarian grounds," that will "always be a contradiction in terms," because all wars make humanitarian conditions on the ground much worse.[13]

David Rieff's conclusion in the face of the humanitarian dilemmas of our time sounds suspiciously like the language of being with. Humanitarianism, he suggests, through tending to victims and saving some lives, despite compromises, is a witness to the more affluent parts of the world that so many live in perpetual suffering, misery, and grief. In other words it is being there, and not closing one's eyes, that matters most.

> Humanitarianism's core assumptions – solidarity, a fundamental sympathy for victims, and an antipathy for oppressors and exploiters – are what we are in those rare moments of grace when we are at our best. But there are limits. If one has a terrible disease, one may wish for a cure. But if there is no cure, then no doctor should say, "I know what to do for you." … So many people talk these days about "mere charity" … As if coping with a dishonorable world honorably, and a cruel world with kindness, were not honor enough.[14]

It seems that some things are worth doing, even if they do not make everything come right.

Perhaps the most creative and wide-ranging critique of working for comes in James C. Scott's study of the failure of central planning.[15] Scott argues that "Formal order is always parasitic on informal processes which it does not recognize, without which it could not exist, and which it alone cannot create or maintain" (310). One could say the same of working for and its dependence on working with and being with.

Scott describes the Greek term *mētis* – practical knowledge, or *savoir-faire* – in such a way that it becomes a kind of working with the environment, complementary to the notion of working with the disadvantaged. The term is rooted in Odysseus' ability to hold his men together, improvise tactics in the face of a constantly changing environment, and outwit his adversaries. What matters is developing rules of thumb, often through practice, and discovering how to adapt them in complex and nonrepeatable environments. A typical example is a ship's pilot, or a guide through the

medina of an ancient Arab city. Thus, "When the first European settlers in
North America were wondering when and how to plant New World cul-
tivars, such as maize, they turned to the local knowledge of their Native
American neighbors for help. They were told by Squanto ... to plant corn
when the oak leaves were the size of a squirrel's ear."[16]

But there are personal elements too: practical knowledge is acquired by
those who have an intense personal stake in the results of close observation.
Often the poor are better placed to acquire this wisdom, because they depend on it for their survival. Thus they build up "a community that serves
as a living, oral reference library for observations, practices, and experiments."[17] Such a community has a large repertoire of practices and visual
judgments for responding to unexpected events or appearances. While often being labeled "traditional," such a community is best placed to adapt
and incorporate ideas, practices, and products: what this label highlights
is that key elements of preindustrial life seem conducive to enhancing the
elaboration and transmission of the insights of *mētis*. Marginal communities rely on it – because they have no choice. Their secret is to take small,
reversible steps and to plan on surprises and human inventiveness.

Scott's analysis is highly illuminating in what it exposes about the assumptions of working for and the potential of ways of attending and part-
nering. He does not seek to abandon scientific knowledge or working with;
he shares Blaise Pascal's judgment, that the great failure of rationalism is
"not its recognition of technical knowledge, but its failure to recognize any
other."[18] The same could be said of working for. He points out that "Modern
research institutions, agricultural experiment stations, sellers of fertilizer
and machinery, high-modernist city planners, Third World developers, and
World Bank officials have, to a considerable degree, made their successful
institutional way in the world by the systematic denigration of the practical
knowledge that we have called *mētis*."[19] In similar ways working for tends
to assume there is no other way.

While Scott isn't describing engagement with social disadvantage, many
of his insights resonate with and describe the pathology of working for.
What his analysis also does is assume that the sources of the poor's redemption lie wholly or largely with the poor themselves – within their existing
practices of survival and networks of subsistence. To be poor and to live
requires ingenuity and adaptability. This is an insight that working-for assumptions seldom seem to grasp.

The Episcopalian lawyer William Stringfellow, reflecting on his experience in the 1950s and 1960s of living in East Harlem, notoriously the

poorest neighborhood in New York City, and on his conflicts with the group ministry of East Harlem Protestant Parish, speaks in similar terms:

> The premise of most urban church work, it seems, is that in order for the Church to minister among the poor, the church has to be rich, that is, to have specially trained personnel, huge funds and many facilities, rummage to distribute, and a whole battery of social services. Just the opposite is the case. The Church must be free to be poor in order to minister among the poor. The Church must trust the Gospel enough to come among the poor with nothing to offer the poor except the Gospel, except the power to apprehend and the courage to reveal the Word of God as it is already mediated in the life of the poor.[20]

The Dynamics of Working With

Returning to the homeless person in Trafalgar Square, we introduced two models in Chapter 2, working with and being with, that differ significantly from and seek to address the deficiencies in working for. Working with and being with both presuppose genuine, serious, and sustained interaction with the homeless person. Such interaction can be demanding, time-consuming, and lacking in adrenalin. The word "with" indicates that both models take for granted that the homeless person must be at the heart of whatever takes place; that there can be no transformation without agency. Working with seeks to gather together a whole range of stakeholders, and sees the homeless person as having a crucial contribution alongside service providers and concerned organizations. It is a much more dynamic model than working for – and it is sensitive to a much wider range of contributions than simply professional expertise.

Perhaps the two figures most closely associated with the practices of working with are Paolo Freire and Saul Alinsky. A survey of their convictions yields a summary of working with.

The Brazilian educationalist Paolo Freire is committed to helping the oppressed become agents of their own stories, artisans of their own destiny. This means helping them transform themselves from being objects into being subjects – something that can only be done by making the journey from for to with.

> The oppressed (who do not commit themselves to the struggle unless they are convinced, and who, if they do not make such a commitment, withhold the indispensable conditions for this struggle) must reach this conviction

as Subjects, not as objects. They also must intervene critically in the situation which surrounds them and whose mark they bear; propaganda cannot achieve this. While the conviction of the necessity for struggle (without which the struggle is unfeasible) is indispensable to the revolutionary leadership (indeed, it was this conviction which constituted that leadership), it is also necessary for the oppressed. It is necessary, that is, unless one intends to carry out the transformation *for* the oppressed rather than *with* them. It is my belief that only the latter form of transformation is valid.[21]

Freire is full of warnings about the dangers of working for. A key mistake is failing to trust the oppressed to become agents in their own liberation: "Attempting to liberate the oppressed without their reflective participation in the act of liberation is to treat them as objects which must be saved from a burning building" (65). "Political action on the side of the oppressed must be … action *with* the oppressed" (66, italics in original). The mistakes of working for are littered throughout the struggle for liberation:

> Certain members of the oppressor class join the oppressed in their struggle for liberation. … However, they almost always bring with them the marks of their origin; … which include a lack of confidence in the people's ability to think, to want, and to know … The generosity of the oppressors is nourished by an unjust order, which must be maintained in order to justify that generosity. Converts truly desire to transform the unjust order; but because of their background they believe that they must be the executors of the transformation. They talk about the people, but they do not trust them … A real humanist can be identified more by his trust in the people which engages him in their struggle than by a thousand actions in their favor without that trust. (60)

Here Freire sets out how deeply working for is written into the DNA of a certain class of people, and how ineradicable it seems to be so long as one assumes one can be the only source of transformation.

For Freire, the journey from working for to working with is cathartic, arduous, and yet crucial. It is nothing less than conversion – because working for is so deeply wedded to paternalism.

> Those who authentically commit themselves to the people must re-examine themselves constantly. This conversion is so radical as not to allow ambiguous behavior. To affirm this commitment but to consider oneself the proprietor of revolutionary wisdom – which must then be given to (or imposed on) the people – is to retain the old ways. The man or woman who proclaims

devotion to the cause of liberation yet is unable to enter into *communion* with the people, whom he or she continues to regard as totally ignorant, is grievously self-deceived. ... Conversion to the people requires a profound rebirth. ... Only through comradeship with the oppressed can the converts understand their characteristic ways of living and behaving. (60–61, italics in original)

As to the actual practice of working with, for Freire it is fundamentally an educational process. In the banking model of education, the teacher possesses all the essential information; the pupils are empty vessels needing to be filled with knowledge. The teacher talks, while the pupils absorb passively. By contrast, in the process Freire calls conscientization, the animator provides a framework for creative participants to consider a common problem and find solutions, asking "Why? How? Who?" The participants are active – describing, analyzing, suggesting, deciding, and planning.

The process can yield results that challenge both the animator and the participants: this is what with has to mean. Thus,

In one of the thematic investigations carried out in Santiago, a group of tenement residents discussed a scene showing a drunken man walking on the street and three young men conversing on the corner. The group participants commented that "The only one there who is productive and useful to his country is the souse who is returning home after working all day for low wages and who is worried about his family because he can't take care of their needs. He is the only worker. He is a decent worker and a souse like us." (118)

It is important to recognize what working with means here; there is clearly tension over the question of being drunk, but this is how Freire handles it:

There are two important aspects to these declarations. On the one hand, they verbalize the connection between earning and low wages, feeling exploited, and getting drunk – getting drunk as a flight from reality, as an attempt to overcome the frustration of inaction, as an ultimately self-destructive solution. On the other hand, they manifest the need to rate the drunkard highly. He is the "only one useful to his country, because he works, while the others only gab." After praising the drunkard, the participants then identify themselves with him, as workers who also drink – "decent workers." (118)

Here Freire shows that working with means the careful interchange of ideas and the reflective enhancement of practice that comes from close listening and deep appreciation of the perspective, experience, and wisdom that comes from all participants. Gone is the assumption that one person is the expert and the rest are waiting to receive their knowledge; no one is being rescued; but outsiders do have a role in animating and scrutinizing a popular movement.

The Chicago-raised broad-based organizer Saul Alinsky had no doubt whose side he was on. "*The Prince* was written by Machiavelli for the Haves on how to hold on to power. *Rules for Radicals* is written for the Have-Nots on how to take it away."[22] Organizing was central to Alinsky's practice of working with. He took membership of his Industrial Areas Foundation and its local branches not as an individual matter, but as an institutional commitment. He did not gather people around issues, but sought first of all to build relationships. Once gathered, the organization sought to be a broad-based coalition, not a narrow or sectional interest group. Political strategy remained nonpartisan, to avoid co-option by influential politicians or by the state. Organizing resembled a craft with rules that members became apprenticed into. One feature that never changed was a strong trickster element – Alinsky delighted to tease, embarrass, and outwit his adversaries in playful and subversive ways.[23]

Among the many tactics Alinsky developed, practiced, and propagated, the following offer a representative sample. Never do for someone something they can do for themselves. No permanent allies, no permanent enemies. Power is not only what you have but what the enemy thinks you have. Never go outside the experience of your people. Wherever possible go outside the experience of your enemy. Make the enemy live up to their own book of rules. Ridicule is your most potent weapon. A good tactic is one that your people enjoy. A tactic that drags on too long becomes a drag. Keep the pressure on. The threat is usually more terrifying than the thing itself. Pick the target, freeze it, personalize it, and polarize it (126–130). It would be hard to find a more succinct summary of the methods of working with.

For Jeffrey Stout, the heart of broad-based organizing is public accountability. "Power minus accountability equals domination," he maintains.[24] He seeks not to level societies, but to establish structures of earned and accountable authority. This requires organizing, because "To achieve a relationship of mutual recognition with public officials and other elites in the broader political community, a citizens' organization has to put officials in a position of needing to negotiate with it" (109). The task of citizens' organizations is to make this culture of accountability a perpetual and vigilant, rather than episodic and occasional, affair. "The spokesperson who, acting on behalf of others, holds officials accountable in meetings of various kinds expects to be held accountable in turn by the ordinary citizens on whose behalf she speaks, as well as by the officials she addresses. Democracy resides in these relations of accountability" (110). Thus every element of for is scrutinized to ensure it never neglects the with; and yet Stout has an abiding respect for for, because of his emphasis on the representative democratic process.

Perhaps the best-known exponent of working with in relation to global poverty today is the Bangladeshi banker and economist Mohammad Yunus.[25] Yunus' Grameen Bank has pioneered and modeled the practice of lending money with no collateral to landless women in impoverished communities and then setting up support structures to help them develop their businesses and encourage one another. The solidarity groups make joint applications for loans and the members act as co-guarantors for repayment, thus making tangible the principle of partnership in enterprise. The women subscribe to a covenant with 16 decisions, including "We shall follow and advance the four principles of Grameen Bank – Discipline, Unity, Courage and Hard Work – in all walks of our lives," and "We shall not take any dowry at our sons' weddings, neither shall we give any dowry at our daughters' weddings. We shall keep our center free from the curse of dowry. We shall not practice child marriage."[26] With a business acumen to match the pedagogy of Freire and the tactical nous of Alinsky, the Grameen Bank offers a complementary model of working with based on empowering women to make their own way out of poverty.

These examples offer a sense of the intellectual, relational, transformational, democratic, and economic appeal of working with. At their most attractive, such initiatives can seem like secular congregations – with all the camaraderie, fellow-feeling, energy, and mutual respect of a church, but with perhaps a greater sense of tangible results, social change, empowerment, forward momentum, and victory through confrontation.

Most criticisms of working with approaches focus not on any perceived weakness of the theory, but more on the inevitable failures to live up to the high ideals. It is not hard to find instances of when money has gone astray in Bangladesh or opponents have been treated without dignity in set-piece organized events or educators have gone off-message in South America. I have no desire to embark on a detailed investigation into the periodic mishaps of well-conceived and carefully construed schemes. My point is that we have seen how a variety of approaches to working with address the deepest flaws that we noted in working for. They trust those who are disadvantaged. They do not assume all expertise has to be imported from elsewhere. They believe the seeds of a community's redemption lie wholly or largely within that community. They harness a diversity of skills, relying on local wisdom and experience but also capitalizing on the responsibilities and commitments of those in positions of wealth, influence, and authority. They are not too ambitious in what they set out to achieve, preferring to identify one thing and do it well, gaining momentum and confidence from small achievements and collective victories to take on larger challenges together. They are founded not on technology, technique, or resources but on relationships, trust, understanding, incremental reflective learning, and communal experimentation.

There is a great deal to be said for making partnerships with a range of stakeholders, and inspiring the agency of disadvantaged persons themselves to work on a project together. This surely is an image of the kingdom, where needy and powerful, expert and volunteer, faithful, member of another faith, and unbeliever can discover solutions and uncover deeper layers of obstruction together. This is Galilee. In particular, in the British postwar context, it is an energizing break away from the assumption that all approaches are rooted in government policy and welfare provision. To use the language of Chapter 3 above, poverty becomes a disease to be healed rather than a mechanism to be recalibrated, and all hands are needed to assault the disease.

What more could one ask for? In many cases, not much. But from the two foregoing chapters two themes emerge that suggest a small but significant difference between the ethos of being with and that of working with. The first is what we might call the "perpetual motion" of working with. Where working with differs from being with is that working with still sees a problem – albeit one that's shared by a range of different people and bodies. In broad-based organizing, the whole dynamic is to focus on a problem, isolate it, polarize in relation to it, and then bring together a short-term coalition of stakeholders to address it and resolve it. The process depends on the energy released and momentum gained by problem-solving. This can be inspiring and constructive and bonding and empowering. The question is, whether it is an end in itself. One might react with horror, and say, but when people are suffering, are oppressed, are discriminated against and marginalized and terrorized, what could be more important than helping them find the strength and the methods to find their own redemption? Of course: but as Freire points out, habits die hard, and the habits formed in addressing poverty and disadvantage may abide in other realms. Working with is an admirable way of seeking change; it simply needs to ensure that it sees being with as its foundation and its goal.

Being with should be the foundation of working with lest working with fall into becoming a technique. Broad-based organizing begins with one-to-one conversations in people's homes, with genuine care and concern for individuals' experiences and aspirations and wisdom and talents. The discernment that brings about the process of isolating and polarizing around a problem arises out of these extensive interviews. Likewise the Grameen Bank began with detailed understanding of the culture and circumstances of women in Bangladesh – that was precisely why it began and has continued to be focused on women, because it was their plight that was perceived to be at the heart of powerlessness and poverty and because, as James C. Scott puts it, they were the living oral reference library of practical wisdom. But when this with is diminished – when the methods of Yunus or Alinsky or Freire are introduced as a technique without the underlying preparation or groundwork or genuine encounter with a people – then it is not a genuine working with, but a different version of the invasion of the experts; in other words, a working for.

But being with should, just as importantly, be the goal of working with. Working with offers more than a glimpse of God's purposes for us, and a profound analogy for the dynamics of church. But it still presupposes an adversarial contest of defeating and overcoming, it still speaks the language of problem and solution, and it still assumes an occasionalistic picking-off of challenges one-by-one. If life is nothing but a series of small victories, of momentum and good spirits maintained by the building of coalitions with no permanent allies or enemies, then there builds up a fear of this process ever stopping: conflict and its overcoming through organizing or conscientization becomes the lifeblood of a people rather than the means to its liberation. The question for the meek is not just how and when will they inherit the earth – it is what they will do with it so as to enjoy it and keep it. Being with, as the subsequent chapters will show, is more than anything else an eschatological notion – a depiction of what it means to live everlastingly, to enter eternal life, to feed on the nourishment that never runs out and to share the things that are always in abundant supply. If working with does not long for and articulate these things, it is in danger of substituting one kind of scarcity for another.

The second challenge being with has for working with is the extent of its reflexive character. In our study of the parable of the Good Samaritan in Chapter 6 we saw that the listeners were being drawn, much against their will, to identify not with the rescuer but with the person in need. Does the working with model encourage or enable practitioners – organizers, educators – to identify themselves as the person in need? Jeffrey Stout's account of Connie, an elementary school principal in Houston, Texas, we may regard as typical. Connie started house meetings and got to know the parents and the real issues of the community – drug dealing, safety, and the well-being of children. They had one-on-ones with the mayor and the chief of police. They started accountability sessions, holding officials to account, stridently and publicly. "'We really became different people, as far as how we saw our role as teachers. … We realized that the parents were the true teachers, because we learned so much from them as we walked the streets … It was our parents … who were the ones making the demands and understood the history of their area and the issues.'" (107–109) The process is a lesson in humility for the organizers.

But what is missing here, and what is crucial in the eyes of being with, is the sense that the organizers understand and *anticipate* this. From the point of view of being with this is, indeed, their principal reason for being organizers – to behold the glory of meeting abundance in the face of the so-called "needy." To make this transition requires nothing less than conversion – the conversion described in Chapter 6; the conversion from seeing oneself as the Samaritan to realizing one is the person in the ditch, and learning to accept the abundance that comes from the despised person rather than assuming all good can only come from oneself. Working for and working with are different: the former assumes all good can come only from oneself, whereas the latter recognizes that good comes from a range of partners, including oneself; but being with assumes from the outset that good comes from the "needy" – that poverty is a mask we put on people to hide their true wealth – and that the purpose of engagement is not to rescue the poor or restore their dignity but to elicit from them the creativity, abundance, and joy that is so deeply hidden by their current circumstances and for that joy to benefit not just themselves but oneself – because it was the search for that joy that motivated one's involvement in the first place.

Altruism is not the goal. Altruism assumes that the only noble way is to seek nothing for oneself and to seek only the benefit of others. But that is not sustainable, and it is not eschatological. It leads to a kind of working for that lauds the self-denial of the giver and deplores the lack of gratitude of the receiver. A truer understanding of with moves beyond the roles of giver and receiver. Here there is something all parties share: in the case of working with it is a sometimes exhilarating sense of being a part of a team that is overcoming obstacles and dismantling barriers together; in the case of being with it is a more abiding sense of finding limitless depth in and through the company of the other, a depth that discloses joy and abundance in ways that anticipate eternal life.

The Limitations of Being For

One could get the impression, exploring the characteristics of these four models, that being for is a straw man. There is an honored place for working for: in a crisis, sometimes it is the only model that makes any sense. An accident happens and an ambulance is needed, an abscess develops that only a dentist can deal with, a lawyer steps in to address a complex immigration tangle, floods devastate a region and helicopters are required to rescue survivors: in such cases working for is largely unproblematic and greatly to be valued. And we have seen how working with and being with in different ways model the life of the kingdom.

But being for seems to lack those positive features, of either necessity or holiness. There are examples, however, of where being for has a distinguished history. When a person is restricted by advanced age, infirmity, or geographical isolation – or when, in retirement or recuperation after years of being with and working with, they are no longer on the "front line" of engagement – there may be much they can do in shaping consciousness, fostering cultures of commitment, supporting with money or the written word, practicing a simplicity of life and a witness of intercessory prayer and meekness of heart. After all, the whole tradition of contemplative monasticism assumes that being with God is the single most important thing one can do to be for one's neighbor, and thus that all for is underwritten by a fundamental divine with. What may look like for can include significant elements of with: when a person commits to writing regular letters and messages to a prisoner in death row or to a political prisoner, even the limitations of geography and mobility can turn a commitment of for into the tangible, almost sacramental, reality of with.

Likewise a person may sense a call to step back from the "front line" of with and thus practice being for but in such a way that involves being and working with those who will one day be on that front line. Thus a teacher may resolve to make sure her students understand issues of poverty, grasp the reciprocal nature of with, and are aware of their own neediness and how vital, unavoidable, and precious awareness of that neediness is in inspiring and sustaining their engagement with disadvantaged people; such a teacher may also create opportunities for limited interactions across social divides and explore with the students a range of methods of interacting with such questions. All of this is being for – but exercised in such a way that it involves a profound degree of working with and being with many who may themselves be inspired to go beyond being for. In the same way a parent may believe his most important role, for a season, is not to be face-to-face with disadvantage, but to provide an environment where his children may come to cherish and practice commitments of working with and being with, perhaps without the risk of overexposure at too tender an age.

All these forms of being for are plausible and appropriate in their own contexts: but it is significant to note that all of them presuppose the priority of with. For may have its place for a period, due to reasons of pedagogy, infirmity, or indisposition – but with is the norm.

The weakness of being for is exposed by the sociologist Paul Lichterman in his illuminating study of community and church groups in a town he calls Lakeburg.[27] Lichterman looked at a wide range of well-intentioned groups with admirable ideals. Many had utopian visions, prophetic convictions, and radical critiques of government and the wider culture. But almost none of them had any significant influence or impact beyond its own members. Only one of all the groups Lichterman studied succeeded in breaking out of its own ideological purity and internal politics. What that single group managed to do was to form relationships of cooperation with other groups in the town, especially including those whose views of promoting change differed from their own, and genuinely listen to the members of those groups, whose members were drawn from all sections of local society. It was able to learn from these interactions, and alter some of its ways of working accordingly, making such alterations part of its identity.

What Lichterman's study does is to highlight the flaws in being for. Being for may vote, being for may write editorials, being for may donate money, being for may compile research: but being for, while assuming Something Must Be Done, generally assumes it is for someone else actually to do the Doing. Being for shares with working for the assumption that the destiny of disadvantaged people fundamentally lies elsewhere than in their own hands: it tends to be just as committed as working for to solutions, but is inclined to find greater reasons for inaction, sometimes underwritten by complex suspicions about the true holders of power or the real dynamics behind the exercise of control. It often generates a great deal of anger, much of which may be directed toward those whose salaries or lifestyles seem impervious to the claims of the disadvantaged other or the nostrums of arm's-length solidarity. But this anger hints at a sense of powerlessness – and that powerlessness is precisely what the other three approaches seek, in their different ways, to dismantle. The trouble with being for is that it often increases the sense of powerlessness, by finding endless complexities and complications and reasons for being sensitive and not imposing and being respectful and avoiding risk. Being for can get so preoccupied with the right language or the best starting point or the purity of its motives or the guarantee of its outcomes that the poor remain at as great a distance as they would were there no good intentions at all.

These are all the reasons that being for does not default to the working for model (and it seldom if ever defaults to any other model). There is an appropriate fear of quietism and cynicism and passive disengagement – the sins of the priest and the Levite who walked by on the other side; and there is an attraction in solutions, in the sense that problems can be fixed, in the heritage of the great social reformers and philanthropists who righted the wrongs of the early industrial era. This is the appeal of working for, particularly when it highlights and harnesses one's own particular skills. Working for is indeed usually a good deal better than being for. Working for at least assumes we ourselves must be part of the Doing. But, as the illustration of the homeless person in Trafalgar Square showed, in working for just as much as in being for we seldom know the homeless person by name and almost never regard them as our teacher: and to that degree, working for is a model that ensures the homeless person remains a stranger to us.

But the distinction between working for and being for is helpful in disclosing something not just about for, but also about being. Being loses its value when it is not with. There is no particular merit in withholding proactive engagement – no essential hierarchy in which contemplation lies above action. The reason for arguing the merits of being with is fundamentally theological, as we shall shortly see – being with is the nature and purpose of God's interaction within the Trinity and with humankind and the creation, and thus the model for human relations with one another. But being is not primarily a negative statement about the temptations and excesses of working. It is a positive statement about a series of responsive and interactive ways to be present – even, perhaps especially, when much in oneself recoils in fear or boredom or weariness or lack of compassion from being present. Thus being – which is inherently about being present – is emptied of meaning if it is shorn of with. Being for lacks the energy of working and lacks the presence of with. It is not a place to abide for very long.

Notes

1. John McKnight describes how human service programs "can create, in the aggregate, environments that contradict the potential positive effect of any one program. When enough programs surround a client, they may combine to create a new environment in which none of the programs will be effective." See his *The Careless Society: Community and its Counterfeits* (New York: Basic Books, 1995): 107.

2. John McKnight, *The Careless Society*: 97.

3. John McKnight, *The Careless Society*: 52.

4. John McKnight, *The Careless Society*: 42, italics in original.

5. John McKnight, *The Careless Society*: 52, italics in original.

6. John McKnight, *The Careless Society*: 53.

7. John McKnight, *The Careless Society*: 106–107.

8. John McKnight, *The Careless Society*: 109.

9. David Rieff, *A Bed for the Night: Humanitarianism in Crisis* (New York: Simon and Schuster, 2003): 91–92.

10. David Rieff, *A Bed for the Night*: 332; quoting Hugo Slim, "Fidelity and Variation: Discerning the Development and Evolution of the Humanitarian Idea," *The Fletcher Forum of World Affairs* 24(1) (Spring 2000).

11. David Rieff, *A Bed for the Night*: 95–96.

12. David Rieff, *A Bed for the Night*: 99–100.

13. 330.

14. 334–335.

15. James C. Scott, *Seeing Like a State: How Certain Schemes to Improve the Human Condition Have Failed* (New Haven and London: Yale University Press, 1998).

16. James C. Scott, *Seeing Like a State*: 311.

17. James C. Scott, *Seeing Like a State*: 324.

18. James C. Scott, *Seeing Like a State*: 340.

19. James C. Scott, *Seeing Like a State*: 332.

20. William Stringfellow, *My People is the Enemy: An Autobiographical Polemic* (Eugene, OR: Wipf and Stock, 2004): 99.

21. Paolo Freire, *Pedagogy of the Oppressed* (New York and London: Continuum, 2003): 67. Further references in the text.

22. Saul Alinsky, *Rules for Radicals: A Pragmatic Primer for Realistic Radicals* (New York: Vintage Books, 1989): 3. Further references in the text.

23. For helpful discussions of these features, see Mark Warren, *Dry Bones Rattling: Community Building to Revitalize American Democracy* (Princeton, NJ: Princeton University Press, 2001); Luke Bretherton, *Christianity and Contemporary Politics: The Conditions and Possibilities of Faithful Witness* (Oxford: Wiley-Blackwell, 2010): 80–81; and Jeffrey Stout, *Blessed Are the Organized: Grassroots Democracy in America* (Princeton, NJ: Princeton University Press, 2010).

24. Jeffrey Stout, *Blessed Are the Organized*, 63.
25. See David Bornstein, *The Price of a Dream: The Story of the Grameen Bank* (New York: Simon & Schuster, 1996).
26. See http://www.villagevolunteers.org/wp-content/uploads/2011/06/Grameen-Bank-Sixteen-Decisions.pdf (accessed December 10, 2014).
27. Paul Lichterman, *Elusive Togetherness: Church Groups Trying to Bridge America's Divisions* (Princeton, NJ: Princeton University Press, 2005).

Part III
Being With

Parts I and II were designed to address all the reasons why being with seldom gets serious attention in addressing social engagement, and indeed why it has seldom been articulated as the nature and destiny of God and God's purpose for humankind and the creation. Those reasons are: because the human predicament is widely assumed to be mortality rather than isolation, because restored relationship is widely taken to be a means to an end rather than the goal of salvation, because the Bible is widely read as the account of God's action for us rather than God's yearning to be with us, because Jesus' ethic is widely thought to encourage us to work for others in their scarcity rather than find ways to receive God's abundance through them, and because the other approaches – working for, working with, and being for – in their different ways affirm our sense of ourselves, of others, and of the world.

It is time to articulate explicitly and in suitable detail the principles and practices of being with. This central part of the book does this in three ways. First, it describes the ways the inner life of the Trinity establishes and elaborates the dynamics of being with. To begin with the Trinity is to make a statement about whence all knowledge, all reality, all being comes. The Christian belief in God as Trinity is a straightforward claim that the fount and origin and sustaining and completing energy of all being is fundamentally being with. Being with is the true nature and ultimate destiny of all things. Considering the Trinity first also enables us to explore being with in a context that is not submerged in sin. If being with is a claim about creation and consummation, it has to be able to speak about perfection in a dynamic and interactive way; I suggest being with is able to do this much more fully than other understandings of the heart of things. And in Chapter 8 I also develop an eight-layered description of what being with entails – a description that will prove useful in the subsequent chapters. This description is by no means exhaustive, but is intended to be sufficiently illustrative that it sets

A Nazareth Manifesto, Samuel Wells © 2015 John Wiley & Sons, Ltd. Published 2015 by John Wiley & Sons, Ltd.

the balance between the created and the eschatological in such a way that we can see replicated or imitated elsewhere.

Second, this part of the book moves in Chapter 9 to consider the ways the Jesus of the gospels embodies what it means to be with us. This chapter looks briefly at whether Jesus indeed assumes being with as a model. At more length it explores whom Jesus is with – and thus by implication whom the church is called to be with. Finally, employing the eight layers developed in Chapter 6, it illustrates how Jesus sets about being with.

Third, we survey the work of the Holy Spirit. Pentecost is the fulfillment of God's promise in Jesus to be with us always, to the end of time. Pentecost is the church's confidence that the church is both human and divine, hard as that may sometimes be to appreciate; and that God is with people beyond the church, making Jesus present to friend and stranger, and making such people witnesses to the church. In three chapters we discover the work of the Holy Spirit in making Jesus present across different contexts. If the reader wonders why there is no chapter entitled "Our being with God," concerning the Holy Spirit, the answer is that these three chapters are that chapter. The conviction is that, while working for and working with and being for may or may not be experienced as being in the presence of God, truly to be with another, in the terms elucidated in Chapter 8, is to be with God. The three chosen contexts aim to cover a diversity of social locations.

One, in Chapter 10, entitled Nazareth, considers abiding presence in the company of lifelong chaotic behavior: the setting is male, the reality impoverished, the experience often violent, the temptation to walk away very great, the absence of theological narration notable, the failure of alternative approaches total. Employing the eight layers of being with offers a chance to assess being with in a very challenging but chronic context. A second, in Chapter 11, entitled Galilee, explores the experience of a hospital. The narrator is female, the theological themes extensive but latent, the wrestling over ethos constant, the journey of the narrator compelling, the discovery of being with moving, the examples of the clinical promise of being with arresting. A third, in Chapter 12, entitled Jerusalem, considers a classic context – opposing genocidal tyranny – through a familiar figure – Dietrich Bonhoeffer, and through a man who sought to be with him across geographical and hostile divides – George Bell. If being with can be narrated in this most archetypal working for context – the decision to assassinate Hitler and thus foreshorten the war – then it is engaging perhaps its strongest challenge.

By the end of Part III the reader should have a thorough, if not complete, understanding of the grounding, the principles, and the practices of being with, articulated through a variety of methods and embodied by a range of people in a diversity of contexts.

8

God Being With God

Being with is, before anything else, a description of what it means for the persons of the Trinity to be so eternally with one another that they are called one, and yet one in such a dynamic and creative way that they are called three. I want now to outline the dimensions of what the persons of the Trinity "being with" one another entails. The ethical implications of this account will emerge in subsequent chapters in considering what it means for Jesus to be with human beings and the creation and for human beings to be with one another: consideration of the inner relations of the Trinity at this stage enables us to perceive what being with means when not waterlogged by sin. My account layers eight aspects, cumulatively, one upon another. Each rests and builds upon the layers below it.

Presence

Being with means, first, *presence*. Presence is in four dimensions – height, breadth, depth, and time. It is the coincidence of all four in the appearance of one person being before another. In the case of the Trinity it is hardly adequate to use the term "physical": the Trinity is certainly not less than physical, and without doubt so much more; but physical, used analogically, implies tangible, here-and-not-elsewhere, utterly given over without remainder, undivided, wholehearted, and receptive. It means to be available for unmediated interaction – not a voice only, or written words only, but incorporating all the communication that occurs non-verbally. In this sense the persons of the Trinity are, without question, fully present with one another – one might even say, perfectly present with one another. We may thus call presence a necessary but not sufficient aspect of being with, upon which rests all the others.

A Nazareth Manifesto, Samuel Wells © 2015 John Wiley & Sons, Ltd. Published 2015 by John Wiley & Sons, Ltd.

This simple prerequisite – loosely termed "just showing up" – would seem a banal criterion with which to begin if it were not so commonly neglected or widely ignored. There can be no with without presence: any assertion or reassurance of "with" that excludes presence ("Even though we're all these miles away, we're with you in your grief") either assumes the intermediary grace of the Holy Spirit to make present that which is, in fact, absent, or is a straightforward denial, however well-meaning, of tangible reality. The mutual indwelling of the Trinity is the model of what presence definitively means. God is unalloyed, unambiguous presence – no remainder, nothing withheld. Unlike human presence, that presence is always blessing. Human presence has the capacity to alter everything without a single word being said: a profound sense of attraction or repulsion, calm or anxiety, charm or manipulation invariably runs far ahead of words. The divine presence, though it may evoke Godly fear, not only has this wordless power, but is always on our side (Rom. 8:31).[1]

The echoing spiritual "Were you there when they crucified my Lord?" identifies the significance of presence. One can describe the scene in immense detail – they nailed him to the tree, they pierced him in the side, the sun refused to shine, they laid him in the tomb; but such description only enhances the conviction that one had to be there – and the only way to make up for not having been there is to be present where such suffering and glory is embodied in God's world today. "You had to be there" is the conclusion to countless descriptions of events so wondrous or hilarious as to be beyond adequate rendition; being there, being present, not only exposes a person to general as well as particular impressions, but also means that person was there and not somewhere else – had made that place the location of their being, at least for that time. In such a way presence implies a solidarity of wordless association – and is thus the foundation of being with.

Attention

But presence on its own does not automatically secure "with." In fact it could be a form of being without with – a negative exposure to being, that made being a withdrawn or uncooperative form of minimalism; a kind of theological "working to rule": as if to say, "I'm here, aren't I? What more do you want?" The layer above presence may be termed, *attention*. Attention is the practice of loving study, of noticing and remembering minute particulars, of engaging the senses to register and cherish unique and characteristic qualities, of digesting and savoring and dwelling upon appearance, gesture, texture, and tenderness. Attention introduces the dimension of desire – the recognition that being in another's presence does not simply represent a numerical increase, but potentially a deepening, an enriching, an inspiring, a revealing. The mutually indwelling persons of the Trinity look upon one another with rapt attention, seeing all, aching to hear all, missing nothing, so fixed in their gaze that they absorb one another's wisdom and grace by osmosis. Presence is "showing up"; it could be reluctant or truculent. But attention is eager, intent, sharp, poised, alert – never assuming something is about to happen, but always ready should it be so. This layer makes clear that being with is a vibrant, dynamic, demanding activity, rather than a passive, static one. Attention to the other need not imply, still less require, neglect of the self: but it does assume that the flourishing of the self is not the principal reason for existence or relationship. The Trinity is sometimes described as a dance: to dance requires the constant attention of each partner to each other's rhythm, energy, imagination, and direction. This is the language of loving attention.

If presence risks being minimalist, attention risks being sentimental. Sentimental attention absorbs the other into a web of pre-existing projections and assumptions, not permitting oneself to see in the other the sharp edges and inconsistencies that constitute the contrary, intractable stuff of existence.

> Most of our loving is more an assertion of self than a recognition of the other. We seldom love the other as he is; rather we love the other by imposing upon him our own preconceived image of who he is. For we cannot stand to love the other, in his particularity, as a contingent being destined for death. To love such an object is sure to bring pain, since we are destined to lose it. We therefore love the other only as we make him an aspect of our plan; we assume this assures his eternity (and ours).[2]

By contrast attention – loving attention – assumes suffering, assumes that there is no way truly to apprehend the other without being grieved by the other's complexity, or their difference, or their imperfections, or their loss, or all four.

This need not be an action limited to interpersonal relations. The point is to divest the self of self-absorption and be formed so as to be able to take in the reality of other beings in their utter particularity.

It may be a profound moral experience to take self-forgetful pleasure in the sheer alien pointless independent existence of animals, birds, stones, and trees. The profound relationship between beauty, good, and the truth is the fact that each of them provides the occasion for such "unselfings." The beginning of moral life may be nothing more dramatic than the recognition of an inanimate object in all its particularity and detail.[3]

Attention requires such a degree of "unselfing," a concentration on the details of another's existence. The persons of the Trinity have such an "unselfed" regard for one another – one that may inspire many such faithful imitations. Martin Buber, in characteristically lyrical and allusive language, describes the cost of attention.

> Love is a responsibility of an I for a Thou. In this lies the likeness – impossible in any feeling whatsoever – of all who love, from the smallest to the greatest and from the blessedly protected man, whose life is rounded in that of a loved being, to him who is all his life nailed to the cross of the world, and who ventures to bring himself to the dreadful point – to love *all* men.[4]

A term closely related to attention, which amplifies its meaning, is *disponibilité* – as employed by Jacques Lecoq and Gabriel Marcel. For Lecoq, *la disponibilité* is the condition of relaxed awareness attained by improvisers in the theater. An actor in this condition has trust and respect for self and other performers, alertness, attention, engagement, narrative skills, facility with status roles, memory, and the ability to develop character and reincorporate discarded material.[5] For Marcel, *la disponibilité* means availability, or being at the disposal of another, on all levels – physical, spiritual, practical, emotional. It is the opposite of pride, which seeks to find all its resources within itself. *La disponibilité* embodies the notion of attention in that it regards the other as a you (thou) and not simply as a he/she, and incorporates the notion of presence in that it assumes the interaction of two physical beings.[6] Treating others in the third person, by contrast, is regarding them as if they (or oneself) were absent. It is to encounter the other in a fragmentary way, to treat them as an abstraction – an example or incidence of certain generalizable characteristics or tendencies. In terms close to the purpose of this study, Marcel explains,

> The person who is at my disposal is the one who is capable of *being with* me with the whole of himself when I am in need; while the one who is not at my disposal seems merely to offer me a temporary loan raised on his resources. For the one I am a presence; for the other I am an object.[7]

The interaction of the Trinity is the image of utter *disponibilité*: complete availability, vulnerable openness to the communication of the other; for which the only word is communion.

Mystery

To pay loving attention to the other discloses a third layer of being with – *mystery*. The language of mystery begins to take the perspective beyond that of the interpersonal: the broader dimensions of being with start to emerge. The nature of a "mystery" becomes clear when it is set in contrast with a "problem." A problem is something I can stand outside and walk around. It's something I can usually solve by technical skill. A broken window is a problem, but I can solve it by fixing a new one. Often a problem can be solved using a technique developed by somebody else. But a mystery I cannot solve. A mystery I cannot stand outside. I have to enter it. A mystery is something I cannot just look at. It absorbs me into it. Someone else's answer is unlikely to work for me. I have to discover my own. "A problem is something which I meet, which I find complete before me, but which I can therefore lay siege to and reduce. A mystery is something in which I myself am involved."[8] The desire to translate something into a problem is likely to stem from a desire to resist its taking too large a presence in one's life, too intractable a place in one's imagination. "When people talk of the problem of evil, even when they are theologians, they are usually on the way to degrading a mystery."[9]

It is not so much that I identify the other as a mystery to be entered rather than a problem to be solved. It is more that I realize the other person is part of a web of relationships and circumstances – and it is that web that constitutes the mystery. Simply isolating the other from such a setting and context and treating her as a problem has no prospect of success. At best it creates an insuperable challenge – that of reinserting her back into her network of relationships and circumstances; more likely, it makes her existence incomprehensible. An example might be the difference between the customary approaches to treating physical and mental illness. A physical illness – let us say, a repetitive strain injury – may generally be treated by isolating the occasions when the limb in question is extensively used, and either significantly reducing the strain or finding other ways to achieve the ends that have hitherto been pursued by use of that limb. Likewise, a broken bone can be set straight and supported with a splint until the time comes when the bone has healed and the patient can begin to use the limb again. This is the treatment of a problem.

But mental illnesses are almost never a "problem" of this kind. They are a mystery. They can seldom be treated except by engaging the web of relationships and circumstances in which the patient is set. To treat them as a problem is either to become exasperated with these tiresome circumstances or to render the illness incomprehensible. There may well be a place for medication; but what is almost always the case is that a physician or carer has to "enter" the life of the patient to a degree largely unnecessary in the case of a person who has experienced a broken bone. The resolution or healing of the patient's condition is unlikely simply to stem from the employment of a formula or application of a technique: it is much more likely to require the adaptation of the efforts and openness of the patient together with the imagination and patience of the physician, in the context of a community of care and support. If treated as a problem, mental illness can seldom be "fixed." All involved must, to some extent, be prepared to enter the mystery.

It perhaps goes without saying that the Trinity is a mystery and not a problem. The persons of the Trinity can never exhaust, still less master, one another in their loving play of interaction. This explains why the Trinity can be described, but never defined – for every definition is a kind of reduction. The term mystery discloses two further dimensions of being with, both amply displayed in the life of the Trinity: wonder and abundance.

As to wonder, one does not wonder at a problem: one scrutinizes, investigates, calculates, hypothesizes upon, experiments on, and eventually solves it. But one does wonder at a mystery. Wonder is a different mode of discourse from inquiry, description, or request – from interrogative, indicative, or imperative. Wonder is an invitation to an imaginative relationship, to a shared exploration of possibility and resonance, to a form of discovery where knowledge is less important than curiosity and playfulness and a willingness to be open to multiple interpretations. It is not the static settling of a problem but the dynamic unfurling of a mystery.[10]

Abundance belongs with wonder. It is the conviction that if something is of God, there is no shortage of it; that joy lies in learning to love the things God gives in plenty, while misery awaits those who set their hearts on the ephemeral objects of scarcity; that God gives everything needed for a life devoted to faithful following. Anxiety, by contrast, perceives scarcity everywhere; and is constantly inclined to hoard or to steal, to trespass into envy or greed, and to miss the value and pleasure of what it has in the restless pursuit to protect it and acquire more. The persons of the Trinity exist in a mystery of wonder and abundance: theirs is a wonder that goes beyond knowledge, an abundance that knows the joy of the other will never run out. It is a dynamic contentment, an inexhaustible awareness, an understanding that there is discovery without end, reward without limit, play without defeat, perception without diminishment. Here are some words that echo the language of *disponibilité*, meanwhile demonstrating the significance of abundance: "Even a modest gift of oneself, tentatively, shyly offered, can be qualitatively different from listening with half the soul ... Some people never give themselves completely, sometimes because they fear there will be nothing left if they do."[11] In this contrast we see abundance exhibited despite shyness contrasted with fear founded on scarcity.

There is some correspondence between the notion here described as mystery and Emmanuel Lévinas's notion of infinity. The term "face" in Lévinas's work is often related to an ethic of responsibility for the other. But in its initial use it is more closely tied to the idea of infinity, an idea close to our notion of mystery. Here is how Lévinas first introduces his idea of the face.

> The way in which the other presents himself, *exceeding the idea of the other in me*, we here name face. ... The face of the other at each moment destroys and overflows the plastic image it leaves me, the idea existing to my own measure .... To approach the Other in conversation is to welcome his expression, in which at each moment he overflows the idea a thought would carry away from it. It is therefore to *receive* from the Other beyond the capacity of the I, which means exactly: to have the idea of infinity. But this also means: to be taught. ... Teaching ... comes from the exterior and brings me more than I contain. In its nonviolent transitivity the very epiphany of the face is produced.[12]

Lévinas goes on to affirm the relationship of the face, the other, and infinity, in language that speaks profoundly of abundance. "The idea of infinity is transcendence itself, the overflowing of an adequate idea. If totality cannot be constituted it is because Infinity does not permit itself to be integrated. It is not the insufficiency of the I that prevents totalization, but the Infinity of the Other" (80). This Other remains "infinitely transcendent, infinitely foreign," and "speech proceeds from absolute difference" (194). And the importance of this is that this utterly different Other becomes one's teacher, and the undergirding all right action. "The idea of infinity ... conditions nonviolence itself, that is, establishes ethics. ... The other is ... the first teaching. A being *receiving* the idea of Infinity, ... is a being ... whose very existing consists in this incessant reception of teaching, in this incessant overflowing of self (which is time)" (204). Thus our notion of mystery brings together much of what Lévinas has to say about infinity, the Other, and the face.

Perhaps the key dimension of mystery is its inexhaustibility. One approaches a problem with a roving eye: there is always the prospect of another, more significant, more challenging, more rewarding problem ahead and beyond, over the shoulder of this one. But since a mystery can never be solved, still less fixed, one can never expect wholly to leave it behind. There is, in entering every mystery, always the possibility that this will be the final resting place: this will be the place of encounter from which all else finds its perspective and depth. "Sit in your cell," said Abba Moses, the Desert Father, to his inquiring visitor, "and your cell will teach you everything." To be with is to treat each person as if they might be that cell – as if each person, if given presence and attention in full measure, could teach one everything. Problems are solved by being delineated, detached, and dismantled. Mysteries, it may turn out, could all somehow be connected, by labyrinthine tunnels of wisdom, mysticism, and truth. In such possibility lies one aspect of their inexhaustible character. This is how the persons of the Trinity contemplate one another.

Delight

The next layer, resting on mystery, attention, and presence, is *delight*. Thus far all that has been said about presence, attention, and mystery may make being with sound like a long travail of endurance, patience, and duty. But that is not the witness of the Trinity. The persons of the Trinity take delight in one another, in one another's existence, diversity, activity, and expression. One of the most compelling arguments for the practice of being with is that that is where the true joy is. It is not fundamentally a self-denying orientation; it does not assume the attainment of an altruistic ideal; it rests on a conviction that, like consequential ethics, working for and even, sometimes, working with, take for granted a goal that turns out to be somewhat too proximate. Being with is eschatological, because it anticipates the communion of persons with their environment, with one another, and with God that will be their joy forever. Rather than prioritizing those activities that are instrumental in bringing about such a goal, being with celebrates the goal itself by seeking to practice its habits right now.

It is common for those whose whole orientation is directed toward working for or working with to be suspicious or dismissive of being with as "doing nothing." A counter argument is to point out how much working – especially for but also with – is an end in itself, a displacement activity rooted in fear or reluctance in the face of being with. How much is this fear truly about the elusiveness of joy? When one's life is constant work, constant deferral of the moment of reward, constant avoiding the gaze of the persons one is serving or eschewing the opportunity to name the security one is pursuing, how much of this is taking refuge in the journey because of profound doubts about the destination? Being with is not inactivity. It is activity that is seeking to be the goal itself, to be the destination, rather than perpetually regarding the destination as an unspecified, distant chimera, or a prosaic, measurable quantity.

The other key dimension of delight, beyond its eschatological character, is that it is reflexive. To take delight in another is simultaneously to allow the other to take delight in me. It is part of the assumption of working for that any joy the recipient may find in me is strictly limited to satisfaction in the service I perform and the results derived from it. Any further joy is not to be sought, and certainly not to be invited; it is bound to distract from, if not undermine or even discredit, the service I perform. But delight longs to be shared, or risks becoming impoverished – even perverted. Part of the self-denying character of working for is denial of the opportunity to make a genuine relationship – one in which both parties may know and express joy and delight. Yet this self-denial masks its limited perception of human flourishing. Integral to human flourishing is the sharing of mutual joy – not necessarily exuberant, or erotic, or egregious: but to be truly joy it must go beyond the utilitarian and glimpse the eschatological, and to be truly mutual it must be something experienced by both parties, not simply respectively at the same time, but in some degree through the recognition of the wonder of one another. The life of the Trinity is the mutual evocation of joy in one another, the delight taken in beholding the other equaled by the joy discovered in causing delight in the other.

Participation

The fifth dimension of being with, resting on those that precede it, is *participation*. Here, perhaps most explicitly, belong the positive aspects of with. The Trinity displays that God is a shared enterprise. The purpose of all things is not to get to the destination quickly, efficiently, and then move on to other business; the purpose is to find ways to be (and do) with. Participation is all. There is no getting there unless all get there. Every action of the Trinity is an action of all three of its persons, and is the richer for that texture of participation. It is a commonplace to speak of athletic honor lying not in the winning but in the taking part; yet the satisfaction – and the superficiality – of athletic contests arises from the fact that life as a whole is not fundamentally made up of victory or defeat, and only becomes so if one isolates and valorizes those parts that can be so described. There is nothing of eternal value that can be achieved or secured in isolation from other beings: there is nowhere to secure the booty of such a conquest, no way to protect it from the ravages of time or the oblivion of eternity, no person to whom to entrust it for safekeeping. All that is not participation is transitory. Put more positively, all that is participation is connected to the eschatological with, the abiding being with of God the Holy Trinity and humanity restored in the new creation. Every mundane with carries a hint of that final with.[13]

We saw earlier in the dimension of delight that being with is not primarily a matter of self-denial – more the discovery of joy in a location other than one's own creative and successful activity, a deeper joy than can be had alone. But there is still a place for self-effacement. Part of taking joy in the presence and activity of others is to realize that the story is not fundamentally about oneself. To be with is to seek to be a saint and not a hero – one who assumes that the decisive action takes place elsewhere, that the story is not about celebrating one's own qualities, that if one fails all is not lost, and that faithful existence is fundamentally in the plural.[14] The emphasis on with discloses another difference between the saint and the hero. The hero performs for the watching, anonymous, crowd, and the intangible, yet quantifiable, glory. The saint has no sense of any watching eye beyond those whose company the saint has chosen (or been chosen) to keep. The saint is not sustained by applause, or inhibited by the lack of it. The saint's presence, attention, mystery, and delight are evaluated by their eschatological nature – more tangibly, the degree to which they are shared, and translated into with. This is the degree to which they resemble the inner relations of the persons of the Trinity.

Martin Buber's concept of the I–Thou relation is fundamentally a theological notion. "Every particular Thou," he says, "is a glimpse through to this eternal Thou. … He who speaks the word God and really has Thou in mind … addresses the true Thou of his life, which cannot be limited by another Thou, and to which he stands in a relation that gathers up and includes all others."[15] Buber is quick to insist that what I am calling participation is not an obliteration of the self. It "does not mean a giving up of, say, the I, as mystical writings usually suppose: the I is as indispensable to this, the supreme, as to every relation, since relation is only possible between I and Thou."[16] The reason Buber's work is so significant is that he is describing what he believes to be the foundation of existence. There is no prior identity that exists outside relation: "in the beginning is relation" (13) – our hearts are restless till they find their telos in relation. "The aim of relation is relation's own being, that is, contact with the Thou. For through contact with every Thou we are stirred with a breath of the Thou, that is, of eternal life."[17]

Buber makes clear that participation, unlike other forms of experience, is all-encompassing. "The primary word I-Thou can only be spoken with the whole being. The primary word I-It can never be spoken with the whole being." [18] He goes on to add, "I become through my relation to the Thou; as I become I, I say Thou. All real living is meeting."[19] (9)

Partnership

A closely related, but subtly different, dimension of being with is *partnership*. Together they cover much of the ground often spoken of in the language of reciprocity. The emphasis of participation is on recognizing the centrality of with, the anticipation of the eschatological involvement of all in the new creation before God. Partnership explores the nature of that with somewhat further, noting variegations and complementarities. The Trinity is made up of three persons entirely with one another; so with, that every action of one is in some degree an action of all three – and that no action of one can contradict the action of another. But the three persons of the Trinity are not identical with one another; they are complementary in their diversity, and creative in their difference. The life of the Trinity incorporates both the purposeless joy of participation for its own sake, and the purposeful intent of partnership for the exercise and enjoyment of the diverse gifts of the respective persons. What it never has is a task so urgent or a goal so unambiguous that one member sees fit to drop the with and go it alone to get the job done.

Partnership is the recognition that each party brings different and vital qualities to the table. In this sense it is a dimension especially pertinent to

working with, but is also important to being with; after all, the two categories are highly permeable. Partnership is a development of attention in the
way participation is a development of presence. That is to say, as attention
notices and highlights particularities and unique qualities, so partnership
translates those qualities into complementary activity. Partnership brings
out the dynamism in attention: more than just noticing and registering difference, more than just tolerating difference or even appreciating it, it rejoices in difference and puts it to work.

It is important to note that being with, while it pays close regard to process, and is skeptical of overemphasis on product, does not thereby exclude
or denigrate activity in general or productive activity in particular. The
skepticism about focusing too much on the end product arises because such
a focus invariably neglects or undermines the with. In other words it deval-
ues or downgrades the telos in the quest – usually the eager, urgent quest
– for something more achievable, tangible, and less costly or demanding.
Re-emphasizing the with means exploring all forms of shared existence and
enterprise, from the more sedentary to the more physically engaged.

For example, when a grandparent has had a stroke, being with, for the
grandchild, does not mean the grandchild going and buying a walking
frame or searching the Internet for herbal remedies: these are for, rather
than with. There is a place for such support, but such support is not to be
regarded as with, and cannot take the place of with. Instead, being with
may mean sitting beside the bed in silence, perhaps holding a hand; it may
mean telling stories and acknowledging fears, making plans and exploring
possible therapies, watching television or listening to the radio together; or
it may mean walking side by side, as the grandparent learns to walk again:
these are all forms of with. And they show the ways with goes beyond participation to partnership. Participation says, "It doesn't matter what it is,
what matters is that we do it together." Partnership says, "If you do your part
and I do mine, we can do something beautiful together."

The significance of this is that, for the stroke victim, it is often assumed
(particularly from a working for point of view) that there is no part the victim can in fact do. Yet partnership, through presence, attention, and delight,
comes to perceive many things the victim can do, and stays around to discover many more that the victim unearths for themselves. Partnership says,
"You have had a stroke, but you can help me with my color-blindness, with
my dyslexia, with my anger, with my depression. In fact, because you have
to take things slowly, and to set aside the thirst for productivity, I can show
you those parts of myself that I wouldn't have entrusted to you before, for

fear I would be wasting your precious time." Healing is not simply taking medication or receiving physical therapy that restores lost brain and limb and speech function; healing means learning to enjoy to the full one's new range of abilities and discovering aptitudes one always had but previously had not thought relevant or necessary. This latter is a journey that depends on participation and flowers in partnership.

Enjoyment

If there is a single word that sums up the character of being with in Trinitarian perspective, and draws together all of the themes explored hitherto, that word is *enjoyment*. For Augustine, there are some things we use, some we enjoy, and some we both use and enjoy. Life is fundamentally about enjoying, and enjoying makes us happy. To enjoy something is "to rest with satisfaction in it for its own sake."[20] (DDC 1.4.4) We use things to the extent that they assist us in pursuing the things we enjoy. The human condition is that of a profound confusion between what we should use and what we should enjoy. The result is that we frequently use what we should enjoy and enjoy what we should use. Here is Augustine's analogy of how we come to enjoy what we should instead use:

> Suppose, then, we were wanderers in a strange country, and could not live happily away from our fatherland, and that we felt wretched in our wandering, and wishing to put an end to our misery, determined to return home. We find, however, that we must make use of some mode of conveyance, either by land or water, in order to reach that fatherland where our enjoyment is to commence. But the beauty of the country through which we pass, and the very pleasure of the motion, charm our hearts, and turning these things which we ought to use into objects of enjoyment, we become unwilling to hasten the end of our journey; and becoming engrossed in a factitious delight, our thoughts are diverted from that home whose delights would make us truly happy. Such is a picture of our condition in this life of mortality. (DDC 1.4.4)

Having made this helpful distinction, Augustine then states, "The true objects of enjoyment, then, are the Father and the Son and the Holy Spirit," because they are eternal and unchangeable. All else is to be used, that one may enjoy God. Then comes the crucial question: should human beings be enjoyed or used?

> Among all these things, then, those only are the true objects of enjoyment
> which we have spoken of as eternal and unchangeable. The rest are for use,
> that we may be able to arrive at the full enjoyment of the former. We, how-
> ever, who enjoy and use other things are things ourselves. For a great thing
> truly is man, made after the image and similitude of God, not as respects the
> mortal body in which he is clothed, but as respects the rational soul by which
> he is exalted in honor above the beasts. And so it becomes an important
> question, whether men ought to enjoy, or to use, themselves, or to do both.
> For we are commanded to love one another: but it is a question whether man
> is to be loved by man for his own sake, or for the sake of something else. If
> it is for his own sake, we enjoy him; if it is for the sake of something else, we
> use him. (DDC 1.22.20)

Augustine's answer is that persons, including oneself, should be loved not
for their own sake, but for God's sake. Thus they should be used rather than
enjoyed.

Commentators have taken two directions in engaging this significant
theme in Augustinian thought. For some, the distinction and hierarchy
represents all that is wrong in Augustinian-inspired Western theology. Augustine underwrites a separation between the material and the spiritual,
implying the former be employed in the service of the latter; hence the ecological crisis, because humanity has used the created environment with no
sense of reverence or limit.[21] For others, what matters is to gain a truer
sense of the term "use" – which, in its original Latin form, means "treat" and
lacks the negative, instrumental connotations of the English translation. To
use things thus means to treat them with respect for exactly the purpose for
which they were made – just as we treat persons for the purpose for which
they were made. By "use," Augustine simply means to make something the
object of purposeful engagement.[22]

Eric Gregory offers a helpful alternative to these engagements. "Augustine's intellectual energies," he points out, "are devoted to an exploration
of how one is to love without desperately trying to consume any good."
He goes on, "To love an eternal and incomprehensible God, for Augustine,
stretches the soul to allow for a qualitatively different kind of love which can
now include all that is not God. God is not an exhaustible or scarce resource,
subject to competing claims." A person that is a creature of God is not God
but participates in the divine life. This participation means there is no inherent exclusiveness in love: "Augustine's God does not compete with the
neighbor for the self's attention, as if God were simply the biggest of those
rival objects considered worthy of love."[23] These qualifiers become highly

significant when one considers some of Augustine's later clarifications of his influential distinction. Augustine says that "The greatest reward is that we enjoy him and that all of us who enjoy him may enjoy one another in him" (DDC 1.32.35); and, echoing our earlier discussion, that "Enjoyment is very much like use with delight" (DDC 1.33.37). Elsewhere Augustine argues that life in the heavenly city involves "The enjoyment of God, and of one another in God" (*City of God* 19.13), and he encourages Christians to "enjoy both ourselves and our brothers in the Lord" (*On the Trinity* 9.13)[24]

These engagements tend either to project Immanuel Kant's distinction of means and ends on to Augustine's notion of use and enjoyment, or to be so concerned to rehabilitate "use" that it begins to sound suspiciously like "enjoy." Rather than pursue either of these lines of engagement, I propose a third. I suggest we expand the notion of enjoyment from simply relating directly to God, to realizing that a joyful encounter with God's good creation is enjoying God. Few commentators dally long on the notion of enjoyment, preferring to investigate the meaning of use. But I believe enjoyment is Augustine's most helpful term.

The crucial point, in expanding the notion of enjoyment, is to see that enjoyment is not self-explanatory: it requires all the dimensions described in my foregoing account. The point is crucial, because what must be avoided is any sense of idolatry. Enjoying another is *a participation in God's enjoyment of that other*, not an idolatrous displacement of God by that other. The other remains other, and is enjoyed in their otherness – especially in their otherness – rather than made one's own creature. God remains God, and enjoys us as we enjoy the other, and enjoys the other in and with our enjoying the other. As Rowan Williams states, summarizing Augustine's outlook: "We cannot properly enjoy what we swiftly and definitively possess: such possession results in inaction and ultimately contempt for the object."[25] To render the same insight in the language of our study, enjoyment must always respect the with – it is always a participatory and generative, never an exclusive or consuming process. The result of enjoyment is always more, always abundance, and never less, never scarcity.

The persons of the Holy Trinity enjoy one another. That is the most succinct description of how they relate to one another; of what God being with God means. To enjoy is to be in one another's presence, to bestow profound attention on the other's differences and particularities, to enter the mystery of the other and the other's relational world, to delight in one another and thus discover joy, to participate with one another simply for the sake of the with that is involved, and to see complementarities in partnership with one another. The persons of the Trinity enjoy one another with no thought to use. It is not that using is flawed and manipulative – a pejorative term to describe second-rate activity. It is that using names the habit of endless deferral, the reluctance ever to say or feel or know or communicate that *this* – this moment, this place, this person – is the site of encounter, the resting place, the angle of repose, the occasion for genuine worship (Augustine says to enjoy something "is to use it with an actual, not merely anticipated, joy"[26]). Here the threeness of the Trinity is particularly significant: enjoyment is always an open, inviting activity. It is not the possessive, jealous, exclusive absorption of two beings, one in the other, but a participation in an enjoyment that has already begun.

To enjoy another is not simply not to use them: it is to say that, at least for a given period, one has nothing more important to do than to be entirely focused on them, to be with them, in all the ways described thus far – to relish the ways they have been fearfully and wonderfully made, and to bring oneself into joyful relationship with them. Enjoyment is perfect activity: it is a moment when the means and the ends so fold into one another that the distinction ceases to jar; when participants experience their activity as effortless, because they cannot imagine doing anything else. For humans, it is the moment when it becomes impossible to tell what is I, and what is the grace of God in me. For God, it is the moment when the immanent and the economic Trinity are indistinguishable.

To argue that enjoying another is to participate in God's enjoyment of them is to assume one further thing that Augustine does not assume. It is to understand that God enjoys us. *How* God enjoys us is the subject of the next chapter; here what matters is to grasp that salvation is the extension to the good creation of the persons of the Trinity's enjoyment of one another.[27] God bestows upon us presence, attention, mystery, delight, participation, and partnership: this is what the process of salvation looks like; this is what enjoyment looks like; this is what grace looks like. Eternal life is our enjoying God in best imitation of and response to God's perpetual and utter enjoyment of us. God does not use us, in either the instrumental sense caricatured by Augustine's critics or the humane sense advocated by his rehabilitators; we are not part of some grander plan: we *are* the plan. There is no beyond to which God is reaching that includes (and therefore uses) us; we are the beyond. God's life is shaped never to be except to be with us. God enjoys us, now and forever. That is the gospel.

Let me offer two analogies. In many cultures a birthday is an occasion to celebrate a person, not for their productivity, talent, skill, wealth, wisdom, or beauty, but simply for their existence as a created being. Anxiety can turn a birthday into an exercise in working for – the making of cakes, the purchasing of expensive but not necessarily appropriate gifts, the arrangement of elaborate but not necessarily welcome surprises. But the heart of a birthday is the desire to be with the celebrant, simply to express the goodness of their being alive and the uniqueness of their place in the world – a moment of thankfulness, particularity, and relish. It is a day to tell stories, share memories, dream dreams, delight in eccentricities, name insights, and treasure consolations. A birthday, when celebrated in such a way, is one of the most common experiences of being with. To enjoy someone is to regard them, every day, as if it were their birthday: not to give them things, or to applaud their triumphs, or to manufacture happiness on their behalf, but to take delight in them and pay attention to them and relish them in sunshine and in rain. This is how the persons of the Trinity regard one another.

To turn to another analogy, technologically shaped existence enables human beings to undertake a fast-increasing number of activities with just one hand. The contemporary West is a culture committed to multi-tasking; cars, computers, and telephones are designed so that one can operate them with one hand while doing something else with the other. Few things interrupt the one-hand culture: most innovation is oriented to enhancing it. One might say the things we do with one hand are those we use; those that take two hands are those we enjoy. To enjoy another person is to take them in two hands, to offer them time, to cherish their particularity and their irreplaceability – to make it clear that experiencing them requires the whole of one's attention. It is to enjoy them in the way God enjoys them – to participate in God's enjoyment of them. The persons of the Trinity enjoy one another, as it were, with both hands; there is no multitasking involved. And God enjoys the good creation with both hands.[28]

Glory

At every stage in laying out these seven dimensions of being with I have described it explicitly as an alternative to instrumentalizing the other, especially the other who offers you no discernible material, social, or emotional benefit. I have played down the telos, precisely because most forms of engagement highlight tangible, specific, measurable, achievable goals that reduce the telos to the proximate target of that which can be immediately foreseen, thereby making the other a means to that end. But there is a telos. And that telos constitutes the eighth layer of the description of being with, in which each of the layers rests on, requires, and incorporates the previous layers. That telos is *glory*.

Here is perhaps the central verse of Christian faith: "And the Word became flesh and lived among us, and we have seen his glory, the glory as of a father's only son, full of grace and truth" (John 1:14). This verse brings together several of the themes we have been exploring. God's life is shaped to be with us; being with us is of a piece with the persons of the Trinity's existence as being with one another; being with is full of grace and truth; and both the Trinity's being with one another and the Trinity's being with us in the Word made flesh are best described as – indeed become the epitome of – glory. God being with God and God being with us are what we mean by the term, "glory."[29]

The scriptural notion of glory is one suffused with both presence and mystery. The heart of scriptural faith in Old and New Testaments is not that God exists as spirit and truth, but that God is made present in love and justice and mercy, in seeking, forming, and restoring relationships. Presence and mystery are focused specifically on the Jerusalem Temple – on the ark, the fire, and most of all the Shekinah, the brightness of God's appearance. The tension in the post-exilic period is whether God is present in the same way in the Second Temple as in the First – given that several of these key features are missing. Many of these associations cluster around the person of Jesus. Even the Urim and Thummim in the high priest's sacred breastplate (1 Samuel 14:41) are fulfilled in the "grace and truth" of Christ's glory in John 1:14. When Paul refers to the "light of the knowledge of the glory of God in the face of Jesus Christ" (2 Cor. 4:6) he is bringing together a host of such resonances. This sense of glory is vividly portrayed in the conversation between Jesus, Moses, and Elijah that constitutes the Transfiguration. The same sense of glory as being with God is exhibited in Stephen's martyrdom, where "he gazed into heaven and saw the glory of God and Jesus standing at the right hand of God" (Acts 7:55). In John's gospel, Christ's glory becomes especially focused on the cross. This means that glory is not primarily associated with sovereign power (as in the aura of Sinai) but also and centrally with vulnerable exposure and suffering presence. Glory is not just the power that delivers those in peril – as at the Red Sea – but is also manifested and witnessed in those in peril themselves.

For Hans Urs von Balthasar, this clarifies who God in Christ is, as much as it clarifies the notion of glory. "God comes to us primarily not as teacher ('the true') or as 'redeemer' with many ends for us ('the good'), but to show and radiate himself, the glory of his eternal Trinitarian love, in the 'disinterestedness' that true love has in common with beauty."[30] Giorgio Agamben points out that glorification (a human activity, external to God) within a Christian context, becomes the reciprocal glorification of the persons of the Trinity, and thus "The Trinitarian economy is constitutively an economy of glory. ... The Trinity is a doxology. ... God is composed of praise."[31] Christ's work on earth is the glorification of the Father, but also the glorification of the Son through the work of the Father. Summarizing Augustine's insistence that the glorification of a person of the Trinity by another creates no asymmetry in glory, Agamben concludes, "The economy of glory can only function if it is perfectly symmetrical and reciprocal. All economy must become glory, and all glory become economy."[32] Thus does glory, and the glory of the Trinity, epitomize being with.

In his high priestly prayer in John 17, Jesus offers to the Father two petitions that have a particularly rich bearing on our discussion. The first is in verse 5: "Father, glorify me in your own presence with the glory that I had in your presence before the world existed." Here Jesus affirms that glory consists fundamentally in the persons of the Trinity being with one another: but he implies that this glory can exist in the presence of human beings, as is about to happen in his own passion. The second is in verse 24: "Father, I desire that those also, whom you have given me, may be with me where I am, to see my glory, which you have given me because you loved me before the foundation of the world." Here Jesus connects the notion of being with to the ultimate revelation of glory. Glory precedes the foundation of the world: it is "the doxological nucleus of the intradivine relation."[33] Being with was the purpose of God from before creation. Glory thus becomes the theme that connects the relations of the persons of the Trinity, the purpose of God in founding the world, the presence of God among human beings, and the notion of being with.[34]

We have seen how these eight layers – presence, attention, mystery, delight, participation, partnership, enjoyment, and glory – build on, incorporate, amplify, and enrich one another as they describe the notion of being with. To employ language I have introduced elsewhere, each layer overaccepts the previous, and is overaccepted by the subsequent layer – in much the same way as each member of the Trinity overaccepts each of the others.[35] One can thus see this account of being with as an amplification of the notion of overaccepting. All the wonder and mystery of being is joined to the delight and participation of with. Being with is not an abstract ideal, but a rendering of the inner relations of the persons of the Trinity, manifested in those persons' relations with humanity and the good creation, and with clear implications for humanity and the good creation's relations with one another; and it is to these relations we now turn. Once we depart from the inner relations of the Trinity, the flawed and fragile nature of human relations emerges as a pervading limitation. But having seen the way being with abides within the Trinity, we are able to perceive that being with is not simply God's (and our) adaptation to human sin; being with is the epitome of human participation in God – indeed, of God's glory itself.

Notes

1. I am reluctant to associate this notion of presence too closely with Martin Heidegger, but it is fair to say presence in this sense bears some correspondence with Heidegger's notion of Dasein, or "being-there." I mention this because Heidegger insists through the notion of Dasein that being is invariably some form of being-in-context and more specifically being-in-relation, and his whole project presupposes that being is not a self-evident synonym for existence, but needs exploring in its own right – both of which emphases I am seeking to affirm in this notion of presence. See Martin Heidegger, *Being and Time*, translated by John Macquarrie and Edward Robinson (Oxford: Blackwell, 1962). Adam Kotsko describes Heidegger's notion of "being with" but his discussion makes clear that this is a notion elucidated in only the most formal terms – that the "with" does no real work and means little more than relatedness is inherent to being. See Adam Kotsko, *The Politics of Redemption: The Social Logic of Salvation* (London and New York: T & T Clark, 2010): 15–23.
2. Stanley Hauerwas, *Vision and Virtue: Essays in Christian Ethical Reflection* (Notre Dame, IN: University of Notre Dame Press, 1974): 33.
3. Stanley Hauerwas, *Vision and Virtue*: 39. Hauerwas is expounding Iris Murdoch, *The Sovereignty of Good over Other Concepts* (Cambridge: Cambridge University Press, 1967): 11.
4. Martin Buber, *I and Thou*, translated by Ronald Gregor Smith (London: Bloomsbury, 2013): 11. Buber goes on to amplify this notion of attention helpfully: "What distinguishes sacrifice and prayer from magic? – Magic desires to obtain its effects without entering into relation, and practises its tricks in the void. But sacrifice and prayer are set 'before the Face,' in the consummation of the holy primary word that means mutual action: they speak the Thou, and then they hear" (*I and Thou*: 58).
5. See Samuel Wells, *Improvisation: The Drama of Christian Ethics* (Grand Rapids, MI: Brazos; and London: SPCK, 2004): 80–82.

6. Wesley Vander Lugt helpfully suggests that Marcel uses the term *la disponibilité* in four senses: (1) it is not vacant, passive availability, but active receptivity and a readiness to give and receive, involving responsiveness; (2) it is the path to discover true freedom in communion with others – it is availability for communion; (3) it is being fully present to someone, present in a mysterious way, not treating people as problems to be solved (a combination of my first three dimensions as elucidated in this chapter); (4) it is being a participant, who accepts the premise of the overall plot in which one is being invited to take part, rather than being a spectator, who rejects such a plot (my fifth dimension, below). Thus Vander Lugt poignantly contrasts Jean-Paul Sartre, for whom, in his play *No Exit*, hell is other people, with Gabriel Marcel, who states, in his play *Le Coeur des Autres*, "There is only one suffering, it is to be alone." See Wesley Vander Lugt, *Available Actors, Appropriate Action: Theodramatic Formation and Performance* (PhD thesis, University of St. Andrews, 2013): 120–122.

7. Gabriel Marcel, *The Philosophy of Existentialism*, translated by Manya Harari (New York: Carol Publishing Group, 1995): 40, italics added.

8. Gabriel Marcel, *Being and Having*, translated by Katherine Farrer (London: Dacre Press, 1949): 100.

9. Ralph Harper, *On Presence: Variations and Reflections* (Baltimore: Johns Hopkins University Press, 2006): 41.

10. For my understanding of wonder I am, as often, indebted to the example and work of Jerome Berryman. See his *Godly Play: An Imaginative Approach to Religious Education* (Minneapolis, MN: Augsburg, 1995).

11. Ralph Harper, *On Presence*: 43.

12. Emmanuel Lévinas, *Totality and Infinity: An Essay on Exteriority*, translated by Alphonso Lingis (Pittsburgh: Duquesne, 1969): 50–51 (italics in the original). Further references in the text.

13. For exploration and explanation of the precise ways participation is a Christological notion, see Adam Neder, *Participation in Christ: An Entry into Karl Barth's Church Dogmatics* (Philadelphia: Westminster/John Knox Press, 2009).

14. Samuel Wells, *Improvisation*: 42–44.

15. Martin Buber, *I and Thou*: 53–54.

16. Martin Buber, *I and Thou*: 55.

17. Martin Buber, *I and Thou*: 44. Robert Bernasconi maintains that Emmanuel Lévinas has the same view. "The philosophy of existence retained the priority of truth, whereas these 'philosophers of coexistence' maintained a sociality which was 'irreducible to knowledge and to truth.'" Robert Bernasconi, "'Failure of Communication' as a Surplus: Dialogue and Lack of Dialogue between Buber and Levinas" in *The Provocation of Levinas: Rethinking the Other*, edited by Robert Bernasconi and David Wood (London: Routledge, 1988).

18. Martin Buber, *I and Thou*: 3.

19. Martin Buber, *I and Thou*: 9.

20. Augustine of Hippo, *On Christian Doctrine* 1.4.4. Available online at www.ccel .org/a/augustine/doctrine (accessed December 10, 2014). Further references in the text.

21. Lynn White, Jr., "The Historical Roots of Our Ecologic Crisis," *Science* 155(3767): 1203–1207 (1967).

22. See the discussion in Charles Mathewes, *A Theology of Public Life* (Cambridge: Cambridge University Press, 2008): 74–104; and Eric Gregory, *Politics and the Order of Love: An Augustinian Ethic of Democratic Citizenship* (Chicago: University of Chicago Press, 2008): 339–343. Oliver O'Donovan, "Usus and Fruitio in Augustine's *De Doctrina Christiana I*" *Journal of Theological Studies* 33(2): 361–397 (1982) offers a characteristic note of caution about rehabilitating "use" too sanguinely.

23. Eric Gregory, *Politics and the Order of Love*: 40–41.

24. Eric Gregory, *Politics and the Order of Love*: 338; O'Donovan, "Usus and Fruitio" at 390–396 offers many further such texts.

25. Quoted in Eric Gregory, *Politics and the Order of Love*: 380.

26. Augustine, *On the Trinity* 10.4.17. See www.newadvent.org/fathers/1301.htm (accessed December 10, 2014).

27. In *On Christian Doctrine* 1.6.6, Augustine writes that God "desired us through the medium of our own words to rejoice in his praise" (Latin "laude"). This is the closest Augustine comes to suggesting God enjoys us. I am grateful to Maureen Knudsen Langdoc for pointing this out to me.

28. For a longer meditation on this theme, see Samuel Wells, *Be Not Afraid: Facing Fear with Faith* (Grand Rapids, MI: Brazos, 2011): 200–204.

29. In this sense of being with as the telos, and in the sense of it bringing together all of these scriptural themes, glory resembles what I have elsewhere described as reincorporation – the reintegration of stray and discarded narrative themes in anticipation and imitation of eschatological fulfillment. See Wells, *Improvisation*: ch. 10.

30. Quoted in Giorgio Agamben, *The Kingdom and the Glory: For a Theological Genealogy of Economy and Government*, translated by Lorenzo Chiesa and Matteo Mandarini (Stanford, CA: Stanford University Press, 2011): 197.

31. Giorgio Agamben, *The Kingdom and the Glory*: 201, 206, 220.

32. Giorgio Agamben, *The Kingdom and the Glory*: 210.

33. Giorgio Agamben, *The Kingdom and the Glory*: 202.

34. This sense of glory in some ways resembles Oliver O'Donovan's use of the term "praise" as the final cause of Israel's activity, the last and climactic element of the four dimensions of Israel's life. See his *The Desire of the Nations* (Cambridge: Cambridge University Press, 1996).

35. Samuel Wells, *Improvisation*: 127–142.

9

God Being With Us

Having outlined what it means to describe God the Holy Trinity in terms of "being with," and having developed several dimensions of what being with involves, I now turn to the second aspect of being with: the relationship and presence of God to humankind and the creation. The chapter comes in three parts. First, an investigation of *whether* and to what extent being with characterizes Jesus' ministry; second, a discussion of *who* (and what) Jesus is with; third, revisiting the dimensions set out in the previous chapter, a probing of *how* Jesus is with.

Taking With for Granted

A great part of the exegetical argument of this book is an argument from silence. If the gospels truly believe the thirty years in Nazareth were so crucial, why do they say so little about them? If Jesus' ministry is so crucially about with, why does he say such obviously for things like "The Son of Man came not to be served but to serve, and to give his life a ransom for many" (Mark 10:45)?

I suggest that Jesus took the centrality of with for granted. Part of my evidence for this comes in the frequent controversies in which Jesus reacts with exasperation when disciples and others don't grasp what seems to Jesus to be something that goes without saying. Here I offer a number of examples.

In John 12 Mary, sister of Lazarus and Martha, makes an extravagant gesture. She "took a pound of costly perfume made of pure nard, anointed Jesus' feet, and wiped them with her hair" (v. 3). Judas reacts strongly and suggests the perfume could have been sold and the money given to the poor. Jesus chides Judas and says, "You always have the poor with you, but

A Nazareth Manifesto, Samuel Wells © 2015 John Wiley & Sons, Ltd. Published 2015 by John Wiley & Sons, Ltd.

you do not always have me" (v. 8). Here Jesus makes a statement, reacting to Judas' misconstruction, that affirms with in the face of a pressing argument of for. As we shall see, it is in controversy that Jesus exposes what he most deeply takes for granted; his exasperation arises because he struggles to realize that the disciples hardly grasp what he assumes goes without saying. In this case, if the disciples follow Jesus, they will always have the poor with them, because the poor are always with Jesus. They will always be with the poor. Jesus, at the same time as pointing out his passion is near (and thus that anointing is appropriate and timely), shows he takes for granted that he and his disciples are with the poor.

Staying with Mary the sister of Lazarus but turning to a different gospel, in Luke 10 Martha chides Jesus for not chastising Mary on seeing Martha has been left to do all the work by herself (vv. 38–42). Again the issue is what Jesus takes for granted. Martha assumes what Jesus takes for granted is basic good manners: one person should not be left to do all the housework on their own. But it turns out what Jesus takes for granted is that with is more important than for. The reason for all the work, presumably, was that when the important moment came, the sisters would be ready. Surely there could not be a more important moment than Jesus coming. By continuing to work Martha suggests by her actions that there is something more important than Jesus. Thus for subtracts from with. Mary has chosen "the better part" because her actions show she is, in Augustine's language, truly enjoying Jesus, with rapt presence, attention, and delight. For Jesus, this goes without saying.

The gospels are replete with such controversies. In Mark 7:24–30 (and Matt. 15:21–8) Jesus has an argument with a Syrophoenician woman. The argument is about whom Jesus is with. What is unique about this argument is that Jesus loses it. What the woman takes for granted turns out to be truer to the heart of God than what Jesus initially says. The woman perceives that Jesus has a somewhat limited notion of whom he is called to be with: "I was sent only to the lost sheep of the house of Israel" (Matt. 15:24). The woman's agile argumentation outmaneuvers Jesus and persuades him that he is called to be with her people too, or at least to be with her in her distress.

Over and again Jesus is in debate about the company he keeps – about whom he is with. The birth narratives in both Luke and Matthew give a detailed account of the array of people Jesus is with as a baby – from outcast shepherds to mysterious Gentile magi, from worthy Simeon and Anna to lofty angels. The narratives conclude with the curious story of Jesus and his parents coming to Jerusalem for the Passover when he was twelve years old (Luke 2:41–50). The story amplifies many themes – Luke's insistence on the centrality of Jerusalem and the temple, the prefigurement of his passion in the festival of Passover and the resonant "three days," and Jesus' ambivalent relationship with his parents. But once again it offers a controversy in which Jesus takes for granted – while others remain unaware of – whom he is called to be with. "After three days they found him in the temple, sitting among the teachers, listening to them and asking them questions" (v. 46). He does not seem in much doubt: when his mother berates him for being so inconsiderate, he simply replies, "Did you not know that I must be in my Father's house?" (v. 49). Being with his Father determines the shape of Jesus' life: it is a basic doctrinal statement in narrative form.

Examples abound, but perhaps the most familiar arises in the controversies over whom Jesus eats with. Eating with is a particularly significant form of being with, not least because it brings together all of the dimensions of being with we explored in the previous chapter. The opening verses of Luke 15 make this point vividly. "Now all the tax collectors and sinners were coming near to listen to him. And the Pharisees and the scribes were grumbling and saying, 'This fellow welcomes sinners and eats with them'" (vv. 1–2). This interchange prefaces the parables of the lost sheep, the lost coin, and the prodigal son. Once again what people take exception to – that Jesus' mission is to the outcast – is what Jesus takes for granted. Similarly in Luke 7:36–50, Simon the Pharisee takes offence at who Jesus allows to be with him: "If this man were a prophet, he would have known who and what kind of woman this is who is touching him – that she is a sinner" (v. 39). Jesus counters by pointing out that she, at least, knows how to be with him – whereas Simon appears not to – "I entered your house; you gave me no water for my feet, but she has bathed my feet with her tears and dried them with her hair. You gave me no kiss, but from the time I came in she has not stopped kissing my feet. You did not anoint my head with oil, but she has anointed my feet with ointment" (vv. 44–46).

All these stories demonstrate the same principle: that Jesus takes for granted that being with the Father means being with this whole range of people; and that it is so intrinsic to his ministry that he only articulates it when he is criticized by those who find that practice of being with problematic. There are obviously aspects of Jesus' ministry that go outside the practice of being with. But this brief survey makes clear that being with emerges as central to the prophetic embodiment of Jesus' person and work.

Being With Us in Nazareth

Having addressed the ways in which Jesus takes for granted that his ministry is to be with people, and with the Father, we now move to the more specific question of whom and what Jesus is with. This is a complex question, not just because the answers are various, but because the manner of being with varies. The manner of being with is the subject of a later section. In simple terms there are five answers to the question of who Jesus is with: Jesus is with his own people, with the disciples, with the crowds, with the authorities, and with the creation. We shall investigate each of these constituencies in due course. But we start with the most complex of these, which is "his own people" – a constituency so significant it needs a section on its own.

The definitive experience in *Nazareth* is the delivery of the so-called Nazareth Manifesto (Luke 4:16–30).[1] The story comes in two parts. Jesus reads from Isaiah 61: "The Spirit of the Lord is upon me, because he has anointed me to bring good news to the poor. He has sent me to proclaim release to the captives and recovery of sight to the blind, to let the oppressed go free and to proclaim the year of the Lord's favor." He announces that "Today this scripture has been fulfilled in your hearing." This is well received. Then there is a dialogue (similar to Mark 6:1–6), in which Jesus compares the unbelief of the community to the difficulties of Elijah and Elisha in being received in Israel, largely because of their ministry among Gentiles. This is not well received, and the people intend to throw him off the brow of the hill, but he mysteriously evades their malicious intent.

The encounter in Luke 4:16–30 raises two questions in the light of my argument. The first is, does the quotation from Isaiah 61 constitute a "for" program on which Jesus is about to embark? The second is, what is the significance of Jesus' rejection by his own people?

The passage quoted from Isaiah 61 makes five proclamations. Jesus declares good news to the poor, release to the captives, sight to the blind, freedom for the oppressed, and the favor of the Lord. These all sound like "for": they sound like God acting on behalf of the people to release them from their chains to live in harmony in divine and human partnership. It is worth looking in more detail at each of these proclamations. In turns out each makes an important statement about the people Jesus is looking to be with.

Jesus speaks of the poor – those deep in debt, with no reliable source of income; who find that most of the people they meet are predators and that no one will trust them; for whom all relationships have been soured by the stain of unpaid loans and the fear of stolen goods; who are vulnerable to the slightest break in the weather or the economy. Jesus speaks of the captives: those in slavery of another's scheming, like Israel was in Egypt, or in the exile of their own folly, like Israel was in Babylon; those in a tiny space with no room to express themselves or grow or play or dance; those who have done something wrong and will always regret it or been punished for something they never did. Jesus speaks of the blind – those we might describe more broadly as oppressed by illness, addiction, or disability, imprisoned in their own body, weighed down physically by limbs or organs or senses that can no longer work as they should (or never have), beset mentally by panic or disintegration or hallucination or addiction. Jesus speaks of the oppressed: of those whose home is a scene of hidden violence and stifled secrecy, whose workplace is a site of exploitation and fear, whose society is one in which they cannot show their face without a mask, or their country is one in which they cannot speak the truth without being disappeared, whose nation is in the grip of aggressive occupiers or willful militias or merciless oligarchies. And Jesus speaks of guilt: those who have done or are doing something that doesn't belong in God's covenant, who long for an honest life but feel crippled by shame and fear, who spend every day dreading that God or the world will find them out; who exist in an internal prison.

Jesus is talking about the social dimensions of the power of forgiveness. These are all areas where the poison of resentment and hardheartedness and bitterness and cruelty has become encrusted in such a way as to leave whole swathes of people in prison, either literally or metaphorically. He is talking about Jubilee: release from economic, legal, physical, and relational bondage. He is talking not just about resentment and guilt on an interpersonal level, but about prisons in which whole peoples put themselves, the paralysis of guilt felt by a whole race or a whole city or a whole gender. This is a comprehensive account of social bondage. Jesus is offering a personal, spiritual, social, political, psychological, and physical vision.

But what Jesus is not doing is outlining a for program to be carried out on behalf of the needy by those with a social conscience. So much is clear from his words, "Today this scripture has been fulfilled in your hearing." It is not talking about the future. It is talking about the fulfillment of something in the present. Jesus' presence fulfills all the promises of Isaiah. It is a call to each person – and to the people of the occupied land of Israel – to recognize that they are poor, that they are in prison, that their body is in prison, that they are oppressed, that they cannot hide their lies and deceit from God. It is an invitation to each person, and to the nation, to be set free, to open their life to the most powerful force in the world, to receive forgiveness, from God and one another, to enter the Jubilee year – today. It is a proclamation of the hope that lies in the words, "God is with us."

Being with Jesus, we can see from the outset, is not a passive, anodyne, stationary condition. It is a challenging, thrilling, inspiring, and transforming discovery. Jesus' presence alone exposes one's own poverty, one's own incarceration, one's own incapacity, one's own oppression, one's own guilt. Jesus' being with a community brings to light and celebrates all in that community that evokes joy, and burns up and threatens all that evokes cruelty and distrust. In this sense, Jesus' visit to Nazareth in Luke 4 is a straightforward fulfillment of Simeon's prophecy to Mary – that her child is destined "to be a sign that will be opposed so that the inner thoughts of many will be revealed" (2:34–35). It is not so much that Jesus proclaims the kingdom – Jesus is the kingdom.

And being the kingdom – being the embodiment of God's fierce and utter holiness – means that Jesus is not easy or pleasant for everyone to be with. Jesus' relationship with his own family and with his own town, Nazareth, is far from smooth.

The ambivalence runs both ways. Jesus hardly goes out of his way to affirm his own family. When voices in the crowd tell him, "Your mother and your brothers and sisters are outside, asking for you," He looks at those around him and replies, "Here are my mother and my brothers! Whoever does the will of God is my brother and sister and mother" (Mark 3:32–35; Matt. 12:46–50 refers specifically to the disciples as Jesus' mother and brothers). Jesus' pointed neglect of his parents on his twelve-year-old visit to Jerusalem has already been noted; another sharp word is given to his mother at the wedding at Cana: when the mother of Jesus says to him "They have no wine," Jesus replies, "Woman, what concern is that to you and to me?" (John 2:1–11).

Jesus' indifference toward his family is matched by outright hostility from his community. Mark 6:1–6 records how Jesus came to Nazareth and taught in the synagogue. People were astounded and said, "Where did this man get all this? What is this wisdom that has been given to him? What deeds of power are being done by his hands! Is not this the carpenter, the son of Mary and brother of James and Joses and Judas and Simon, and are not his sisters here with us?" Mark also records that "they took offence at him." Jesus notes that "Prophets are not without honor, except in their hometown, and among their own kin, and in their own house." Mark adds that Jesus "could do no deed of power there, except that he laid his hands on a few sick people and cured them." Their unbelief took him by surprise.

As John's prologue puts it, "He was in the world, and the world came into being through him; yet the world did not know him. He came to what was his own, and his own people did not accept him" (1:10–11). The experience in Nazareth is not counter-evidence to what we have explored about the theological significance of the 30 years Jesus spent there. It is simply a reminder not to be sentimental about those 30 years. The people of Nazareth, despite substantial exposure to Jesus, are no better than anyone else at seeing him, accepting him, recognizing him, or worshiping him. They simply resent him: the more wondrous he becomes, the more they take it as some kind of criticism of them. This is not a pretext to downplay the Nazareth years: more a stimulus to see the Nazareth years as being as challenging, in their own way, as the Galilee ministry – even as the passion in Jerusalem.

The rejection in Luke 4 brings together these other accounts of the indigestibility of Jesus – the ways in which his own people found him impossible to be with. It is not just Jesus himself that his townspeople cannot abide – it is, more especially, those others whom he chooses to be with, to whom he alludes in his accounts of Elijah and Elisha. By offering seven verbs – stood up, was given, unrolled, found (read), rolled up, gave back, sat down – Luke is offering a miniature summary of Jesus' coming, ministry, and return to heaven. This highlights the way Nazareth is a synecdoche for the people of God as a whole. Jesus' experience in Nazareth is a metaphor for the whole experience of his ministry. Nazareth is a symbol of Israel. But the conclusion of the story, in which the people drive Jesus "out of the town," and lead him "to the brow of the hill," explicitly anticipates Jesus' final rejection; and thus Nazareth becomes a symbol of Jerusalem. The mysterious manner in which Jesus "passed through the midst of them and went on his way" evidently anticipates the resurrection and ascension. But in our terms the rejection story can be read as affirmation that Jesus is committed to being with even people who find it disagreeable or intolerable to be with him. In such a way Nazareth comes to represent not just the whole of Jesus' ministry, but the perpetual suffering presence of God before humankind.

Whom Jesus is With

Nazareth is thus the template for all the ways in which Jesus is with us, and discloses some of the complexity of what being with entails when it comes face-to-face with human sin. But there are four other contexts in which Jesus' ministry displays what it means for God to be with us. In each case we shall consider what it means for Jesus to be with in this context, and what it means for this group of people to be with Jesus.

The first is Jesus' being with the *disciples*. Like Nazareth, the disciples dispel any assumption that regular, close, and sustained proximity to Jesus consolidates faith, eradicates discomfort, or removes misunderstanding. We can see the disciples as Jesus' most explicitly chosen context in which to embody being with: he is with the other groups considered here, including Nazareth, but the disciples are those he most evidently chooses. We can narrate the story of the disciples as their struggle to be with Jesus – to stay with him, most obviously in his passion, but more generally to keep pace with him in his vision, ethos, and instructions.

Jesus being with the disciples means first calling them – bestowing or unearthing their vocation, crystallized in the conversion of Peter, James, and John from fishers of fish to fishers of people. It means teaching them, shaping their imaginations, giving them parabolic perception, and helping them see the significance of Jesus' symbolic actions. It means clothing them with power and sending them, first on missions, then, after the resurrection, to the ends of the earth. It means disclosing to them his true identity, and calling them to share his suffering servanthood. In all these things it means recognizing their timidity, folly, weakness, blindness, and fecklessness; challenging, correcting, trusting again, forgiving, and recommissioning. There is much here of working with – Jesus is like a community organizer, spending endless time in conversations, carefully correcting misinterpretations, testing out scenarios, upbraiding for inappropriate implementations.

Thus the disciples long to "command fire to come down from heaven and consume" a Samaritan village (Luke 9:54); Jesus rebukes them. They discuss which among them is the greatest; Jesus tells them, "the greatest among you must become like the youngest, and the leader like one who serves" (Luke 22:26). They see someone casting out demons in Jesus' name and prevent him; Jesus tells them not to (Luke 9:49–50). They speak sternly to those who are bringing children to Jesus; Jesus says "Let the little children come to me" (Matt. 19:14). In all these ways Jesus displays what it means for God to be with a people who are teachable yet flawed, willing yet sometimes unable, eager yet weak. His patience is tested: he says, "You faithless and perverse generation, how much longer must I be with you?" (Matt. 17:7); but he never fails to be with each person he meets.

Some, of course, cannot be with him. The rich young man who cannot obey the command to "go, sell what you own, and give the money to the poor, and you will have treasure in heaven; then come, follow me" (Mark 10:21) is one such. Judas, slinking away from the supper table, is another. The disciples are repeatedly humiliated and exposed when others model being with Jesus in ways that go beyond the disciples' own imagination and practice. Three times Jesus has predicted he will go up to Jerusalem and be killed; but it is not the male disciples who anoint Jesus for burial with costly ointment. The disciples see miracles of many kinds, but when a centurion assumes Jesus has authority over his servant's desperate illness, Jesus says "I tell you, not even in Israel have I found such faith" (Luke 7:9). The disciples have been called to take up their cross, but when Jesus dies it is not them but the centurion who declares, "Truly this man was God's Son" (Mark 15:39). For Mark, the term "with" expresses the irony of the disciples' betrayal: Peter is cornered by the words, "You also were with Jesus, the man from Nazareth" (Mark 14:67); but when it comes to the climax, "with him they crucified [not Peter but] two bandits" (Mark 15:27). Here we have the paradox of God's being with us: the Old Testament is shaped around a lament that God is somehow not sufficiently with Israel, that the exile is not yet over, and Israel still cries out "How long?"; but when God is fully, utterly present to and with Israel, fully disclosed and in flesh and blood, somehow Israel finds it cannot fully be with God.

The next constituency Jesus is with is the *crowds*. The crowds do not represent Israel in the same way that Nazareth, the disciples, and the authorities do. They represent more specifically the poor. Jesus' being with the crowds is undoubtedly costly: they throng around him – "Great crowds came to him, bringing with them the lame, the maimed, the blind, the mute, and many others" (Matt. 15:30) – and he has compassion on them. But in order to be with the crowds, he needs time to be with himself and with the Father: "After he had dismissed the crowds, he went up the mountain by himself to pray" (Matt. 14:23) This dispels any suggestion that being with others means never being with oneself, that with obscures within, that imitating Jesus requires extraverted exhaustion. Being with the crowds is not only costly but dangerous. After feeding the 5,000, Jesus "realized that they were about to come and take him by force to make him king" (John 6:15). Despite their joy on Palm Sunday, the crowds turn against Jesus and demand that he be crucified, finally taunting him on the cross. This amply demonstrates the dangers that lie in Jesus' being with us. Being with evokes not just rejection, but execution. Within the crowd, the gospel writers isolate individuals who give texture and complexity to the crowds. Jesus is with the woman with hemorrhages even though he is almost unaware of being so; nonetheless his being with her heals her. Jesus is approached among the crowds by penitents like Zacchaeus, demon-possessed figures like Legion, and chronically sick people like the ten lepers. Each stranger that approaches Jesus in different ways challenges, affirms, or enriches the nature of the crowds and what it involves for Jesus to be with them.

What these more personal encounters, particularly when taken together, suggest is that, for members of the crowd, to be with Jesus is in some significant way to cease to be part of the crowd. The crowds are by no means always bad, and Jesus certainly has compassion for them; but Jesus never sweeps his hand over a great crowd and heals them all. To be with Jesus means an important detachment from the crowd, a forming of some kind of side channel. Being with Jesus seems to require some kind of face-to-face, personal encounter. It is part of the healing, part of the conversion, that the person senses their uniqueness and is seen, touched, heard, recognized, accepted, forgiven, sent.

With some, few, exceptions, the *authorities* – what John calls the Judeans, and all the evangelists speak of as the scribes, the Pharisees, the Sanhedrin, and the Herodians, together with their Roman masters, are hostile to Jesus. Here we discover what being with means when in the face of sustained antagonism. Jesus is sought out by representatives of each of these groups for debate and possible entrapment. He is under no illusions about their motives or their malicious scheming. On more than one occasion he refers to the Pharisees as a "brood of vipers" (Matt. 12:34; 23:33). When brought before Herod, he has nothing to say (Luke 23:9). Likewise Jesus is far from seeing the Roman occupiers as benevolent. The reference to unclean pigs and the egregious name Legion make it highly likely the story of the Gadarene swine refers to the Romans as a demonic force that will one day be exorcized (Mark 5:1–20). Yet Jesus still finds ways to be with even these collaborators, oppressors, and tyrants. He speaks at length with Nicodemus. He attracts enough interest from Joseph of Arimathea for the latter to provide a tomb for his burial. He heals the centurion's servant. He dines with Simon the Pharisee. He makes tax collectors his dinner hosts and disciples. He dialogues with Pilate even in the hour of his crucifixion. And at the end he says, "Father, forgive them; for they do not know what they are doing" (Luke 23:34). The gospel accounts are in no doubt of how corrupt and fallen the authorities are, and of how deeply Jesus threatens their collaborations and compromises; yet there is a straggle of instances where Jesus is able to be with even the most vile, and is prepared to dialogue with representatives of even those groups who wish his extermination.

In his teaching Jesus describes how to be with enemies; in his passion he embodies it. He offers seven actions that constitute what being with the enemy entails.

> Love your enemies, do good to those who hate you, bless those who curse you, pray for those who abuse you. If anyone strikes you on the cheek, offer the other also; and from anyone who takes away your coat do not withhold even your shirt. Give to everyone who begs from you; and if anyone takes away your goods, do not ask for them again. (Luke 6:27–30)

These are the ways to be with the enemy. First, "Do good to those who hate you." Say by your actions, "However much you hate me I will never hate you." Remember this will end. Don't let these people turn you into a monster. Repay evil with good. Second, "Bless those who hate you." Mind your speech. Try not to lose your temper. Think of those who are hating and hurting you and see them as the tiny children they once were, longing for trust and safety, and speak to them as if they were still those children. Third, "Pray for those who abuse you." Abuse can be very difficult to become disentangled from. Remember God is always as much a part of any story as you are. In prayer, ask God to be made present not just to you but to your enemy. Fourth, "Offer the other cheek." In other words, not just do not get into a fight, because then there will be no difference between you and them, but do not let those who hate you think you can be intimidated by violence. Offering the other cheek means saying "I am not going to accept that violence trumps everything else." Fifth, "Do not withhold your shirt." In other words, surprise your enemy with your generosity, and thus show your enemies you have not become like them. Sixth, "Give to everyone who begs." Remember that, even when you can only think of how you've been hurt, there is always someone worse off than you, and reaching out to them is a way of rescuing yourself from self-pity. And seventh, "Do not ask for your property back." Remember you will lose everything when you die so start living toward your possessions in such a way that they don't determine who you are.

Jesus describes on the Plain what will happen to him on Golgotha. Jesus went to the cross because he loved his enemies. As he went to the cross he was hated, he was cursed, he was abused, he was struck, he was stripped of his clothes and humiliated. And yet at every step he responded not with hatred but with love. His Sermon on the Plain is a prediction of the passion. His passion is the embodiment of his teaching about being with the enemy.

An understanding of forgiveness is a vital dimension of being with. Among the seven ways of being with the enemy, it turns out that forgiveness does not appear. Jesus says do good to them, bless them, pray for them, offer the other cheek, give to them, let them take from you, do not ask for restitution. But he does not say "forgive." Why not? Perhaps the answer is, because he is talking about hatred and abuse and violence that is still going on. To forgive something that is still going on is a category mistake. Jesus offers several ways to respond and engage while hostile and cruel and destructive actions are still going on. But forgiveness waits until the activity is over. Being with, it seems, does not mean a requirement to forgive something that is still going on – because that would imply that what is going on is somehow plausible, even right. There are certain relationships in which trying to avoid confrontation and using the language of forgiveness prematurely can be a form of collusion, a way of denying what is really going on, a way of suppressing anger and deepening the cycle of despair. In some relationships there is such a level of self-deception and compulsion and profound disorder that the hurt really is "going on" until the day one or other person dies. Only when the harm done to him was almost over, when he was nailed to the cross, did Jesus go beyond the discipline of love and make the last step. Up to that point he had loved his enemies. When it was over he forgave them.

The final context of Jesus' being with in the gospels is Jesus being with the *creation*. Of course his incarnation is his signal way of being with creation: he takes on human flesh, contingent existence, and the challenges of creaturely circumstance. Since this whole book is a book about the dynamics and implications of incarnation, I shall in this brief section be a little more specific.

The sea invariably indicates the waters of creation and the barrier of the Red Sea. When Jesus calms the storm and walks on the water, he is not only showing the ways he is deeply with – in tune with – creation, but also inheriting the mantle of creator and liberator, fulfilling the expectations of Genesis and Exodus. Jesus finds ways to be with even the forces of oppression and chaos. When Jesus experiences the wilderness, the place of temptation and trial, he is with the wild beasts (Mark 1:13) – just as, when in the manger, he is, by popular assumption, with the farm animals. He is with even those whom no one regards as good company. He feeds crowds in the wilderness, just as Moses did before him; he is able to make the wilderness his home. He spends a Sabbath in the cornfields: he is able to be at peace with creation, and yet not let creation be his master. He brings about a miraculous catch of fish, thereby showing the disciples how in the power of the Spirit they may face impossible odds and be more defined by abundance than scarcity. His parables encompass vineyards, sowing, sheep, wheat, goats, yeast, a mustard seed, fields, shepherds, and a whole range of characters who relate to creation in acquisitive, sensitive, and imaginative ways.

Most significant in how Jesus is with creation is how he is with human limitation, sickness, and death. Jesus is constantly seen overcoming sickness and disability and demon-possession; on a number of occasions – including the raising of Lazarus and the raising of the widow's son at Nain – he even transcends death. His birth, resurrection, and ascension all defy conventional norms of creation. These events raise two questions pertinent to the pattern of being with. The first is, are these miracles not incontrovertible evidence of the primacy, in Jesus' ministry of for, rather than with? Drawing attention to the significance of with does not gainsay that there is much in Jesus' ministry that is for. The miracles – particularly the overcoming of sickness, disability, and death – are the most explicit kinds of for. But as this chapter has made clear, that for is rooted in a profound with – Jesus brings about miracles in contexts where he is deeply with people; and the areas of controversy – healing on the Sabbath, curing a Canaanite girl – are precisely about whether Jesus is sufficiently with (in one case with Jewish law, in the other the Gentiles) to make for appropriate. What Jesus' ministry demonstrates beyond dispute is that God can be with without being for but God can never be for without being with.

The second question raised by these miracles is, are these arbitrary interventions not against the spirit of being with? The answer is, they are not arbitrary interventions. God is not an outsider. God is utterly with the creation. When God is utterly with, there can be no talk of "intervention." There is no such thing as nature, understood as a self-sustaining system to which God is alien. Instead there is creation, which God initiated, upholds, and is perpetually with. Jesus' conception, cross, and resurrection change the possibilities of creation: but more significantly they reveal the true heart of creation – that Genesis refers more to God's never-changing decision to be with us than to the beginning of life; that the cross refers more to God's taking the consequences of what that being with entails than to God's eradicating of all negativity; and the resurrection refers more to the inseparability of God from us than to the conquest of all barriers to our flourishing. Thus the miracles don't so much change reality as make the veil between life and eternal life momentarily transparent.

How Jesus is With

The purpose of the previous chapter was threefold: to examine how deeply the notion of being with is rooted in the life of the Trinity; to explore the dimensions of being with when unencumbered by sin, lack, deficit, scarcity, perversity, or vice; and to enumerate eight of these dimensions – not exhaustively or definitively, but allusively and cumulatively. Having set out the contours of whom Jesus is with, and begun to see what happens to the notion of being with when it encounters oppression, cruelty, and violence, it is time to discover how Jesus is with us by putting the eight dimensions of being with to work.

Jesus is with us first of all by being *present* to us. This is the principal and most significant element of the incarnation: God is with us – not far away, not simply for us, but near, here, tangibly with us. Søren Kierkegaard tells a story of a king who has everything but who loves a lowly maiden – a person without fame or fortune or fine features or fair favor. How is the king to win this lowly maiden's love? He considers using his money, influence, and power. He could communicate to her, probably through an emissary, that she is his chosen one, and she would be lifted from obscurity and brought to him like a banquet on a platter. But he realizes that this would provide him with her body, but not her soul, her will, or her heart. She would have no agency, no say in the question. He would remain a tyrant at worst or a benefactor at best. So he has a second idea: to raise her to his social level and so overcome the distance between them. But he realizes all she would know of him is his wealth and grandeur. If she came to love him, he would never really know why. A third, much riskier plan emerges. He could remove the trappings of majesty and adopt the clothes of a poor man. Then she would truly be choosing him for the right reasons. How could real love begin with so giant a lie? Thus there is only one way to realize his desires. He must become like the one he loves. He must become poor.[2]

Thus God in Christ set aside the trappings of majesty, and, while never ceasing to be a king, was voluntarily stripped of all the comforts and acclaim and protection we associate with the kingly picture of God. When he stood on trial before Pilate, when he hung naked on the cross, Christ had nothing left but his love of us. This is a parabolic rendering of the nature of being with – of God being with us. In Luke's description of the crucifixion, the leaders, the soldiers, and the first thief all goad Jesus into going back to being the king in his castle, the king who can remove the mask and snap his fingers and use power and influence to fix everything. "Come down from the cross," they say. "Save yourself and us." Only the second thief understands what almost everyone in the gospel story has missed: not only that this truly is the king, but also that this king has laid aside his majesty because of love for people just like these two between whom he's being crucified. Here, at the moment of greatest rejection and greatest sacrifice and greatest agony, finally Jesus sees the glory of being loved in return. Paradise breaks through when for the first time someone looks at Jesus and sees not the opportunity of what Jesus can do for them but the sheer joy of his being with them. The poignancy of that discovery coming at the most utterly horrific moment in the history of the universe is the heart of the mystery of God being with us. At this most precious, most painful, most intimate moment of loving and dying finally the lowly maiden (in the mouth of the repentant thief) responds to the king, and says, "Jesus, remember me." It is the only moment in all four gospels when anyone simply calls the Son of God by his simple name, "Jesus." With has done its work. In that simple, naked, name humanity has finally, in the form of this dying thief, realized what the whole story, the whole parable of the Bible, was about. It is the epitome of with: a glimpse of paradise.

When it comes to *attention*, the passion offers positive and negative models of what being with means in the persons of Jesus' male and female disciples. One negative model is the disciples in Gethsemane. When the eleven remaining disciples get to Gethsemane, eight stay near the edge of the garden, while Jesus takes three with him to the place where he is going to pray. Here we see more than a hint of two levels of discipleship – those who are with Jesus, and those who are with Jesus to the end. Jesus gives Peter, James, and John the privilege of being close to him at this most tortured moment of his life, in this most intimate exchange between him and his Father, where he says, "If it is possible, let this cup pass from me" (Matt. 26:39). But Jesus also expects more of these three disciples than of the others: the fact that Peter, James, and John fell asleep has been held against them and seen as a sign of the church's faithlessness for 2,000 years.

By contrast several women offer what the male disciples, it seems, cannot. The woman at Bethany "came with an alabaster jar of very costly ointment of nard, and she broke open the jar and poured the ointment on his head" (Mark 14:3), thus anointing Jesus for his burial. She has been with Jesus in a way the regular disciples have not: her attention has made her realize what the other disciples have missed. Thus "wherever the good news is proclaimed in the whole world, what she has done will be told in remembrance of her" (v. 9). Likewise, in Matthew's and Mark's accounts, women were with Jesus in loving attention, at three key moments of his passion: at his death ("Many women were also there, looking on from a distance," Matt. 27:55); at his burial ("Mary Magdalene and the other Mary were there, sitting opposite the tomb," Matt. 27:61); and as soon as the Sabbath was over ("as the first day of the week was dawning, Mary Magdalene and the other Mary went to see the tomb," Matt. 28:1).

Attention is not restricted to the intensity of the moment; it also means sustained engagement with detail, appropriateness, and fittingness. Thus Jesus' post-resurrection conversation with Peter exhibits attention to precise details. Three times Jesus says, "Simon son of John, do you love me?" (John 21:15–17); this threefold commission mirrors the threefold denial in the high priest's courtyard (18:15–27). Jesus precisely addresses the depth of Peter's betrayal through the manner of his restoration. Likewise the Samaritan woman exclaims, "He told me everything I have ever done" (John 4:39). Attention includes attention to sin as well as attention to creative wonder.

Turning to *mystery*, the transfiguration discloses both positive and negative aspects of how mystery is integral to being with. The story begins as a statement about the degree to which Jesus is with Peter, James, and John. Jesus "took with him Peter and James and his brother John and led them up a high mountain, by themselves" (Matt. 17:1). The disciples see the mystery within the reality of God's presence in Jesus: "he was transfigured before them, and his face shone like the sun, and his clothes became dazzling white" (17:2). The veil is removed, and humanity comes face-to-face with the glory of God. But then a further element of with emerges: "Suddenly there appeared to them Moses and Elijah, talking with him" (17:3). Jesus is always understood in conversation with the law and the prophets. Jesus is always with scripture, with Israel, with the liberation of the exodus and with the struggle of the people to be faithful in settled times. But quickly a negative aspect surfaces: Peter said to Jesus, "Lord, it is good for us to be here; if you wish, I will make three dwellings here, one for you, one for Moses, and one for Elijah" (17:4). Once again the disciples cannot fully grasp what it means to be with Jesus. They see a problem and miss the mystery. But mystery is reasserted in what happens next. "Suddenly a bright cloud overshadowed them, and from the cloud a voice said, 'This is my Son, the Beloved; with him I am well pleased; listen to him!'" (17:5) "Listening" distils the essence of being with in the presence of mystery. Peter's response discloses an impulse toward working for: he is out of his depth and reverts to the safest mode of engagement. But the added mystery of the cloud and the voice is something that cannot be managed: it must simply be enjoyed. The disciples, however, do not enjoy it: "they fell to the ground and were overcome by fear" (17:6). It takes Jesus to be with them in a much more tangibly incarnate, reassuring way to make the mystery one they can truly enter: "Jesus came and touched them, saying, 'Get up and do not be afraid'" (17:7). What the story has given us is a vivid portrayal of the mystery of Jesus' being with us, with the law and the prophets, and with God, all at the same time, and an invitation to us to enter that mystery. It demonstrates how much we resist doing so, and how Jesus finds a way to be with us regardless.

The key features of *delight* are eschatological joy and reciprocal mutuality. The most widespread portrayals of these characteristics come in shared meals and in the parables. Once again the examples are negative as well as positive. Thus the parable of the rich fool (Luke 12:13–21) demonstrates the wrong kind of delight in its lack of mutuality. The rich man has a conversation with himself. He has no one to have a conversation with, no one whose wisdom he seeks out, no one for whom he feels responsible, no one to whom he regards himself as accountable. He is alone: surrounded by money and food and resources, but starved of people and of love. The rich man finds a way to cushion himself from contingency, and thereby insulate himself from dependence on other people and on God: bigger barns. He talks about a party: "Eat, drink, and be merry," he says. But he has no one to attend the party but himself. It is a ghastly parody of heaven, with no God, no companions, and no eternity. It is delight without eschatological joy and reciprocal mutuality. The rich man is a fool because he thinks he can obtain security by insulating himself from God and other people; it turns out that by so doing he is putting himself in solitary confinement now and forever.

Other parables demonstrate the delight of being with and the grief of not being so. The parable of the prodigal son articulates the joy of the restoration of with: "Bring out a robe – the best one – and put it on him; put a ring on his finger and sandals on his feet. And get the fatted calf and kill it, and let us eat and celebrate; for this son of mine was dead and is alive again; he was lost and is found!" (Luke 15:22–24). It also shows the agony of the elder son's not being with the father, despite the latter's plaintive words, "Son, you are always with me, and all that is mine is yours" (15:31). Telling of the delight of the shepherd at his found sheep and the woman at her found coin, Jesus exclaims, "Just so, I tell you, there is joy in the presence of the angels of God over one sinner who repents" (Luke 15:10). Here is the camaraderie of the delight of being with, together with its eschatological anticipation.

Perhaps the most vivid contrast of delight and despair is the story of Dives and Lazarus. By failing to be with Lazarus at a time when only the dogs were willing to be with Lazarus, indeed by erecting significant barriers to render it impossible to be with Lazarus, Dives makes it impossible to be with Lazarus eternally, when Lazarus has the company of Abraham. By calling on Abraham to send Lazarus, first to dip the tip of his finger and water and cool Dives' tongue, and second to warn Dives' brothers of the impending fate, Dives shows how, even in extremis, he has no notion of a reality that contains any notion of being with, only of a social arrangement made up of working for relationships in which Lazarus is his slave.

Jesus' meals are a tour through many features of delight, in positive and negative aspects. One he shares with Zacchaeus, evoking considerable controversy, to which Jesus responds, "Today salvation has come to this house, because he too is a son of Abraham. For the Son of Man came to seek out and to save the lost" (Luke 19:9–10). We have already noted the contrast between his reception by the notorious woman and by Simon the Pharisee at dinner (Luke 7:36–50). The Last Supper is a poignant study in being with. Jesus immerses himself in the company of his disciples: "I will never again drink of this fruit of the vine until that day when I drink it new with you in my Father's kingdom" (Matt. 26:29). Here there may not be joy, but there is certainly eschatological anticipation. Yet there is also pain: "But see, the one who betrays me is with me, and his hand is on the table" (Luke 22:21). Thus being with brings out the complexity and the multi-dimensionality of what is taking place at the Last Supper.

The most explicit account of *participation* in the gospels is the temptation narrative. The question asked by Satan is, "Are you going to be with your people or not?" Each of the temptations is a proposal for Jesus to work for Israel rather than be with Israel – and each offers a much more comfortable ride than the journey to which Jesus is called. Being with Israel is a rather greater challenge than working for Israel. Thus the first temptation is, "If you are the Son of God, command this stone to become a loaf of bread" (Luke 4:3). This promises to give relief to Jesus in his desert hunger; it also promises to deliver Israel from its apparent scarcity, its dependence on food and supplies and farming. Jesus chooses to be with rather than to retreat into for: it is the choice on which the incarnation rests. The second temptation is, "To you I will give their glory and all this authority; for it has been given over to me, and I give it to anyone I please. If you, then, will worship me, it will all be yours" (Luke 4:6–7). Here Jesus has an even starker choice between for and with. He could be magnificently for the world – he could rule in justice and equity; the only cost would be to be with the devil. Who Jesus is with again turns out to be more telling than who he is for. Finally Satan tempts Jesus, "If you are the Son of God, throw yourself down from here" (Luke 4:9). To make such a dramatic gesture is a classic act of for: it involves no relationship with Israel, no participation, simply the visual impact of the angels' intervention. It is the polar opposite of the pattern of the savior who is crucified in ignominy among criminals and resurrected in obscurity among mistrusted women. Later, when Jesus compares Peter to Satan, it indicates that Peter's perception of Jesus' mission is disturbingly reminiscent of these temptations in the desert. Jesus "rebuked Peter and said, 'Get behind me, Satan! For you are setting your mind not on divine things but on human things'" (Mark 8:33). Peter assumes a working-for model where Jesus will be spared his own suffering; and perhaps Peter also assumes no necessity on his own part to be with Jesus in such suffering.

Partnership, unlike participation, highlights the different but complementary ways God is with us. Perhaps the representative center of partnership is to be found in Jesus' words in Matthew 18:20: "where two or three are gathered in my name, I am there among them." Here is the assurance that when disciples are truly with one another, Jesus is with them. Partnership is, in theory, the heart of Jesus' relationship with his disciples, because it affirms not only the solidarity, the way they are together in all things, but also their complementarity, the good ways in which they are different. Again we may observe a positive and a more complex example. At the feeding of the five thousand, the disciples make the mistake of thinking everything falls to them; and they despair because they have no resources to feed the crowd. But it turns out they have two roles, both of which arise out of being with the people and being with Jesus. Their roles are to bring the sufficiency of the people to Jesus and to bring the abundance of Jesus to the people. Both are working roles (a mixture of working with and working for) but they make little sense without the being with relationships that undergird them. Once the disciples' eyes are opened, the feeding story is a perfect instance of partnership.

A rather more challenging portrayal of partnership is to be found in the footwashing in John 13. The footwashing is a study in the interrelationships and tensions to be found in being with, working with, and working for. Peter is adamant that if there is any working for to be done, it is he who is going to do it. Jesus has adopted a thoroughly working-for role – the slave who washes feet. Peter says Jesus may not adopt such a role. Jesus responds by telling Peter they can share no with unless Peter is prepared to accept this moment of for. Peter immediately changes his tune. For Peter, being with Jesus is everything. That is why he swears he will never abandon the with: "Lord, I am ready to go with you to prison and to death!" (Luke 22:33). But that is also why his failure to be with Jesus in the High Priest's courtyard is more galling for him even than it would have been for the other disciples. In the light of the terms of our study, it is not hard to see the footwashing as a microcosm of the whole gospel: Jesus is utterly with his people and his disciples; the cross is the moment of for that is entailed by and inseparable from the with.

The great paradigm of *enjoyment* is the parable of the sheep and the goats (Matt. 25:31–46). The parable depends on the recognition that Jesus has been or shortly will be in all of the conditions the story portrays. He has been hungry in the desert, tempted by Satan. He will be thirsty on the cross, when offered a sponge of sour wine. He was a stranger when he returned, unwelcome, to his home town, and when his parents came, unknown, to Bethlehem. He was naked in the manger and will be on the cross. He will be sick in Gethsemane, when his sweat will fall like great drops of blood. And he will be in prison at the hands of the High Priest and of Pilate. So he is with people in each of these circumstances. The customary challenge in this story is to see in the disadvantaged the face of Jesus. But from the point of view of this study, there is a slightly different challenge: it is to respond to the disadvantaged in being with ways – ways of enjoyment – rather than principally in working for ways. Thus "I was hungry and you gave me food, I was thirsty and you gave me something to drink, I was a stranger and you welcomed me, I was naked and you gave me clothing, I was sick and you took care of me, I was in prison and you visited me" (Matt. 25:35–36). Six simple gestures of mercy.

Feeding a person or giving a person a drink may sound like a working-for activity. But it is important to notice the ways in which it is counteracting a working-for mentality. "You gave me food" is not "You invested in dietary sciences that look into malnutrition" or, "You dug a well in the developing world" or, "You provided a year's supply of water purification tablets." It requires face-to-face encounter with the person in desperate need, and a humble recognition that one cannot hope to fix their problem but that it is more than worth being with them anyway – because maybe they might be your savior – maybe they might be Jesus. "I was a stranger and you welcomed me" is not "You transformed immigration policy" or, "You provided sufficient public housing for a generation." It requires hospitality

– it requires you to change the shape of your own life to accommodate the flourishing of another's; with the promise that you might be entertaining an angel unawares. "I was naked and you gave me clothing" is not "You invented incredible fibers that actually breathe so you only need to wear one layer whether it's sweaty summer or snowy winter." It involves being close to those who face the humiliation of being without a shirt to cover their modesty and not turning your back on them. "I was sick and you took care of me" is not "You cured me" or, "You labored night and day in a laboratory and science park to find and test a crucial vaccine." These are good things, but the parable is an invitation to presence, attention, and enjoyment: to care, not for an issue, or even for the alleviation of suffering, but to care by being present with a person in need. Finally, "I was in prison and you visited me" is not, "You undertook extensive statistical research into various indicators of crime rates in order to be better able to track ex-prisoners and reduce recidivism." It is not even, "You defended me and spoke up for me when I feared my cause was lost." It is a simple affirmation of the indelible and irreplaceable value of being with those whom society has ostracized, in the expectation of seeing revelation in them.

The accounts of the resurrection and ascension of Jesus are the great gospel depictions of *glory*. Thus on the road to Emmaus we find a vivid description of the glory of God being with us: "Were not our hearts burning within us while he was talking to us on the road, while he was opening the scriptures to us?" (Luke 24:32). The Emmaus road story is a paradigmatic account of what it means for the resurrected Lord to be with us. In being with us, Jesus challenges our practice ("What are you discussing with each other while you walk along?" 24:17), invites our testimony ("a prophet mighty in deed and word before God and all the people," 24:19), accepts our fragility ("But we had hoped that he was the one to redeem Israel," 24:21), traces his mission through the scriptures (24:27), walks with us on our journey toward understanding, takes, blesses, breaks, and shares bread with us (30), and inspires us to tell of all we have heard and seen.

Likewise Jesus' appearance to Mary is an invitation to share the glory. Jesus says to Mary, "Do not hold on to me, because I have not yet ascended to the Father. But go to my brothers and say to them, 'I am ascending to my Father and your Father, to my God and your God'" (John 20:17). In other words, if Mary insists on Jesus' being with her alone, Jesus cannot be with the Trinity and all creation. And Jesus' final words in Matthew sum up his promise that being with is not limited to his earthly incarnation: "Remember, I am with you always, to the end of the age" (Matt. 28:20). In the end,

Jesus does not have to choose between being with humankind and being with God. And neither do we.

Notes

1. André Trocmé's treatment of Luke 4:16–30 as Jesus' announcement of the Jubilee year remains extraordinarily illuminating. See his *Jesus and the Nonviolent Revolution*, translated by Michael H. Shank and Marlin E. Miller (Scottdale, PA: Herald Press, 1973).
2. Søren Kierkegaard, *Philosophical Fragments*, translated by Howard V. Hong and Edna H. Hong (Princeton, NJ: Princeton University Press, 1985).

10

Being With One Another
in Nazareth

Being With One Another

What kind of discipleship does the foregoing theological description of being with assume and entail? Having explored what being with means in
the life of the Trinity and the relation of God in Christ to humanity and the
creation, what does being with imply or require for human relations one
with another?

This chapter and the two that follow seek to illustrate and deepen the
notion of being with, understood as the heart of Christian discipleship. The
three perspectives adopted correspond with the three dimensions of Jesus'
life outlined in Chapter 2. Just as there we noted that Jerusalem might be
taken to represent working for, Galilee working with, and Nazareth being
with, but that in fact the quality of being with pervaded, undergirded, and
most truly expressed the nature of each part of the story, so in these three
chapters we shall see the same pattern at work. In each chapter the focus is
on a particular context that both affirms and challenges expectations. The
portrayal is done in two ways: there is an element of narrative, challenging
the conventional way of telling the story; and there is a testing of that narrative more specifically through the eight dimensions of being with elucidated in Chapter 8, originally in relation to the Trinity – a reciprocal process
in which the narrative sheds light on the categories and the categories give
shape to the narrative.

We begin with Nazareth. Let me be clear what I mean by Nazareth.
Nazareth refers to the quotidian character of life – the abiding, largely une-
ventful, ordinary pattern of birth and death, work and rest, dawn and dusk,
misunderstanding and insight, companionship and controversy, play and
planning, that fills a week, a month, a year. But just as for the people of
Nazareth in the first century, living under Roman occupation, the emphasis

A Nazareth Manifesto, Samuel Wells © 2015 John Wiley & Sons, Ltd. Published 2015 by John Wiley & Sons, Ltd.

of this book is toward those for whom the ordinary is oppressive, the daily is distressing, the habitual is hard. So the subject of this chapter concerns problems that cannot be solved, cannot be significantly alleviated, and will not go away by themselves.

Thus here we consider a person among the most excluded members of British society – one of what could be called the "chaotic homeless." In this account there are two default dynamics at work. One is the optimism and urgency and sense of duty that such people "must be helped" by a series of interventions – a combination of working for and working with. The other is more weary and perhaps cynical, a resigned sense that such people "cannot be helped," a combination of containment and helplessness, with a touch of being for – that is, a sense that some resources must be directed toward such people's well-being, but it is not a worthwhile focus for individual commitment or statutory investment. All the observations of this chapter are made against the backdrop of those two dynamics. Being with incurs the impatience of the one and the derision of the other. It is a profound challenge to both.

In Chapter 11 we move to Galilee. Here we see a unique institution – a hospital in a culture dominated by working for that has somehow retained many of the qualities of being with. A new doctor arrives and is inculcated into and entranced by what being with can mean in medicine. But as fast as she is drawn into the culture of this institution, that culture is changing in the opposite direction. We are given a narrative account of the pressures and values that push a hospital increasingly toward working for. What emerges is a portrayal of what being with and working with truly mean in medicine, and how they can abide and be made more explicit against a backdrop of an irresistible slide toward working for.

We complete this series in Jerusalem. Here we look at a genuine, re-nowned, and terrifying crisis – and the way it pushed two famous men, Dietrich Bonhoeffer and George Bell, to search the roots of their understanding of Christian witness. Bonhoeffer, in particular, is conventionally portrayed as the epitome of working for, and his participation in the plot to assassinate Adolf Hitler as the epitome of the way "Jerusalem" cannot avoid violence. But we discover that the key to Jerusalem lies in Nazareth – that there is no way to understand Bonhoeffer's story without perceiving the virtues of being with, so amply expressed in the life of his close friend, Bell.

This series offers a balance between charitable (or non-profit) work, professional engagement, and the life of the church; between the contexts of social exclusion, ill-health, and war, between the secular, the spiritual-but-not-religious, and the Christian, between the underclass Stuart Shorter, the middle-class Victoria Sweet, and the patrician Dietrich Bonhoeffer. Rather than attempt an analytical or anecdotal survey, I have chosen to look with careful attention into encounters that portray being with in unsentimental depth.

A Life Backwards

In December 1999 two charity workers, Ruth Wyner and John Brock, the director and day-center manager of the Cambridge homeless support organization Wintercomfort, were sent to prison after drug-dealing was discovered to be taking place on charity premises. They eventually served seven months inside. Wintercomfort was both traumatized and galvanized by their arrest, trial, and incarceration: staff and homeless people joined forces to campaign for their release. It was thus that Alexander Masters, a member of staff, met Stuart Shorter, who had spent much of his life living outside, but who had recently appeared to have "turned over a new leaf" (5) and had got himself a flat in the nearby village of Waterbeach.[1]

Alexander starts with a straightforward enquiry into when and how Stuart became homeless (38). As Alexander begins to unravel the complex and multilayered answer to this question, he discovers that homelessness is "not about not having a home. It's about something being seriously fucking wrong" (39). It turns out Stuart belongs to what is described as the "chaotic" homeless. These are people whose lives are characterized by multiple addictions, regular bans from hostels, repeated arrests, and frequent stays in prison. Alexander comments that what the chaotic have in common is "the confusion of their days" (4). What happens is that cause becomes detached from effect. They aren't under their own governance; and they are well out of reach of anyone else's. Any moment they might spring into violent life or collapse into sobbing despair. They attract the greatest attention from agency staff because they are pitiable or hateful in more or less equal measure; they constitute the extremity of life on the streets. Thus when the Wintercomfort staff first discovered Stuart, he was ostracized by the regular homeless and was lurking on the lower basement floor of a multistory car park. The other homeless people called him "Knife Man Dan" and "that mad bastard on Level D" (4).

Alexander sets out to write a biography of this chaotic man. But not an arm's-length biography, of detached and objective judgments, and not an ordered sequential narrative that sets each event carefully in the context of its antecedents and consequences. The form Alexander adopts is as distinctive as his subject matter. This is Stuart's doing: the book begins with the words, "Stuart does not like the manuscript" (1). Stuart's dislike of the original manuscript with its academic quotations and background research prompts his suggestion that instead it should be like the novels of Tom Clancy and that Alexander should do things the other way round. He should adopt the style of a murder mystery. The key question would be what murdered the boy Stuart originally was. This would mean writing Stuart's story backwards (6).

So Alexander does exactly what Stuart suggests. He writes Stuart's story backwards, interspersed with episodes of their shared encounters and growing companionship. This leads to a complex book, the chaos of which mirrors that of its subject's life. In contrast to the familiar biographical style that illustrates the development and construction of the subject's identity, at Stuart's request, the book instead illustrates the deconstruction of his identity, the loss of the boy he was, or how, in the words of his mother, he changed from being a happy-go-lucky, considerate child, into the nightmare *Clockwork Orange* figure of his adult years (5).

Alexander quickly takes to the backwards idea. At a stroke, it addressed the problem of narrating the life of a person outside the public eye. There is no need to plod through the opening chapters with their tedious details about childhood and grandparents. Instead here is Stuart – a terrifying, nightmarish figure demanding attention and inviting scrutiny. Thus childhood details are no longer idle circumstance but potentially vital clues (13). Perhaps such an approach can only truly work when a person's sense of their own existence constantly lingers on the edge of incoherence (13).

Working backwards like a mineworker sifting back through a dark tunnel, Alexander forges a tentative path through a slurry of misfortune and malevolence, eventually reaching the well-buried years of Stuart's childhood (272). There is plenty of sleeping outside, abuse of alcohol, drugs and solvents, fragile and scarred relationships; endless crime, arrests, and imprisonments, endemic conflagrations of wild violence, frequent self-harm and repeated suicide attempts; and various psychotic episodes. And then there emerges the truth beneath all the terror: the ghastly moment when he threatened to kill his son; the death of his father who had led a violent life and deserted his mother; his brother's suicide; the discovery of his disability (muscular dystrophy); the long history of being bullied; and finally the relentless sexual abuse he suffered at the hands of both his brother, Gavvy, and the babysitter – a pattern that was replicated in yet more damaging ways by senior members of staff when he was taken into care.

We shall now consider Alexander's relationship with Stuart under the eight dimensions of being with that we elaborated in relation to the Trinity in Chapter 8.

Presence

The most remarkable part of this zig-zagging story, besides the depth of the suffering Stuart underwent in his childhood, is the way Alexander continues to be present with Stuart despite Stuart's chaotic, sometimes hostile, and perpetually unpredictable behavior. Presence is the most basic element of being with: but presence itself is tremendously challenging in this context. Part of presence is the habit, perhaps discipline, of not seeking solutions. Stuart is not a problem to be solved – however much of a challenge he presents to almost everyone he meets. The only way to be with Stuart is to renounce the impulse to "fix" him – sympathetically or destructively. The catharsis of this discipline comes when Alexander, Stuart, and others go down to London to protest about Ruth and John's arrest by sleeping on the street outside the Home Office.

Earlier in the book, Alexander observes, "You'd think the homeless would despise the rest of us, but it seems the thing they want to do most is talk" (70). He speculates that if homeless people could just hold the attention of the rest of society long enough to tell their whole story then their problems would be largely over. Alexander is straining to make the transition from companion to savior. But it turns out the transition is not so simply made – as the days sleeping outside the Home Office make clear. What cannot be hidden is how irritable and angry Alexander and Stuart get with one another, and how impatient and frustrated Alexander becomes at Stuart's constant talking. Presence is no straightforward matter. On Sunday evening, Stuart "loses it": "You fucking, wanky, middle-class cunt-fuck, Alexander, always saying 'What's the answer?' That's the difference, in'it? No answers! You want to know how I become what I am? Write a book what don't have no answers. But that won't make your fucking name, will it? Nah, see? Fuck off. Go find your fucking answers" (92). In significant ways, this is the center of the book. Can Alexander be with Stuart, a man who finds it so hard to be with himself?

Alexander does not hide his difficulty in continuing to be present to Stuart. Soon after Stuart has delivered his rant at Alexander, he turns his anger toward a police officer, repeating the same question, about why they don't arrest hostel managers in London, no less than 15 times. Alexander stands his ground and tells him to shut up. Stuart calls Alexander a "middle-class geeky cunt" yet again. Alexander begins to grasp what Stuart has been trying to tell him: that it is not the cold or the hardness of the streets that makes life intolerable, it is the people whose company one is forced to keep. "It's the people like *fucking* Stuart, ranting and raving. *Shut up, will you!*" (93, italics in original). When the police officer drives off, Alexander reflects on the disagreeable nature of Stuart. He regards Stuart's ugly, twisted demeanor, his hinched, animal gait. And Alexander fantasizes that Stuart might die, there and then – and thus at least achieve a publicity coup (94–95). But the passage of time and a humorous twist in events bring reconciliation. The next day Alexander and Stuart are laughing together on the train back to Cambridge after they are both absent from the camp when the Home Secretary finally visits it (98).

Stuart's stay in hospital illustrates the ways presence requires from Alexander both faithful action and the challenge of inaction. Presence is fundamentally abiding; but it also involves resisting powerful temptations to rescue, solve, fix, or become a guardian angel. When Stuart goes to hospital to seek a cure for his premature ejaculation, the doctors discover there is a problem with his heart: it turns out he needs a pacemaker (148). Alexander visits him on a number of occasions, even when the patient is asleep for most of his second visit (152). Presence does not always require that the other person be conscious of the one who is abiding with them.

But there is another more challenging dimension to presence. After his operation at the specialist heart unit at Papworth Hospital, Stuart is reminded explicitly and unambiguously by the doctor that he should no longer inject, due to the risk of infection in his pacemaker (153). Alexander notes that Stuart cannot seem to grasp what the doctor has been saying – that the problem is Stuart's method of inserting the heroin into his body, not the heroin that constitutes the danger. He is still welcome to eat, snort, or smoke to his heart's content. By being present, Alexander is hearing what Stuart is not hearing; but does that mean he automatically acts on Stuart's behalf? No. Alexander says nothing. Drugs have frequently come close to taking away Stuart's life; if his life comes to an end because he cannot make out what the doctor is saying, "then that is as good a way as any" (154). To emphasize the point, perhaps more strongly than many could countenance, when Alexander does work for Stuart, he gets Stuart exactly what Stuart asked him for: a bottle of gin, which he puts into the empty water jug (155).

This might to some take the uncritical dimension of presence to excess. The point is, Alexander is present to Stuart: if he were to flip into rescue mode, where would he start – and where would he end? Alexander never says he has no aspiration for a better life for Stuart, and never suggests he feels Stuart's life as it is is without need of improvement; but he never lets those concerns get in the way of being present to Stuart – the first dimension of being with.

Attention

When it comes to someone as chaotic as Stuart, offering attention, like being present, is no small thing. The process of writing the book is a form of paying close attention. But it is traumatic for both parties.

The grief of Stuart's personal history is not something Alexander tries to soften or avoid. Paying attention to Stuart means being with him even – especially – through his recall of the most painful memories of his past, memories that are often extremely distressing and drive him to find refuge in drugs. Alexander observes that Stuart will only talk about what is known as the Unmentionable Crime on a Thursday morning. It has to be in the morning, because he needs time to recover, and if it is a Thursday he will just have got his benefits, so he will have the £30 required by his dealer. The hit will be part of his recovery from broaching the unspeakable (119). Likewise Alexander attends to the details of Stuart's self-harm, even when Stuart has mixed feelings about continuing to talk about it. When it comes to the abuse Stuart suffered at the hands of his brother, Gavvy, and the babysitter, Alexander notes that the subject can only be mentioned when Stuart has had a calm week and has the prospect of distraction. If such stars are not aligned, Stuart may well spiral into a pattern of depression, drink, self-harm, and injecting citric acid, followed several times by grabbing a nearby implement and taking to self-butchery (259–260).

Alexander is not trying to be an angel: the process of being with involves profound feelings of outrage, disgust, and horror. Registering those feelings, without them becoming a reason to terminate the conversation, is the key to writing the book and maintaining the relationship. Both book and relationship are unsentimental and honest. Alexander does not attempt to conceal his continued frustrations with Stuart, his struggle to write the book, or his disapproval of Stuart's past misdemeanors. He is dismayed and infuriated by Stuart's season in prison after the post office robbery. It is a season when Stuart "ceases to be (to me) human." The subtle, soft-spoken, tender side of Stuart is utterly displaced by "Stuart Fury, the set of bloody incidents. Events replace character" (99). Alexander makes no secret of the fact that the Unmentionable Crime appalls him. Reflection on this and Stuart's spell in prison propels Alexander into self-loathing at the pointlessness of trying to find any gold in such a swamp. The chaos of Stuart's life is always in danger of seeping into the lives of those that pay close attention to him. And yet close attention is its own reward. Stuart is more than capable of encompassing the issues in absorbing and less threatening terms: he points out that this is what life is like with chaotic people. Episodes of time do not connect together in any conventional way. "Every day is like no day and, at the same time, it's a hundred different days" (118). The challenge is to pay attention to such intensity and diversity in the face of such unpredictability and hostility.

But wisdom can be gained, and the heart can be sustained, amid the extremes of language and emotion. By attending to Stuart, and others, Alexander learns to listen beyond the immediate words, and not to be manipulated by emotive language. The first time that Alexander sees Stuart, Stuart is wedged into a doorway close to Sidney Sussex College in Cambridge (14). Stuart tells Alexander that he is going to kill himself as soon as he gets the opportunity – though he will make his suicide look like murder because his brother had already killed himself and he didn't want to put his mother through that again. Attention doesn't mean taking every statement at face value. Alexander states later in the book:

> Working at a hostel, one gets used to bold comments about violence and self-destruction from the homeless. The first three or four times they alarm you. By the fifth or sixth, they're becoming old hat. You learn to try to change the subject, tell a joke, treat the person like a petulant schoolboy: "Now, Tom, I don't think it's really a good idea for you to pick a fight with Jenny this morning. She's already beaten you up three times, and that's quite enough for one day." Or, "No, Adam, if you slit your wrists with that razor it will not be 'all my fault.' It will be your fault, because they're *your* wrists and *you're* the one who's spent the last ten minutes breaking the blade out of your Bic shaver." (57)

Alexander always has before him both the horror of what Stuart can be, and the deeper horror of what Stuart has been through. Attention means seeing each face simultaneously. Throughout the book, the despair in Stuart's brain is unraveled, nowhere more so than in the transcript of the Dictaphone cassette that Alexander finds among the wreckage of Stuart's flat:

> There are times regular when I sit in this flat and I look around, and I look what's here in my life – do I really want to be here? If the truth is known, I've used alcohol every night recently, just to go to sleep. If I've got my drink inside me I sit here having mad conversations with meself, talking about mutilating myself, killing myself, killing those who I think have done me wrong, from me babysitter to tracking down those who were responsible who abused me in care to executing the police officers who never gave me any justice. I wanted just to lay down and die. I felt so dirty, and fucking horrible and hated and attacked anyone I got close to. I can't even have a relationship if I want it because I think sex is dirty and disgusting. I just wish there could be an escape from this madness. (194–195)

Alexander's struggle to be with Stuart is always a sideshow to Stuart's main quest to be with himself.

Alexander never says so explicitly, but from the start of his friendship with Stuart, he must have lived with the knowledge that one of Stuart's frequent suicide attempts might be successful. He seems to make the judgment that he cannot rescue Stuart even if he were to want to. At one point he reflects, in regard to people like Stuart, that the best that can be done is to steady them with drugs. The worst approach is to incarcerate them, and hope not to be close by when they tie a noose around their own neck (193). It is a bleak outlook. Accordingly, after a particularly violent incident in Stuart's flat, Alexander reflects that if Stuart's story is what counts as success, then the cost of real help will exceed the national budget. A host of the sad or the unfortunate might be comforted, but chaotic cannot be mollified with employment and a bed-sit – they require "a new brain" (192). Such is an unflinching assessment of what it means to be with Stuart.

Mystery

Being with means regarding the other, not as a problem to be solved, but as a mystery to be entered. Stuart looks to almost everyone like a problem. But no one comes anywhere near solving that problem. The book tells many stories, one of which is how Stuart becomes, in Alexander's eyes, a mystery rather than a problem.

Perhaps the simplest level of mystery is a kind of misunderstanding that discloses a deeper truth. Stuart constantly challenges Alexander to question and re-evaluate his own background, his own class assumptions, and his own perspective as a "nine-to-fiver." Alexander's tussle to understand the mystery of Stuart continues throughout the book. Stuart challenges Alexander's impulse to find purpose in life put perspectives on things (225). Yet there are moments of misunderstanding which lead to understanding. During a discussion about driving cars into brick walls, Alexander identifies a "classy misunderstanding": he and Stuart mean different things by the words "good" and "bad" (241). Such a glimpse into another world exhilarates and inspires Alexander, as if he were looking through a break in a hedgerow during a car journey and seeing poppies and cornflowers (242).

But not every misunderstanding leads to revelation. Alexander struggles in head, heart, and gut to understand the choices Stuart has made and how he has become the person he is. Thus Alexander asks Stuart over and again why he puts himself on the streets. Initially Stuart attributes it to his part-Romany background of itinerant independence. But Alexander quickly points out that Stuart is not adopting an itinerant life: he just sleeps on the street of a nearby city and does not move (58). Alexander tries to rationalize Stuart's choices, but Stuart fails to understand them himself (59). Sometimes "why?" is a question that runs into the ground. "Why?" is perhaps not a question in the spirit of mystery.

Mystery may be an attitude of exploration and awareness; yet it may be a state resulting from bewilderment and exasperation. Sometimes Alexander just cannot resist spiraling down to a single issue or tragedy which is the cause or source of all other woes. Thus he asks Stuart what one thing he would have changed "to make it right" (290). Stuart replies, philosophically, that he does not know. Can he change his brother? Would that change his getting "rageous"? If he changed the muscular dystrophy it would not have altered the abuse or the system. "Be easier just to change me" (290). There is no simple answer, no solution, no outcome that involves retracing steps to a fault on the line. It is their last recorded encounter before Stuart is killed – hit by the late night London to King's Lynn train on July 6, 2002.

Yet, mystery is not simply a one-directional phenomenon. Being with is a reciprocal practice, even with someone as complex as Stuart. Throughout the book there are moments when Stuart, in turn, wrestles to understand the mystery that Alexander is to him. After he was given a role at the end of the open campaign meeting at Wintercomfort, for example, Stuart acknowledges how surprised he is. He had assumed middle-class people had something wrong with them. But it turned out they were not so out of the ordinary. He was rather shocked (27). Stuart is shocked because his experience of people like Alexander, the people of "the System" (or "the nine-to-fives" as he calls them), has not been positive. For Stuart, order has meant police, prisons, courts, care homes ... and pedophiles. The system has been a malevolent force in his life (146). The alternative to abusive order was culpable ineffectuality, in the form of the social worker assigned to Stuart when he was expelled from school. She would drive to see him, make a foray into some kind of soothing conversation, and simply drive off again – having transformed nothing (265).

Being with means attending to the mystery that lies beneath even the most clumsy, loud, and infuriating relationship. It does not mean soothing the unsoothable.

Delight

There is little in Stuart's story, or Alexander's account of being with Stuart, that spontaneously evokes delight. Delight is an eschatological mood – activity that seeks to be the goal itself, to live now the way we are called to be together forever, to leave aside the utilitarian concern about getting there and to enjoy the journey for its own sake. It turns out there is delight in Stuart's story, delight brought about by absurdity and by victory. One example comes when Stuart gets into a knife fight with his neighbor in his flat, is arrested, and has several court appearances. Alexander walks with Stuart through this entire episode. He goes to the destroyed flat with Stuart's mother while Stuart is banned from returning to it (192). He also accompanies Stuart to his various court appearances. The first is at Cambridge Magistrates' Court (220ff.). Stuart objects to his bail conditions, which stipulate that he has to live with his mother and stepfather, who live in the pub they run in Midston: being an alcoholic, it seems unwise for him to live in a pub (223). Stuart, however, continues to be under police curfew at his mother and stepfather's pub, where Alexander goes to visit him (236). Alexander makes no attempt to "rescue" Stuart from the pub, even when Stuart tries to stab his stepfather (238). Yet he does accompany Stuart on his next two visits to the court at King's Lynn (239–245; 280–282). The case is thrown out by Judge Howarth (282). At this point there is joy and delight in abundance: Alexander and Stuart are ecstatic. Yet Alexander confesses the whole adventure leaves him a little alarmed – wondering if people like Stuart are to be allowed to wield knives and square up to the police with no punishment at all (282). Here the rollercoaster of life with Stuart leaves Alexander almost dizzy.

But delight comes in the process by which they first meet – campaigning for and with homeless people. Alexander goes with Stuart to his meeting with the MP for Cambridge, Anne Campbell. Stuart takes charge. He complains that this year there is going to be no emergency winter shelter for rough sleepers – and that means, almost inevitably, that there will be more deaths. Stuart concludes his argument with the incongruous words, "because there's been two new dog litters" (253–254). Alexander assumes Stuart has finally parted company with sanity. But Stuart explains that the homeless love their dogs, more than they love people, and choose to sleep out rather than enter a hostel which doesn't allow them to keep a dog with them. "Unless the government stops their Singapore-style social fashioning and provides an emergency winter shelter *with* pet facility," Alexander summarizes, there will be more drugs, more trouble, and more deaths. As Alexander puts it: "Vintage Stuart. A vast conclusion exposed to have a tiny cause" (255). Alexander is actually *proud* of Stuart – his ingenuity, his insight, his quick thinking, his compassion, his logic. And this is a man that others see as doing nothing but wreak havoc.

This is how being with can breed delight in the most extraordinary and unpromising places.

Participation

The key to participation is to focus in a disciplined way on the word with. There may be a hundred quicker, more efficient, more satisfying, more exciting ways to pass time, but being with means concentrating on how that time can genuinely be time with.

Alexander's participation with Stuart gives him genuine insights into what it feels like to be Stuart. This particularly arises through the campaign for the release of the Cambridge Two. When Ruth and John were arrested the staff of the hostel felt they were under attack – they for the first time experienced what homeless people become used to – being the object of public loathing. With shock, we realized we now had something in common with the homeless (19). Another instance is Alexander's experience of sleeping rough for three nights in front of the Home Office which, for Stuart, was to teach Alexander and his like, who "had life 'so fucking easy'" about the realities of sleeping rough. To earn the right to campaign about it meant having to learn about it first-hand. There was to be no for without with. Alexander finds that, with no place of his own, he must invent one. He realizes he is eyeing a part of the pavement to be able to call a handful of concrete slabs home (72).

Participation is not something Alexander arrives at by design. He begins with no theory or commitment or ideal of being with. Through the campaign to release the Cambridge Two, and in particular through his friendship with Stuart, we see him discover what being with means. As a writer, he is not setting out to "fix" Stuart or to "rescue" him from his predicament. About his biographical project he states that he has no hope of justifying or explaining Stuart: his best plan is simply to "staple him to the page" (118). Gradually the biographer and his subject tussle over the writing of the book; and a real and honest friendship begins to develop. It is not a friendship which begins with altruistic concern on Alexander's part, however, just as his motive for beginning as a part-time fundraising assistant at Wintercomfort was not altruism but financial reward: "I did it for the money" (17). So, in a good description of the lack of interaction which characterizes working for, Alexander states how he "worked in an attic, beyond the lawless alcoholics many floors underneath, and on a good day he could arrive early enough to dodge past the art group's alarming paintings and shoot up to his office without speaking to a single homeless person" (16).

From there a genuine participation, with moments of reciprocity, begins to emerge. Alexander visits Stuart's flat and Stuart makes him "Convict Curry," which he learned to cook in prison. Crucial to this developing participation is Alexander's discipline in not rescuing Stuart or attempting to save him from himself. Stuart says that he overdosed last week; and that "the bills on the bedside cabinet are red" (29). Stuart's kitchen is in unspeakable state – Alexander cannot even see the sink, which is obscured by a "swarm of dishes trying to escape down the plughole" (30). But instead of helping him to sort his bills or clean his kitchen, let alone address the issue of overdosing, Alexander eats Stuart's "purple" Convict Curry and watches television with him. After which, Stuart lends him the bus fare home (32). At every stage Alexander resists for and sustains with, even to the point of allowing a for (the loan of the bus fare) in return.

Participation rests on trust, and trust, in these circumstances, is slow to build. There is an inevitable degree of suspicion on both parts as they start the process of writing the book and as they wrestle to understand the "mystery" of the other. Alexander is nervous about Stuart's first visit to his house: his crazy existence and amusing jailbird stories seem rather different when he is about to be a guest in Alexander's home. Will he turn out to be a compulsive thief? The women at his mother's pub treat him so (35). Gradually the trust grows. Alexander reflects that he is not frightened of this apparently dangerous man. Not in the least. If pushed to name why, he would suggest that Stuart's anger is not random, but is directed at the sources of his pain – "care homes and pedophiles and prison and the police." None of these touches on Alexander, and Alexander is able to keep a critical distance: "To be honest, I find his remarks a little silly" (57). Alexander's ability to hear Stuart's anger but not take it as directed toward him is crucial for the relationship.

Partnership

Thus does participation flow into partnership. Whereas participation emphasizes togetherness and accompaniment, partnership stresses complementarity.

Partnership is most evident in the relationship of writer and subject. There would be no story without Stuart, and no book without Alexander. "Alexander, sort it out – you're the writer. I just done the living" reads the epigraph at the start of the book.

There is no suggestion of them becoming partners in crime: this is not a road movie, with an unlikely Thelma and Louise, or a more knockabout *Of Mice and Men*. But there is no question of Alexander being the expert and Stuart being the pupil – or the patient. Partnership flourishes in two senses. First there are ways that Stuart is simply tougher than Alexander, for the challenges their friendship and common cause brings. This is closer to the territory of working with. When it comes to sleeping out, Stuart's sturdiness and experience makes up for Alexander's fragility.

Alexander finds that, after three days, homelessness is getting too much for him. By midday he felt like crying. He was losing control. He contemplated that at this rate there would be nothing left of him in a matter of days. He would be "like the dead, a function of other people's thoughts." He was losing perspective on everything, and becoming totally exasperated with Stuart (91–92). And this is the moment when he needs Stuart's support: "'Don't get stressed, mate,' he says softly and lifts his Stella. 'You done alright, Alexander'" (92).

The other kind of complementarity comes in Alexander and Stuart's way of seeing the world. The dynamic of the book is created because the two characters are alternately intrigued, attracted, and repelled by each other's worldview. This is epitomized by their respective views of the "System." Stuart hates the "System." The description of it epitomizes working for. The System is a shapeless agglomeration of state-sponsored agencies that has pursued him since he was twelve. Many organs of the System including welfare benefits and charities are expressly tailored to help people like Stuart. But what might to others appear a reasonable channel to integrate a homeless person into regular society appears to Stuart as "an approach that patronizes you at one end and swipes you raw at the other." Homelessness represents the fallout from this System. The System is to Stuart a bit like the Market is to economists: unpredictable, unreliable, ruthless, operating in a haze of sanctimonious self-justification, and almost human manner toward health professionals and support workers, he has little respect for them. Some might almost be friends; others are simply examples of the demeaning effects of the System (24–25).

By contrast Alexander cannot understand why Stuart cannot make the System work for him. To Alexander it is simple: you go to a homeless agency, and you get a place at a hostel. From there you find an assignment on a job program, you move into a shared house or establish a private tenancy. The 24-hour support staff structure is there to facilitate this process. There is no reason to sleep outside (45). But Stuart can no more understand Alexander's defense of the System than vice versa: Stuart regards Alexander as if he is beyond hope. "You fucking nine-to-fives believe everything you read in the bloody newspaper or watch on the telly, when the reality of it is so fucking different, it's unreal" (45–46).

The book as a whole shows that Stuart's perspective is not as bizarre as it appears. But Stuart also learns there are people within the system he can trust – indeed Stuart wants Alexander to write the book to thank certain family members and those at Wintercomfort who have helped him, and is always singing the praises of Linda (a member of the outreach team) as "someone who stuck by him in his thousands of hours of need" (71) – in whom he saw the blessing of with.

Enjoyment

Enjoyment is the heart of being with – what distinguishes it from the other kinds of engagement. To use is always to have one's eyes half a moment beyond, to be constantly looking for an outcome or a result or a further purpose or a likely consequence. To enjoy is to revel in the abundance of the present moment, to soak up all that is here, now, present and available, to put one's hope and trust and energy in the things that never run out, to plumb depth rather than anxiously scan for breadth.

Alexander enjoys Stuart, and enables the reader to do the same. Stuart is someone whom society has no "use" for; Alexander doesn't deny this – indeed, he gives plenty of evidence why this might be the case – but, crucially, he realizes that having no use for someone doesn't mean you can't enjoy them: it might even be a provocative stimulus for learning to enjoy them. For this is the shape of the incarnation: Jesus shares our humanity, and relishes our vibrancy, while never ignoring either our plight or our perversity. God enjoys us – God's life is shaped to enjoy us in Christ.

From time to time Alexander brings together all the foregoing elements of being with in a statement of true enjoyment of Stuart: "So here it is, my second attempt at the story of Stuart Shorter, thief, hostage taker, psycho and sociopathic street raconteur, my spy on how the British chaotic underclass spend their troubled days at the beginning of the twenty-first century: a man with an important life" (6–7). Again, at the end of the discussion about ramming cars into brick walls, Alexander states, "The boy's a freak, surely" and then muses that people like Stuart, rejected even by those the world despises, who have had their social development terminated at the age of twelve, "simply don't understand the way the big world works." Their isolation from mainstream society is as great as vice versa. The astonishing thing about Stuart is that "he has had the superhuman strength not to be defeated by this isolation." He has found a way to relate to Alexander without terrifying him (242).

This is perhaps the secret of the book's success. Whether Alexander and Stuart's relationship can truly be called a friendship is never a settled matter. But this creates part of the tension in the book. The book enables the reader to enjoy Stuart, and thus to learn to enjoy people and things that cannot be used – for which or for whom there is no use. There is no helping some people: but perhaps there is being with them.

Glory

It may seem wholly absurd or fanciful to suggest it, but this train wreck of a life and rollercoaster of a relationship offers glimpses of glory. The last time the two friends see one another, Stuart has called to see Alexander to discuss the first two chapters of his second attempt at the book – the backwards version (285). They laugh about potential titles. Stuart wants to borrow £20. Alexander reassures him, "No need to explain, Stuart. You borrow money off me when you need it. I borrow money off you when I need it. What's the fuss about?" (289). Reciprocity has been reached. Alexander offers him a lift and highlights the irony that he now owns Stuart's old car "which he has sold to me for £275, plus alloy wheels, a £25 discount on what he was planning to raise" (289). In other words, this is not a working for, it is a genuine being with along with moments of working with. Alexander drops Stuart at a pub and asks him a final question – what is his date of birth? Stuart calls him "mate," and Alexander comments, "I love that word, 'mate.' Stuart uses it with me very rarely" (291). They have become, at last, true companions. Off Stuart goes into the pub. It's the last time Alexander will see him.

Stuart dies under a train. It could be suicide – but is probably not. Nonetheless it seems to be transfiguration. Alexander believes so: "For a moment, I believe, there was a stillness. A shocking realization by all things – beetles, dormice, the spiders spinning their webs in the moonlight, even the hot metal of the tracks and the wind in the trees – that Death has just shrieked past like a stinking black eagle and made off with a remarkable man" (293).

Looking Back to Nazareth

Jesus spent 30 years in Nazareth accompanying us. We are at least as wayward, feckless, flawed, troubled, effervescent, and fragile as Stuart. Inhabiting Stuart's story enables us to see how challenging it is for God to be with Israel, and for Jesus to be with us. Challenging as it is, God's faithfulness and improvisation sustain the relationship. And bring out surprising grace in us. The relationship between Alexander and Stuart is thus a metaphor for God in Christ's relationship with humanity and the creation. Jacob wrestles with the angel all night, and both parties discover they have received a blessing.

But it is not a simple correspondence. Alexander undoubtedly offers a way to be with Stuart analogous to God's way of being with us. But there is a dimension to human being with one another that is different to God's being with us – or God's being with God. Reciprocity is not just the goal: it is the starting point. The encounter with difference, social disadvantage, distress, suffering, hostility, or in this case explosive chaos cannot always be a somewhat predictable journey from assuming one is the patient benefactor to discovering one is the receiver – from Samaritan to traveler in the gutter. At some stage the starting assumptions have to change. The single word for that change is Nazareth. Nazareth names the way God blesses relationships that are entered into where, despite disjunction of power, privilege, influence, or social stability, both parties expect to discover glory through presence, attention, mystery, delight, participation, partnership, and enjoyment.

Stuart may seem an extreme example. Besides the quality of the interactions and the intensity of the way they are recorded in Alexander's book, he was chosen for two reasons. First, his is not obviously a narrative that assumes a direction – from suffering to healing, for example, or from crisis to death. The very shapelessness of his story, and in particular its open-ended character, correspond with the characteristics of Nazareth. If one is to engage Stuart, one can't intervene – one can only abide alongside him. Second, its extremity makes an important point: both that God faces this kind of extremity in engaging us, and that if a person can be with Stuart, then perhaps it is possible to imagine being with almost anybody – and finding glory there. That is what Nazareth is finally about.

Notes

1. All the references in this chapter come from Alexander Masters, *Stuart: A Life Backwards* (New York: Delta, 2006).

11

Being With One Another in Galilee

Galilee

Jesus spent a week in Jerusalem, three years in Galilee, and thirty years in Nazareth. This book considers the theological significance of those thirty years in Nazareth. But it also discovers that being with, the quality most associated with Nazareth, in fact undergirds the whole of Jesus' ministry – and thus it proposes that being with should undergird the whole of the church's mission. This chapter considers Galilee, the season most associated with working with – building a social movement, offering moments of training, truth, healing, controversy, confrontation, learning, revelation, and challenge. The two forms of life most associated with such moments in the contemporary West are education and health care.

Thus this chapter examines health care. It does so through the eyes of a woman who begins her story by assuming that medicine is about working for. But she falls under the spell of an unusual institution that transforms her understanding of what it means to be a doctor and changes her life. She discovers being with. Victoria Sweet's book *God's Hotel* is subtitled *A Doctor, a Hospital, and a Pilgrimage to the Heart of Medicine*. The irony of the book is that the institution that is teaching her so much is making a journey in the opposite direction. It is incrementally rejecting being with in favor of working for. "The practice of medicine had become the delivery of health care. I had changed, too, but in a diametrically opposed way" (325).[1] Thus the author of the book is impelled to set in writing the spirit of the institution – the spirit of being with – to ensure it is not lost.

Whereas the relationship of Alexander and Stuart, in Chapter 10, largely bypassed institutional procedures and professional boundaries, an account of a hospital, with its responsibility for thousands of patients, inevitably involves a more complex set of relationships. Thus Victoria Sweet's experience

A Nazareth Manifesto, Samuel Wells © 2015 John Wiley & Sons, Ltd. Published 2015 by John Wiley & Sons, Ltd.

combines the intensity of Alexander Masters' account with the more professional environment more familiar to those who try to engage social and
material disadvantage. But the treatment of the material will be largely the
same: demonstrating ways in which the experience of Victoria Sweet –
ostensibly a balance between the working with of Galilee and the working
for of Jerusalem – in fact displays profound dimensions of being with at
every stage.

God's Hotel

Laguna Honda sounds like a car but it turns out it is a hospital. It is an almshouse in San Francisco, a place of refuge for several thousand people – the
last such institution in America: not a homage to high-tech mechanized
medicine, like so many other hospitals in the country, but more of a garden
in which waifs and strays, who cannot go home because they have no home
to go to, and cannot be cared for in the community because they have no
community, can instead be regenerated. Once every county in the United
States had a county hospital, which saw to the acute cases, and an almshouse, which cared, in theory, for the chronically disabled – but in practice met a variety of needs, for shelter, rehabilitation, a place of transition,
and a refuge for unemployed people (7). Now America has only one left –
this one.

This unusual setting, an inheritor of the Hôtel-Dieu in which the poor
were cared for in medieval Europe, becomes in Victoria Sweet's book the
stage for a fourfold pilgrimage. It is a study in patience with patients: the
narrator carefully explains the details of a series of memorable people who
taught her and trained her as they opened her eyes and her soul to the nature
of healing. It is a study in the hospitality of a hospital: every chapter tells of
an ongoing (and often comic) battle between administrators with their new
schemes for counting, measuring, improving, and evaluating; and doctors,
nurses and patients who continue to elude and evade the constraints of the
bureaucrats while discovering what health is really about. It is a study in the
nature of medicine itself: *God's Hotel* is not taken in by the sophistication of
the awesome American medico-educational complex; instead it disarmingly offers a complementary ethos, imagination, and practice. It is, in the end,
a personal pilgrimage: the author – in her studies, in her visits to Europe,
in her walking the path to Santiago de Compostela, in her remaining faithful to the hospital, its staff and patients, through sunshine and rain – finds

wisdom. All four pilgrimages are interlaced throughout the book: they are not, finally, detachable from one another.

In a crucial passage, the narrator encounters a Mrs. Muller, who, it seems, is diabetic, demented, and psychotic. On close inspection Mrs. Muller turns out to have a dislocated hip: her other conditions gradually and movingly evaporate as it becomes clear they all arose in response to the poor treatment of the hip. The narrator calculates that her own practice of "slow medicine" – paying close attention to patients and letting them remain in hospital rather than resorting to interventions and medications from the outset – had, in this one case alone, saved the health-care system about $400,000. In exasperation she points out that, in the pervading culture, huge sums were spent on the medical process, but the human parts of that process such as food and staffing were pared down to nothing. All these extremely expensive interventions were necessities, but doctors and nurses were a luxury. She estimates that slow medicine, by discontinuing perhaps ten or twelve unnecessary medications per person, outdid "efficient" health care by around $70 per day.

But the real intent of the book is above and beyond health-care budgets. Victoria Sweet brings out of her treasure a continual array of gifts and insights about medicine and hopeful life that infuse her account with wisdom, challenge, and encouragement. And at the root of that wisdom lies the unlikely medieval figure of Hildegard of Bingen. She notes there are two Hildegards in academic discourse: the theological woman of letters, and the medical infirmarian, who knew a lot about the body you wouldn't expect a medieval nun to know. Sweet's academic project, against the grain of the field, is to synthesize the two.

The setting for this synthesis is a year in a Swiss hospital, where Sweet finds, astonishingly and symbolically, that the emergency room is comfortable, pleasant, congenial – and empty. This discovery epitomizes the revelation intended by the whole book; and synthesizes the personal, medical, administrative and intellectual challenge Sweet's cumulative argument represents. The empty Swiss emergency room is a visual, unforgettable, undeniable, and compelling critique of American medicine: for the crisis of American medicine is, without doubt, crystallized in its emergency rooms.

Sweet offers a model of witness. Hers is not a style of denunciation or campaign or protest or demand. Instead she combines research and practice; she sets out to learn before she proclaims; she realizes the answers may lie outside her own experience; she pays close regard to patients as the potential source of their own problems; she holds off from techniques and solutions until it is clear what their role might be; and she knows she is on a pilgrimage, which, like all pilgrimages, becomes a lesson not only in the destination but in the discoveries to be made on the way there.

Slow Medicine

The tension between modern medicine, with its technology, bureaucracy, and solutions and slow medicine (Sweet's term for the spirit of Laguna Honda) plays such a large role in the book, and is in many ways an exemplary account of the contrast between working for and being with, that it is worth a separate treatment before examining the dimensions of being with in detail.

Sweet paints a picture of modern medicine by describing the first autopsy she ever witnessed. Medicine is now limited to the physical; it is mechanistic; the breakdown of the body is a problem in need of solution. She sees contemporary health care as an "industrial, mechanical, and democratic" approach to the human body: it is "a factory with workers; a machine with parts; a democratic republic of cells, each obedient, hardworking, and united for the common good" (179). The body is regarded as a machine to be fixed – a problem in need of a solution. What was a craft became a profession: now it has morphed into a commodity. This commodity is sold like any other in the marketplace (6). Doctors are now "health-care providers" and patients are "health-care consumers" (272). Sweet recounts the many visits of different "health-care efficiency experts" (56) who attempt to change Laguna Honda into a modern health-care facility.

Thus head nurses are replaced with "nurse managers" to oversee the staff. Managing means putting in place a system characterized by speed and efficiency (73). The key is the relationship to the computer and the manager-generated forms. Into the background fall the duties of speaking to relatives, assisting physicians, picking up the telephone, and assisting one another (75). And efficiency is not the result: once the role of head nurse was abolished, a plethora of symptoms proliferated: sick days, illness, and early retirements among the staff; falls, bedsores, fights, and tears among the patients (76). So Sweet questions whether the new, "efficient" system is in fact what it claims to be: reflecting on one of a series of efficiency reports, she says that it taught her "the inefficiency of efficiency" and "the efficiency of inefficiency" (76). Sweet points out, as the epitome of attention, presence, and care, the head nurse that knitted blankets for each of her patients (75).

Unassigned time appeared inefficient to the researchers but was among one of the secret ingredients of the hospital. This is how Sweet discovers the link between inefficiency and what it means to care (76).

This connection she illustrates extensively. The most striking example is one of a simple working for that arose out of being with. Dr. Curtis serves the rehabilitation ward. He has a patient who has been ready for discharge for three months. Finally he discovered that special shoes had been ordered, but Medicaid was taking a long time to approve them (80). So Dr. Curtis went straight out and bought a pair of shoes for $16.99. And the patient left the hospital the same day. Sweet confesses she would have stayed in the tangle of filing requests and filling in forms. But Dr. Curtis taught her the truth of the old aphorism that the secret in the care of the patient is in caring for the patient (81). Sweet finds the source of the aphorism in a lecture given by Dr. Francis Peabody to the graduating medical class of Harvard in 1927. What he meant was doing the little things like "adjusting the patient's bedclothes or giving him sips of water." Such "time-costly caring was what created the personal relationship between patient and doctor. And that relationship was the secret of healing" (82). This reminds Sweet of an old Indian account of the good doctor, the better doctor, and the best doctor. The good doctor diagnoses correctly and prescribes properly. The better doctor also accompanies the patient to pick up the medication. The best doctor abides until the patient takes the medicine (82). By this reckoning going out to purchase the shoes was precisely the action of the best doctor. Sweet suspects that Laguna Honda's inefficient care might not in fact be more efficient than the researchers' cost-effective approach. Even in spreadsheet terms (83).

This irony becomes acute when Laguna Honda fails its recertification as a hospital (239ff.). Patients had fallen, call lights had gone unanswered, and bedsores had developed. Why could the hospital not prevent these? Because all the money had gone on staffing assessments, policies, and procedures. The administrative staff despised Miss Lester, "who toured each ward daily with set mouth and eagle eye." The trouble was, "without that scrutiny, all the plans, policies, and procedures didn't clean any gurneys, turn any patients, or pick up any slippers off the floor" (240). A further irony is that as the administrators attempt to move Laguna Honda closer toward "health care" and prepare for a move to a new building, it is proposed that as part of the re-branding, the institution should henceforth be known as a center for "health, wellness, and rehabilitation" and no longer called "Hospital" at all. The staff object: "If Laguna Honda was not a hospital, we asked, then who were those sick, demented, frail, one- or no-legged, coughing, yellow people we took care of everyday? In their wheelchairs, gurneys and beds? With their IV's, feeding tubes, catheters, casts, oxygen, and tracheotomies? What were they doing here? And so they kept the name 'Hospital' after all" (319–320).

Sweet illustrates the way working for assumes no relationship by repeatedly noting that the growing number of administrators did their best to distance themselves from the patients (324, 327). Instead they read charts and forms (202). Meanwhile the designers of the new hospital had never toured the existing hospital, nor met with any of the patients (232). They had not taken into consideration patient needs, so they had designed it without space for wheelchairs (234). Nor had they considered the doctors, with the result that there were no doctors' offices in the new hospital. Most tellingly the new hospital also included technology which would limit the need for interaction, especially presence – including cameras in each room which would enable families to view their relatives without the trouble of having to visit (233) and a two-way monitor under each pillow so nurse and patient could talk to each other without needing to meet face-to-face (330).

Putting the relentless battle for the soul of the hospital to one side, Sweet has a great many constructive examples of what Galilee might look like, undergirded by Nazareth. Each of the dimensions of being with are reflected and refracted through the story of Victoria Sweet and Laguna Honda.

Presence

Sweet gives several examples of ways in which presence is basic to medicine. One is the account of Janice Gilroy. Janice was a heavy cocaine, heroin, and alcohol user. She had a stroke on the right side of her brain. It looked like she would require a brain scan, a bone scan, and a spinal tap. She might also need perhaps biopsies and extended hospitalization. Although it was quiet and cool in her room, Janice was lying stark naked on the bed, and refusing to cooperate. Sweet decides simply to sit with her. She felt like crawling out of her skin; but then realized Janice was acting as if she'd been poisoned (291).

Maybe Janice had indeed been poisoned. It turned out, that was it: there was so much serotonin in the medications, it was about to become fatal. Taking her off all her medications made the symptoms clear up. Sitting beside Janice in the dark crystallizes a great deal for Sweet. "I'd done so little for her." What she means is, she hadn't examined her or looked over her records or touched her. But what she had done was to be with her. "The diagnosis had appeared without me sending her to the emergency room, without additional tests, scans, or biopsies. Somehow, just by sitting with her, I'd understood what was wrong" (293). So after Janice Gilroy, Sweet takes time to "just sit" in this way with all of her patients for five or ten minutes: "and something, somehow, would happen" (293). Being with turns out to be the best way to work for.

Meng Tam is another patient with whom presence was everything. He was listed as "do not resuscitate" and he seemed to have developed ventricular tachycardia, which meant he had about 20 minutes to live. But Sweet and her colleague noticed signs of movement. Sweet also noticed that his eyelids opened. They looked upon one another, deeply. "And it was as if I saw him, all of him, present at the back of his eyes" (310). Gradually, in ways no one who was there had ever known, Mr. Tam came back. His eyes became clear. And Sweet knew he had made up his mind to stay (310). Though Sweet had attended many resuscitations, she had never before watched the soul stop in the tunnel of death and weigh its options. This revival of his demeanor and blood and countenance was "an experience of pure life" (312). Here is a profound discovery of presence, yielding glory.

Returning to our argument in Chapter 3, what Sweet's account of presence makes clear is that isolation really is the predicament, rather than mortality. Disease isolates us. The temptation in the face of the sick is to solve their problems. What Sweet articulates is that mortality is not the predicament. But to address isolation, the first step is presence.

Attention

In many ways *God's Hotel* is a paean to presence and attention. Attention is the key to the difference between modern medicine and Sweet's "slow medicine." Sweet is inspired to deepen her practice of attention through her study of the medieval theologian and physician Hildegard of Bingen. Study of medieval manuscripts disclosed the existence of palimpsest. This occurs when one realizes that a shadow text lies underneath another text. Because parchment used to be expensive, people would reuse it, scraping the ink off each page to do so. But the earlier text was still discernible underneath the new. Sweet takes this as a metaphor for her experience of medicine at Laguna Honda: beneath modern medicine she could begin to see an older understanding of the body (29). Palimpsest is also a good description of what Sweet discovers when she brings presence and attention to the symptoms of her patients.

Sweet finds colleagues who understand the centrality of attention. Christina is a Filipina nurse who loves everyone she looks after and recalls every detail about them (214). She remembers who they were married to, who they used to be married to, and what they called their children. She remembered their favorite foods and all the different medicines they had taken and which ones had not worked. "She remembered the tests whose results our over-zealous medical records department removed from the chart" (216). Together, Christina and Victoria attend to Mr. Gillon. Mr. Gillon is blind; has seizures; and can do nothing (214). But Sweet finds, amid all the damage and sadness of the ward, Mr. Gillon reminds her what matters: "that there were more ways to be of use than to be of use; that there was something to be said for pure existence; that none of us knows what is valuable to God" (215). Christina boasts to Victoria about what Mr. Gillon can do. She brings Victoria over and says to Mr. Gillon, "Clap your hands!" After a long wait Mr. Gillon clapped his hands. These were the kinds of things Christina knew about every patient. In Mr. Gillon's case, his ability to clap his hands remained the most reliable way to tell if he was sick.

Mr. Jackson taught Victoria a further lesson. Dr. Romero calls Victoria in to look together at an X-ray of a homeless man who's been at the County Hospital for two months and is losing weight. When they go to see the patient, there is no explanatory sign; until they turn him on his side, whereupon immediately they see a lump the size of a fist: cancer – lung or kidney cancer. The nurses at the County must have seen it. How come it hadn't been treated in two months? Were the nurses not on speaking terms with the interns? For Victoria, the lesson lies in attention. It was not simply that the patient should have an X-ray which the doctor should look at; neither was it just that the various medical practitioners should speak with each other about such cases. The key lesson was, "The diagnosis is written on the body – look for it. Turn the patient on his side; examine him thoroughly. Don't miss the obvious" (20).

Steven Harp brought yet another lesson – which was, again, another version of the same lesson. Steve was a "bad boy": he'd had a stroke at 34 and again at 38, both while using cocaine. He couldn't walk, he had heart failure, and he couldn't manage his saliva. Victoria pays attention to him, even though he isn't her patient. She describes his appearance in great detail. He does not, on close attention, seem quite like a stroke victim. It turns out he has been a commercial truck driver until only a year before – three years after the first stroke. And he can write – in neat, sophisticated sentences. This does not look like dementia from multiple strokes. Looking through his records, only one diagnosis adds up: muscular dystrophy – affecting only three in 100,000 adults; including, without question now, Steve Harp. When Victoria calls Steve's sister she is not surprised – it turns out one of Steve's brothers has it. And a cousin. And an uncle. Victoria reflects that she was turning into a physician from an earlier era, who simply listened to the patient and looked at his eyes. There was something special about those old doctors: they were slow, quiet, uncomplicated, unstressed. They were connected to the quiet that lies beneath all activity. "Once you key into it, there are no emergencies, and you have all the time you need" (261).

Mystery

For Gabriel Marcel, as we saw in Chapter 8, there is a profound difference between a problem, which one seeks to solve, and a mystery, which one can only enter. Victoria learns this lesson through Mrs. Tod. Again, she was not Victoria's patient, but her bed was between two of Victoria's patients and she passed her several times a day. Mrs. Tod was 35 and had brain cancer growing out of her right eye. She was very hard to look at. Victoria had to work out what it meant to care when she could not cure. "Is there anything I can do for you?" Victoria asks – it sounds like the epitome of a working for question, but it is asked in the humiliating context of the doctor assuming the answer is "no." Mrs. Tod has a simple answer: nicer food and a new pair of glasses. Victoria learns that there is such a thing as a soul: Mrs. Tod's lesson is one of a solid rock of courage (31). And she learned about medicine: "Even when there is nothing to do for a patient – no cancer to discover, no paradoxical pulse to take – there is still something to do." Such things may not be grand gestures – they may simply be small fidelities. "The big thing – the hand of God, fate – can be accepted, perhaps because it is so big and fateful, so unchangeable. But the small things are correctable, or should be, if people only cared to notice" (31–32).

If Mrs. Tod showed Victoria the mystery of courage, Terry Becker revealed the mystery of *viriditas*, or vitality. Terry was a prostitute, and she had inflammation of the spinal cord, paralyzing her from the neck down. She was 37 but looked much older. She kept being checked out and abused by her boyfriend, Mike. Finally she was found in her wheelchair on the streets, unarousable and without a heartbeat: clinically dead. Resuscitation warmed her up and in two hours she was awake. Not long after she was delivered back into the hands of Mike. A few months later she returned to Laguna Honda with an enormous, deep, horrifying open wound on her back. Victoria draws on Hildegard's notion of *viriditas* – the body's ability to heal itself. Give a patient deep sleep, fresh air, sunlight, good food, peace, and safety, and, most of all, time – in this case, two and a half years – and the body would do the rest. Which it did. As Hippocrates said, "What heals disease is nature" (99).

Time was the most important ingredient. Victoria reflects that the health-care system offered endless medicines and procedures, at limitless cost – and yet after every $50,000 hospitalization, Terry went back to squalor and was soon no better off. Laguna Honda offered the vital gift of time. What captivates Victoria is beholding the process of healing – a sight seldom seen in the days of efficient medicine: "it seemed magical, a sleight of hand" (98). It is this sense of mystery, this sense of healing as fundamentally something that the patient experiences and the doctor watches, rather than a commodity the doctor manufactures and the customer purchases, that for Victoria lies at the heart of medicine. Medicine is not fundamentally a science, or even an art: it is participation, by doctor and patient together, in a mystery.

Delight

Delight refers to moments of joy and an emerging dance of wonder. Victoria discovers both at Laguna Honda.

Joy comes through Mr. Teal. Mr. Teal taught Victoria community, unselfish love, and resurrection (188). Mr. Teal had dementia. He thought he was in Florida and it was 1983. He had been picked up by a paramedic team after a heart attack and resuscitated – but was, thereafter, demented. He would not cooperate and behaved more and more like a "homeless wino" (191). They could not discharge him because no hostel would take him – he had a record of setting fire to his room. But everything changed when he met Jessie, a patient on the women's ward. His personal habits were transformed, and preparations for a wedding began. The whole panoply of the hospital turned out – physical therapists, speech therapists, activity therapists, nurses, social workers, volunteers, and limping or wheeling patients. The bride arrived "like a queen on a wheeled throne ... smiling so widely that even the paralyzed side of her face was lifted" (194). When the minister declares he may kiss the bride, there is a shuffling of wheelchairs: "Mrs. Teal couldn't move her left side, and Mr. Teal couldn't walk" (195) but he threw himself out of the wheelchair and gave her a passionate kiss nonetheless. For Victoria this "Wedding at Cana" was about miracle, about change, and about relationship in community (196). It was a moment of delight.

The emerging dance of wonder refers to a discovery Victoria initially makes on pilgrimage to Santiago de Compostela. On that journey she realizes the difference between two kinds of stranger. *Hostis* describes a stranger as the host sees things – a person who comes to the door. *Peregrinus* describes a stranger as a pilgrim sees things – a person who goes to the door. When a pilgrim sets out on a journey, they become a stranger and inhabit a language, experience new foods, live among new customs (207). The root of *hospital* is *hospitality*, and the root of *hospitality* is *hospes*, which can mean either "guest" or "host" (175). In Rome, travelers, strangers, and pilgrims were all of the same class, "one's identity as guest or host was interchangeable," because every host was a guest somewhere else. But because of the tradition of Matthew 25:31–46 – that any stranger could be Christ, and therefore needed to be treated accordingly – a new kind of hospitality arose.

Victoria realizes that in medicine, guest and host are the same, and interchangeable – this is the world made possible by a hospital: "every host will for sure become a guest; every doctor, a patient" (176). She realizes that Laguna Honda was not principally about medicine but about hospitality – the practice of taking in the stranger at the door. A stranger that could be – had been – her.

Here is delight: a profound sense of connectedness and fellow-feeling, based on mutual assistance, reciprocal compassion, and eternal companionship.

Participation

Victoria learns from Hildegard of Bingen what it means to accompany the patient. Hildegard devised for each of her patients, as part of their recovery, a "regime." A regime was a rule of life – for food, sleep, exercise, sex. It varied with the season, your age, the climate, and your internal make-up. Its principles were summarized in the words, "Even without a doctor you have three doctors at hand: Dr. Diet, Dr. Quiet, and Dr. Merryman." Dr. Diet was concerned with what you should eat or drink; Dr. Quiet covered exercise, sleep, and rest; and Dr. Merryman stipulated how much sex you had and what kind of emotions were salutary (142).

What this leads to, for Victoria, is a gradual realization that her concerns about boundaries, transference, and countertransference, while having an honored place in her professional training, had to be significantly reconsidered if she was to function at Laguna Honda. One nurse cooked a whole pig on his day off for breast cancer patient from Tahiti who was homesick. One doctor accompanied a musical patient to the opera. Some staff members paid out of their own pockets for birthday dinners for their patients (229). All of these were in the spirit of the charity that was at the root of why the almshouse had been built in the first place. "In the Middle Ages, charity was accepted as doing as much for the giver as it did for the receiver, the 'goodness of charity being a bond of love that draws us close to God.'" (228).

And this is how Victoria came to discover charity and reciprocity through one of her patients, Paul Bennett. The data on Paul suggested he was a cocaine and alcohol user, who was homeless, angry, and destructive, and had an incurable physical illness. "Which shows you how wrong a form can be, even one with 1,100 little boxes" (220). He had peripheral vascular disease – unusual for one as young as 47 – and the attendant circulation difficulties had already cost him one leg. In trying to keep off his left side he had developed terrible bedsores on his right. Eventually the right leg had to come off too; and he was facing a slow death from gangrene. At a colleague's suggestion, Victoria administered a high concentration of oxygen – and the wounds began to heal. And then reciprocity set in. It transpired that Paul had the ability to construct computers out of their constituent parts; and he built one while recuperating in the hospital (226). Quickly patients were fascinated and nurses brought him all their computer problems. He developed quite a following.

Victoria was moved to ask Paul if he wanted a Christmas gift. He asked for a fishing vest. He had no legs, so he lacked the pockets that trousers would provide. A fishing vest, with all its pockets, would make up the shortfall. Giving Paul a fishing vest for Christmas gave Victoria enormous pleasure. She saw such acts of charity all around the hospital – in clear contravention of conventional doctor–patient boundaries. She recognizes it as partly selfish. She joined in something that was going on all around her. And so it seemed natural (230).

Thus the commitment to be with meant a careful regime, closely monitored; it meant recognizing that charity, when "evoked by dearness" is about finding mutuality between giver and receiver – about basing every for on a genuine with; and it meant discovering reciprocity when a patient was truly given space to discover his abundant gifts.

Partnership

Partnership means being with someone in such a way that complementarity develops – that something occurs or is perceived or discovered that it takes both parties to elicit. This happens for Victoria in the story of Mr. Rapman. Mr. Rapman had cirrhosis of the liver, and he was soon going to die, from bleeding, infection, or coma. His scrappy, argumentative character might save him, but only if he ceased drinking. He stabilized enough to go to the rehabilitation unit for a while; and the next time Victoria saw him he was a changed man. He had been sober for 264 days and was on stage four of a twelve-step program. The credit for that went to Don Taylor, a substance-abuse counselor at the hospital. At first Mr. Rapman had thrown Don out of his room; but Don would not be so easily put off, and eventually Mr. Rapman began on a program of recovery. Victoria observes: "While medicine had done a good job of saving Mr. Rapman from death, it was something else that had made him well. And that something seemed to have been Don Taylor" (336).

After some while Mr. Rapman returned to attend Don Taylor's funeral. Don had emerged from a drug-laden household: in prison he had joined a twelve-step program; since then he had spent his life directing people to see their own powerlessness, the existence of a higher power, the discovery, in love, of true happiness. Mr. Rapman spoke at the funeral. He recalled how Don came back every day. Don had saved his life – and the life of many others. Victoria looked around and realized that there was a whole nexus of life at the hospital among the addicted that she had never been aware of – and that their conversation was about the same things the doctors talked about – patients dying, the purpose of life, "how to live, and how to die" (339). She sees that the hospital is a partnership, where each member contributes to the community of healing. And that she is not their superior – but one like them. Indeed, they have much to teach her: a crucial aspect of being with.

Mr. Rapman provided the capstone to what Victoria had learned at Laguna Honda, summarizing everything she had learned there.

There was the importance of modern medicine, with its intensive care units, transfusions, and antibiotics. Without that "medical model of care," Mr. Rapman would never have survived his fatal liver disease. But modern medicine was not enough. Mr. Rapman also needed the Way of Laguna Honda, the Way of Hildegard and premodern medicine – tincture of time, the little things, Dr. Diet, Dr. Quiet, and Dr. Merryman – to heal completely. But even that had not been enough. It took Don Taylor, with his enactment of meaning and of love, to save Mr. Rapman's life for good. (340)

Enjoyment

Pilgrimage teaches Victoria that medicine is a practice to enjoy, rather than to use. She describes a day in the pouring rain, far from the day's destination. She was wet and cold, and she and her companion had to sing to stay warm. But she wasn't eager to reach her next stop: she was as happy as she could ever recall having been (209–210). So much of her life had been spent trying to avoid such an experience; but thereafter she wanted to keep that place with her in every interaction with her patients. She had learned what it means to enjoy: being a doctor is in so many ways about going against the grain of how things are – but thereafter she started increasingly to appreciate her patients "just for who they were" (210). In other words, conventional medicine assumes a role of working for: something is wrong, I can fix it, only my intervention will make a difference, and that difference is what medicine is all about. By contrast Victoria was discovering a different kind of medicine, which appeared at Don Taylor's funeral – a community of acceptance, appreciation, reciprocity, partnership, patience, and healing, in which the body's own powers are appreciated and the disciplines of time, rest, and food are respected.

By the end of her journey, Victoria finds that medicine seemed a lot simpler. Only a few things ever happened to the human body. Much of the medical textbook was much less important. "I began to enjoy my patients and know that I enjoyed them and that they enjoyed me." She did not have to do a great deal. "With just a little bit on my part, my patients would get better" (253–254).

It seems that even in medicine – what our culture might term the epitome of working for – enjoyment can become the heart of the practice. Victoria *enjoyed* her patients: and her patients *enjoyed* her. Henceforth all her practice was predicated on being with.

Glory

In the end Victoria senses she has been brought to the edge of a holy place. This is something she hints at throughout her account. Perhaps the simplest description comes when she talks about a late afternoon ward round with Dr. Fintner. They came to the bed of Mrs. Georges, who had been admitted suffering from what seemed to be no more or less than old age. Victoria and Dr. Fintner stand for a while on either side of her bed, in silence. Mrs. Georges is concentrating, though her eyes are closed. She is remembering her high school prom. "The girls were so pretty!" Victoria became aware in the ensuing silence, of a deep, healing peace. It was as much for the doctor as for the patient: "a quiet space of non-asking and non-answering, of non-doing" (39). This is the essence of being with: an entering into glory.

Victoria concludes the book with a summary of how she has discovered glory in a transformation of her understanding of the doctor–patient relationship. "Before, I'd stood back from my patients – not a lot, but a little; I was wary of the transference and the countertransference. I threw myself in, but not completely, only for that fifteen-minute visit, that two-hour workup, that two-month or even six-month period." But she learned from all the characters in her narrative that "that wasn't being the best doctor." To be the best doctor meant walking alongside the patient to collect the medication and standing beside the patient while they drank it. "They taught me that the real name for the transference and countertransference was love, and that the doctor–patient relationship was, above all, a relationship" (348). As she had been told on her first day, Laguna Honda had proved to be, for Victoria, a gift.

Thus does Galilee begin in service – and end in worship.

Notes

1. All the references in this chapter come from Victoria Sweet, *God's Hotel: A Doctor, a Hospital, and a Pilgrimage to the Heart of Medicine* (New York: Riverhead, 2012).

12

Being With One Another in Jerusalem

In choosing examples of our being with one another, I have had an eye to the abiding criticisms of the notion of being with. To speak in detail about a chaotic homeless person was to address someone whom it is very difficult to be with (and almost impossible to work for or work with). Thus it is clear being with is not an easy option. To discuss at length contemporary health care is to consider perhaps the most obvious context in which working for seems helpful, effective, and uncomplicated; thus to find how deeply working for depends on being with in such a situation makes a vital point about the extent and inextricability of being with, and an insight into how working for, working with, and being with may be complementary in circumstances where systems are running in a conventional way. In this chapter I take an extreme example of what it means to be with when there is nothing benevolent whatsoever about a force that has almost unlimited power and evil intent. Just as pacifists are invariably asked "What about Hitler?" so in considering being with I look at the case of Dietrich Bonhoeffer, a man who I perceive was with the German people even in the most trying circumstances imaginable. Hence this chapter addresses the question: Surely, there are some circumstances so demanding that being with becomes a luxury and working for must take over?

John Howard Yoder offers what would seem, at first glance, to be a serious challenge to my account of being with. Yoder is concerned to dispel any sentimentalities or domestications regarding the ways in which Christians are called to imitate Jesus. It would seem that Yoder might have little time for an account that affirmed the centrality of Nazareth in the following of Christ. Consider these words:

> There is no *general* concept of living like Jesus in the New Testament. According to universal tradition, Jesus was not married; yet when the apostle Paul,

---

advocate *par excellence* of the life "in Christ," argues at length for celibacy or for a widow's not remarrying (1 Cor. 7), it never occurs to him to appeal to Jesus' example, even as one of many arguments. Jesus is thought in his earlier life to have worked as a carpenter; yet never, even when he explains at length why he earns his own way as an artisan (1 Cor. 9), does it come to Paul's mind that he is imitating Jesus. Jesus' association with villagers, his drawing his illustrations from the life of the peasants and the fishermen, his leading his disciples to desert places and mountaintops, have often been appealed to as examples by the advocates of rural life and church camping; but not in the New Testament. His formation of a small circle of disciples whom he taught through months of close contact has been claimed as a model pastoral method; his teaching in parables has been claimed as a model of graphic communication; there have been efforts to imitate his prayer life or his forty days in the desert: but not in the New Testament.

There is thus but one realm in which the concept of imitation holds – but there it holds in every strand of the New Testament literature and all the more strikingly by virtue of the absence of parallels in other realms. This is at the point of the concrete social meaning of the cross in its relation to enmity and power. Servanthood replaces dominion, forgiveness absorbs hostility. Thus – and only thus – are we bound by New Testament thought to "be like Jesus."[1]

This chapter is an extended anecdotal response to Yoder's assertion. I seek to do two things: to show that what Yoder calls "the concrete social meaning of the cross" is equivalent to, and amply expressed by, the language of "with"; and to show how Jerusalem and Nazareth have more in common than might at first appear – in other words, that it is precisely in the face of danger, and through sacrifice and courageous witness, that the qualities of being with are most fully tested and revealed.

There is no way to address, even by survey, the range of issues evoked by the theme of this chapter. Thus what I shall do is to discuss George Bell and Dietrich Bonhoeffer – two prominent figures of the twentieth-century church – their witness, and the relationship between them, hoping to demonstrate in depth what cannot be envisaged in breadth.

Bonhoeffer is often taken to be someone who, in joining the plot against Hitler, set aside being with and in its stead placed working for; and, by the depth of his witness, is thereby taken to validate and even require such an exchange in others – under frequently invoked names like "responsibility" and "realism." By renarrating Bonhoeffer, I seek to challenge that influential invocation. I am also aware that, even allowing that Jesus assumes disciples will face persecution, and are likely themselves to have to take up their cross, Bonhoeffer was a man facing an extreme situation.

That is why I have set alongside him George Bell, Bishop of Chichester (1929–1958), the close friend to whom Bonhoeffer wrote his final letter before his execution. Bell could easily have avoided controversy, even – perhaps especially – in wartime; he could have concentrated on the internalities and pastoral domesticities of the Church of England, or simply waved the flag over the British war effort. But, at the cost of his personal popularity, to the dismay of some who saw in him the likely future leader of the Anglican Communion, and at the risk of his life (in traveling, for example, to Sweden during the war to meet Bonhoeffer), Bell remained in solidarity with his ecumenical partners and his overseas friends. His witness was precisely one of being with those whom most others had felt now lay out of reach. And the way Bell and Bonhoeffer were with each other, at such poignant moments, constitutes an intimacy that helpfully offsets the public, political commitments for which both men are more widely remembered. These were two friends who remained with God in great part because of their determination to continue to be with one another.

George Bell

George Bell (1883–1958) discovered the depth of being with first of all through the ecumenical movement. Bell encountered ecumenism at seminary in Wells in the early 1900s; ten years later in 1914 he became Archbishop Randall Davidson's chaplain for international and interdenominational relations. He worked ecumenically during the 1914–1918 war, to assist orphans, and upon the end of hostilities, to partner in the exchange of prisoners of war. He was active in international ecumenical meetings while Dean of Canterbury in the 1920s and, after becoming Bishop of Chichester in 1929, became president of the Universal Christian Council for Life and Work. It was in that capacity that he was in Berlin in February 1933 as Hitler rose to power.

On April 30, 1934, Bell visited the German Ambassador to protest about the autocratic rule of the Reich Bishop, and to threaten the severing of relations between the Council and the German Christian Church that was loyal to Adolf Hitler. On May 10, Ascension Day, Bell published an official letter regarding the German Evangelical Church. In it he spoke of "the assumption by the Reich bishop, in the name of the leadership principle, of autocratic powers unqualified by constitutional or traditional restraints which are without precedent in the history of the Church." Bell noted the disastrous results on the internal unity of the church, the disturbing introduction of racial discrimination, and the painful impression on Christian opinion abroad. Already we can see the significance of being with: for Bell, the issue was not primarily one of justice, but of how Christians in Germany could be one body and how Christians outside Germany could be one with Christians in Germany.

Likewise Bell's quarrel with the German Christians was their failure to remember their baptism and be with other Christians, in Germany and abroad. Dietrich Bonhoeffer, with Bell's support, was a sometimes lonely voice striving to ensure the Confessing Church remained a church, and did not simply become synonymous with the opposition to Hitler. Hideous, ruthless, and reckless as Hitler's regime already was, Bonhoeffer and Bell could see that what was required was not simply the removal of Hitler, but a wholesale renewal of the church in Germany. That was what the Confessing Church was really to be about. For the German Evangelical Church's support of Hitler had not come out of the blue, but was of a piece with a theology that had been flawed for some time. It is perhaps his ability to grasp this insight that makes George Bell unique among the few prophets speaking up for the Confessing Church from outside Germany.

It is important to note that Bell's famous commitment, in the face of widespread mistrust and criticism, to hold the British government to the principles of a just war, arose also from an international and ecumenical desire to be with even the (temporary) enemy. Bell perceived that there are no permanent enemies and thus that nothing should be done to hamper eventual reconciliation. He said,

> The Church then ought to declare in both peace-time and war-time, that there are certain basic principles which can and should be the standards of both international social order and conduct. ... It must not hesitate, if occasion arises, to condemn the infliction of reprisals, or the bombing of civilian populations, by the military forces of its own nation. It should set itself against the propaganda of lies and hatred. It should be ready to encourage a resumption of friendly relations with the enemy nation. It should set its face against any war of extermination or enslavement, and any measures directly aimed to destroy the morale of a population.[2]

One biographer summarizes his further remarks:

> The church "cannot speak of any earthly war as a 'crusade,' for the one thing for which it is impossible to fight with earthly weapons is the Cross. Its supreme concern is not the national cause." ... It must "do whatever it can

to maintain brotherly relations with all the Churches it can reach ... through the help of the Churches in neutral countries. Every effort should be made, with the same help, to preserve former contacts between Churchmen whose nations are divided by war, not for conspiracy but for spiritual community. ... In particular, the Churches should work in such ways as are open to them for a just peace and try, through the Ecumenical Movement itself, to discover what terms of peace would appear right, and likely to be lasting, to Churchmen in enemy and neutral countries."[3]

Just as the task of the Confessing Church was the reconstruction of the church in Germany, so the purpose of the war was to establish a new order in Europe. As always, Bell had in mind what it meant to be with his friends in Germany. He wanted to be able to tell them with integrity that the British government had no ambitions to humiliate or dismember Germany, and thus that Hitler's rhetoric in this regard was unfounded. Knowing those in Germany who were eager for peace, and did not assume Nazism and Germany were identical, and knowing their desire to create a new Germany at peace with its neighbors, Bell needed to know from the British government what terms would be regarded as making for a lasting peace. Hence his words in October 1942:

I could wish that the British Government would make it very much clearer than they have yet done that this is a war between rival philosophies of life, in which the United Nations welcome all the help they can receive from anti-Nazis everywhere – in Germany as well as outside – and would assure the anti-Nazis in Germany that they would treat a Germany which effectively repudiated Hitler and Hitlerism in a very different way from the Germany in which Hitler continued to rule.[4]

When Churchill and Roosevelt announced in January 1943 their resolve to pursue the unconditional surrender of Germany, Bell responded in the House of Lords by pointing out that this betrayed those within Germany who had opposed Hitler to the point of death; and simply lined up "the Nazi assassins in the same row with the people of Germany whom they have outraged."[5] In due course, Bell's persistence met with some reward, and on March 10, 1943, the Lord Chancellor acknowledged in the House of Lords that while "the Hitlerite State should be destroyed, ... the whole German people is not ... thereby doomed to destruction." Bell had refused to stop being with the German people, and especially their faithful Confessing Church, even while at war with their government and military forces.[6]

Bell's solidarity with the Confessing Church and with the humanity of the German people embodies the solidarity we explored in Chapter 5. It gained most attention with his outspoken (and extremely unpopular) opposition to the Allied bombing campaign. The situation in the summer of 1940 was that Hitler was poised to invade Britain, while Churchill's only means of hurting Germany was from the air. By late August Allied bombing had strayed from direct targets such as ports to general ones, especially Berlin itself. Bell denounced this policy as initiating a spiraling competition in destruction, neither moral nor winnable.

When the tide of the war began to turn, he was no less attuned to the moral significance of the bombing campaign. Having failed to enlist the advocacy of Archbishop William Temple on the question, he wrote, in September 1943,

> When a Minister of the Government speaks in exulting terms of a ruthless and destructive bombing of the German people; or quarters, supposed to be authoritative, contemplate the subjection of fifty German cities to the same terror as Hamburg (or Coventry) has suffered, or the wiping-out of Germany as an industrial unit; then we have real cause to grieve for a lowering of moral tone, and also to fear greatly for the future. ... To bomb cities as cities, deliberately to attack civilians, quite irrespective of whether or not they are actively contributing to the war effort is a wrong deed, whether done by the Nazis or by ourselves.[7]

When Bell expressed similar sentiments in the House of Lords in February 1944 he received a torrent of indignation in much, though not all, of the press. Bell's ability to discriminate between the bombing of centers of transport and war industry, which he endorsed, and the carpet bombing of whole towns, was based on his conviction that war could only be justified as a departure, in extreme and very unusual circumstances, from a fundamental commitment to peace. The language of "teaching Germany a lesson" and "giving the Germans what they deserved" had no resonance for him.

Bell was perhaps the only figure in church and Parliament who was able to perceive both the need to be with the German people and the need to address the refugee crisis. This was because neither concern began with the outbreak of war – they both traced back to solidarity developed long before. Here one observer comments on Bell's commitment to refugees.

> Among the Bell papers at Lambeth eight box files are labelled "refugees." They bear witness to his care and labour on behalf of the so-called "Non-Aryan" Christians from 1933 onwards. Perhaps English people who discuss

the failure of the German Church with regard to the Jews, might, with the Swiss and the French, do a little heart-searching on their own and reflect how slowly this cause made its way into the English conscience. ... High up as he was on the Nazi blacklist, he visited Germany in April 1938 to make enquiries at first hand ... Then in 1938 came the news of the fearful "Christall-nacht" ... Immediately ... Bell announced that he had been to the Home Office and had personally guaranteed to support twenty Non-Aryan pastors and their families. ... They included ... Franz Hildebrandt, friend of Bonhoeffer and assistant to [the Confessing Church leader Martin] Niemöller ... Hildebrandt tells how a vast correspondence came flowing into Chichester, how the floors of the palace were littered with dumps of letters and how, when he suggested that some formal printed acknowledgement be sent to each, George Bell turned on him with a look of horror, insisting that each be sent a personal reply.[8]

It was the plight of the refugees that was the subject of Bell's maiden speech in the House of Lords. He described his visits to the internment camps located at Huyton in Liverpool and on the Isle of Man, and in a speech in August 1940 went on to emphasize that "there is all the difference in the world between aliens of enemy nationality and refugees from the enemy." That difference was not evident in the conditions in which the internees were held, and, as the threat of German invasion became imminent, all male refugees between 16 and 70 were rounded up.[9]

Franz Hildebrandt, one of the internees, whom we have already quoted, describes Bell's reaction in visiting the camp on the Isle of Man. Bell

was almost speechless and could only stammer and stutter. ... The sight of the refugees in their new captivity was just too much for him – it was not only a question of a wrong to so many of his personal friends, it was a moral burden on the English people. It was clear to him that something must be done immediately. ... On returning from the Isle of Man he called on the central postal censorship office in Liverpool, inspected the stacked postbags of the past six or eight weeks for which the internees had waited in vain, and suggested quietly but firmly that the letters might be delivered to the people to whom they were addressed. Three days later the camp post office was inundated.[10]

Bell was a public figure: he had plenty of opportunities for working for as a bishop and a member of the House of Lords and a patron of the arts and an ecumenical leader. But all of his public and prophetic actions were profoundly rooted in being with his clergy, his people, his friends in Germany and elsewhere, and those who were in peril and distress. At every turn his calls for others to implement change or take risks is backed up by his own willingness and history of doing precisely the same. When he calls for the government to consider overtures for peace, he himself is meeting with key partners from the enemy side and facing the dangers of doing so. When he is calling for public and private institutions to respond with imagination and compassion to the refugee crisis, he himself is visiting internment camps at the other end of the country and housing refugees in his own quarters. When he deplores the carpet bombing of German cities, and highlights the distinction between Germans and Nazis, he himself is striving through ecumenical engagement to model what it means to encounter difference and historic enmity yet keep a high moral aspiration amid conflict and never forget all parties' common humanity. When he calls on the government to declare its war aims and envisage a new international order beyond the destruction of Nazism, he himself is modeling in his diocesan relationships and his promotion of the arts the kind of culture and civic commitment for which he is calling. His working for and working with always has a being with to point to and be grounded in. He journeys to Galilee and Jerusalem, but his practice is rooted in Nazareth.

I now want to describe at greater length and with more precision how George Bell's imitation of God's being with us was fulfilled in different, but overlapping, circumstances by his friend Dietrich Bonhoeffer.

Dietrich Bonhoeffer

On July 21, 1944, the day after a turning point in German history, Dietrich Bonhoeffer wrote from prison to his friend Eberhard Bethge,

> If one has completely renounced making something of oneself … then one throws oneself completely into the arms of God, and this is what I call this-worldliness: living fully in the midst of life's tasks, questions, successes and failures, experiences, and perplexities – then one takes seriously no longer one's own sufferings but rather the suffering of God in the world. Then one stays awake with Christ in Gethsemane. And I think this is faith; this is *metanoia*. And this is how one becomes a human being, a Christian.[11]

Three weeks earlier he had written these words to Bethge: "Christians do not have an ultimate escape route out of their earthly tasks and difficulties into eternity. Like Christ … they have to drink the cup of earthly life to the last drop, and only when they do this is the Crucified and Risen One with them, and they are crucified and resurrected with Christ."[12]

In the quest for the historical Bonhoeffer, one comes across a wardrobe of conventional guises: the pacifist who discovered responsibility, the humanist who proclaimed a world come of age, the uncompromising radical who heard Christ calling each disciple to come and die, the prodigy who had published two doctorates before the age most scholars today have even embarked on one, and the scornful European who dismissed American Christianity as Protestantism without reformation. What I want to suggest is that we cherish Dietrich Bonhoeffer not so much in these conventional guises, but more because, in his own words, he "drank the cup of earthly life to the last drop," because he "lived fully in the midst of life's tasks, questions, successes and failures, experiences, and perplexities," because when he did this "the Crucified and Risen One was with him," and because "this is how he became a human being, a Christian." And most of all because, walking in his steps, this is how we may do the same.

Dietrich Bonhoeffer has been remembered mostly as a man "for" others. He wrote theology *for* the academy, he stood up *for* the Jews, he spoke up and established a seminary *for* the Confessing Church, he joined the bomb plot *for* Germany's salvation. But I suggest he should be even more remembered as a man "with" others. At three defining moments in his life, he resolved that to be a faithful disciple meant to be *with* God by being *with* the church, by being *with* his people, and by being *with* his family, friends, trusted companions, and fellow conspirators.

I suggest that John 11 offers a narrative shape that defines the arc of Jesus' life, and I wish to highlight how a measure of Dietrich Bonhoeffer's faithfulness is that his life has a corresponding narrative shape. In the process I want to identify three moments in Bonhoeffer's life that disclose his deepest commitments, and to comment on ways in which those commitments were ones that I have already begun to describe as an embodiment of an incarnate ethic of being *with*. Jesus' words in John 11:4 resonate deeply with the story of Dietrich Bonhoeffer: "This illness does not lead to death; rather, it is for God's glory, so that the Son of God may be glorified through it." This was Bonhoeffer's prayer for the crisis of the German churches and of Germany and Europe as a whole: that this crisis, for all its horror and terror, and for all its slaughter, speak not, finally, of death but of the glory of God.

Jesus crosses three key thresholds in John 11. First, he crosses the threshold into Judea. The message comes from Martha and Mary that Lazarus is ill. Curiously, Jesus stays two days longer in the place where he is. It is not entirely clear why. There follows an intense and illuminating interchange. Jesus announces it is time to return to Judea. The disciples say "But they were all ready to stone you when you were last there." Jesus is not to be deterred. He discloses the true reason for his journey: "so that you may believe." And Thomas gets the message, proclaiming: "Let us also go, that we may die with him."

Here lies the first defining moment of Bonhoeffer's life. It is June 1939. He is in New York. The Executive Secretary of the Federal Council of Churches has made an offer to employ him for three years coordinating work among German refugees in the city. He ponders his situation for two weeks, echoing Jesus' delay after receiving Martha and Mary's message. When he meets with the Executive Secretary on June 20, he declines the offer, to the consternation and bemusement of those making it. His motives are partly a mystery to himself: in his journal he writes, "We are acting in a plane that is hidden from us, and we can only ask that God may judge and forgive us."[13] But with Reinhold Niebuhr he is less equivocal, explaining,

> I have made a mistake in coming to America. I must live through this difficult period of our national history with the Christian people of Germany. I will have no right to participate in the reconstruction of Christian life in Germany after the war if I do not share the trials of this time with my people. Christians in Germany will face the terrible alternative of either willing the defeat of their nation in order that Christian civilization may survive, or willing the victory of their nation and thereby destroying our civilization. I know which of these alternatives I must choose; but I cannot make the choice in security![14]

Of all the dimensions of Bonhoeffer's momentous decision to return to Germany in 1939, one in particular stands out. And that is his conversation, in Chichester, with George Bell. The conversation took place in early April 1939. In a letter dated March 25 to Bell before the meeting, Bonhoeffer expressed his anxiety about the prospect of being called up to military service and his reluctance to take the military oath.[15] He also communicated his recognition that very few of his Confessing Church companions would approve of his attitude. He acknowledged, "I should have to do violence to my Christian conviction, if I would take up arms 'here and now'"; but he admitted, "I have not made up my mind what I should do."[16] The meeting took place a few days later. Bethge describes it vividly. Bonhoeffer, he says, sought out Bell,

> the man who stood in another world, but could listen to him calmly and yet realize the force of the alternatives: Confessing church and family, pacifism and theology, political conspiracy and ecumenism. Within his family he could expect no close commitment to church theology, and among his friends on the Council of Brethren no freedom toward the political realm. Bell understood both. ... [Bonhoeffer] confided in the older man who, as he knew, understood how to pray and how to demand what was necessary.[17]

Bethge comments that Bell "probably eased Bonhoeffer's conscience about temporarily leaving Germany."[18] Keith Clements captures the spirit of the meeting by saying that Bell, "as a good counsellor, simply let him talk and talk, and listened." Citing Bonhoeffer's subsequent letter of April 13, in which he expresses gratitude to Bell and says "it means much to me to realize that you see the great conscientious difficulties with which we are faced,"[19] Clements describes the meeting as "a classic case of a good pastoral conversation."[20]

The reason this conversation is so significant is that in his compassionate concern and listening spirit toward Bonhoeffer, George Bell modeled the attitude Bonhoeffer would come to adopt toward Germany. Bell was profoundly with Bonhoeffer, in much the same way as Bonhoeffer came to understand himself as called to be profoundly with Germany. Only Bell truly comprehended the diverse commitments and characteristics of Bonhoeffer's personality, and perhaps only Bonhoeffer truly recognized the pathos and yet abiding possibility of Germany's situation. What Bell was helping Bonhoeffer to see was that there was no solution to his predicament, either in an appointment outside Germany or in simply consenting to being called up. Instead he was going to have to live without a solution. He was called to find a way to be with his people, not in a dramatic and conclusive decision, but in an extended series of daily discernments. Only thus was he going to imitate how God is with us. Let me repeat Bonhoeffer's letter to Bethge:

> If one has completely renounced making something of oneself ... then one throws oneself completely into the arms of God, and this is what I call this-worldliness: living fully in the midst of life's tasks, questions, successes and failures, experiences, and perplexities – then one takes seriously no longer one's own sufferings but rather the suffering of God in the world. Then one stays awake with Christ in Gethsemane ... this is faith.

That exactly how Bonhoeffer lived with the German people in the years after 1939.

The second threshold Jesus crosses in John 11 is into Bethany. Why does Jesus come to Bethany? Because, we are told in 11:5, "Jesus loved Martha and her sister and Lazarus." Bethany becomes a synecdoche for the world that Jesus enters because God so loves it. Martha and her sister and Lazarus become a synecdoche for the people of God with whom Jesus identifies. The conversation about discipleship took place before crossing into Judea. But the more profound conversation, about the resurrection and the life, takes place on this threshold, the threshold of Bethany. Mary says to Jesus, reproachfully but in words full of faith, "Lord, if you had been here, my brother would not have died" (11:32). These words sum up the quandary of the Confessing Church. Had Christians in Germany been more faithful, would the soul of Germany have descended to the point where Hitler captivated the national imagination? There is no certainty that it would not. Jesus does not affirm Mary's statement. He never says that if he had been there, Lazarus would not have died. God's action, it seems, is not to make bad things not happen. God's glory is revealed in that God does not leave us alone when they do.

Here lies the second defining moment of Bonhoeffer's life – a moment that came only a year after the first. Bethge describes sitting in the sun at a café in Memel, a small town in East Prussia, now a part of Lithuania, on June 17, 1940. Over the café's loudspeaker came an announcement that France had surrendered. Everyone stood up, sang *Deutschland über alles*, and saluted Hitler. Edwin Robertson sums up the significance of the moment like this: "Since the rise of Prussia almost a century earlier, the two contenders for the dominance of Europe were Germany and France. … The harsh terms of the Versailles treaty were thought to be the work of France." Thus the capitulation of France meant the erasure of Versailles and the undisputed supremacy of Germany in Europe. Bethge describes the scene in the café in withering terms. "The crowd jumped onto the chairs and forgot, in the jubilant tumult, both the means and the end of the victory. [Bonhoeffer] felt only shame at the success of the crime."[21] What the moment really meant for Bonhoeffer and his circle was this: no one was going to get rid of Hitler for them. If they wanted Hitler gone, they would have to do it themselves. As Bethge puts it, "The expectation that the first military difficulties would topple the hated regime had proven false, and all dreams of its removal had vanished. The victory in France sealed an immense miscalculation by Bonhoeffer's informants and friends in the resistance movement. The professionals … were wrong, and Hitler the amateur was right."[22]

This moment was a turning point. As Bethge puts it, momentously, "It was then that Bonhoeffer's double life began. ... He was acting out of an inner necessity for which his church as yet had no formulas. By normal standards everything had been turned upside down."[23] It's interesting and important to note that June 1940, rather than, for example, January 1933, is the date Bethge identifies in such shuddering terms. What it meant is expressed vividly by Mary Bosanquet. "As Bonhoeffer became more and more deeply enmeshed in the evil of his time, he was driven quietly to accept the loss of that particular personal treasure which he had many times struggled to abandon, but which had yet clung to him, wrapping its powerful tentacles round his inmost being; the sense of his own righteousness."[24] One can hear resonances of this moment in Bonhoeffer's *Ethics*, written four years later. Here Bonhoeffer maintains that responsible action involves "the willingness to become guilty," just as Christ entered into human guilt and took it upon himself out of selfless love for his brothers and sisters.[25]

Edwin Robertson expresses what being with risks in the realm of Christian character. "Little by little this Christian man became completely a man of his time. His involvement in the conspiracy would require the abandoning of much that Christian life demands – expert lying built up gradually into closely woven deception, and ultimately the willingness to kill."[26] Here Robertson points out the connection between these painful transformations and Bonhoeffer's words from Tegel prison four years later:

> We have been silent witnesses of evil deeds. We have become cunning and learned the arts of obfuscation and equivocal speech. Experience has rendered us suspicious of human beings, and often we have failed to speak to them a true and open word. Unbearable conflicts have worn us down or even made us cynical. Are we still of any use? Will our inner strength to resist what has been forced on us have remained strong enough, and our honesty with ourselves blunt enough, to find our way back to simplicity and honesty?[27]

The key point, again, is that Bonhoeffer's participation in the plot to kill Hitler was not a lonely hero's quest to save Germany even at the risk of his own soul; it was his much humbler participation in the communion of saints. It was not something Bonhoeffer did for; it was something he did with. In this lies its profound continuity with the previous threshold, the return to Germany a year earlier. The return to Germany was an incarnate expression of with: to have remained aloof and beyond Germany would still have permitted Bonhoeffer to work and be "for" a new Germany. Yet it would not have permitted him truly to work and be with Germany in its most benighted hour. Having committed himself to being with Germany in 1939, it was not an incomprehensible step to begin to work with those who sought to remove the single force that was propelling Germany deeper and deeper into the mire. Bonhoeffer was under no illusion that the death of Hitler would be the salvation of Germany: that would have been the fantasy of working for, the presumption that he could have the fate of a nation in his own hands. What Bonhoeffer was seeking to do was to help Germany get to a place from which it could begin to row back from catastrophe, to prevent things continuing to get worse, to bring about circumstances in which sanity could begin to break through the storm clouds of demonic fanaticism. In this he saw himself in solidarity (of the kind highlighted in Chapter 5 above) with a diverse group of people whom he regarded as representing the best in German character and spirit. For that reason, it is appropriate to see his efforts in the resistance as a humble identification with Germany, rather than a high-handed action for his nation. It was a genuine working with.

Bonhoeffer's being "with" Germany extended to his willingness to share the guilt for what Germany, collectively, had done. In a poem written in Tegel prison, he speaks of the "we," rather than the "they," who had brought about Germany's descent into apostasy, in words reminiscent of Romans 1:

> We the offspring of devout generations,
> once the defenders of justice and truth,
> became despisers of God and humanity,
> as Hell looked on, laughing. ...
> Only before thee, Fathomer of all Being,
> before thee we are sinners.
> Afraid of suffering and lacking good deeds,
> we have betrayed you before humankind.
> We saw the Lie raise its head
> and failed to pay homage to Truth.
> We saw others in direst need
> and our own death was all we feared.[28]

The fact that Bonhoeffer was not an advocate of his nation's fall did not mean he thought he could avoid its cost. Like Jesus, he bore in his own body the sins of his people. He lived the logic of Christ's incarnation.

George Bell highlighted his friend's commitment to be with in his sermon at Bonhoeffer's memorial service in London in July 1945. For Bell, Bonhoeffer was with not just his family and his country and the Confessing Church, but with the saints and martyrs everywhere and always.

As one of a noble company of martyrs of differing traditions, he represents both the resistance of the believing soul, in the name of God, to the assault of evil, and also the moral and political revolt of the human conscience against injustice and cruelty. He and his fellows are indeed built upon the foundation of the Apostles and the Prophets. And it was this passion for justice that brought him, and so many others ... into such a close partnership with other resisters, who, though outside the Church, shared the same humanitarian and liberal ideals.[29]

And that brings us to the third threshold Jesus crosses in John 11:38 he comes to Lazarus' tomb. It takes 38 verses of a 44-verse story for Jesus to reach the tomb. Just as Bethany, in the persons of Mary and Martha, corresponds to Israel, so the tomb, the place of horror and of transformation, represents Jerusalem. This is the place where Jesus performs the seventh miracle in John's Gospel, the miracle that perfectly anticipates the definitive miracle upon which all the others converge, the miracle of his own resurrection. And it is the place where we witness the confrontation that epitomizes the scandal of the cross. Jesus says, "Take away the stone." Martha responds, "Lord, already there is a stench because he has been dead four days." Jesus insists, "Did I not tell you that if you believed, you would see the glory of God?" So they took away the stone (John 11:39–41). Martha wants there to be a way to redeem her brother that does not involve the stench. Jesus asks if she is serious about wanting to see the glory of God.

This abiding presence of faith in the face of horror characterizes the third defining moment in Bonhoeffer's life. Bonhoeffer was kept in Tegel prison in the northwest of Berlin from the day of his arrest, April 5, 1943, until his transfer to Central Security Office in central Berlin on October 8, 1944. In the summer of 1944 he had the opportunity to escape. But he didn't take it. That was his moment of facing the stench of the tomb, out of a deeper desire to see the glory of God.

The unexpected, absurdly unlucky, but nonetheless devastating failure of the plot to kill Hitler at his Wolf's Lair headquarters near Rastenburg in modern northeast Poland, on July 20, 1944, was described by one observer as "perhaps the most tragic day in modern German history."[30] It marks a turning point at least as significant as the fall of France. After the fall of Paris, it was clear no one could get rid of Hitler but the Germans themselves. After the failure of Claus von Stauffenberg's attempt on Hitler's life, it seemed that all who had plotted Hitler's downfall were set to be eliminated. Any hope for a solution to the demonic possession of Germany seemed at an end. Bonhoeffer's extended prison stay and delayed trial was predicated on the case against his brother-in-law Hans von Dohnanyi, and beyond him Admiral Wilhelm Canaris and the whole spider's web of officers grouped around the *Abwehr* office that shielded the resistance under the pretext of military intelligence. But after July 20, 1944, their exposure was no more than a matter of time. Thus Bonhoeffer began seriously to plan for escape, and persuaded his prison guard, Corporal Knobloch, to disappear with him while Bonhoeffer would don a mechanic's uniform procured by his family. The clothing was transferred on September 24 and the chaplain to the Swedish embassy was put on standby.[31]

But on October 1, 1944, just days before the planned escape, Klaus Bonhoeffer, Dietrich's brother, was arrested, along with several others whose involvement in the plot had been hidden until this point. Dietrich perceived that his window for escape had closed. Any adventure now would cast a shadow of guilt upon his brother and expose his parents and his young fiancée Maria to significant danger. Within 24 hours he informed Corporal Knobloch and, through him, his family, that there was to be no escape. Once again with had displaced for. In this case with meant his brother and his family and his fellow conspirators. We may look back and imagine what it could have meant if this great theologian and visionary German intellectual had escaped the demise of the German war effort, and what by this stage had become his almost inevitable death. The stench, to us, may seem unbearable. But Bonhoeffer withstood the stench. He was concerned to see the glory of God. He knew that when he would stand before the divine judgment seat he would face the question "Where are the others?" If he was going to spend eternity with them, he had to be prepared to remain with those others now.

To enter the mystery of this solidarity, a solidarity that finally took him to his own death, we may draw on Bonhoeffer's own words. In *An Account at the Turn of the Year 1942–3* he says, prophetically, "We must learn to regard human beings less in terms of what they do and neglect to do and more in terms of what they suffer. The only fruitful relation to human beings – particularly to the weak among them – is love, that is, the will to enter into and to keep community with them."[32] Keeping community was exactly the with that inhibited him from escaping. He goes on to say,

> Christ withdrew from suffering until his hour had come; then he walked toward it in freedom, took hold, and overcame it. Christ … experienced in his own body the whole suffering of all humanity as his own. … We are not Christ, but if we want to be Christians it means that we are to take part in

Christ's greatness of heart, in the responsible action that in freedom lays hold of the hour and faces the danger, and in the true sympathy that springs forth not from fear but from Christ's freeing and redeeming love for all who suffer.[33]

If one were to choose a title for a biography of Bonhoeffer, one could do worse than call it "taking part in Christ's greatness of heart." Here again the emphasis is profoundly on being with.

In the same vein he writes to Bethge on July 28, 1944: "not only action but suffering, too, is a way to freedom. In suffering, liberation consists in being allowed to let the matter out of one's own hands into the hands of God. In this sense death is the epitome of human freedom."[34] These sentiments crystalize what it means for God to be with us in Christ and for us to imitate Christ in being with one another. In this spirit the poignancy of these words of Bonhoeffer's *Ethics*, written in prison, becomes piercingly clear:

In Christ the reconciliation of the world with God took place. The world will be overcome not by destruction but by reconciliation. Not ideals or programs, not conscience, duty, responsibility, or virtue, but only the consummate love of God can meet and overcome reality. Again, this is accomplished not by a general idea of love, but by the love of God really lived in Jesus Christ. This love of God for the world does not withdraw from reality into noble souls detached from the world, but experiences and suffers the reality of the world at its worst. The world exhausts its rage on the body of Jesus Christ. But the martyred one forgives the world its sins. Thus reconciliation takes place. *Ecce homo.*[35]

Here he is clearly speaking of his own imitation of Christ in being with Germany.

It is instructive to look back to how Bonhoeffer had anticipated these commitments in his words in *Life Together*, as follows:

The first service one owes to others in the community involves listening to them. Just as our love for God begins with listening to God's Word, the beginning of love for other Christians is learning to listen to them. ... The other service one should perform for another person in a Christian community is active helpfulness. ... Those who worry about the loss of time entailed by such small, external acts of helpfulness are usually taking their own work too seriously. ... Third, we speak of the service involved in bearing with others. ... The law of Christ is a law of forbearance. Forbearance means endurance and suffering. … In suffering and enduring human beings, God maintained community with them. It is the law of Christ that was fulfilled in the cross. Christians share in this law.[36]

Finally, in his *Ethics*, Bonhoeffer brings together the first, second, and third defining moments of his life in the following section. This short passage holds profound resonances of how the resolutions he made in June 1939, June 1940, and October 1944 coalesce in a Christological formulation. It is a perfect summary of how Bonhoeffer's life and death were constituted by being with:

> [Love] is the reality of being drawn and drawing others into an event, namely, into God's community with the world, which has already been accomplished in Jesus Christ. [Love] does not exist as an abstract attribute of God but only in God's actual loving of human beings and the world. Again, "love" does not exist as a human attribute but only as a real belonging-together and being-together of people with other human beings and with the world, based on God's love that is extended to me and to them.[37]

It is because love "does not exist as an abstract attribute of God" but *existed* as the "belonging-together and being-together" of Dietrich Bonhoeffer "with other human beings and with the world" that Bonhoeffer deserves to be regarded as the epitome of being with. The three key moments of his life are the places where the veil between heaven and earth is especially thin, and God's divinity is most evidently shown in Bonhoeffer's humanity. They are moments when Bonhoeffer's with most aptly reflects Christ's with, a with that embodies God's being with the world.

What we have seen is that the key moments of Bonhoeffer's story are episodes where he most keenly identifies with Jesus' birth and death. They are moments of embodying Christ's incarnation and crucifixion. Bonhoeffer embodies Christ's incarnation in the way he realizes he has to be with Germany, be with the conspirators, and be with his brother and brother-in-law, however flawed and fallen and fragile this fellowship might be. Jesus' incarnation united his divine and human nature: it did not, at a stroke, redeem human nature, but it identified human nature and destiny definitively and permanently with the nature of God. This is the most evident outcome of God's decision never to be except to be with us in Christ. Despite the damaged character of human nature, the incarnation did not besmirch the divine nature of Jesus: but it certainly exposed Jesus to the distress of

the thousand natural shocks that flesh is heir to; most extremely, crucifixion. Bonhoeffer was committed to be with his nation, with his family, and
with those who, like him, discerned they could not look to others for an end
to governmental insanity. These commitments led him into danger, into
detention, and into death. This is how he embodied Christ's crucifixion. He
took on the sins of his people, and the pathos of a pacifist joining the plot
against Hitler is that it raised the fear for him that being with, and being
faithful to, his people might make him somehow less with, and less faithful
to, God.

Perhaps the most tangible sense of Pentecost in Bonhoeffer's biography is
his experience with the international ecumenical movement, and the depth
of the relationships he made there. The fact that his final message before his
execution was directed to George Bell expresses that debt, and its significance, succinctly. Being with, for Bonhoeffer, was not just a sober matter of
incarnate humanity, or the inevitability of crucified sacrifice; it was also the
Pentecostal joy of wondrous companionship across time and space.

In his epiphany in New York – in his realization that he had made a
mistake in coming to America, and needed to live through this difficult
period of their national history with the Christian people of Germany –
Bonhoeffer displays the kind of epiphany that has appeared repeatedly
in the new developments in theology in recent generations. Theologians
have realized more and more kinds of people that they are called to be
with, because God has always been with such people. Increasingly, for
example, theologians who have seen how God is with those oppressed
due to race, class, disability, age, or gender, are describing how God is
also with the created ecological order and how Christians are called to be
with the creation in a corresponding way. This being with is not simply
incarnate – it is subject to the experience of crucifixion, resurrection, and
Pentecost too.

And what of the Jews? It may be said that Bonhoeffer spoke up for the
Jews. But I would suggest that, in the light of the argument I have been
making, Bonhoeffer did not so much speak up for the Jews as perceive the
Jews as part of the Germany with whom he was called to abide.[38] The failure
of the church in Germany in the Nazi era was obviously a failure to *do*. But
prior to that it was much more fundamentally a failure to *see* – to see the
Jews as those whom Christians were called to be with. The parable of the
Last Judgment (Matt. 25:31–46) is often interpreted as a call to activism; but
it is more fundamentally an identification of those the church is called to be
with. In the same spirit, Jesus' words in John 12 that "the poor will always

be with you" presuppose that the majority of church members throughout its history have always *been* poor.[39] They are words that identify the poor as those the church is always called to be, or at least to be with.

One of Saul Alinsky's most uncompromising rules, repeatedly expressed by his successor Ernie Cortés, is, as we saw in Chapter 7, "Never do for others what they can do for themselves."[40] Bonhoeffer's return to Germany, his joining the plot to kill Hitler, and his renunciation of escape from prison – the three defining moments of his life – were not actions for others. They were actions of solidarity empowering others to act for themselves. This is a profound challenge to conventional notions of activism, in the churches and elsewhere. Take the Millennium Development Goals as an example. These are ambitious targets, largely identified by Western experts, almost entirely to be realized in developing world contexts. They are not, as we saw in Chapter 3, based on indigenous practical wisdom, on small, reversible steps, or on nuanced understandings of local histories, climate, rites of passage, conflicts, or health maps.[41] They are the thinking of what William Easterly calls "planners" rather than "searchers" – in other words, they are concerned with a superimposed blueprint rather than an engaged, listening presence.[42] In my language they are about achieving outcomes "for" people without the extensive and time-consuming commitment to be "with" them. By contrast Bonhoeffer had no plan when he returned to Germany. He had no plan when he renounced escape from prison. William Easterly, reflecting on years of failure in world development, insists, "The right plan is to have no plan."[43] He would be proud of Bonhoeffer.

In this sense, Bonhoeffer's most radical step was to become an educator. In setting up the seminary at Finkenwalde, Bonhoeffer trained students, as Alinsky and Cortés would have advised, to learn to do what they could do for themselves. In *Life Together*, Bonhoeffer's whole attention is upon the challenge, gift, imperative and grace of learning and "being with" one another. In that sense, and in the light of my argument, we can see *Life Together* as the book that sums up Bonhoeffer's theology – as well as his own life. We *can* find life, it claims – so long as we do so together.

In his dissertation *Sanctorum Communio*, commenting on Galatians 6:2 ("Bear one another's burdens"), Bonhoeffer says, "The possibility of this 'being-with-one-another' does not rest on human will. It exists only in the community of saints, and goes beyond the ordinary sense of 'being-with-one-another.' It belongs to the sociological structure of the church community."[44] The challenge Dietrich Bonhoeffer presents is to make "being with" the sociological structure of the church.

Being With One Another in Jerusalem

In this extended discussion of the narratives of George Bell and Dietrich Bonhoeffer I set out to illustrate what Yoder calls "the concrete social meaning of the cross" and to draw parallels, even equivalences, between that meaning and the language of "being with." I have sought to dispel any quietist notion of being with by demonstrating the kinds of commitments being with entails. I have argued that, while being with is rooted and grounded in the Nazareth of abiding, patient presence, it is also integral to both the Galilee of constructive common action and the Jerusalem of vicarious sacrificial courage. All three are found in the narratives of Bell and Bonhoeffer.

To what extent does the human dynamic of being with one another resemble God's being with God? I shall now briefly review the qualities of the latter (as detailed in Chapter 8) through the lens of the former.

Both Bell and Bonhoeffer's witness depends on *presence*. That was the heart of the crucial conversation between the two men in the spring of 1939. Bell was such a figure in the ecumenical movement, in parliamentary debates, in refugee support, because he was incarnately present in his diocese, among his people, living through the hungry thirties and the war years just as they were. Bonhoeffer realized he could only be a witness for Germany if he was with the German people. He could only be part of Germany's future if he was part of its present, even if – perhaps only if – he did not have a plan.

Likewise the two men's narratives presuppose loving *attention* – to God, to the church, local and ecumenical, to their respective peoples, to one another. In a certain way Bonhoeffer's whole project in returning to Germany in 1939 rested on his confidence in the quality of his attention – that is, that he understood and saw and read and heard the German people more truly than Hitler had, and that the future of Germany was closer to his perception than to that of the Nazis. The condition of *disponibilité* is an apt description of Bonhoeffer's disposition throughout the 1930s.

The term *mystery* similarly articulates the nature of the questions facing Bell and especially Bonhoeffer. Germany wasn't a problem to be fixed. Carpet bombing was not the answer; and, it turned out, assassinating Hitler was not the answer either. To return to Marcel's distinction, cited in Chapter 8, "A problem is something which I meet, which I find complete before me, but which I can therefore lay siege to and reduce. A mystery is something in which I myself am involved." Both Bonhoeffer and Bell realized that the German crisis was something with which they were, in this sense, involved. Bonhoeffer's faith enabled him to see the abundance of Germany – that there was a Germany beyond Hitler, outside the imagination of Nazism, out of which postwar reconstruction could emerge.

And so to *delight*. To those who are familiar with Bell's extensive wartime engagements, his care of refugees, his interventions in the House of Lords and in the convocation of Canterbury, his ecumenical engagements, and his writing, not to mention his diocesan responsibilities, it is almost incredible to behold him hosting a conference at the Palace in Chichester for four days in September 1944 attended by such figures as T.S. Eliot, Dorothy Sayers, and Henry Moore. Here was a man not merely interested and active in the reconstruction of international order in Europe; his vision was for the reconciliation and flourishing of Christianity and all aspects of life, not just in conditions of strife and deprivation but equally of the vision glorious. Ronald Jasper summarizes Bell's vision for the arts.

> Throughout all his efforts to further the association of the Church and the arts, Bell was impressed by the need for spiritual unity. The life of the Spirit had been gravely threatened by the mechanization of culture no less than by dictatorship and war; and it could only be strengthened and sustained by communion with the Creator. Such communion required expression in a life in which contemplation and service combined: and it was in the developing of this communion that Bell realized the artist had a contribution to make in re-association with the Church.[45]

The many activities of parish life – printing a magazine, digging a churchyard path, sewing altar linen, embroidering vestments, mending books – all of these had sacramental quality, reuniting people with beauty through communion with God and one another, and implicitly challenging the world to be renewed in the same way. Even in the intensity of sacrificial attention, Bell found delight.

The choice of subject-matter for this chapter presupposes *participation* and *partnership*. Bell and Bonhoeffer understood that there is nothing of eternal value that can be achieved or secured in isolation from other beings; what makes their participation more fascinating is that they found that conviction exemplified nowhere more deeply than in one another. They realized that the story was not, finally, about themselves – and certainly there could be no story of any abiding truth that did not have a place for each other. And yet part of the poignancy of the spring 1939 meeting between the two men was what I am calling partnership – that sense that they had complementary, but nonetheless quite different, roles to play, and neither could perform his own role with the same sureness of hand if he had not known that his friend was playing the corresponding role. Bell's parliamentary witness assumed that there were Germans of courage and integrity; Bonhoeffer's engagement with the conspiracy assumed that there were Allies of mercy and a desire for a justice that was not simply contained in the word "victory."

The final two dimensions of God's being with God, enjoyment and glory, are amply fulfilled in the story of Bonhoeffer and Bell. This becomes clear perhaps most explicitly in their meeting in Sweden in May 1942. Edwin Robertson succinctly summarizes the circumstances surrounding this occasion.

> Plans were afoot for a dramatic *coup d'état* to which Bonhoeffer was privy. Its success would, of course, depend on having the right support in Germany. And that depended upon some word of encouragement from Britain. A message and an explanation had to be communicated to Churchill, or at least to Anthony Eden [the Foreign Secretary]. It is likely that the conspirators overestimated Bell's influence and underestimated his unpopularity. However, for a meeting with Bell, Bonhoeffer was the natural choice as courier.[46]

This extraordinary rendezvous seems more the material of a spy thriller than a genuine moment in history. It produced no result because in the thick of war there was no notion of *enjoying* – only using. Churchill had no time for any initiative that might in any way undermine the sacrifices he was calling the British people to make, and had no hesitation in pointing out the number of promises and undertakings already broken from within Germany. Does Bell's enjoyment look naïve? Or does Churchill's use look cynical? Perhaps both. This was an extreme circumstance. What is clear is that Bell and Bonhoeffer's complete (divine) enjoyment of one another – with no thought to use – made conceivable an alternative path to peace; a road not taken. The alternative, the path of use, assumed total war.

Such *glory* as Bonhoeffer and Bell knew was eschatological. Their glory was that they never forgot the true telos – even when everyone around them had. Such a realized, embodied, final cause is, perhaps, the very heart of being with.

Notes

1. John Howard Yoder, *The Politics of Jesus: Behold the Man! Our Glorious Lamb*, 2nd edition (Grand Rapids, MI: Eerdmans, 1994): 130–131.
2. Ronald C. D. Jasper, *George Bell: Bishop of Chichester* (London: Oxford University Press, 1967): 257.

3. Ibid.

4. Ibid.: 273.

5. Ibid.: 274.

6. One could describe this stance as being for, or even working for, given that Bell was not physically with the German people; but in that he put solidarity as the focus of his efforts, it still more nearly resembles being with than the other two categories.

7. Jasper, *George Bell*: 276

8. E. G. Rupp, *"I Seek My Brethren": Bishop George Bell and the German Churches* (London: Epworth Press): 16–17.

9. E. H. Robertson, *Unshakeable Friend: George Bell and the German Churches* (London: CCBI): 66.

10. Ibid., 69.

11. Dietrich Bonhoeffer, *Dietrich Bonhoeffer Works, Volume 8: Letters and Papers from Prison* (Minneapolis, MN: Fortress Press, 2010): 486.

12. Ibid.: 447–448.

13. Edwin Robertson, *The Shame and the Sacrifice: The Life and Preaching of Dietrich Bonhoeffer* (London: Hodder and Stoughton, 1987): 172.

14. Ibid.

15. Bonhoeffer was subject to the draft because he had been born in 1906.

16. Eberhard Bethge, *Dietrich Bonhoeffer: A Biography*, revised edition(Minneapolis, MN: Fortress Press, 2000): 637.

17. Ibid.: 638.

18. Ibid.: 639.

19. Ibid.: 996 n.105.

20. Keith Clements, *Bonhoeffer and Britain* (London: Churches Together in Britain and Ireland, 2006): 100.

21. Robertson, *The Shame and the Sacrifice*: 187.

22. Bethge: 682.

23. Ibid.

24. Quoted in Robertson, *The Shame and the Sacrifice*: 174.

25. Dietrich Bonhoeffer, *Dietrich Bonhoeffer Works, Volume 6: Ethics* (Minneapolis, MN: Fortress Press, 2005): 275.

26. Robertson, *The Shame and the Sacrifice*: 175.

27. Bonhoeffer, *Letters and Papers from Prison*: 52. This quotation is longer than the one Robertson cites, which concludes at "Are we still of any use?"

28. Bonhoeffer, *Letters and Papers from Prison*: 467–468; see also Robertson, *Bonhoeffer's Heritage: The Christian Way in a World Without Religion* (London: Hodder and Stoughton, 1989): 178.

29. Eberhard Bethge, *Bonhoeffer Gedenkheft* (Berlin: Haus und Schule, 1947): 9. I am grateful to Rebekah Eklund for discovering this document.

30. Robertson, *The Shame and the Sacrifice*: 261.

31. Bethge: 827–828.
32. Bonhoeffer, *Letters and Papers from Prison*: 45.
33. Ibid.: 49.
34. Ibid.: 493.
35. Bonhoeffer, *Ethics*: 82–83.
36. Dietrich Bonhoeffer, *Dietrich Bonhoeffer Works, Volume 5: Life Together* (Minneapolis, MN: Fortress Press, 1996): 98, 99, 100, 101.
37. Bonhoeffer, *Ethics*: 241.
38. This is trespassing on complex and disputed territory. Stephen R. Haynes, *The Bonhoeffer Legacy: Post-Holocaust Perspectives* (Minneapolis, MN: Fortress Press, 2006), argues that Bonhoeffer always had a paradoxical view of the Jews, as both God's chosen people and the people who uniquely rejected God and murdered Jesus (106–107). Thus: "Nowhere does Bonhoeffer encourage Christians to view Jews simply as human beings whose rights must be respected. For Bonhoeffer, the Jew is always the other who is also Christ's brother; the other with whom is tied up the fate of the West; the other whose suffering reflects God's providence and whose treatment discloses the moral condition of church and society. Bonhoeffer's commitment to defend Jews may have formed the basis for a theology of solidarity with others more generally, but he never conflated the two categories" (142). According to Haynes, Bethge tries to make the point of Bonhoeffer's "deep solidarity" with the Jewish people, but Haynes remains skeptical. Haynes complains: "Bonhoeffer's use of [*Judenfrage*], coupled with his claim that the church exists wherever Jew and German 'stand together under the Word of God,' gave unwitting credence to a conviction … that 'Jews' were an alien people whose very existence posed a threat to ethnic Germans" (67).
39. Stanley Hauerwas, "The Appeal of Judas," in *A Cross-Shattered Church* (Grand Rapids, MI: Brazos Press, 2009): 95. Hauerwas writes, "The one who said 'You always have the poor with you' was poor himself. … Christianity is determinatively the faith of the poor. That is why we, the moderately well off, are puzzled by the undeniable reality that the church across time and space has been constituted by the poor" (95).
40. Jeffrey Stout, *Blessed Are the Organized: Grassroots Democracy in America* (Princeton, NJ: Princeton University Press, 2010): 136. See also Saul D. Alinsky, *Rules for Radicals: A Practical Primer for Realistic Radicals* (New York: Random House, 1971).
41. The most articulate advocate of such approaches is James C. Scott. For his notion of metis, see his *Seeing Like a State: How Certain Schemes to Improve the Human Condition Have Failed* (New Haven, CT: Yale University Press, 1999).
42. William Easterly, *The White Man's Burden: Why the West's Efforts to Aid the Rest Have Done So Much Ill and So Little Good* (New York: The Penguin Press, 2006): 3–32. I acknowledge this is a generous reading of Easterly. In Easterly's

eyes Searchers are still trying to "solve problems" and thus continue to embody a "working for" model: "Planners fail to search for what does work to help the poor. … Yet Searchers in aid are already finding things that help the poor" (12). The commitment to "being with" on Easterly's terms is valid to the extent that it leads to a more effective working for and/or working with. The goal is still to help the poor. The key point, for Easterly, is that one goes in with no *preconceived* plan. Bonhoeffer clearly had a plan, in joining the plot against Hitler. But it was not a preconceived plan in that it did not predate his return to Germany.

43. Ibid.: 5.
44. Dietrich Bonhoeffer, *Dietrich Bonhoeffer Works, Volume 1: Sanctorum Communio* (Minneapolis, MN: Fortress Press, 1998): 180. In fact, Bonhoeffer writes about the inseparability of being-with and being-for, when he discusses "the social acts that constitute the community of love" (i.e., the church): "(1) Church-community and church member being structurally 'with-each-other' [*Miteinander*] as appointed by God and (2) the members' active 'being-for-each-other' [*Füreinander*] and the principle of vicarious representative action [*Stellvertretung*]. In reality, however, one is possible only through the other; they depend on each other" (*SC*, 178). "This being-for-each-other must now be actualized through acts of love [i.e., through being and acting for one another]" (*SC*, 184). I do not regard this as a convincing argument for the complementarity of being with and being for – I believe it invites an expanded notion of being with, which is what I seek to offer in this chapter.
45. Ibid.: 134.
46. Ibid.: 84–85.

Part IV

Explorations

Having in Part III set out the dimensions of being with, and illustrated the notion in a broad but not comprehensive range of contexts, the question that next needs addressing is: how far does this renarration of Christian theology and ethics go?

Here in Part IV I offer the beginnings of an answer to that question. A fuller treatment would take each of the conventional loci of theology and address them through the lens of each of the eight dimensions of being with, as outlined in Chapter 8. A fuller ethical enquiry would in similar vein explore what presence, attention, mystery and so on would mean for ecological questions or euthanasia or the just war. Such exploration would fill at least two further volumes.

What instead I attempt to do here is to offer two chapters, one broadly in the area of theology and the other in the area of ethics, that hint and gesture toward what a renarration through the lens of with might look like. The theological chapter takes some key themes such as creation, salvation, and eschatology, and digs a little further into each one in the spirit of with. These proposals are not conclusive, but suggestive. The ethical chapter adopts a different approach: there I take one form of community development, known as asset-based community development – a model I perceive as deeply in sympathy with the trajectory of my overall argument – and explore its extent and potential through the eight dimensions of being with outlined in Chapter 8.

If the book has succeeded the reader will want more than this part can provide – and my proposals will stimulate further and deeper discussion in these and many other areas.

A Nazareth Manifesto, Samuel Wells © 2015 John Wiley & Sons, Ltd. Published 2015 by John Wiley & Sons, Ltd.

13

Theological Ramifications

The contention of this book is that with is the most important word in theology. The purpose of this chapter is to investigate how far-reaching are the theological ramifications of that claim. To entirely renarrate theology through the lens of with would be a whole new project. Here I attempt no more than to touch on some key contours of what that might involve, by exploring creation, redemption, and fulfillment – thereby offering a sense of what might lie elsewhere.

Creation

In Chapter 3 we considered the proposal that the essential problem of human existence, widely thought to be mortality, is, in fact, isolation. Here we may push the question one stage further back. What is the fundamental purpose of creation – what is creation's final cause? There are two traditional answers to this question. The first answer is that creation arises from God's overflowing goodness, understood as God's profound selflessness. This goodness issues in a creation brought about for the sake of the creatures. Creation was thus triggered because God already loved that which had not yet been made. The second answer takes the opposite view: it suggests that creation occurred as an expression of God's perfection. Thus creation is a demonstration of the glory of God – regardless of whether anyone else is watching; it is a perfect synthesis of power and glory. From the point of view of this study, both conventional answers display the poverty of an imagination dominated by for. The notion of for assumes imbalance, assumes a gesture of goodness that disadvantages the one to benefit the other. Such an imbalance is not assumed from the perspective of with. With does not assume all is equivalence: that is, the difference between participation,

A Nazareth Manifesto, Samuel Wells © 2015 John Wiley & Sons, Ltd. Published 2015 by John Wiley & Sons, Ltd.

which is side-by-side with a disappearance of differences, and partnership, which is complementary in its affirmation of different but indispensable contributions.

Creation thus arises from God's desire to be with us – generally, in flourishing life, in presence, attention, mystery, and so on – but pivotally and definitively in Jesus, whose virgin birth and resurrection are both inherent in the creation. If creation is rooted in with, rather than for, we need not be distracted by the imbalance of whom creation is for – whether creation is for us or for God. There is, from the perspective of with, no inconsistency between the two. Indeed, creation is not principally *for* anybody – God or us. Creation is to bring about with. With means creation is God's decision never to be except to be with us. We have no existence without this original decision; we have no flourishing without the participation and partnership that make up our side of creation. Creation is not inherently necessary to God, because the inner life of the Trinity already offers a plenitude of with; but creation becomes inseparable from our knowledge of God, since without the original decision to be with us, nothing whatsoever could be known by us, for good or ill.

The incarnation is the epitome of with; together with the resurrection, it is the epistemological center of a theology conceived around the notion of with. The question that discloses the dividing line between a theology grounded in with and a theology rooted in for is, as we saw in Chapter 4, "If there had been no fall, would Christ still have come?" A theology rooted in for invariably replies, "No – since what would there be for the Messiah to do?" Such a perspective presupposes sin, in that it makes Christ's humanity dependent on a deficit – on a problem to be solved. By contrast a theology oriented to and shaped by with takes for granted that Christ would have become incarnate had there been no fall – since Christ being incarnate was the *raison d'être* of the universe. The incarnation is the heart of a mystery, not the solution to a problem. Irenaeus writes, "Since the Savior was preexistent, it was necessary that what was to be saved come to be, lest the Savior be pointless."[1] From our point of view, this makes a crucial point, but is still only half right. The crucial point is that the humanity of the Son is prior to the existence of the world: that the incarnation is prior to the fall; that God's desire to be in relationship is the trigger for the universe's coming into being. But a theology of with assumes more than this. It does not define the Son through the lens of the term "Savior": the Son is the principal, determinative way in which God is with us – but God is with us not primarily to do things for us, even to secure our salvation; God is with us because that is the purpose of creation. Immanuel is prior to Savior. God's working for is subordinate to and designed to restore God's being with. The fall does not determine the shape or character or purpose of God; such things are defined by the original decision of God – the decision to be with.

The notion of being with sheds further light when we consider God's providence and human agency and the vexed question of free will. In discussing the resurrection, Paul says, "By the grace of God I am what I am, and his grace toward me has not been in vain. On the contrary, I worked harder than any of them – though it was not I, but the grace of God that is with me" (1 Cor. 15:10). In this simple phrase, "the grace of God that is with me," Paul offers a window on how the notion of with can reshape an understanding of agency. From the perspective of for, agency is a zero-sum equation: either we act for ourselves, or God acts for us, to bring about an outcome, distant or proximate, in the interests of creation's fulfillment, if not always of our own immediate well-being. This creates a host of philosophical problems, from the integrity of human action, to theodicy, to the nature and purpose of intercessory prayer. But from the perspective of with, so much changes. God does not seek to act for us; God seeks always to act with us. God seeks to act through what Paul describes as "the grace of God that is with me." Pure act is therefore action that is wholly God's and wholly ours. There remains a difference between participation and partnership. Some acts are ones of participation: we and God seem perfectly aligned and wholly in tune, walking step by step with a shared melody. Others are ones of partnership: we and God are playing different tunes, and walking at different paces, but are nonetheless in harmony. Grace may be present either as participation or partnership; it is God's attention, and ours, that discerns the difference. The Chalcedonian formula, which presents Jesus as two natures in one person, shows how Christ embodies the with that is at the heart of God's intention for all creation: full human will and full divine will in melody and harmony.

It is perhaps theodicy that shows the difference between a theology of for and a theology of with most sharply. In the words of the Jewish actor and director Woody Allen, "You know, if it turns out that there is a God, I don't think that he's evil. I think that the worst you can say about him is that, basically, he's an underachiever."[2] Such a view, in Christian terms, can be traced back to a view of Israel's season in exile.

Here is a one reading of the story. God delivered the chosen people from Egypt and made a covenant with them, with Promised Land and king and temple as its outward signs. But disobedient people lost land, king, and temple, and went into exile in Babylon, and stayed there 50 years – and even when many of them returned they did not have a king and they did not govern the land and the ark of the covenant was lost and it was only a partial restoration of the glory they had left behind. But God visited the people in their internal exile and came in human form. In signs and words Christ proclaimed that the exile was finally over, and that God's promise to redeem the whole world through Israel was fulfilled. By raising Christ from the dead God changed the notion of exile from Babylon to earth and changed the notion of Promised Land from a restored territory to a heavenly destiny. Henceforward the tension in Christian life is between material, transitory earth and spiritual, eternal heaven, and the question always is, "How much of the limitless reserves of heaven is God prepared to bring forward into the current account of earth? Given the exponential everlasting inheritance, how big is the tangible downpayment?" The prayer is always, "Thy will be done on earth as it is in heaven," and the longing is that, "The earth shall be filled with the glory of the God as the waters cover the sea," and the cry is the Advent cry of "How long, O Lord, how long?"

And it is due to this configuration that God always appears to be an underachiever – because the advance payment never seems to be adequate. We never seem to get enough heaven on earth to reassure us that the full dose is coming later. To return to Woody Allen's way of putting the matter, "If only God would give me some clear sign! Like making a large deposit in my name at a Swiss bank." We get into the habit of constantly deferring the expectation of God's fulfilling our earthly needs, let alone desires. And this habit gradually transposes from wondering why God won't fully reveal the final glory to assuming God is unable to do so.

But the notion of with invites a slightly different telling of the story. The Trinity is utter relationship – Father, Son, and Spirit are boundlessly open and available to one another, utterly attending and present to one another, constantly responding and understanding and listening and reflecting. God is constantly looking to expand this circle of relationship, this utter presence and attention and delight and partnership. Israel is the name we give to the people through whom God sought to extend this partnership to all creation. Like all relationships, the love between God and Israel has two dangers. Either Israel becomes too *independent*, and sees God as an appendage it can cast off and God's action as an instrument it can use or neglect at will. Or Israel becomes too *dependent*, and is so needy that it never finds abundant life because it is constantly lurching from one crisis to the next.

How does God address this problem? What we see is a thread that runs through the Old Testament by which God is made known to people in situations of adversity. God is not simply the rescuer. A series of people in the most daunting moments in their lives become aware that God's purpose was not to fix the world or to fix them, but to be with them and share life with them at least as much if not more in adversity than in times of plenty. Hagar laments her situation, facing the death of her son Ishmael. But, says Genesis 21:20, "God was with the boy." Jacob ran away from conflict with his brother Esau. God wrestled with Jacob all night in a microcosm of Israel's experience of the God who, in doubt and sorrow and wilderness and wandering, will never let us go (Gen. 32:22–32). Elijah ran away so much that God continually asked, "What are you doing here, Elijah?", but finally met God not in the fire, or the earthquake, but in the sound of an echoing silence (1 Kings 19:5–18). Shadrach, Meshach, and Abednego, who were not saved from Nebuchadnezzar's fiery furnace but found in the midst of the fire that there was one with them who looked like God (Dan. 3:1–30).

These stories, as we saw in Chapter 3, portray in different ways the experience of Israel in exile in Babylon. God had not rescued them: yet they felt closer to God at what was assumed to be the lowest moment in Israel's history than they had ever felt during the times of plenty in the Promised Land. That is the discovery on which the whole Bible rests. This time in exile was the period when the Bible was written. The story of the Old Testament is precisely this: that Israel had always assumed that God was the liberator, and that the covenant made at Sinai was a guarantee that God would continue to liberate Israel forever and a day as long as was necessary. But in exile in Babylon Israel was learning that God is not a device, like a get out of jail card in a Monopoly game; God is longing to be in relationship with us. The covenant is not a contract that we wave in God's face when we feel let down: it's a token of the entire purpose of God to be with us in good times and bad.

This means the coming of Jesus is not the final, grandest rescue act of them all. It's the utter manifestation of God's commitment to be with us, come what may. Eternal life without God is useless to us: it's no more than a perpetual prison. God is offering us something much richer, much deeper, much more challenging and wonderful: everlasting relationship, a relationship that holds through adversity, danger, disaster, and death. As soon as we ask the question, "Do I get eternal life out of this?" it is proof positive that we want something else more than we want the relationship.

But for God it is always about the covenant. The Christian faith does not have a prescription for how God fixes our problems. It does not have a simple formula for how and when healing happens or how and when eternal life follows death. Instead, Christians simply believe that the greatest power in the universe is God's desire to be in relationship with us. And that desire and that relationship are stronger than the other forces in our lives – evil, sin, and death. To be a Christian means to be transformed by the discovery that God is with us in such a way that we stop noticing or counting what God does for us. It's not about the *for*. It's about the *with*.

Such an argument identifies the distortion of faith and of God involved in the conventional quest known as theodicy. But it still leaves open the more general question – why there is evil and sin and suffering in the world if the God who created the world is good. This question is often approached as a problem but from our point of view it should rather be considered as a mystery. Cross and resurrection do not fix this problem; miracles do not or would not; in part because it is not a problem but rather a mystery. If the human predicament is that of mortality and limitation, evil and suffering are major problems – *the* major problems – that need to be fixed. But if the human predicament is that of isolation, the evil and suffering are contexts – challenging ones, granted, but not determinative ones – in which to explore, exercise, attempt, practice, and display the with. Jesus says, "Let us go to Judea again." Let us enter the mystery. The disciples reply, "Rabbi, the Jews were just now trying to stone you, and are you going there again?" Judea is a problem – if we cannot fix it, let us avoid it. Thomas answers differently: "Let us also go, that we may die with him." Let us enter the mystery (John 11:7–16). And the reward for entering the mystery, as Jesus reminds Martha, is something those who perceive only a problem could not imagine: "Did I not tell you that if you believed, you would see the glory of God?" (John 11:40).

The Power and the Glory

The exchange between Jesus and Martha at the entrance to Lazarus' tomb discloses perhaps the most evocative distinction between for and with. The long history of alchemy involved a cluster of secrets that promised to turn base metals into gold and create a "philosopher's stone" that could bring about rejuvenation and usher in immortality. Today in the West we expend far greater energy, and shape our lives far more systematically, on a similar search: the quest for power. This relentless quest for power has its own philosopher's stone. And that elixir is power over death. That is why medicine is the greatest focus of worship in Western culture: because it appears to promise this elusive power – power not just to prolong or enhance life, but power over death itself.

From the point of view of our study, this quest for power is based on a fundamental mistake. The problem with power is not just that power over death, which is the goal of all quests for power, is and will remain out of our reach – although that is true. The problem is that our quest for power, and for the eternal life we hope that power will bring, is one colossal detour from the quest on which God invites us and the gift that God truly offers us. This accumulation of power is one enormous insurance policy against there being no God. But the insurance policy fails because it is unable to deliver eternal life – which is the one thing for which we need it. What God offers us more than anything else is not power. What God offers us is glory.

Glory, as we saw in Chapter 8, is the culmination of all the layers of being with. Glory is more than praise or fame. Praise is one-way and conversational; glory is shared and beyond words. Fame is empty and transitory; glory is wondrous and eternal. Holiness is part of the identity of God; glory is something that comes to fulfillment as God shares it with us, like a cloud that billows out as we enter it. Ecstasy is a word that conjures up the intensity of glory – the sense that everything else pales by comparison. But ecstasy is an out-of-the-body experience we discover on our own, whereas glory is deeper than the ordinary rather than outside it, something we fundamentally share with God and others. Joy is something wondrous and godly and eternal, but joy is simple and direct whereas glory is mysterious and trembling in a fabulous place beyond joy.

Glory is the wonder of the full presence of God that reveals God's utter desire to be present to us in joy and delight and attention and love; and at the same time it is the magnetic, billowing aura that draws us inexorably into intimate, thrilling, everlasting, and fulfilling discovery of our destiny in God. It is both the cloud of unknowing and the seeing God face to face, all at the same time. But it not for keeping; it is something for sharing. Glory is what God created us to enter, to enjoy, and to share. Glory is the complete and overwhelming revelation of God's character: God's character is ever-expanding, ever-embracing, ever-enfolding enjoyment of us.

A theology based on for is always in danger of making one key mistake. That mistake is to think we need the power to get the glory. Glory seems elusive and distant, whereas power is something tangible and only just out of reach. So we concentrate all our energy on getting the power. We sacrifice, we train, we betray, we lie, cheat, and steal to get the power; we dream about the power, work to get the power, shape our whole existence to get the power. But then we face a double tragedy. Either we fail in our quest, and we die regretting that we never *got* the power, influence, recognition, strength, achievement, money, acclaim – yet still believing as much as ever that our quest is really about the power. Or, even worse, we *do* get the power, and we have turned our whole life to get the power, so we have nothing left to offer when we realize that the power does not get us anything – certainly not the glory. In other words we die a poor fool or a rich fool. This is the pathos of the philosophy and ethic of for.

But the philosophy and ethic of with maintains that the power is not the way to get the glory. On the contrary, the glory is the way to get the power. It is not that power is pointless, useless, or wrong. There is a kind of power that comes from God, and it is precisely what the alchemy of human quests for power has always searched for. It is the resurrection of the dead. But this is the crucial point that turns with from a theology into an ethic: you only discover that power if you are prepared to enter the glory. The Word became flesh and lived among us, and the disciples saw his glory – in other words they saw in Jesus God's ever-expanding, ever-embracing, ever-enfolding enjoyment of each one of us. The cross, where Jesus was emptied of every ounce of power, where Jesus hung naked, stripped, shamed, humiliated, defenseless, was the moment more than any other when we behold his glory – his ever-expanding, ever-embracing, ever-enfolding encircling of us. If we discover the glory of the cross, we shall receive the power of the resurrection. That is the Christian faith. There is no true power that is not discovered through glory.

Despite the misapprehension of the church, which has often thought it needed the power to see the glory, God continues to disclose true power through the power of the resurrection. Resurrection is power subsumed into glory. Eternal life is not a product of our power. It is a side-effect of God's glory. The ethical message of the resurrection is this: seek the glory, and you will be given the power. Seek only the power, and you will never find your way to the glory.

Graham Greene's novel *The Power and the Glory* is set in Mexico in the 1930s.[3] The Mexican government is determined to suppress the Catholic Church, sending paramilitary groups into the provinces to persecute priests. The story centers on a whisky priest, a flawed and fallible man who has fathered a child, likes a drink, and is always on the run. Pursuing him is a lieutenant of the police, a disciplined socialist who wants to obliterate the church. Two factors inhibit the priest's escape. First, he truly loves his child, awkward and ugly as she is, and shameful as her existence may be. Second, he comes out of hiding to hear the confession of a dying man – even though deep down he suspects that he's being lured into a trap. Sure enough, the priest is captured and the lieutenant orders his execution. The lieutenant wins the power, but cannot comprehend the glory. Meanwhile the fallible, gullible, pitiful priest loses all his power: but nonetheless – or maybe consequently – he glimpses, and reveals, the glory. It is almost as if the more fragile and foolish the priest becomes, the more he sees and manifests the glory. The challenge of the story is that, only as the priest, and through him the church, are crucified, do they see the glory. One only truly, finally, fundamentally enters the realm of with if one lets go of the promise and pretension of for.

Atonement

It is not entirely flippant to suggest that, by the terms of this study, the notion of "at-one-ment" might be reconfigured as "re-with-ment." In other words soteriology is usually conceived as the study of the ways through Jesus we are reunited – made once again at one – with God. Whereas soteriology through the lens of with becomes the assessment of the ways we are restored to God's company – the ways we become once more *with* God. To scrutinize this invites a closer study of sin.

"Negative although sin thus is, God's people are from first to last of Scripture given to it, that is, to rebellion against their own communal hope," says Robert Jenson. "God's history with us is decisively shaped by our betrayal of the 'with us.'"[4] Righteousness is being with God; sin is being not-with God – living, or attempting to live, without God. That not-withness can take two, or perhaps three, forms.

One form – perhaps the root form – is idolatry. Idolatry and unbelief may be regarded as similar if not identical, if one assumes it is impossible to live without trust, and not to trust in God requires one to trust in something or someone other than God. God's most notable act of self-description is as a "jealous" God (Exod. 20:5, Deut. 6:15). While envy is the desire to gain something someone else has, jealousy is the determination to retain something one has oneself. Thus jealousy is an appropriate attribute of a God who wants to be with us forever. Idolatry is not just the adopting of the wrong target for devotion or the placing of treasure in clay jars; it is using God as for instead of enjoying God as with. All the layers of being with detailed in Chapter 8 become, in humanity's waiting upon God, ways to prevent us instrumentalizing and objectifying God and therefore lapsing into idolatry. Sin, as construed through idolatry, is our desperate effort not to be with God, and instead to be with anything and everything that is more pliable to our own purposes and constructions. It is not necessarily opposed to being with as such; it is resistant specifically to being with God.

A consequent form of sin is our being not-with not God, but one another. This can surface in a variety of forms. One is being with one another, but in such a way that is not truly with: impoverishing, humiliating, using, toying with the other. These are forms of lust. Love is a true being with the other that is at the same time a true being with God. Lust is an attempt to be with the other without being with God – a furtive, secretive, perhaps hurried and hidden desire to use what is given to be enjoyed. It is relationship without attention, mystery, enjoyment, or glory, but with possession, control, manipulation, and deceit. A similar failure to be with one another is injustice, or, in its extreme form, cruelty. This is the failure to be with the person who is vulnerable, whether by actively taking advantage of and therefore worsening their plight or by passively neglecting to see – to be present and attentive to – their need. It is the deliberate or tacit assumption that there are some people one has no call or obligation to be with. For sure one cannot be with all persons in the same way: discerning how best we are each to be respectively with one another is the business of politics. But injustice and cruelty begin the moment one makes the transition from saying one cannot be with all people in the same way to assuming there are some people one has no need or duty to be with at all. And increasingly the church is coming to understand that such destruction and neglect are just as much features of human interaction with the created order as they concern relation to the human other.

A third form of sin is some kind of hybrid of the first two: being not-with ourselves. Jesus calls us to "love the Lord your God with all your heart, and with all your soul, and with all your mind, and with all your strength;" and "love your neighbor as yourself" (Mark 12:30–31). Thus loving oneself stands alongside loving God and one another. The reluctance to be with oneself, the drowning of solitude in distraction, the abolition of silence and stillness, the rush to fill each unforgiving minute, the translation of aloneness into loneliness, the conversion of disappointment into self-pity: these are all forms of despair. The apparently narcissistic contemporary jargon of self-care can be, at its best, a form of training in what it means to be with oneself. Self-care is not necessarily selfishness or hedonism. Likewise the discomfort in being with oneself is unlikely to be a form of desire to be with others or with God. The ability and willingness to be with oneself are more likely correlatives of the eagerness and desire to be with others and with God. John Wesley counseled his followers to consider themselves as the first among the poor they were called to serve.[5] Being with oneself can be a form of training and preparation for being with one another and with God.

How then, does God overcome sin? How does God achieve "re-with-ment"? The historic notions of atonement divide between working for and working with. The classic theory, by which Jesus defeats death or tricks the devil and is vindicated in the resurrection, and the Anselmian theory, by which Jesus is the perfect sacrifice as a human who is also God (only a human should, only God could) thereby paying the necessary price of sin, are both solidly working-for narratives. The so-called subjective theory, by which Jesus' cross moves the believer to a transformed life, is very much a working-with approach. Is there such a thing as a being-with view of the atonement? In Chapter 5 we saw how Jesus, on the cross, has a choice be-tween being with the Father and being with us; and that in choosing us, Jesus opens out the path of our salvation. This way of telling the story presupposes the claim we explored in Chapter 3: that isolation, rather than mortality, is the fundamental human predicament. Thus by overcoming our isolation, Jesus saves us: his death is the cost of that, rather than the achievement of that. The resurrection is the reassertion that he is not isolated from the Fa-ther forever. Rather as we just saw, that one can only find the power if one is prepared to see the glory, so the resurrection, the overcoming of mortality, is a gift given to Jesus, and thence to us, because he places the overcoming of isolation above the preservation of his own life. Our faithfulness, our disci-pleship, thus resides in the same place: putting being with Jesus and one an-other (the overcoming of isolation) above averting our own mortality. This is the lesson we discovered in the story of Laszlo in Chapter 3.

How does this being with notion of atonement affect our reading of the New Testament? First of all, as we have already claimed, Jesus is Immanuel before he is Savior. For many approaches, Jesus is a rescuer who comes to deliver us from captivity. My argument seeks a different perspective. It in-sists on making God's being with us in Christ the epistemological center of theology: all other wisdom and insight and logic is derived from this conviction. It refuses to begin with the deficit of sin, and see the life of God as shaped to respond to this primordial setback. It makes no claim about the origin or purpose of evil and sin – about whether it arose and abides through God's strength in creating it or through God's weakness in being unable to abolish it or through God's patience in harboring it. Any answers to such questions can only be sought in the narrative of Jesus' cross and resurrection.

In contrast to conventional atonement theories, which portray God orchestrating creation from problem to solution, my argument rests on God's improvisatory love and on the two words that sum up that love: "whatever happens." As we saw in Chapter 9, Jesus' ministry is one of being with his own people, with the disciples, with the crowds, with the authorities, and with the creation. Being with these respective constituencies is what takes Jesus to the cross. The poignancy of the cross is enhanced in that all of these constituencies are represented there to a greater or lesser extent: Nazareth in Mary, the disciples in the beloved disciple, the crowds in the tumultuous onlookers and the neighboring thieves, the authorities in the mocking scribes, and the creation in the darkness and earthquake. Being with God is what brings about the resurrection.

We have seen that sin can, in significant ways, be characterized as being not-with: not-with God, not-with one another, and not-with ourselves. In this abandonment, the crucified Jesus is subject to the full impact of sin – and in this sense it makes sense to say he takes our sin on his shoulders on the cross. But Jesus finds a way to be with us even when we have abandoned him. By saying "Father, forgive them" he is with people who have cruelly been not-with him; by saying "Why have you forsaken me?" he is still in dialogue with the Father who has abandoned him. He embodies the love that is sustained whatever happens. It is this love that overcomes isolation and therefore saves us.

Looking more closely specifically at the cross as the center of the re-with-ment, we may see that at the foot of the cross, in Matthew's account, there are three kinds of mockers. The first are members of the crowd, who say, "You who would destroy the temple and build it in three days, save yourself! If you are the Son of God, come down from the cross." Then there are the chief priests, along with the scribes and elders, who say, "He saved others; he cannot save himself. He is the King of Israel; let him come down from the cross now, and we will believe in him. He trusts in God; let God deliver him now, if he wants to; for he said, 'I am God's Son.'" Finally there are the bandits (a parody of the disciples, who should be being crucified with him) who taunt him in the same way (Matt. 27:38–50). This threefold taunting at the climax of Jesus' ministry echoes the threefold temptation at the outset of his ministry.[6] Both the devil and the mockers goad Jesus with his apparent inactivity. Surely a real divine being would offer fireworks and spectacle, not silent resignation? How can Jesus be the Messiah if he does nothing?

But there is many a true word spoken in jest. Between them this array of mockers gathered around Jesus succeeds in summarizing and affirming almost every truth the Gospel of Matthew seeks to communicate. Of all the ironic statements at the foot of the cross, the most poignant are the words of the temple authorities, who say, "He saved others; he cannot save himself" (27:42). This perfectly sums up the story that Matthew tells. It is a double irony because the authorities think the joke is on Jesus, and that they are identifying the irony that Jesus cannot do for himself what he can do for others. But meanwhile what they cannot see is that the joke is finally on them, because first of all they have been drawn into identifying that Jesus has indeed saved others, a major acknowledgement for them to make, and secondly that there is something unique about Jesus that makes both him and his suffering different from others. And that sums up the gospel. Jesus saves us but at terrible cost to himself.

This is the second miracle in Jerusalem. One is obvious – the miracle of resurrection. The other is more subtle: it is the miracle that Jesus did not come down from the cross. He stayed there. He outlasted humanity's hatred, cruelty, and enmity. After everything the crowds and the authorities could throw at him, physically and verbally, he was still there. His endurance demonstrated the love that holds on, whatever happens – the love that will never let us go. His perseverance showed that nothing can separate us from the love of God. Our isolation has been overcome – from his side: forever after we can connect to God, not through our striving, but through Jesus' suffering, not through our longing, but through his lingering, not through our achieving, but through his abiding.

It is not the Jesus we want. We want the Jesus that comes down from the cross, the Jesus that rights wrong, ends pain, corrects injustice, sends the wicked away empty, sets the record straight, and makes all well with the world. We want answers, we want solutions, we want our problems fixed now. This Jesus will not come down from the cross. This Jesus bears all things, endures all things, and never ends. This is not the God we want. But answers, explanations, solutions – they fail to give us what we fundamentally need in the face of suffering and sin. What we need is love that overcomes our isolation. The passion account displays how little humanity knows its need of that love, how much humanity contributes to its isolation: thus Pilate washes his hands, the disciples run away, Judas loses patience, and Peter settles it with a sword. And so all the more what humanity needs is a love that abides, perseveres, remains present to us whatever happens, however bad things are, for however long it takes. What humankind needs is a love that sticks around, a love that stays put, a love that hangs on. A being-with love. That is what the cross is. A love that hangs on. Nothing can separate us from the love of this God. God's invitation is, hang on to that love; God's promise is, that love will never let you go. That promise is fulfilled in the resurrection. In this lies our salvation.

Such is a being-with notion of the atonement – the "rewithment." Does it eradicate working for? It certainly harmonizes the person and work of Christ more thoroughly than most conventional treatments. But it is not true to say that it eradicates working for. Because, as many theologians have pointed out, the real work of atonement does not take place between God and the devil, but in the inner-Trinitarian relations – the inner life of God. Jesus' struggle, his being not-with the Father at the crucial moment and yet still being with us, however firmly we rejected him, before finally being with the Father again in the resurrection: this struggle is done *on our behalf*. It is an act – *the* act – of working for, the paradigmatic moment of working for that enables and inaugurates all subsequent being with, on God's part and ours – God being with God, God being with us, and our being with one another.

But working for should not have the last word. Again it is important to reiterate the telos of working for. Just as creation was a divine working for (making the universe) that was wholly designed to bring about being with (God being with us), so cross and resurrection was similarly a divine working for wholly designed to bring about being with. Salvation is not a problem fixed; humanity is not left to continue as before, like a household whose drain is fixed by a plumber and whose members can happily wash dishes and take a shower once again. Salvation is a mystery entered: humanity may have thought its problem was mortality, but in Jesus it discovers its curse is isolation from God and one another, and through Jesus it finds the way to overcome isolation and thus discover the gift of resurrection – being with God and one another forever. Such is a theology of rewithment.

Eschatology

It has been a repeated theme of my argument that being with is an eschatological notion. And so it is important not to end a chapter exploring the theological ramifications of being with without giving a sense of what being with means eschatologically. How does one conceive of everlasting being with God and one another in a way that remains dynamic and does not become anodyne? Isaiah 65 offers a helpful answer to this question. What might redemption look like for a struggling neighborhood, nation, or world?

When the prophets of the Old Testament talked about regeneration and social hope they tended to do it in one of two ways. One way, favored by the book of Zechariah, was to long for political restoration, to put King David back on the throne and to have Israel king among the nations once again. The other way, portrayed by the book of Daniel, was to imagine a dramatic apocalyptic intervention of God that brought history to an end. We could call the first way earth and the second way heaven. Zechariah's way appealed to an activist spirit; the main drawback was that it was so much about Israel taking its destiny into its own hands that it didn't leave much room for faith in God's action. Daniel's way was all about God's action, but so much so that it risked encouraging a passive resignation among the people. Little has changed. Those who talk about salvation today tend to be either those who assume it comes from us (and adopt their own working-for model) or those who assume it all comes from God (and thus assume it is God alone who works for).

Such is the context that explains why the vision of Isaiah 65 is so significant and so compelling. It is about God's action. It talks about "new heavens and a new earth" – so it is obviously about the dramatic and decisive intervention of God. There is a significant and indispensable dimension of working for in eschatological consummation. But its mundane details are about children's well-being, people building houses and growing crops. The picture offered in Isaiah 65 is poised between heaven and earth – poised between God's action and human action, between hope and pragmatism, between astonished wonder and hard-won realism, between the unknown future and the very ordinary present tense. It is a model of what in Chapter 8 we called partnership.

Isaiah offers three dimensions to this vision of God and humanity in partnership. The first is about health and well-being. "No more shall there be … an infant that lives but a few days," it says, "or an old person who does not live out a lifetime." Salvation means health. Salvation means safety, and permanent relationship with God – being with God whatever happens. The second dimension is security – that those who build a house get to live in it, and those who plant vineyards get to enjoy their fruit. Isaiah offers a manifesto for an alternative to slavery or indentured labor or oppressive social structures. Here is a picture of a happy, productive world where everyone gets to make and grow and enjoy and no one has to be exploited or used or alienated. Isaiah assumes it is good to work. Work is at the heart of earth and heaven. Working with is integral to how human beings turn earth into heaven and bring heaven to earth, blending the gifts of God with the labor of human hands. Here is endeavor in the knowledge that the conditions of work are fertile and all labors are fruitful.

The third dimension is about the relationship to the soil, to food, and to the animals. "The wolf and the lamb shall feed together, the lion shall eat straw like the ox." The message here is that the wider relationships that make human habitation possible are not fundamentally conflictual. Isaiah goes on, "They shall not hurt or destroy on all my holy mountain, says the Lord." This is Isaiah's great philosophical claim: that when heaven and earth meet there is not war, but partnership; not battle, but beauty; not a contest for scarce resources, but an act of worship centered around the sharing of food. A Eucharist, perhaps. This is a vision of our being with one another, with animals, and with the soil.

But Isaiah infuses his vision with the presence of God. God is more intimately involved in redemption than the people themselves. God says, "Before they call I will answer, while they are yet speaking I will hear." God knows our thoughts and our interests and our flourishing better than we do, but lets us enjoy the work of our hands anyway. God says, "I am about to create Jerusalem as a joy, and its people as a delight. I will rejoice in Jerusalem, and delight in my people." Here is the creative and salvific picture of God working for in order to be with – creating, saving and fulfilling so as to take delight and enter the mystery and share enjoyment. This is heaven – the discovery that God's whole life is shaped to bring about our flourishing and to share in it: that God's joy is us.

Notes

1. Quoted in Robert Jenson, *Systematic Theology: Volume 2: The Works of God* (New York: Oxford University Press, 1997): 20.
2. Woody Allen, *Love and Death* (USA: MGM, 1975).
3. Graham Greene, *The Power and the Glory* (London: Vintage, 2001).
4. Robert Jenson, *Systematic Theology Volume 1, The Triune God* (New York: Oxford University Press, 1997): 72. My argument in this section is indebted to Jenson, who proposes sin as idolatry, lust, injustice, and despair.

5. The sentiment can be found in John Wesley, Sermon 51.3.5, available online at http://wesley.nnu.edu/john-wesley/the-sermons-of-john-wesley-1872-edition/ sermon-51-the-good-steward/ (accessed December 10, 2014). See Kelly Johnson, *The Fear of Beggars: Stewardship and Poverty in Christian* Ethics (Grand Rapids, MI: Eerdmans, 2007): 84–88, for a helpful discussion of this strand in Wesley's thought.
6. In case there is any doubt of the connection, we get the same phrase used on both occasions – "If you are the Son of God" (Matt. 4:3 and 27:40).

14

Social Embodiments

Seeking Nazareth

In the course of this study we have explored summary statements of the commitments and dimensions of being with. In Chapter 8 we followed the pattern of the Trinity and elucidated eight dimensions of being with. Meanwhile in Chapter 2 we set out ten commitments in the form of a manifesto.

It is time to put those two lists together and examine what being with might entail when translated into a modest program for social renewal. I have had two opportunities to embark on such a program myself, in very different contexts. First, in 1998, while I was vicar of a Church of England parish on the western side of Norwich, East Anglia, the Labour government announced a program called New Deal for Communities. In this scheme, 17 socially disadvantaged areas would be identified and £37 million would be made available to each one if its local residents could organize themselves into a board and committees to run their own regeneration. It turned out my neighborhood was identified as one of the 17. Quickly I found myself taking on a new unpaid additional job as a community organizer and helping to lead a mass democratic regeneration movement. I continued to do so for another five years. We eventually formed the first development trust in the Eastern region and set about doing community surveys and elections and hiring actuaries and solicitors and funding and overseeing all manner of initiatives.

The challenge was to imagine what redemption might look like for such a neighborhood, long perceived as an underclass drain on the rest of the city. Should we strive to make it look as much like one of the more middle-class suburbs as possible? Was it distinctive only for what it was not, or was there an elixir of life at the heart of the neighborhood around which could cluster a whole host of initiatives and green shoots of regeneration? I went to live in the neighborhood and I got involved in the regeneration process because I wanted to be with people in their sorrows and struggles, and find beauty and abundance where some might only see shame and scarcity. But then I had to allow my imagination to be stretched to a vision of what it might mean for this community genuinely to flourish, to be happy, settled, and at peace with itself. And that was somehow harder.

The second opportunity came in 2005, while I was Dean of Duke University Chapel in Durham, North Carolina. If the underclass neighborhood in Norwich was a symbol of powerlessness, Duke Chapel was a symbol of power. An elite research university like Duke is a place of immense power, because it marks the intersection of knowledge, wealth, and social influence. None of these forces are decisively powerful on their own, but when all three are put together they are dynamite. Duke Chapel was and remains unique for three reasons. Duke University lies on the longitude of the Ivy League and the latitude of the Bible Belt; hence religion remains a subject of legitimate public discussion, and the appetite for sophisticated presentations of Christianity among faculty, students, administrators, and townspeople is extensive. The university has an outstanding divinity school, and so Christianity remains a credit to the university, rather than an embarrassment. Meanwhile the architecture, liturgy, music, and preaching of the Chapel have a national reputation.

Yet Durham is a town of 200,000 people – made up of African Americans, Caucasians, and Hispanics – with a complex and sometimes troubled history. The widespread assumption was that Duke Chapel was a place to escape from raw religion and chaotic community relations. Duke Chapel was accustomed to enhancing its social capital – but not to putting that social capital to work. So a year after becoming Dean of the Chapel I set about facilitating ways in which the Chapel and the poorer parts of Durham might become more visible to one another, through showcasing community initiatives, creating residential opportunities for students, hiring a community minister incarnationally resident in a disadvantaged neighborhood, and seeking to bring people into conversation, relationship, and partnership across social divides. The plan was not to "fix" anything: more to display and to discover what was possible when one approached the disadvantaged other in expectation of discovering God's abundance in them.

Whereas the examples discussed in Chapter 10, Chapter 11, and Chapter 12 above are all ones that to some degree involve a crisis – of a chaotic lifestyle, significant sickness, or political tyranny – and while much of the discussion in Chapter 7 concerned the context of humanitarian aid in troubled circumstances in the developing world, my experiences in Norwich and Durham, and the explorations of this chapter, are much more about the quotidian, the mundane, the local, the unremarkable, the everyday. In that sense they are perhaps a more suitable subject for a discussion of the ethic of Nazareth. To help translate what I learned in these two very different experiences of seeking to be with, I shall draw extensively on a recent study in the field of community regeneration to set the contours of the discussion.

The Plight of the Contemporary Nazareth

In their book *The Abundant Community*,[1] John McKnight and Peter Block distil the wisdom of a lifetime of community development. Because their vision parallels my argument at many points, I am going to describe it at some length. Their argument and its public policy implications are simply summarized.

> The greatest "service" our society provides is the opportunity to express our unique capacities, to have a decent income, and to join with our fellow citizens in creating productive communities. No human service professional or program will ever equal the healing and empowering effect of those three democratic opportunities. Therefore, policies that support citizen capacity, income, and community should have preference over other forms of intervention that are necessarily second-rate and second-best responses.[2]

McKnight and Block begin with their own diagnosis of what is wrong with contemporary North Atlantic societies. They do not limit their account by economic categories – they go out of their way to point out that the malaise they describe transcends class and income. The tragedy that they perceive is that of ungiven gifts, unexpressed potential, imprisoned wisdom, unused talent, suppressed longing, and, fundamentally, unfulfilled freedom. They tell a story of how this tragedy has come about. What has happened is that "what was once the province or function of the family and community [has migrated] to the marketplace" (27). Following Jeffrey Kaplan, they see this as having arisen, in the USA, from a deliberate policy of the nation's business and political elite "to defuse the dual threat of stagnating economic growth and a radicalized working class in what one industrial consultant called 'the gospel of consumption' – the notion that people could be convinced that however much they have, it isn't enough" (27). This is a story of the successful manufacture of dissatisfaction.

McKnight and Block perceive two elements of the gospel of consumption. One is the systems and management that have emerged to cope with its scale, particularly in government, health, and the corporation. Such systems "expand the message that prosperity and peace of mind can and must be purchased"; it is the aim of systems also to "maintain control by taking uncertainty out of the future." The result is that "All that is uncertain, organic, spontaneous, and flowing in personal, family, and neighborhood space is viewed … as a problem to be solved" (29). The trouble is, that systems, in offering answers, are making a false promise. They dangle more than they can deliver. "The more important dimensions of being human have no clear answer" (31). "The fundamental romantic illusion is that better management and better systems can essentially eliminate fallibility, that they can 'fix' the human condition" (43). Meanwhile, replicability has its costs: personal lives, with their complications, are seen as a threat to the system – systems make relationships instrumental and commercial. In short, "Systems are good for making automobiles and fighting wars. They are good for monetized commerce. But as soon as you create a world that ensures sameness and predictability, you have created conditions where the real humanity of citizens and employees is marginalized" (35). Systems can deliver "order, consistency, and the cost value of scale" (43); but nothing more – and they do so at great cost to the social fabric.

The other element of consumerism is the professional industries that feed off it. Suffering is extracted from the family and neighborhood and subcontracted to the marketplace.

> Professionalization is the market replacement for a community that has lost or outsourced its capacity to care. The loss of community competence is the price we pay for the growth of the service economy. What I once went to an uncle or neighbor for, I now pay a professional to do. What this produces is a hollow neighborhood that does not value coming together around troubles. (36)

But while community is impoverished, there are of course those who stand to gain from this change in culture. "What was a condition of being human becomes a problem to be solved. … Care becomes commodified, then reduced into a curriculum so that it can be categorized, taught, and then certified" (37).

Systems are designed to produce a cure: even aging is medicalized such that death is considered no longer a mystery but "a failure of the medical system, the fixing system" (38). Such an approach takes a human condition, describes it as a problem, and then sells a purported solution. Universities begin to control who can be certified as providers of such solutions. When the work becomes sufficiently extensive and complex, a manager is needed. The community is rendered incompetent: all deviancies from the norm are taken secretly away to the confidential oversight of strangers. People who deviate seriously from the norm are isolated and cut off from their communities. The aggregation of deficiencies "makes personalized care impossible. … Collecting people by their needs isolates them from the commerce and affection of everyday life" (41–42).[3]

Put together, these two elements of the gospel of consumption infantilize, instrumentalize, and impoverish the informal relationships that are fostered in communities and families. "I have organized a life of consumer purchasing as a substitute for my capacity to grieve, relate, welcome, and share wealth and resources with others" (56–57). Kindness, generosity, and civility disappear, to be replaced by entitlement.[4] Being with ourselves becomes impossible: we have no resources or competence to tolerate our own imperfections. As a result we look to fill our hollowness with purchased experience and entertainment. "The price we pay for living in a consumer world … is living a dissatisfied life. An incomplete life. A life where the harder we try, the more hollow it becomes. Individuals become useless, families lose their function, neighborhoods lose their competence. We are then left to purchase what we might have chosen to produce" (62).

Neighborhoods are thus left both hollow and dependent.

> First, institutions fail to deliver on their promise to keep us healthy, safe, and prosperous; and thereby all of us, institutions and citizens alike, become more skeptical and cynical, and keep calling for more control and accountability. We see this in our growing distrust of government, public schools, physicians, and institutional services of all shapes and sizes.
>
> Second, citizens grow rusty from failing to do what only they themselves can do. Their community skills are weak from lack of use. They succumb to isolation and being "well serviced." They reduce their trust in their neighbors who live three dwellings away and farther. Their community vision is blurred from the dependency created by focusing on nothing but big systems. (99)

In the language of my argument, what has emerged is the pathology of working for. When working for becomes a default, not just for addressing crisis, but for engaging every challenge, then mysteries become problems, attention is episodic and devolved to professionals, presence is unnecessary, participation is eradicated, partnership is eroded, and delight and enjoyment disappear. Being with is not just difficult; it is incomprehensible. What McKnight and Block describe is what I would call the pathos of working for; and they narrate how working for has practically become a religion.

My experience in Norwich was different from, but recognizable within, this description. In Norwich there had been 60 years of paternalistic local government; 90 percent of the residents lived in local authority-owned social housing, and almost inevitably the local authority was seen as the only source of resources, support, and innovation. There was thus a long history of being on the receiving end of a working-for model. Not only was there a profound lack of expectation of breaking out of this cycle; even within the cycle there was a tragic aura that things were unlikely to get any better. When working for is surrounded by expectation that problems can be "fixed" it is deeply problematic; when there is little expectation that problems can be fixed, yet a working-for culture still abides, the plight of all concerned is even worse.

The Capacities and Properties of Nazareth

How can people break out of the all-pervasiveness of a working-for mindset? How can relationship displace professionalized clienthood, and the citizen emerge out of the shell of the consumer? For McKnight and Brock, the key is a world-view shaped around abundance. What gives McKnight and Brock hope is that each person, in their idiosyncratic and unique configuration of characteristics, is a cornucopia of gifts.

> Gifts are inborn and not subject to management. Gifts don't need to be trained into us; they are inherent. They are who we are and they cannot be taken away. They are also nearby, though often unseen. Since we cannot manipulate the gifts of another, they are not subject to external management, and therefore they are an antidote to system life. (56)

Such gifts simply await a nurturing context in order to emerge. A community's power resides in its ability to manifest and mobilize the gifts of its people and to exercise and express those gifts through the quality and extent of its associations. "A gift is not a gift until it is given. Before [that] it is a capacity held in exile. ... The tragedy of a dysfunctional family or

neighborhood is that the potential gifts of its members are never given"
(70). This is a perfect summary of what I observed in Norwich: a community whose capacities were held in exile. Developing permission, confidence, encouragement, and hope to release these potential gifts was a huge
but worthy task.

The abundant community believes that what we have is enough; we have
the capacity to provide what we need in the face of sorrow, aging, illness,
celebration, fallibility, misfortune, and joy; we organize in a context of cooperation and satisfaction; we are responsible for one another, in that if one
is not free, valued, or flourishing, none of us can be (66). Such convictions
and the practices that derive from them enable a community to avert much
of the sense of dissatisfaction for which the marketplace offers answers,
and to provide for itself much of "what systems and consumerism would
have us purchase" (67). In such a setting poverty is no longer considered
to be fundamentally or even primarily about money: because abundance
is about things that money cannot buy. Well-being is about overcoming
isolation and finding ways to make material limitation a source of mutual
interdependence.

One of the signal convictions of the abundant community is that adversity and hardship can become entry points into plenitude. In a conviction
that resonates with what we saw in Chapter 5 of God's pattern with Israel
and Jesus, troubles, and their sharing, are seen as the seedbed of community and growth. It may be that a single father seeks counsel from a neighbor when his teenage daughter absconds. Or that an Irish family next door,
rather than turning to bereavement experts, hold a wake for family and
friends.

> The range and variety of the sorrows we bear gives us the fuel for community
> and connectedness. … Sharing the personal is how the consumer cycle is
> broken. … At this moment, the restoration of community competence has
> begun. … This is a political act in the best sense – reclaiming power from
> professionals who are sworn to secrecy and putting it in the hands and hearts
> of citizens who choose to disclose, discuss, imagine, and act. (70)

The goods of the abundant community can be aggregated as properties
and capacities. The three properties, or organizing principles, commend-
ed by McKnight and Brock, are focusing on gifts, nurturing associational
life, and offering hospitality by welcoming strangers. Hospitality was the
way the initiative in Durham began. From the start the emphasis was on

learning to be both a host and a guest. When one was a host the guests were the center of attention, and all the questions and sense of expertise focused on them. When one was a guest one sought to bring something of oneself to the table to share. Evenings were held in a variety of churches and community centers around the city, and activities took place that gave both residents and visitors opportunities to showcase established gifts and to discover new ones. Monthly meals took place in the student residential house in which neighborhood figures were treated as sources of wisdom on life, community, and well-being. The emphasis throughout was to highlight common commitments, respect histories and differences, but most of all to make shared ventures into territory new to all parties. Thus hospitality became the key to both releasing gifts and making new associations. Perhaps most important of all was learning to be present on others' territory in unstructured time – to attend clubs, children's playschemes, and other gatherings and learn to feel useless but still take an interest and pay close attention to individuals and rituals, until one was accepted and, when absent, missed.

The six capacities are kindness, generosity, cooperation, forgiveness, acceptance of fallibility, and mystery. These are all aspects of the fostering of gifts. A community that sees troubles as potential gifts requires *kindness*, because kindness is a respectful awareness of the vulnerability and fragility of the troubled other. In Durham, the community minister found that times of hardship or even tragedy were opportunities to show through presence and memory a simple pattern of kindness: thus the remembering of anniversaries after bereavement focused a sustained and abiding presence in the face of sadness. Whereas many neighborhood residents and most outsiders objected strongly to those who conducted drug deals at the bus stop in front of the student residence, it was an appropriate act of kindness to learn the names of the those involved, speak to them with courtesy and respect, hear something of their stories, and seek out their family members to understand them better – rather than simply decry them as enemies or report them as criminals.

Generosity is the virtue of abundance. Unlike charity, which assumes scarcity and "is really an unstable and false generosity because it is oriented around the needs and deficiencies of just one party in the transaction" (85), and is thus demeaning, generosity assumes abundance by investing in the still-not-fully disclosed gifts of the other. In the Durham initiative, a key element was helping the congregation's local mission committee to move beyond seeing its role as giving "grants" to local non-profits, and instead to realize that "showing up" and sustaining regular presence at events of local community joy and sadness was a more significant investment of care and interest – one which issued in acts that deepened relationship, like taking a new friend to a hospital appointment. Thus people discovered the depths that could be found when money was no longer the principal form of investment.

Cooperation is a fruit of abundance because it believes there are enough gifts for everyone – whereas competition is a fruit of scarcity because it assumes there are limited gifts which can only be acquired by winning. It corresponds to the being-with notion of participation.

Forgiveness is "the willingness to come to terms with having been wounded" (87). It is vital for a community that seeks to accept fallibility, and distinguish between fallibility and transgression. Again the secret is the unleashing of gifts: "our unwillingness to forgive keeps us imprisoned and unable to either offer our gifts or receive the gifts of those around us who are most problematic" (88). Not all fallibility is a transgression to be forgiven: accepting fallibility, such as addiction, or mental illness – the "stuff we leave off our resume" and that systems seek to eradicate – means seeing people beyond the label of their shortcomings, and ensuring that all get to contribute their gifts (88–90). One of the more humbling aspects of my experience in Norwich was to witness the community's ability to live with both fallibility and transgression. On one occasion two members of the community who had been very actively and closely involved in the regeneration process, became angry and went to the local newspaper with a complaint which, when published, embarrassed and exasperated many board members. But in only a matter of weeks the two had found their way back into the process. On another occasion there was a stand up fight in the office itself, with community members throwing files at one another; but again, in a few days everyone realized we all needed each other and space and grace were rediscovered. I wish I could say I had seen such accommodation within the life of the church.

Like Alexis de Tocqueville, McKnight and Brock see the unique energy of the United States and its greatest potential as lying in affinity groups and associations – because "associations are a primary place in community where individual capacities get expressed" (71). But they are not "responsible" or charitable, and this is a significant way in which they avoid the pitfalls of working for: "Few associations come together to do a social good. For people to do a real social good, they come together for some other reason and do a social good out of their peripheral vision. Otherwise, it is a system" (72). Associations can be defined by location (a neighborhood), by function (preserving a woodland, caring for the elderly), or by common interest (a dog club or book club). They may be formal, with elected officers and a recognized name such as the local Peace Fellowship; or less formal, yet often sites of dialogue and the exchange of opinion, like a poker club; or they may center on a bar or a barber's shop, where interaction blends with transaction. Such mark precisely the kinds of contexts from which labeled people such as developmentally disabled or ex-convicts tend to be excluded. [5] Such associations provide the context and process through which gifts are exchanged. "The power of associational life is that money is taken off the table. It's all about 'We do it,' not 'We buy it'" (74). People are there because they want to be there and be together. No one is getting paid. There is thus "exchange but no commerce" (77). It is not necessarily efficient: "No one claims a community system is efficient. ... [But] the purpose of community is community" (76).

The notorious problem with associations, besides inefficiency, is their insularity and social conservatism – the exclusion of some and the subordination of others. That is why McKnight and Brock insist on the property (or practice) of *hospitality*. "The extent of hospitality becomes a measure of the belief that people have in their community. ... Hospitality is generated because people feel so good about themselves that they want others to share it and they want to share the joy of others. ... Hospitality generates from trust and produces trust" (79). "A community forms when people have enough trust that they can combine their properties and capacities into gifts. Friendship and trust are the means through which something that was an individual quality now becomes a communal reality" (79–80). In the abundant community, friendship and trust form a covenant that in the system is replaced by payment and contract.[6] The reason why McKnight and Brock put so much store by associations is that they are settings where people develop trust in one another and generate cooperation, generosity, forgiveness, and hospitality. Associations produce properties and capacities and thus generate abundance, whereas systems produce services and products and thus generate scarcity.

What I observed in the community-led regeneration program in Norwich was the way the money followed the association, but how hard it was for the money to generate the association. In most cases the best the money could do was to give the association the chance to expand its horizons. For example a modest school-watch scheme became a more ambitious community warden project. But no amount of money could spark into life initiative without any existing association. At the end of some years there was money left unspent because there were important development areas where no accountable, authentic associations had emerged to spend the money wisely.

Underlying McKnight and Brock's account is a conviction about the power unearthed by releasing gifts through association, and the consequent creation of a local marketplace, in which capacities, resources and talents either enrich the local economy or are exchanged without being monetized. The community's competence creates an integrity that releases it from dependence on the system world. Communities ask what they are purchasing, where it comes from, and whether they could just as easily (and with more enrichment) supply it from within their own efforts and skills. "You don't know what you need until you know what you have. Then you know what you need to buy from the outside" (98).

The Abundant Community as Nazareth

It will by now be clear why McKnight and Brock's treatment is so significant for distilling my account of being with. A survey of the eight dimensions of being with should make the connections transparent.

The abundant community takes *presence* for granted. Presence, in the sense of shared location, is not the only form of association – there are also function and common interest. Without question the rise of social media has altered the degree to which physical location is crucial to association. Nonetheless presence names the incarnate, material quality of human relationship, and affirms that virtual communication is ancillary to physical interaction. Presence over time bestows authority, deepens trust, establishes credentials.

Not long after I moved into the socially disadvantaged neighborhood in Norwich, I had lunch with the head of a local non-profit organization. She was one of the chief movers and shakers in the town, and she invited me to lunch. I was keen to show her I knew all the jargon of social regeneration, so every time she used a phrase like "capacity building" I made sure I replied with a term like "community stakeholders." Every time she referred to "social exclusion" I countered with "leveraging private sector buy-in." I thought I was holding my own pretty well until we reached the end of the meal. Then she looked up at me, over her napkin, and held my gaze, and said, "Are you staying?" It was a searching question about presence. She meant, "Can I rely on you? Are you serious about this? I've given my life to this work – is that what you're going to do? Or are you one of those people who waltzes in for a while, talks a good game, and then heads off in search of another transformative experience elsewhere? Are you truly going to allow this place to change you?"

Albert Schweitzer stayed at a little West African hospital on the Ogooué River at Lambaréné in Gabon. There he treated countless thousands of local patients, with conditions ranging from dysentery to sleeping sickness to leprosy to malaria to sandfly fever. He saw his work as an act of penance for the sins of European colonizers. While some critics felt he, and his methods, perpetuated some paternalistic qualities, few could doubt the courage and devotion he brought to his work. And some atonement it was. He spent the majority of the 52 years from 1913 to his death in 1965 caring for and seeking to cure all who came to his hospital at Lambaréné. He was probably a better theologian and musician than he was a doctor. But being a physician was where he "stayed." He allowed Lambaréné to change him. When he was asked about what he had learned, he said, "Everyone can have their own Lambaréné." Albert Schweitzer's witness was that when we ask God, "Where are you staying?" God's answer is, "I'm staying with you." This is the ministry of presence. It is the opposite of the frenzied, anxious motion sometimes to be found in the working-for approach. It is a visible, simple statement of confidence in the abundance of the neighborhood.

One way in which I discovered presence in Durham, North Carolina, was in learning the significance of the porch. The rocking chair, the idle time, the half-begun conversation in a climate of almost year-round outdoor interaction: this setting both offered the opportunity to be present to quite a number of people in the course of an afternoon simply by walking along a street, and gave the timid and inhibited a chance to put a foot in the water simply by sitting on a porch together and initiating half-dialogues with passers-by. Because the student residence was close to a bus stop, its porch became the scene of numerous half-conversations, any of which had the potential to be resumed later or to stand alone as a gesture of acceptance and acknowledgement, a recognition of common humanity. The porch was, literally, a liminal space.[7]

Attention goes beyond but is dependent upon presence. If the potential of a neighborhood lies first in its unlocked gifts, attention is the slow and purposeful listening to stories, abiding in silence, befriending time, and the acceptance of fallibility that leads to the discovery of gifts. It relies on qualities like vigilance and virtues like patience. In many ways McKnight and Block's whole project is one of patient attention, willingness to notice detail where the system perspective notices deficit, awareness of creativity where professionalized service sees bland inertia. In particular patient attention applies to what McKnight and Block call forgiveness and acceptance of fallibility. Neither fragility nor transgression can be accommodated in a sweep of the hand; both, in different but overlapping ways, require firm but gentle incorporation into a larger story.

This is the process I elsewhere describe as overaccepting.[8] Fallibility and transgression may be curious and unwelcome gifts – but the important thing is that they are still gifts. They cannot be blocked. (McKnight and Block describe how difficult it is for systems to talk about failure, fallibility, imperfection and transgression, and how a culture of silence grows up around such attributes because they are absurd within the institution.) They are not problems that can simply be solved. The choice is whether simply to accept them and thereby allow their negative undertow to damage the culture of the community, requiring denial and compensatory action and evasion; or whether to *overaccept* them – to live into a story that would not have been possible without them, a story that is not destroyed by them but which yet is the richer and more dynamic for their having been obstacles and challenges to navigate and reintegrate. This is not a story that is imposed on a community but a story that adapts to embrace a community in its new reality. To discover such a story requires loving attention.

The dimension of *mystery* is one to which McKnight and Block themselves refer many times. Their use of the term lacks a transcendent dimension, but it acknowledges and perceives the need to "make space for what is unknowable about life" (90). As they put it, realizing there is more than what you know is enlivening; mystery is the source of all learning, the catalyst for creativity, and the freedom from the burden of answers that "are just a restatement of the past" (90–91). Mystery is also a protest against the culture of planning, goals, blueprints, measurability, and certainty. To enter mystery is to jettison the myth of safety for the adventure of discovery.

Mystery is also the name for hidden connections. On the day of the dedication of the student residential house in Durham, a cluster of people gathered on the porch for a commissioning ceremony. A woman who was walking by lingered to watch and was invited to join. She disclosed that she had been a resident of the house when it had been notorious for drug-taking and low life. Her reflections became the center of the dedication service.

Of all the dimensions of being with, perhaps the most apt to McKnight and Block's project is *delight*. This is the case on several levels. Most importantly, delight treats as a gift what others might regard as a burden. Of all the dimensions of being with, delight is most attuned to the expression and celebration of gifts. And the expression and celebration of gifts is the heart of the abundant community. Again, my earlier work on theatrical improvisation is instructive here. The following game makes the point succinctly.

> Divide people into pairs and call them A and B. A gives a present to B who receives it. B then gives a present back, and so on. At first each person thinks of giving an interesting present, but then I stop them and suggest that they can just hold their hands out, and see what the other person chooses to take. … The trick is to make the thing you are *given* as interesting as possible. … Everything you are given delights you. …
>
> … When the actor concentrates on making the thing he *gives* interesting, each actor seems in competition, and feels it. When they concentrate on making the thing they *receive* interesting, then they generate warmth between them.[9]

This game, and the different ways of playing it, aptly summarizes McKnight and Block's argument. Indeed it goes beyond their argument: for they tend somewhat to regard gifts as self-explanatory, needing only release to become salutary for the community. Whereas what the game demonstrates is how much work there is training the eye of the beholder. Delight is not simply a spontaneous reaction: it is in significant ways a learned behavior. In Chapter 8 I describe this as an eschatological anticipation: that is to say, heaven is an experience of all our gifts being released and evoking delight – delight beyond our imagination, and gifts beyond what we knew we had. McKnight and Block recognize the joy that resides in the expression of gifts, but they do not fully articulate the work involved in receiving these gifts with delight, or the degree to which that delight comes to exceed even the joy involved in giving. It is more challenging, community-building, and ennobling to receive with delight than to give. McKnight and Block also underplay the reflexive character of delight, and thus of gift exchange more generally. Working for is impoverished in part because of its resistance, reluctance, unwillingness, and finally inability to make a genuine relationship. This hollows out the professional person as much as it does the client. The joy to be found in delighted reception of gifts is not just that it releases imprisoned talents but also that it encourages the recipient to disclose and thus discover hidden gifts in themselves.

The abundant community, as a genuine community, is evidently one that prizes *participation*. McKnight and Block like to use the word citizen, and see themselves, rather like Jeffrey Stout as we saw in Chapter 7, as part of a movement to renew American democracy as a participative, rather than

passive, exercise. The energy of abundance comes about not just in the release of gifts, but more mundanely in the recognition that this is not a society where most have problems and just a select handful have the solutions,
but instead that everyone has a part to play. This is the simple everyday
dynamism of participation. Association is the great celebration of participation, as De Tocqueville noted in the 1830s.

McKnight and Block enrich our notion of participation by distinguish-
ing between two ways that a property can be generated. One is the simple
doing of things together. The other is the way that a community can release
the gifts of an individual. They give the example of two people getting together to cook a meal for a person across the street who has lost a loved
one. This is collective kindness. Meanwhile if one cooks the meal alone,
yet within a culture where kindness is welcomed and valued, it may be on
the surface a working-for activity but it is part of a being-with narrative.
The first way builds community among the community offering kindness
– a mixture of working with and being with; the second way affirms the
habits of kindness, and is a mixture of working for and being with. Either
way, the meal is an excuse to enter a conversation about bereavement with
a vulnerable person, and is, at best, a pretext and a preliminary for being
with, where the true participation takes place. When one says the purpose
of community is community, one is talking about participation.

The goal of the process is to create true *partnership*. McKnight and
Block's vision is to create community inventories in which everything from
babysitting and tree-pruning to sewing and accounting is made visible in
the neighborhood, with the aim of harnessing all such gifts in service of the
community's core concerns for children, land, enterprise, food, health, the
vulnerable, and safety. Then a cross-generational sharing and cooperative
culture can spring up, by which many help repair a neighbor's home (like a
modern barn-raising), or create a barter exchange of skills like haircutting
and minor electrical work, or create support groups for single parents or the
recently bereaved. In the process a community takes responsibility for one
another, discover new connections and relationships, understand the limits
of money, develop a new kind of trust, feel powerful, and create a shared
history (119–124). In this McKnight and Block are inspired by the pioneer
families who together achieved things in the early part of the American
story that no family could have accomplished on its own. They see associations as the agency through which passivity can be translated first into what
we would call participation and thence into the truly dynamic dimension
of partnership.

A different way to put this would be to see this as the point where being with genuinely becomes working with. Here it is important to recognize that John McKnight is widely regarded as the founder of Asset-Based Community Development – an unequivocal model of working with. In *Building Communities from the Inside Out: A Path Toward Finding and Mobilizing a Community's Assets*,[10] John P. Kretzmann and John L. McKnight set out a working-with approach to community development, rooted in the assets, skills, and capacities of residents, associations, and local institutions. The first two chapters seek to release individual and associational capacities, respectively, and cover in more detail similar to what we have been considering, with particular attention to the associational power of churches and cultural organizations. The title of the third chapter however discloses the distinction between being with and working with: "Capturing Local Institutions for Community Building." These institutions include parks, libraries, schools, community colleges, and hospitals. The term "capturing" has an instrumental character that distinguishes the process from being with. The reason for this becomes clear as the subsequent chapter explores how the resources of such local institutions can strengthen the local economy, how savings can be retained in the neighborhood through credit unions, and how abandoned space and waste materials can be reincorporated into the community's asset register. Once assets have been mapped, relationships built, information shared, and visions and plans developed, then outside resources can be introduced to support locally driven development.[11]

There is a vital role for government so long as it supports local invention and does not simply seek to manage, replicate, and proliferate local initiatives. Kretzmann and McKnight note that, as we saw in the work of James C. Scott quoted in Chapter 7, evidence from the developing world shows that "if outside plans and resources dominate and overwhelm local initiatives and associations, massive social and economic disasters occur. ... If all the outside resources did suddenly begin to be available in low income neighborhoods, without an effective and connected collaboration of local individuals, associations and institutions, the resources would only create more dependency and isolation before they were finally dissipated."[12] In other words there is a clear agenda of economic regeneration that goes well beyond the conviction that the purpose of community is community. Yet that regeneration is not limited to economic prosperity. There is genuine delight, mystery, and participation along the way, and human flourishing is principally evaluated in non-material and non-economic terms.

The distinction between participation and partnership offers a vocabulary to articulate what I tried to do as Dean of Duke Chapel, and the ways it seemed strange to many observers. The community I perceived as abundant was Durham – as a whole, not simply its more disadvantaged or its more prosperous neighborhoods. What I sought to facilitate was participation – people being present to, attending to, and enjoying one another and finding mystery and delight in doing so. While I anticipated that partnerships on a micro interpersonal or macro institutional scale might ensue, those partnerships were not the purpose of the participation. I trusted that people would come to relish participation for its own sake. The process was a challenge to the default working-for assumption that engagement means the rich helping the poor; but it was also challenging to the working-with assumption that partnership is the dimension of with that really matters. To me, all of it mattered; the danger of partnership, particularly if it did not emerge organically and naturally, was that it might come to seem that all the other dimensions of being with had merely been instrumental – whereas I saw them as good in their own right, and trusted others would come to see them as such too.

This brings us to *enjoyment*. In Chapter 7 we saw that, while community organizing, perhaps the most visible and outspoken manifestation of working with, has tremendous qualities of bringing vitality and energy and partnership and hope, as well as an impressive track record of achievement, its weakness is its tendency to use that which should perhaps be enjoyed. Not only is community organizing inclined to instrumentalize relationships, but it thrives on the identification of problems and the energy released by solving them. In this sense it requires and exploits deficit, rather than discovering and celebrating abundance. McKnight and Block make a similar point as they both affirm and distance themselves from community organizing. They recognize the shared aspiration to create change "based on the gifts of all: the neighbor, the deviant, the care filled, the troubled, the elected official, and the formal leader." However, community organizing relies on the identification of a common, if impermanent, enemy to create common cause: "Bringing people together against a common enemy is the opposite of hospitality. Community competence based on abundance is about bringing people together around possibility, not disappointment" (78). Thus emerges the subtle but significant distinction between asset-based community development and community organizing. McKnight and Block see their work as relationship-based organizing – a kind of half-way point between being with and working with.[13]

Another subtle point that arises out of enjoyment is the practice of hospitality. The concern of McKnight and Block to avoid the pitfalls of exclusion of the outsider (or newcomer), marginalization of the deviant (or merely different), and subordination of the vulnerable (or simply female) is commendable. They are right to describe hospitality as a sign of a community or household's confidence. Yet hospitality retains a territorial connotation that is not quite in the full spirit of what it means to enjoy. Hospitality requires one to have premises, resources, and to some degree skills, not to mention the cooperation of one's household; in my own experience of religious association in socially disadvantaged neighborhoods, such a combination of assets, particularly the last, was rare. The language of enjoyment opens out a vocabulary of cherishing the other, especially the different, new, and challenging other, that does not assume one has any significant material resources, nor that one's own territory is the best setting for an initial encounter.

Finally, *glory*. McKnight and Block's account has a healthy and encouraging respect for religious association, but their perception of the church is almost inevitably a largely instrumental one. Yet in their notion of abundance, their description of the joy to be found in the release of gifts, and their sense of overflowing community as an end in itself, there is a profound secular analogy of glory that in impressive ways crystallizes the notion of being with. Perhaps the most telling common theme comes in relation to the discussion in this chapter above that, against the widespread assumption in church and beyond, one can only reach the power by pursuing the glory. The devotion to discovering and affirming individual and collective gifts, not (at least initially) as levers of economic development but for the sheer joy and energy to be found in releasing them, is a wonderful picture of what it means to seek the glory, and only thereby to find the power.

By devoting this chapter to expounding, evaluating and making comparisons and connections with the work of McKnight, Brock, and Kretzmann, I have sought an appropriate way to render my own experience of leading and facilitating community development from the inside and engagement from the outside within a critical framework.[14] I have also sought to explore what being with entails when translated into the concrete, complex, and often conflictual world of social deprivation on the scale of a neighborhood. In the process we have amplified and tested some of the constructive commitments of being with, so as to encounter a few of their more demanding and distinctive characteristics. What we have found is a set of behaviors and perspectives that assume and celebrate the abundance of God.

Notes

1. John McKnight and Peter Block, *The Abundant Community: Awakening the Power of Families and Neighborhoods* (San Francisco: Berrett-Koehler Publishers, 2010). Further references in the text.

2. John McKnight, *The Careless Society: Community and its Counterfeits* (New York: Basic Books ,1995): 114.

3. Elsewhere McKnight points out vividly the folly of isolating those whom professionals perceive only in terms of their needs. "Many people labeled 'developmentally disabled' or 'physically disabled' are never going to be 'fixed' by the service professions. Nonetheless, they are frequently subjected to years of 'training' to write their names or tie their shoes. ... For those whose 'emptiness' cannot be filled by human services, the most obvious 'need' is the opportunity to express and share their gifts, skills, capacities, and abilities with friends, neighbors, and fellow citizens in the community. As deficiency-oriented service systems obscure this fact, they inevitably harm their clients *and* the community by pre-empting the relationship between them" (*The Careless Society*: 104). Meanwhile in such contexts human service programs "can create, in the aggregate, environments that contradict the potential positive effect of any one program. When enough programs surround a client, they may combine to create a new environment in which none of the programs will be effective" (*The Careless Society*: 107).

4. McKnight sees community as the alternative to the two conventional forms of addressing social exclusion, both of which I would describe as varieties of working for. The first form is therapy: "a world in which there is a professional to meet every need" and "the ultimate liberty is the right to treatment." The second form is advocacy: "a defensive wall of helpers to protect an individual against an alien community." By contrast the community vision sees "a society where those who were once labeled, exiled, treated, counseled, advised, and protected are, instead, incorporated into community, where their contributions, capacities, gifts, and fallibilities will allow a network of relationships involving work, recreation, friendship, support, and the political power of being a citizen" (*The Careless Society*: 168–169).

5. John McKnight, *The Careless Society*: 118.

6. For further reflections on contract and covenant, see Samuel Wells, *Learning to Dream Again: Rediscovering the Heart of God* (Norwich, UK: Canterbury, 2013): 39–44.

7. "From time to time, I'll get a phone call from someone saying, 'Are you going to be on your porch this evening?' To which I'll reply, 'Yeah, I'll be there. Probably be out about 7.' Sure enough, around 7 the caller will come walking up and join me on the porch. We'll visit, catch up on news, likely I'll tell a story or two, and eventually the visitor will get to whatever it is that's bothering him or her. We're

not in a hurry; it is porching, after all. What I've learned is that conversation on the porch is important ministry. If the caller comes to my study at the church for an appointment, it is called 'counseling.' But if someone drops by my porch and we sit in the rocking chairs, it is just two friends having a conversation. We're visiting." Kyle Childress, "Porching, Friendship and Ministry," *Faith and Leadership*, August 12, 2014, available online at www.faithandleadership.com/content/kyle-childress-porching-friendship-and-ministry (accessed December 10, 2014).

8. Samuel Wells, *Improvisation: The Drama of Christian Ethics* (Grand Rapids, MI: Brazos; and London: SPCK, 2004): 127–142.

9. Keith Johnstone, *Impro: Improvisation in the Theatre* (London: Methuen, 1980): 100–101. See also Samuel Wells, *Improvisation*: 129–130.

10. John P. Kretzmann and John L. McKnight, *Building Communities from the Inside Out: A Path Toward Finding and Mobilizing a Community's Assets* (Chicago: Acta Publications, 1997).

11. This was largely the pattern we followed in Norwich, though hardly any of us, me included, really knew what we were doing, still less that there was a book just published that described what we were doing.

12. John P. Kretzmann and John L. McKnight, *Building Communities from the Inside Out*: 374.

13. McKnight and Kretzmann suggest that the four kinds of organizations on which Saul Alinsky depended, churches, ethnic groups, political organizations, and labour unions are all weaker today than they were in Alinsky's heyday. Meanwhile the visible, local, and capable targets on which he focused are now impossible to identify. Thus "it becomes less and less likely that strategies stressing either the consolidation of existing associations or the confronting of an outside enemy make much sense" (*The Careless Society*: 157). What is required is a reconceptualization of the neighborhood as a locus for production as well as consumption – and an organizing approach "aimed at building community through the restoration of localized political economies" (*The Careless Society*: 160).

14. See Samuel Wells, *Community-Led Estate Regeneration and the Local Church* (Cambridge: Grove Booklets, 2003), for more of a narrative approach to my experience in Norwich.

Part V
Implications

Perhaps the most common criticisms of being with are that it is passive in the face of injustice, naïve in relation to imbalance of power, and ineffective in regard to wrongs that simply need energy and skill to be put right. I take these all to be different versions of the same complaint: that being with is wrong on consequential grounds, in that it does not produce the right effects, and that other approaches would produce better outcomes.

The second most frequent form of complaint is that being with is heartless in the face of suffering, sentimental in relation to human distress, or weak in regard to eradicating pain from the world. I understand these criticisms, again all more or less the same accusation, as maintaining that being with is wrong on deontological grounds: that is, that there is only one right way to engage with suffering, and that is to eradicate it – anything else at best dissipates energy from the simple unquestioned good, at worst questions the determination to eradicate suffering that should, so the argument goes, be a universal human imperative.

I regard these two broad claims as wrong in their understanding of being with, self-serving in their invariably working-for assumptions, and ironic in that they replicate the very haste to action that being with seeks to question. Nonetheless, I have chosen to spend my final two chapters attending to these criticisms, because responding directly seems the best way to draw out their wisdom as well as address their hostility, and because they fit more or less neatly into consequential and deontological categories, thus offering a broadly comprehensive survey of possible criticisms.

Thus in the first of these two chapters I consider injustice. Just as throughout the book I seek not to abolish working for, still less working with, so here I offer good reasons why conventional understandings of justice have a significant role to play – but not a sufficient role on their own. I argue for an approach to justice that more fully embodies being with. This

A Nazareth Manifesto, Samuel Wells © 2015 John Wiley & Sons, Ltd. Published 2015 by John Wiley & Sons, Ltd.

chapter is also intended as an illustration of how a full understanding of being with sits alongside working-for and working-with approaches in a balanced understanding of social engagement.

In the second chapter I turn to suffering. Being with offers itself as the most honest, realistic, faithful, enduring and, in the end, courageous way of engaging suffering; working for, by contrast, overpromises and under-delivers by trying to take suffering away. This is the contrast with which we began the book – with Laszlo staying with Katherine or walking to Cairo. It seems an appropriate way in which to conclude.

15

The Transcendence of Justice

The Problem with Justice

During a summer break in the course of my undergraduate studies I was living in the Middle East. I had cause early one morning to head out to the north side of town, near one of the ancient gates of the city. In the half-light I saw dozens of shadowy figures, not huddled together, but separated individually, leaning against the walls of a huge square, waiting for something. Quite soon I saw a few pick-up trucks draw up, not all at once but every minute or two. I wandered closer to see what was going on. Each truck would park in the square, and the men would cluster around the driver's cabin. Each time some men would drift away, while others would climb wearily into the back. I could not hear the conversations with the driver, but it was obvious what was being said: "Who will work today for this wage? Who will work for half as much? Who will work for a quarter?"

One of those men turned his head around and looked at me. Perhaps he was wondering, "Who are you? Are you one of us, looking for work? Or are you one of them, offering it for derisory wages?" I did not know if his look was a desperate plea for help or a glance of agonized rejection. But I know it went straight through me. And I know I have been trying to answer his question ever since. In the language of this book, his look was a challenge to choose whom I was with – them or us – and to recognize that a commitment to be with the oppressed may mean recognizing one cannot always succeed in being with everybody.

In this chapter I want to explain the conclusions I have come to in relating the concerns of justice to the notion of being with. I do so because when I talk about the notion of "with," and especially "being with," as I have now over many years around the USA and the UK, perhaps the most recurring concern is that it is somehow soft or naïve or ineffectual around the

A Nazareth Manifesto, Samuel Wells © 2015 John Wiley & Sons, Ltd. Published 2015 by John Wiley & Sons, Ltd.

question of justice. And justice is taken, somewhat unthinkingly in some quarters, to be the goal of Christian social engagement. I sense the churches are not at peace about justice. They find it hard to hold together both halves of Jesus' claim, "I am the resurrection and the life" (John 11:25). Resurrection is where Christianity begins. Jesus is risen from the dead. Death is real, but it doesn't have the last word. Love is stronger than death. God's creative and life-giving purpose cannot be permanently thwarted. Nothing can finally separate us from the love of God. That is what Christians celebrate in the beauty of worship and the urgency of evangelism. That is the good news.

But it is not the whole of the good news. There is also life. Christianity is not just faith about the past and hope for the future: it is also love in the present. Christianity is a way of living made possible by the removal of our panic about death. It is a way characterized by joy, peace, gentleness, goodness, and patience. Today we would add words that we associate with the virtues of our era – words like generosity, hospitality, kindness, inclusivity, respect, compassion, trust, and dignity. Jesus says I *am* the life – not "I bring the life" or "I procure the life" or "I promise the life" – but I *am* the life.[1] This is a present tense thing. If you cannot live it now, what hope does it truly give for the future?

The problem for the church is how easy it is for Christians to get a hold of one of these dimensions and not the other. Half the church grabs hold of the resurrection and runs the danger of missing the life. It concentrates on personal salvation, getting into heaven, knowing you are forgiven, having a personal relationship with Jesus, and often a rather narrow range of issues in so-called personal morality that promise to keep us in God's good books. The risk is that Christianity becomes a means to an end, a device to avoid hell and head toward heaven forever; in short a rather self-centered and limited project. People tend to look at it from the outside and wonder whether it really and truly represents the life that Jesus is talking about.

Yet half the church makes the opposite mistake. It concentrates on the life, and talks about justice, and tolerance, and rights, and affirmation, and the planet, and never quite gets round to focusing on the crisis of death, the need for personal repentance, the awesomeness of judgment, the fear of oblivion or everlasting torment or isolation in eternity. The trouble with this is that, while it is admirable, it is not always clear in what sense it is Christianity, because the commitments and perceptions are often shared with a whole range of secular and religious people looking for a better and more equal society; and often reference to Jesus disappears almost altogether.

So whether the church veers toward the resurrection or the life, there's a problem with justice. Either it seems a distraction from the real business of salvation; or it seems so much the center of salvation that it obscures the traditional Christian language almost altogether.

Going back to my youthful experience by the ancient gate of that Middle Eastern city, I had never before witnessed the inequalities of life and the brutal economic humiliation of a mass of people so vividly. I had seen political oppression – I had been to places where one part of the population was marginalized and subjected to discrimination and daily insults. But this was more subtle. It made me feel utterly powerless. It was a little epiphany. This is what in the jargon of our day is known as becoming passionate about justice. What does one do in the face of this daily diminishment, humiliation, and degradation of human beings? What I want to do in this chapter is to look at the two conventional answers to that question, and then suggest a possible third.[2]

Conventional Justice

The first conventional answer is this: justice is about freedom. It is about ordering the affairs of a country such that every person has the greatest degree of liberty compatible with similar freedom for others. These are the classic political liberties – of conscience, assembly, and speech; the freedom to hold property, earn a living, and avoid arbitrary arrest. This is what we could call justice from the government's point of view.

The trouble about this kind of justice is that it begins to look suspiciously like justice for the winners. Over time huge economic inequalities can emerge, and a procedural justice that concentrates on protecting individual liberty can come to underwrite huge swathes of poverty. What I witnessed in that market square in the 1980s wasn't unusual: in countries that prize political liberty to the exclusion of economic equality, it is more or less normal.

There are three questions Christians need to think about in relation to government justice. One, how does the church relate to situations of significant injustice in other countries? So, for example, when Western governments deliberate over military action in the Middle East, they say they are concerned about injustice and oppression and tyranny, but people suspect they are mainly concerned about oil. Again, it is not about simple justice, it is about *whose* justice, and whether the powerful get to decide what justice looks like, and arrange justice in their own interests.[3] The ecological crisis is becoming the biggest example of how the reigning Western conception of justice is simply inadequate to comprehend the unprecedented levels of injustice being visited in our generation to those at most risk from global warming and in future generations on the whole planet. These are challenges where the norms of procedural justice are simply inadequate to the task.

Two, how does the church get involved in helping nations move toward the rule of law in societies where many of the conditions are still fundamentally unjust? If you are living in postcolonial sub-Saharan Africa, the likelihood is that the colonial power monopolized the land for the century or more of its rule. On departing a generation or two ago the colonizers did not, in most cases, make much of a job of returning that land to the descendants of its previous owners – those who constituted their rightful heirs. The meticulous work of identifying those heirs and resolving the complexities of inheritance and family history is crucial to crafting a just peace. But it is well outside the normal understanding of procedural justice.

Three, does the church see its own nation state as a place where the rule of law fundamentally prevails, or does it align itself with those for whom this is anything but the case? A church I know well has hosted a series of worship services to mark significant anniversaries following the racially motivated killing of a young black man in London and the notoriously perverted investigation into his death which has stretched over more than twenty years. As the distressing disclosures around that case have continued to mount, and the disparities in treatment of people of different races have continued, the question becomes, whose side does the church think it is on when it presumes that miscarriages of justice are the exception, rather than the norm? Can the church that sings the Magnificat ever be comfortable siding with a justice that's skewed toward the winners?

And so to the second conventional kind of justice. Justice is about rights. It is about recognizing that every individual has inherent worth as a human being. Pursuing justice means taking up the cause of those whose rights have been ignored or suppressed, even if the person or body whose responsibility it is to uphold those rights is hostile, formidable, or hard to identify. This is what we could call justice for the losers. It does not start with a blank sheet of paper and a theory of good order. It starts with people's experience of pain and suffering and cruelty and seeks to give those people a chance in life that has been snatched from their hands. It does not expect to win every time and it has no template in mind of what the end of all its striving might look like. It does not always know how the resources will be found or the adjustments be made to answer its demands: it just takes up one case at a time and seeks to give each person the honor that is their due and has been denied them.

Let us consider an analogy from pastoral care. When a person comes to see a pastor, they sit down, they explore in subtle ways how much they trust their interlocutor, and when all goes well they tell a story and with the pastor they find a new or better way to locate that story within a wider story of themselves, the world, the church, and God. And when that point is reached, the pastor has a choice. He or she can slap their thighs, and say, "Well, nice talking, time to head off to the youth group, and I'm sure you've got things to do", thus bringing the conversation to a polite end. Or, he or she can say, slowly and gently, "Was there anything else?" I believe it is no exaggeration to say that on this choice hangs a whole ministry. If the pastor takes the first option, and heads off to the youth group, he or she is saying all is basically well with the world, and life can be fitted into a routine. If the pastor takes the second option, he or she will never be bored. Overwhelmed, possibly: but there will never be a need to scratch around for the new mission idea or a bold justice agenda, because it will be provided free of charge.

The second kind of justice is not tidy, smooth, or ever really finished. If a congregation is genuinely close to its community, and aware of a global community in which it is wrapped up even if it is not so tied by bonds of affection and encounter, then issues of justice will arise readily. It just has to pay attention, and keep its eyes open. Then there are two directions it can go. Its members can spend time and care supporting the wronged as they seek to make a journey toward their own vindication, restitution, or restoration. Or they can take up the struggle on their behalf, and join with others seeking to do so. These are the approaches we have called working with and working for.

Embarking on a justice campaign, whether it is the patient accompaniment of working with, or the more strident advocacy of working for, requires a sober estimation of what it means to raise awareness in victims, perpetrators and the wider public.[4] Each of the these constituencies – victims, perpetrators and the wider public – has its own reasons for shielding its eyes from and refusing to name injustice, and, even when it has called it what it is, still not doing anything about it. Each constituency requires a different strategy, a different kind of perseverance, a different kind of cajoling and trickster spirit.[5]

The only tried and trusted way of bringing about change is to awaken anger and compassion. Injustice provokes outrage, shock, horror, disgust, fury. And here lies a major problem. To provoke such strong reactions can involve a degree of simplification, amplification – even an element of deception – in order to achieve the required response. These are bridges one has to find a way to cross. If one is going to campaign on homelessness one needs a picture of a person sleeping rough. If one is up against deadline day and no such picture is to hand, does one dress a colleague up to lie down in a doorway? Or is that a lie that undermines the credibility of the whole organization? These are the kinds of questions justice work turfs up every day. The public can only usually deal with a certain degree of nuance before losing interest or the flow of the story: but people's lives are almost entirely made up of nuance. So in the quest to get a justice message across, one can end up exploiting a victim of injustice by simplifying and thus distorting their story.

And that names the danger in justice work. In the quest to achieve the goal, it can chew people up who get in the way, and thus generate its own kind of injustice. Justice work almost always involves building coalitions, and coalitions require compromise, and compromise is generally something that passionate people who see the world through partial lenses find hard to swallow.

And it is not just about treading on people. George Bernard Shaw's play *Mrs. Warren's Profession* tells the story of Vivie Warren, who goes to Cambridge University to read Maths, and while there is filled with all sorts of righteous and outspoken opinions about the world, about men and women in it, about justice and about morality.[6] But half-way through the play she makes a humiliating discovery. The money that's paid for her education has come from her mother's professional profits. Her mother, Mrs. Warren, has made her fortune by running a chain of brothels all across Europe, in which women have sold their bodies to men for payment. It turns out Vivie's high principles are rooted in her mother's low practicalities. When Christians style themselves according to the fashionable phrase "speaking truth to power," they invariably assume they have the truth and someone else has the power. Too often one or both of these assumptions proves incorrect. Sometimes Christians discover they themselves are Vivie Warren, and their righteous advocacy has been funded or facilitated by deeply compromised commitments they themselves prefer not to see or disclose.

So the first kind of justice concentrates on guaranteeing people's freedom to be able to do things that don't harm others. The second kind of justice is about securing people's right not to have harmful things done to them. The first kind looks to biblical leaders like Moses and Solomon; the second to prophets like Elijah and Amos.

Going Beyond Justice

The church has always been divided between these two kinds of justice. Because it has always, or almost always, sought to be close to the poor, it has always been alert to the second kind of justice. It has always seen the worth of every person in the fact that Jesus came to be one like us, so each of us is precious in God's sight. But to the extent that the church has felt it had a stake in the good ordering of society as a whole, and to the extent that's it is often been more or less in the pocket of the wealthiest and most influential in society, it has always had an interest in the first kind of justice.

One way of dodging the question, and averting the gaze of that man in the square, is to say the only justice that matters is God's justice. This sees each one of us as being in the wrong before God, and rejoices that Jesus stepped in to take God's punishment on our behalf. Our eternal salvation is secured by the merciful justice of God – justification. What is good about this account is that it makes Jesus central to our idea of justice, and insists that mercy is at the heart of God. (After all, it is not clear how the two conventional notions of justice have anything much to do with Jesus.) But what is bad about this retreat into piety is that because it has so little to say to the searing gaze of that man in the market square, in practice it more or less ends up siding with the first kind of justice, because it takes no initiative to change the status quo. It justifies the winners today by saying we can all be winners in the end.

So how can Christians talk about Jesus in relation to justice in a way that doesn't retreat into piety or simply underwrite the shortcomings of the conventional approaches? Christians will continue to pursue both conventional approaches in painstaking and honorable ways. But we need to say something more about justice, something more that does not preserve the problem that we somehow leave Jesus behind when we seek justice.

Here we may turn to Paul's short letter to Philemon.[7] Here are the crucial verses.

> Though I am bold enough in Christ to command you to do your duty, yet I would rather appeal to you on the basis of love. ... I am appealing to you for my child, Onesimus, whose father I have become during my imprisonment.

Formerly he was useless to you, but now he is indeed useful both to you and to me. I am sending him, that is, my own heart, back to you. I wanted to keep him with me, so that he might be of service to me in your place during my imprisonment for the gospel; but I preferred to do nothing without your consent, in order that your good deed might be voluntary and not something forced. Perhaps this is the reason he was separated from you for a while, so that you might have him back forever, no longer as a slave but more than a slave, a beloved brother – especially to me but how much more to you, both in the flesh and in the Lord. So if you consider me your partner, welcome him as you would welcome me. If he has wronged you in any way, or owes you anything, charge that to my account. ... I will repay it. I say nothing about your owing me even your own self. ... Confident of your obedience, I am writing to you, knowing that you will do even more than I say.

Now we have to recognize that Paul isn't being entirely transparent in this letter. He does not actually say what the problem is or what he wants Philemon to do. But let us look more closely.

It seems that Paul is returning a runaway slave to his master, asking the master to treat the former slave with mercy, and, if there is any loss of money or honor, to charge that loss to Paul's account. Paul is talking about the creation of a new kind of community. He regards Philemon as a brother in the faith; he wants Philemon to recognize Onesimus as a partner too; and he hopes so to move Philemon to make Onesimus a legitimately free man. This reconciliation is possible and plausible because Jesus, by laying down his life, has brought about our reconciliation with God. In the same way by saying "charge it to my account" Paul is laying down his life to reconcile Onesimus and Philemon. This is hardly a retreat into piety. This is putting one's life on the line for something better than justice.

Twelve years after that encounter in the Middle Eastern market square, I happened to be on the outskirts of a town in East Anglia, again around 5:30 in the morning. I saw shadowy figures loitering in a lay-by, hoodies up, faces obscured, occasionally speaking to one another in a language I did not know. And then I saw a van draw up. And behold it was a replay of what I had seen in the Middle Eastern square, but this time for day-labor picking East Anglian fruit. It was another epiphany. Oppressive economic relations were not just an issue in a faraway land: they were an issue right here, right now. Twelve years before a man's piercing gaze had challenged me to choose whom I was with. Now that man's gaze was upon me, once again: it was challenging me to step from a place of being for to one of the three other options: to work for, by putting to use the political influence I now had; to

work with, by coming alongside the issues in a local context, of full employment, immigration, a low wage economy, and a seasonal labor market, or to
be with by getting to know the men under the hooded sweaters. That gaze
came straight out of the parable of the sheep and the goats.

And ever since I have had two songs singing in my heart. One is a song of
justice. It is good to pursue justice – especially that second kind. It is good
to be close to those who have been deeply wronged, and walk with them as
they find strength to seek restitution. It is good to awaken victims, perpetrators, and the wider public to things that should not be, to stir grievance
and anger and compassion, to build coalitions to achieve results, to change
laws and alter practices, and to seek a better future together. This is about
dignity and honor and rights and solidarity and setting people free.

But when all this activity is over more often than not people still have not
got what they most need. Because there is only so much the law can do. Justice can give dignity, justice can affirm rights, justice can restore property,
justice can clear one's name, justice can outlaw domination. But while those
things make life possible, they alone don't make life. Life is about more than
getting one's due and living free from harm. Life is about restored relationships, about flowering talents, about passionate friendships, about costly
forgiveness, about the release of hidden joys, about what Paul describes in
his letter to Philemon when he talks about going beyond what he asks and
discovering a beloved brother.

And this is the central point. Both conventional kinds of justice are
handicapped by the ways in which they replicate working-for assumptions.
If Paul had followed the first kind of justice he would probably have had
such respect for the law he would made sure Onesimus remained a slave.
If he had followed the second kind of justice Paul would have made sure
Onesimus was a free man, but Onesimus and Philemon would most likely
have ended up at best strangers to one another, perhaps enemies. Paul was
looking for a way of life that goes beyond justice – a way that goes beyond
working for and requires the dynamic of with. And the name of these practices that go beyond justice is church.

Church is where Christians practice the justice of God, which goes beyond vindication and restitution and legitimation and liberation. Church
is where Christians find there is something beyond freedom and that is
friendship, there is something beyond dignity and that is celebration, there
is something beyond guaranteeing a person's security and that is laying
down one's life for their flourishing, there is something beyond vindication
and that is forgiveness, there is something beyond good order and that

is worship. When I stood in that Middle Eastern market square and that man's gaze went straight through me, I had not read John Rawls' *A Theory of Justice* or John Locke's *Two Treatises of Government* or even Martin Luther King, Jr.'s *Letter from Birmingham Jail*. And I had no innate insight into injustice. But I had read Matthew 25:31–46 many times, I had spent a lot of time in home groups wondering about the hungry, the thirsty, the naked, the stranger, the sick, and the prisoner, and I had been trained to spend my life expecting to see in the dispossessed the face of Christ. Human nature did not teach me that; school did not teach me that: church did. But church did not think confronting injustice was an end in itself; church thought seeing the face of the unjustly treated was a way of being with Christ.

Jean Vanier has a way of describing justice.[8] He says the story begins "with a huge gap of injustice and pain. It is the gap between the so-called "normal" world and people who have been pushed aside." But this injustice cannot simply be rectified by fixing a disability or outlawing discrimination. Vanier says the first time he entered an institution for intellectually disabled people he heard their simple cry: "Do you love me?" And he realized that was his cry too. He realized his need of these people – for they could help him "grow in the wisdom of love" (31). His goal for them was not autonomy – which he describes as the ability to "live alone, watch television and drink beer." What autonomy doesn't grasp is the need for belonging. "The church," he says, "is a place of compassion and fecundity, a place of welcome and friendship" (37). It is bound together by sharing food, prayer, and celebration.

Beyond justice lies transformation. Janine came to L'Arche aged 40 with a paralyzed arm and leg, severe epilepsy, and difficulties understanding and learning. She was angry with her body, her sisters, and God. At L'Arche she discovered she could dance; and she could be loved. She would sit down next to Jean Vanier, rest his tired head on her shoulder, and say, "Poor old man" (26). This mode of life beyond justice is one in which the so-called needy or victim becomes the teacher. In the words of John Paul II, "In revealing the fundamental frailty of the human condition, the disabled person becomes an expression of the tragedy of pain. ... The difficulties of the disabled are often perceived as a shame or a provocation and their problem as burdens to be removed or resolved as quickly as possible. [But disabled people] can teach everyone about the love that saves us; they can become heralds of a new world, no longer dominated by force, violence, and aggression, but by love, solidarity, and acceptance" (38–39). This is a description of the journey from working for to being with, translated into the discourse of justice.

On a rather humbler level than the prophetic work of the L'Arche communities, one church in central London holds a gathering for 45 people every Sunday afternoon. A handful of those gathered are congregation members; the rest are people from outside the European Union with no recourse to public funds. The first encounters come about because most of the latter spend significant amounts of the week relaxing in the pews of the church, having spent the night on overnight buses or on the streets of London or in some kind of ad hoc accommodation. They are used to four kinds of interaction: denial, hostility, human rights lawyers, or sandwiches. The volunteers seek to offer them warmth, washing machines, showers, friendship, a hot curry, and space to recover their identity and dignity. The volunteers hear stories – stories of people who were often highly qualified in some of the more troubled and oppressive countries of the world, stories of people who risked everything to come to London and who now experience untold hardship rather than return to the even worse hell from which they came. Gradually vulnerable people gain confidence, become leaders, recover their inner strength, and Sunday afternoon becomes the focus of their week. Often they help each other: one turned out to be a barber and was happy to cut the hair of all the others on request. The volunteers cannot fix these people's problems and no one knows what their future holds. But together they discover something deeper, more lasting, and more human than bare justice. It is being with translated into the discourse of justice.

Vanier and the Sunday group explain why, while I believe Christians are called to seek justice, I do not believe they can finally be content with seeking justice. Beyond the care for the freedom and flourishing of society and the upholding of the rights of individuals lies the vision of the church as a community of reconciliation, forgiveness, and friendship. It is almost impossible for this church to flourish without justice; and this church should certainly be committed to both kinds of justice, in appropriate degrees depending on its social context. Being with does not mean renouncing working for; it means fulfilling it and going beyond it. Yet justice cannot constitute this church, and it certainly cannot substitute for it. What grieves the world is not simply oppression, cruelty, exploitation and fraud – though of course these need to be outlawed, confronted, and resisted. What grieves the world even more is exclusion, isolation, ostracism, neglect, and loneliness. There can seldom, perhaps never, be a law against these things. Yet they abide when processes of and campaigns for justice have done their work. And it is in their transformation that the church's vocation most truly lies.

So I sing the song of justice. I sing it with those who struggle, with all who seek a world where people are not oppressed, a world where people stand with one another in times of cruelty and hardship. But I also sing another song, a song of worship, a song of forgiveness, of celebration, of unbridled, overflowing joy, reconciliation and resurrection, a song that goes beyond justice, a song that Paul sang to Philemon. It is a song we call love.

Notes

1. This point is made particularly well in B.F. Westcott, *The Gospel According to St. John* (London: John Murray, 1882): 168.
2. My sense of the two conventional kinds of justice has been greatly informed by Nicholas Wolterstorff in his books *Justice: Rights and Wrongs* (Princeton, NJ: Princeton University Press, 2008) and *Journey toward Justice: Personal Encounters in the Global South* (Grand Rapids, MI: Baker, 2013). My position is informed by Wolterstorff, but Wolterstorff's account explicitly favors the second of what here I take properly to be considered three approaches.
3. Alasdair MacIntyre, *Whose Justice, Which Rationality* (London: Duckworth, 1988). See also Stanley Hauerwas, "Whose Just War? Which Peace?" In *Dispatches from the Front: Theological Engagements with the Secular* (Durham, NC: Duke University Press, 1994): 136–152.
4. Wolterstorff has an excellent account along these lines in his *Journey toward Justice*: 166–179.
5. For more on the trickster spirit, see Saul Alinsky, *Rules for Radicals: A Pragmatic Primer for Realistic Radicals* (New York: Vintage, 1971); and James C. Scott, *Domination and the Arts of Resistance: Hidden Transcripts* (New Haven, CT: Yale University Press, 1990).
6. George Bernard Shaw, *Mrs. Warren's Profession* (London: Methuen, 2012).
7. The radical and novel dimension of Philemon in this context was brought to my attention by N.T. Wright, *Paul and the Faithfulness of God: Christian Origins and the Question of God* (London: SPCK, 2013): 1–74.
8. Stanley Hauerwas and Jean Vanier, *Living Gently in a Violent World: The Prophetic Witness of Weakness* (Downers Grove, IL: IVP, 2008): page references in the text.

16

The Transfiguration of Suffering

"The angel of the Lord appeared to Gideon and said to him, 'The Lord is with you ...' Gideon answered him, 'But sir, if the Lord is with us, why then has all this happened to us?'" (Judg. 6:12). If one of the two most pressing challenges to the notion of being with is that it does not offer enough in the face of injustice, then the other is that it is too much to ask in the face of suffering.

In this final chapter I consider the moral configuration of suffering. I begin with a survey of sources of suffering – because so many of the responses presuppose an account of causes. In looking at causes I identify the way much endurance of suffering involves disentangling the causes. In moving on to responses I reflect as elsewhere on the difference between with and for – but for the first time in the book I begin to consider whether there might be something requiring, but nonetheless beyond being with – an action of God to which those committed to being with may yet be exposed. Finally I look into that action more closely and connect being with to the practice of prayer, from which it is, perhaps, ultimately inseparable.

Sources of Suffering

There are broadly three sources of suffering. The first is our own folly, ignorance, and sin. "Jephthah made a vow to the Lord, and said, 'If you will give the Ammonites into my hand, then whoever comes out of the doors of my house to meet me, when I return victorious from the Ammonites, shall be the Lord's, to be offered up by me as a burnt offering'" (Judg. 11:30–31). Shortly after defeating the Ammonites, Jephthah sees his daughter – and berates her for bringing misfortune on him: "'You have brought me very low; you have become the cause of great trouble to me. For I have opened my mouth to the Lord, and I cannot take back my vow'" (Judg. 11:35). In

A Nazareth Manifesto, Samuel Wells © 2015 John Wiley & Sons, Ltd. Published 2015 by John Wiley & Sons, Ltd.

an echo of this story, Herod Antipas solemnly swears to Herodias' daughter, "'Whatever you ask me, I will give you, even half of my kingdom'" (Mark 6:23). In both stories, someone else has to die because of the oath of an exuberant man. These stories are a paradigm of folly, ignorance, and sin.

When we have a road traffic accident, the first question is, was it caused by our own reckless driving? Very often not, but it is still the first question to ask. "Could I have done something differently?" – that is the place to begin when reflecting on a bad situation. The child in us looks for a thousand other people to blame when we get in trouble, for others to lift the burden from our shoulders. The grown-up in us accepts that sometimes we get it wrong. It is important in this regard to distinguish between folly, ignorance, and sin.

Sin is where Jephthah bargains with something that does not belong to him, and thus speaks to God as if any person he might meet is at his disposal. This is arrogance, hubris, pride, the swagger of a reckless man. Herod Antipas is exposed by the meanness and conniving of Herodias. But it is his lust, his forgetfulness of his own responsibility, his world of fantasy kingship that brings about the death of the Baptist. Sin is where we drive without regard for the other cars, mixing selfishness with showing off, impatience with irritation, thrill with denial. Much of the time other cars will succeed in getting out of our way; but not always – and sometimes through overestimating our own ability to control the vehicle while at excessive speed or in the midst of major distraction we will simply hit another object without any other car needing to be involved. Perhaps the greatest suffering is that of King Lear who at the end of his play looks at his dead devoted daughter Cordelia whom he cast off, and his other two faithless daughters, Goneril and Regan, to whom he entrusted himself and his kingdom, and realizes, in his isolation and misery, he has no one to blame but himself.

Ignorance is where we simply do not know what we are doing. Of course one may say we never know what we are doing; but ignorance covers the ground between on the one hand the limitations we each share with the human race about causes and consequences and unexpected outcomes, and on the other hand the heedless trespassing into unknown territory with no good reason to expect to avoid damage or harm. When Jesus prays, "Father, forgive them; for they do not know what they are doing" (Luke 23:34), he is making a distinction between what the church recalls as the greatest sin of all – the putting-to-death of the Son of God – and the reality of the soldiers' situation, as carrying out a relatively routine execution of a man taken to be a seditious threat to the empire. They indeed do not know what they are really doing.

On the one hand ignorance includes not having an advanced understanding of the mechanics of our car, such that we did not realize the red
flashing light on the dashboard meant we should stop right away; on the
other hand ignorance means setting off for a journey in poor weather conditions and not taking due account of the dangers those conditions might
enhance. Ignorance thus dwells in the hinterland between what cannot be
excused as bad luck, but yet stops short of what could be called carelessness.
Its actions, not wrong in themselves, are intended, but its consequences are
neither intended nor anticipated. It is often said that ignorance of the law is
no excuse; but that is not to say that ignorance is the same thing as flagrant
disregard.

Folly is a similar attempt to name that which we did not intend, but for
which we are nonetheless responsible. Jephthah certainly did not intend the
first person he met after defeating the Ammonites to be his daughter – but it
is nonetheless his folly that made a tragedy out of a triumph. It was not just
bad luck. Haman, in the book of Esther, on being asked by King Ahasuerus,
"What shall be done for the man whom the king wishes to honor?" (Esther
6:6), could never have expected the king to be talking about Haman's arch-
enemy Mordecai; but Haman is such an unscrupulous double-dealer that
his machinations were bound to catch up with him eventually. Again, it is
folly – it is hard to call it simple misfortune.

We become used to driving without frequently checking the rear-view
mirror: most of the time it has no adverse effect; this one time it proves
disastrous. Some terrible news on the car radio distracts us from seeing
how close we are to the car in front; it turns out we are too close, and an
accident results. What distinguishes folly from ignorance is that ignorance,
in this context, names a somewhat random constellation of events with an
unpleasant outcome; whereas folly hints at a pattern of behavior, a compulsion, even addiction, that was perhaps bound in the end to come to grief.
The accident is not due to ignorance: we know it is important to look in the
rear-view mirror. In the aftermath of an accident, sometimes what comes
to light is reckless action – this is sin; other times what emerges are wholly
unexpected results arising from uninformed action – this is ignorance; other times again in the fervid search for causes and meanings one can discern
a possible, likely, if not probable turn of events emerging from repeated,
unwise, and yet not necessarily sinful habit. This is folly.

To say "I got that wrong," is not by any means the same as to say "and accordingly I was punished." The psalmist bewails the fact that getting things
wrong and suffering the consequences seldom occur in any kind of logical

sequence. Life rarely works in any such cause-and-effect way. Few people receive their just desserts, positively or negatively. To blame oneself entirely in the face of one's own suffering is to exaggerate one's own power and significance – one's power to build as well as destroy, one's power to ruin as well as ameliorate – and to underestimate the role of other people and other factors in one's story. It may appear pious but in fact can mask a good deal of pride.

The second kind of suffering comes to us from the folly, ignorance, and sin of others. Uriah the Hittite did nothing wrong; David set his heart on Uriah's wife Bathsheba, and would stop at nothing to make an end of Uriah, without Uriah ever knowing the cause for his life being put in such great and eventually fatal danger (1 Sam. 11:1–27).

This in some ways is the simplest kind of suffering. It seems clear who is to blame, and it is not ourselves. If you are subject to racial discrimination, you are on the receiving end of the ignorance and sin of others. The one thing you must not do is to take that sin on yourself – that is, internalize their disregard of your dignity and come to see yourself as lowly and in some way deserving of their contempt. While your suffering is real, morally this second kind of suffering is the perpetrator's problem, not yours. You only make it your own moral problem if you internalize their sin, or if you cling to their sin, and your woundedness by it, as part of your identity, by wearing it as a badge or, in due time, by refusing to forgive or be reconciled. Your suffering is important, but you can only really begin to address it if you disentangle it from the sin – which is someone else's.

That is why this kind of suffering is simpler than the first kind, because it is what we might call pure suffering – suffering unencumbered by one's own sin. If you are on a street and are simply hit by an object thrown apparently randomly from a window, the issues are relatively simple: there is no sin, ignorance or folly involved on your part; in no way did you bring this upon yourself; you would normally seek to endeavor, in due time (which may be a very long time), to be reconciled with the person who foolishly threw the flying object, but aside from that you can concentrate on recovering from the wound and the shock. To say this suffering is pure and simple is not to minimize the very considerable pain and agony sometimes involved; it is simply to recognize that when you detach suffering from your own sin it becomes a lot easier to face up to. A lot of the effort expended recovering from such a wound can involve addressing the anger and powerlessness that are evoked when you realize this really was in no way your fault – not sin, for sure, but not even folly or ignorance either, or at least not ignorance by any conventional estimation.

In making a journey through this kind of suffering it is very important to disentangle the perpetrator's sin, ignorance, and folly. The understandable anger of the victim can easily assume all hurt arises from the perpetrator's sin. (The perpetrator's own sense of guilt can make the same assumption.) But through the gifts of time, narrative, and grace, the victim can often come to perceive that the hurt arose not through the evil that deliberately sought to do harm, nor through the sin that recklessly disregarded another's well-being, but through the ignorance that had never seriously imagined the consequences for others of a particular kind of action, or the folly of a pattern of cutting corners or lacking thoroughness or assuming no one would really notice or care. While forgiveness for sin and evil is immensely difficult, forgiveness for folly and, even more, for ignorance may, when such are seen as almost universal shortcomings, be found to be a little easier.

The third kind of suffering is the most complicated. It is stuff that just happens. Breast cancer just happens. Earthquakes just happen. Floods just happen. In the language of this book, the second kind of suffering is mostly about the breakdown of relationship – the kinds of things that lead to hurt and distrust and resentment and even hatred. This third kind of suffering – stuff that just happens – is the territory of human limitation – and, ultimately, human mortality. Things do not turn out perfectly, do not turn out as planned, and do not last forever. Material things break, organic things decay, and interactions between things produce unexpected results. Few people are content to settle for what might be termed an "Ecclesiastes view" of the world – that time and chance envelop and submerge all things. The result is that all manner of research and enquiry tries to turn this third kind into one of the first two kinds – to turn chance into culpability, by ourselves or by others.

Hence the question, "'Who sinned, this man or his parents, that he was born blind?'" (John 9:2). Jesus' disciples try to turn something that just happened into either of our first two categories – the fault of the sufferer or attributable to a third party. Thus a news story will, on the first day, deal with the drama and gore; on the second day expose the authorities who should have prevented it all happening; and on the third day uncover the human narratives; before searching for a new dimension to sustain the story. All efforts are spent to find negligence underneath accident, oversight behind misfortune, and blunder within disappointment. For breast cancer and other health questions attention turns to diet and exercise; for earthquakes and geological issues the focus is on construction and planning; while for floods and weather events the scrutiny rests upon climactic and agricultural patterns. But the truth is that for most people, most of the time, stuff just happens.

In fact, few forms of suffering fall neatly into just one of these three categories. When a romantic relationship ends, is it the first kind of suffering, where you blame yourself, the second, where you are furious with your former partner, or the third, where you say it just did not work out? When a person is made redundant, is it an appropriate juncture for them to face up to their own shortcomings, is it a good moment for them to lash out and call their employer all the names under the sun, or is it a simply a personal experience of the process by which all organizations change and their employment needs change accordingly? Sometimes reverting straight to the third category can be a cop-out that avoids facing where we or another person really have been foolish or stupid or cruel ("All's fair in love and war."). But, at least as often, trying to blame ourselves or someone else is a desperate attempt to retain some agency, some kind of handle on something that has swept way beyond us and we can't imagine how we can ever control. After 2008 people in the West spent enormous energy seeking a scapegoat for the financial crisis, but most of that energy was expended in trying to bring down to size something that was beyond us all. Sometimes the hardest thing in life is coming to terms with things that are nobody's fault, but still overshadow and terrify us. The greatest example of this is death. Some deaths are somebody's fault; but most deaths are nobody's fault. Our bodies are only made to run a course of years. Our greatest challenge is to face our own mortality and that of those we love. And when we look round for someone to blame, we look in vain.

These reflections on the different kinds and origins of suffering are designed to clarify the following point. Genuine suffering – as opposed to hardship, adversity, or hurt – is seldom pure and never simple. Profound impulses, primally and culturally, insist on translating it into a problem that can be fixed, often in a working-for way – by someone's intervention straightforwardly to remove or extinguish it. The foregoing account is intended to nuance the complexity of suffering, not exhaustively, but sufficiently to show why working-for solutions seldom do justice to the complexity of what they are trying to fix.

Responses to Suffering

How then does one respond to suffering? Again there are three broad responses, although they do not neatly map onto the three forms of suffering that we have noted. The first response is to see if there is anything that can be done. When Lazarus is ill, Mary and Martha send for Jesus (John 11:3).

When the children of Israel faint with hunger in the wilderness, they look to Moses to do something about it (Exod. 16:3). When a tree falls down on two people, and they are still underneath it, and you are close by, your first thought is to see if you can move the tree. When a person has cancer you wonder if some intervention can take the tumor out or somehow attack it so its threat is reduced or nullified. Ideally the person can help themselves; alternatively you can help them or some kind of expert can step in. This is a standard working-for approach. This whole book starts from a twin premise: that most disadvantage, hardship, distress, or suffering is not like that; but that most response to such adversity assumes that it is.

Second, the truth is, not much suffering works in a linear pattern from problem to solution. When you go to see a counselor, whether in a formal contractual relationship or informally with a pastor or mentor or friend, you are not looking to the counselor to fix your problem. What you are doing is putting all the details and contributory factors out in a shapeless heap, rather like a motorcyclist dismembering a bike and placing the pieces on the garage floor. And then what the counselor helps you do is reassemble those confusing pieces in some kind of a coherent story that more or less relates each piece to the others in some way that begins to make sense of what is happening to you.

The abiding claim of Christianity throughout the ages is that it indeed is that story – that it provides the texture and truth that help us understand our stories for the first time, even, and indeed especially, in the face of suffering. One pastor spoke at length with a woman in her forties who had always longed to have a husband and child and was beginning to sense the moment for her was passing. And as they talked the pastor and she together came to see her as symbolizing her community, a place with gifted and hopeful people who yet were beset by unemployment and hardship and dashed hopes. As they spoke further she came to see herself in the passion of the God who in the prophets had over and over again offered love and companionship to Israel and felt the seed landing on the path and never taking root. She was finding her story of suffering in God's story of unrequited love and unrewarded offering. It did not take her suffering away but it gave her suffering meaning and context and purpose. It made it beautiful.

Again, there was one young child who had been diagnosed with Aicardi Syndrome from shortly after her birth, was expected to survive a very short while, and in the end lived for around three years. Reflecting at her funeral, the preacher remarked, "It is *we* who are born blind, blind to the life-changing truth that a child like Lydia carries in her frail little body a glimpse of eternity. She is not an object of pity but of wonder, awe, and reverence. In her gentle, gracious way she points us to the reality that this life is only a minute fraction of God's creation, the blink of an eye." She went on to say that this tiny girl "came into time from eternity and now she has gone before us into eternity. I believe she came to open our eyes, to restore our sight. She did not need to use words. God chose to make his home in her and through her very frailty and seeming brokenness his infinite love and compassion was once more made incarnate." This is simply taking God's story more seriously than our own – inscribing our stories into the slipstream of God's glory.

The struggle for narrative is at least as much at stake in the aftermath of war. When a soldier returns from a conflict zone and is experiencing post-traumatic stress, what a psychiatrist is trying to help him or her do is not to tell a story that is characterized by happy endings and an absence of tragedy, which would be a lie, but rather to find a way to go on as an agent in the world in which he or she is not mastered by past traumatic events – but a world in which also the avoidance of those things doesn't become its own form of mastery by them.[1]

And yet there is a third kind of response to suffering. It arises when there does not seem to be anything you or anyone else can do to alleviate it, and there seems no story that can make sense of it. This is the point when a person finds that many, perhaps most, of their friends will walk away from them, because the majority of people want to fix things, and the remaining people want to make sense of things; and the number of people prepared still to stay around when something cannot be fixed and does not make any sense is very small. It is the point where working for and working with have run their course. It is the moment when being with comes into its own.

Gerard Hughes takes an uncompromising view of suffering. "Most of our suffering," he says, "comes to us not because our lives are dedicated to promoting Christ's kingdom, but from our failure to build our own kingdom."[2] He goes on to refer to our longing for wealth, honor, and power, to our sense of our own incompetence and feelings of inferiority, to difficulties of temperament, to loneliness, to disappointments in love, and to what he calls our "pathetic mediocrity." What Hughes is doing is pointing out the narratives we compose for ourselves for which we then hold God accountable. His is a blunt but perhaps healthy way of dismantling our cloying self-pity, maudlin regret, and self-serving sentimentality.

But removing self-pity, regret, and sentimentality does not remove suffering altogether. The argument of this book has been that there is only one way to address the suffering that cannot be fixed by intervention or reframed by wrapping a story around it. And that is by incarnational presence – being with. Such presence seeks to say, "You may fundamentally know, in your echoing pain or fear, that you are not alone." This is the most important thing we offer one another in times of hardship and distress. This is the heart of the acts of mercy: "When you are hungry I might not be able to get you a job but I will not turn my back on you; when you are a stranger I will not forget you; when you are sick I will sit by your bedside; when you are in prison I will write and wait and remember and visit you." And that is the fundamental way God engages suffering. Not by fixing it; not by renarrating it; but in being with us in the incarnate Christ and in those whom, in the power of the Spirit, God indwells in order to be beside us. Christianity is most transparently embodied when disciples imitate Christ's incarnation and show up among those on whom the world has turned its back, whose suffering the world cannot bear to see. It is not about having the solution or the answer, but about being present even when you have no things to do, actions to offer or words to say. That is what faith means.

What is the role of Christ in relation to suffering? Conventional portrayals of Christian theology have tended to portray Christ's suffering as arising from the second kind of cause from my first list and to involve the first kind of response from my second list. That is to say, Christ's suffering is attributed squarely to the sin of others, rather than his own or "stuff that just happens"; and his suffering is taken to constitute God's way of fixing human suffering in general and sin in particular. But that uncomplicated account does less than full justice to suffering on the one hand or Christ on the other. As we saw earlier, there is a lot of suffering, perhaps most, that is not really anyone's fault. If we see Christ's role as wholly or largely about taking away sin, that still leaves a huge swathe of sadness, grief, and pain with which to deal. What does it mean for Christ to engage with that? Surely God did not leave the job half-done? Christ is not simply about fixing human sinfulness like a surgeon replacing a dislocated joint.

Christ certainly does die at the hands of greedy, cruel, proud, and envious people. But it is not as simple as that. Christ truly enters the human condition and takes on suffering that, though it is nobody's fault, nonetheless impoverishes and depresses and subdues and disables. That third kind of suffering is on and around Christ's shoulder as he walks the way of the cross. And what he embodies is that third kind of response to suffering – the kind that shows up even when it does not have a solution, the kind that hangs on when it does not know what to say. This is how Christ shows God's love for us – that in the face of both the folly of humankind and the contingency of existence, we see God not just setting things right but being with us and suffering with us as long as things hurt and until things come right – and even if things never come right. That is the God Christians worship on the cross. And that is the God Christians meet when they pray.

Three Ways to Pray

An account of engagement with hardship, disadvantage, poverty, and suffering through the lens of being with has to end with a treatment of prayer. The reason is that, if there were no conviction that God is at work outside and beyond human ministry, service, and friendship, then one would almost inevitably have to assume the model of working for. Being with depends on the patience, humility, and hope that are shaped around the eschatological fulfillment of God and the anticipatory glimpses of that fulfillment brought by the work of the Holy Spirit. And it is those anticipatory glimpses that the disciple yearns for in the practice of intercessory prayer.

Perhaps the signal anticipatory glimpse the gospels afford is the transfiguration. Here is an unmistakable sign to the disciples that there is more than one story going on simultaneously. Jesus relates to them, but also to Moses and Elijah; Jesus has a conversation with them, but the voice of the Father is speaking to Jesus too. There are two, perhaps three dimensions to the event; in no way is the disciples' experience central or primary – indeed, they are privileged to be involved at all. Here is the clue to how to identify, recognize, understand, and finally move beyond what we might somewhat harshly call the narcissism of suffering. And more importantly, here is the window onto the ambitions of intercessory prayer.

Let us take the most mundane of congregational experiences: a conversation over coffee after a worship service at a local church. The two parties greet one another, update each other on recent events, discover why they have not spoken so much recently, and catch up on news and comment. And then, just as they are finishing, one conversation partner holds her friend's forearm, and her tone changes and is more serious, and she says, "Say a prayer for my dad, will you, he's not himself, the dementia's really kicking in now, and I feel like he's losing his identity inch by unrelenting inch." And her eyes reveal the cost of what it has required to keep going, and of what it has taken just to put that pain into words, and all there is to say in reply is, "I'm sorry. I'm so sorry. This must be such a bewildering time for you. Of course I will pray for your dad. And I will pray for you too."

But then a promise has been made. A promise that must be kept. How exactly does one pray for a person in such a situation? What words can one find to wrap around this kind of long, slow-burning tragedy, in which lives and souls unravel and there is no sign of the dawn?

I choose this example because, as much as any case of suffering, caring for a loved one with Alzheimer's is as close as it gets to what I earlier called the third kind of suffering – stuff that just happens; because in this context working-for solutions are at best elusive and at worst irrelevant to the point of being absurd; because, in the absence of solutions, the temptation to lose patience and walk away from the patient, or from the carer, is enormous and sometimes insuperable; and because an impoverished notion of the atonement, which simply sees Jesus as having taken away our sins, has so little to offer to the carer, since it either assumes Alzheimer's is somehow connected to the sin that has been taken away (thus adding insult to injury) or it suggests, in taking away sin, Jesus missed the more important part, which is inexplicable suffering and remorseless, in this case mental, limitation. And I choose this example because it offers a hint that there might be something beyond being with – or, perhaps better, there might be a hint of glory that cannot be glimpsed without first accepting the assumptions and undertaking the disciplines of being with.

There are two conventional ways to pray for a friend and her father facing Alzheimer's together. We might call the first way resurrection. It is a call for a miracle. It forms such petitions as these: "God, by the power with which you raised Jesus from the dead, restore this man in mind and body, make him himself again, and bring my friend the joy of companionship and the hope of a long and fruitful family life together." There is good reason to pray this prayer. It comes out of love for a friend. It arises from seeing how watching her father disintegrate before her eyes is breaking her heart. It is rooted in a desire for God to show some compassion, some change, some action. There may well also be a sense of some other Christians, perhaps close at hand, who seem to pray for resurrection all the time, and an abiding uncertainty as to one ought to have more faith and expect God to do amazing things every day. But there is also perhaps a memory of having seen hopes dashed, a knowledge of having seen Alzheimer's only end one way, and thus a deep resistance to saying the word "heal" because it seems to be asking for something that is just not going to happen. That is the prayer of resurrection. There is no question that Christianity is founded on it and it would seem to be understandably what the friend most longs for – but sometimes it is too hard to say.

But resurrection is not the only kind of prayer. The other conventional kind of prayer is the prayer of incarnation. This is the territory of being with. It is a call for the Holy Spirit to be with this friend and her father. It is a recognition that Jesus was broken, desolate, alone, on the brink of death, and that this is all part of being a human being, all part of the contingency that begins at the moment of conception. Human bodies and minds are fragile, frail, and sometimes feeble. There is no guarantee life will be easy, comfortable, fun, or happy. The prayer of incarnation says, "God, in Jesus you shared our pain, our foolishness, and our sheer bad luck; you took on our flesh with all its needs and clumsiness and weakness. Visit my friend and her father now: give them patience to endure what lies ahead, hope to get through every trying day, and companions to show them your love." The irony about this prayer is that the resurrection prayer expects God to do all the work, whereas this prayer stirs us into action ourselves. Those who pray, "Send them companions to show them your love," have to be wondering if there is anyone better placed to be such a companion than they themselves. (In such a context one may speak of a "prayer of Pentecost" – a prayer that God may empower the intercessor and others through the Holy Spirit to deliver the change they long to see in the world.)

Deep down the friend is well aware that the prospects for her father are bleak. What she is really asking for when she nervously puts her hand out to clasp a supportive forearm is, "Help me trust that I'm not alone in all of this." Being with offers a response to precisely that plea. But in the midst of everything anyone would be likely to feel powerless and inadequate in the face of all this friend was going through.

Only at this point in our study, as it reaches its conclusion, is it possible to recognize that resurrection and incarnation are not the only kinds of intercessory prayer. They are certainly the most common, and in many circumstances they say most or all of what the intercessor wants or needs or ought to say. But what the disciples see on the mountain at the central moment in the synoptic gospel narrative discloses a third kind of prayer – a prayer of transfiguration. On the mountain the disciples discover that Christ is part of a conversation with Israel and God and is dwelling in glory in a way that they have no idea of and can hardly grasp and yet that puts everything on a different plane. There is a whole reality going on that is part of their reality and affects their reality, but about which they are unaware and ignorant.

This is an invitation to a third kind of intercessory prayer. "God, in your son's transfiguration we see a whole reality within and beneath and beyond what we thought we understood; in their times of bewilderment and confusion, show my friend and her father your glory, that they may find a deeper truth to their life than they ever knew, make firmer friends than they ever had, discover reasons for living beyond what they'd ever imagined, and be folded into your grace like never before." This is a different kind of intercessory prayer. The prayer of resurrection has a certain defiance about it – in the face of what seem to be all the known facts, it calls on God to produce the goods and turn the situation round. It has courage and hope, but there is always a fear that it has a bit of fantasy as well. The prayer of incarnation is honest and unflinching about the present and the future, but it is perhaps a little too much swathed in tragedy. To take the transfiguration context, it can be so concerned to face the reality of the disciples' situation that there is always a fear that it is going to miss the glory of what Jesus is displaying with Israel and with the Father.

The ingredients of the prayer of transfiguration lie in the transfiguration story itself. There is glory – the glory of the Lord in the face of Jesus Christ. There is the pattern of God's story in Israel and the church, a story that finds its most poignant moments in the midst of suffering and exile. There is the loving, tender presence and heavenly voice of God the Father – a voice that, for the only time in their lives, the disciples hear and understand. And there is the extraordinary realization that, even though all this could have gone on without them, the disciples have been caught up in the life of the Trinity, the mystery of salvation, the unfolding of God's heart, the beauty of holiness. They have been with God.

This is the difference between the prayer of resurrection ("Fix this and take it off my desk!") and the prayer of incarnation ("Be with me and share in my struggle, now and always") set against the prayer of transfiguration. The prayer of transfiguration is something more like, "Make my friend's trial and tragedy, her problem and pain, a glimpse of your glory, a window into your world, when she can see your face, sense the mystery in all things, and walk with angels and saints. Bring her closer to you in this crisis than she ever has been in calmer times. Make this a moment of truth, and when she cowers in fear and feels alone, touch her, raise her, and make her alive like never before."

Beyond Being With

I have spoken about being with in many settings, in several cultures, and among diverse religious and social constituencies. I have in these last two chapters tried to address the two main criticisms I have heard – that being with is wrong because it does not work, and that being with is wrong because it does not care. I take these to be the consequential and deontological objections. In these two chapters I have sought not to give detailed responses to every precise objection, but to locate their assumptions within a wider perspective, and more importantly to offer a vision that renders them unimaginative in their scope as well as inaccurate in their aim.

There is another criticism to address which much of the book has been oriented: the view that the teleological and ethical priority of being with is exegetically unsustainable and theologically unjustified. All I can say to this has already been offered in the foregoing chapters.

However, there is one last criticism that I receive with much more sympathetic ears. Most complaints about being with is that it is too little – it does too little to "make a difference" or "make the world a better place"; it does too little to show compassion or eradicate suffering; it does too little to fight structural evil and systemic injustice; it does too little to acknowledge the abiding (or dominant) "for" aspects of God in general and salvation history and the atonement in particular. But the complaint to which I am more inclined to plead guilty is the opposite one: that being with is too much. Being with asks too much of Laszlo, that he should remain with Katherine rather than walk to Cairo; it asks too much of my friend, that she should abide with her father rather than seek earnestly to fix his Alzheimer's; it asks too much of missionaries, that they should live in the areas they serve, rather than visit them and deliver programs in them; it asks too much of Alexander, that he should rub along with Stuart, the feckless homeless man, rather than tell him to pull himself together and stop shipping the overflow of his troubles onto others; it asks too much that we should all be Bonhoeffers who return to Germany to be with the German people rather than Allies who invade and defeat and emerge victorious from war.

It is true. Being with does ask too much. It is not too small a commission. It is, for many, perhaps most, too great a commission. We therefore find a hundred ways, practical and intellectual, to circumvent it. But by ending my argument with transfiguration I hope I have shown that the imitation of God in Christ is only possible in the power of the Holy Spirit and in the grace made tangible through prayer. Being with is, finally, a gesture of confidence that, like the disciples at the transfiguration, we know the true work of salvation is going on not just here but simultaneously elsewhere; that it is not in jeopardy; and that our joy, and privilege, is found in discovering our invitation to be even a small part of it.

Notes

1. I am grateful to Warren Kinghorn for expressing the work of psychiatrists in cases of post-traumatic stress disorder in these terms.
2. Gerard Hughes, *God of Surprises* (London: Darton, Longman and Todd, 1985): 131.

Epilogue:
Magnificat

This sermon, on the text Luke 1:39–55, was preached in Duke University Chapel, Durham, North Carolina, on December 20, 2009.

The Blessed Virgin Mary is often portrayed as the epitome of sallow, submissive girlhood. But notice how, in the early, physiologically turbulent months of pregnancy, she journeys the 70 miles from Nazareth to the Judean hill country, with no sign of Joseph at her side, let alone a donkey to help her down the dusty road. And when she gets there, she sings a song. And in the song she's pretty articulate about what God's doing and how that's in continuity and contrast with the ways God has worked with Israel up to now.

At the heart of her hymn of praise to the God of reversal and transformation are these unforgettable words. "He has brought down the powerful from their thrones, and lifted up the lowly; he has filled the hungry with good things, and sent the rich away empty."

At first sight, we might ask, what can she be referring to? After all, the Old Testament has no notion of holy poverty. Wealth and possessions are a blessing, and power is a sign of God's favor. So maybe she's talking about herself. Maybe this is what she's saying, "*I* am the hungry one, and God has literally filled me up with a baby who's growing in my womb. And all the powerful ones who thought God was theirs to prescribe and control are out of luck." Or maybe she's talking about Israel. Maybe she's saying, "Israel is the lowly, Israel is the hungry, the other nations are the powerful and the rich, and in the savior Jesus God is turning the tables and restoring the fortunes of Zion."

Or maybe, just maybe, she's showing us the truth about God. Mary's song is really the story of God. God is the mighty, the powerful, who in Jesus comes down from his throne and becomes lowly, and fills the hungry with good things, and then is himself lifted up first on the cross and then in the resurrection and finally in the ascension to the right hand of the Father.

Maybe so. But we're reading these words in Duke Chapel, a mighty throne of the combined powers of academic knowledge, economic leverage, and social influence if ever there was one. It's easy to see why we might want to keep Mary as a sweet teenager, and restrict her song to the personal, historical, or theological sphere. Yet there remains a nagging suspicion about these momentous words. "He has brought down the powerful from their thrones, and lifted up the lowly; he has filled the hungry with good things, and sent the rich away empty." Could she possibly be talking about us?

Now there's a conventional script when it comes to a pastor talking about wealth and power in a setting like the one we're in today. A whole bunch of people will think it's wonderful, it's about time, and maybe even use words like "prophetic." These reactions may in fact be more sophisticated versions of the assumption that Mary isn't really talking about us – she's talking about *them*, that lot over there, who've got more money and power than we've got. After all, I've got a student loan, a house loan, a hundred loans, kids at college, a worrying overdraft, an insecure job, I haven't even had the ready cash to get that rattle underneath my car fixed, so she can't be talking about me. And then another bunch of people will think "It's naïve, it's intrusive, it's inappropriate, you can't just take poetic words from a first-century teenager and translate them artlessly into a financial, social, or economic program; I come to church for heavenly eternities not earthy practicalities."

Well, I'm not planning on following that conventional script today. I don't believe Mary is much interested in that conventional script. This is what her song of praise is really saying. God's divinity has transformed my humanity – personally, economically, socially, politically. God is transforming my life the way pregnancy's transforming my body, making it full of promise and expectation and fertility and joy. And that's what Mary's saying to each one of us today. *Are you allowing God's divinity to transform your humanity?* Are you allowing the Holy Spirit to sing a song of joy and hope through you?

Those are big questions, so I want to break them down into four parts of a conversation. I'd like to ask you to have this conversation with someone over the next few days. If you're feeling short of courage, or a little uncertain, have the conversation with someone with whom you feel very comfortable, maybe someone with whom you're looking forward to spending Christmas. If you're feeling a little more courageous, try having this conversation with someone from a different place in society to yourself, someone you'd usually be worried about offending or ignoring or not understanding or more than likely not even knowing. Here are the four parts of the conversation I'd like to encourage you to have.

Tell me about the ways in which you are rich.
Tell me about the ways in which you are poor.
Let me tell you about the ways in which I am poor.
Let me tell you about the ways in which I am rich.

That's it. Those are the four parts of a conversation I'm encouraging you to have with someone in the next few days. Of course how you're likely to have the conversation depends on who you're having it with. If the person is in desperate need, you're probably going to be starting with discovering the ways in which they are poor. But if the person is in anything other than significant pain, or distress, or hardship, it's most likely you're going to want to begin by discovering the ways in which they're rich. And again, what you say about yourself is likely to depend on what the other person has said about themselves. You're going to want to make human connections, and so if what they've said about their poverty resonates with what you feel about your own poverty, you're likely to want to start with recognizing that. Or if you've felt a sense of common identity in what they've said about the ways they are rich, you're likely to look to start there.

So maybe the conversation might go something like this. You'd say, "Tell me about the ways in which you are rich." And your friend might say, "I appreciate the way you see me for what I am and not just for what I'm not. My childhood was difficult, but I feel rich in the number and variety of people my parents brought into my life. My education wasn't very successful on paper, but I feel rich in the way I learned to read people and look into their hearts. I've never lived in a luxurious home, but I feel rich in the wonder of the birds and their song and the dawn and its beauty and the pouring rain and its refreshment. I've never had many great talents, but I did learn to play the harmonica and I'd love to play you a song I made up myself. I've never had much money, but I have a wealth of friends and somehow, maybe because I've always tried to help people out, there's always been someone who's stepped out of the shadows to help me when I couldn't manage everything myself."

And then maybe you'd say, "Tell me about how the ways in which you are poor." And your friend might say, "You're probably expecting me to talk about how I can't pay the rent and can't find a job. But the real way I feel poor is when I see a person who's a lot worse off than me and I feel powerless to help them. The real times I feel poor are when I see a newcomer to this country trying to make their way and I can't speak enough of their language to be much use to them. The real times I feel poor are when I think of my daughter who died when she was just two and I was just 19 and I miss her with more sadness than I have in my whole heart."

And then maybe you'd say, "May I tell you about the ways in which I am poor?" And your friend might say, "Please do. I'd never thought of you, or someone like you, as poor." And you might say, "My brother was the talented one. I felt like my parents really just wanted boys. I felt I had to apologize for being a girl. All my life I've struggled with envy and jealousy. I've always hated my brother, even though I've never told him and anyone would think we were the best of friends, and I've never been able to trust that the love and achievements and possessions I've had weren't just about to be snatched away from me. In some ways I have a lot but I've never been able really to enjoy what I have. I wonder if I've ever trusted anyone enough to show them who I really am.

"But I'm also rich. Let me tell you about how I'm rich. I've always had the ability to concentrate. I can listen, or read, or even be silent and pray, for hours. And I can paint. I can paint a watercolor, I can paint a miniature, I can paint a wall, I can paint a face, I can paint anything and make it laugh and dance and spring to life. I find it hard to talk to and trust people, but I share my heart through my paintbrush."

When the two of you have shared your wealth and your poverty with one another in this way, you may want to leave it there. But you may choose to go a little further.

Your friend may say to you, "You've told me about how you're rich. Let me tell you about how you're rich. You're rich because you don't have to spend every waking moment of your day earning money so you've got time to do beautiful things and walk with people who're in trouble. And let me tell you how you're poor. You're poor because you've never found a way to love your brother. You're poor because you've never let anyone into your inner circle. You're poor because you don't have enough people like me around you to tell you the truth about yourself."

And then, ever so tentatively, you may find the courage to say to your friend, "You've told me about how you're rich. Let me tell you about how you're rich. You're rich because your laugh is infectious and exciting. You're rich because every child you ever meet loves you. You're rich because you've already been through the worst that life can bring so you live without fear.

But you're also poor. You're poor because you've got a servant heart but no one wants what you have to give right now. You're poor because you're deeply hungry to do something really useful to others but you can't find a way to do it."

That's the point where it's time to ask Mary's question. "Are you allowing the Holy Spirit to sing a song of joy and hope through you?" Through your poverty and through your riches. Can you each see it in one another? Can you each see it in yourselves? Are you letting God turn you into Mary's song?

If you have the first kind of interaction, where you talk about yourselves and how you're each rich and poor, that's great. That's called a conversation. But if you have the second kind of interaction, where you talk about each other, that is even better. That's more than a conversation. That's called a real relationship.

Poverty is a mask we put on a person to cover up their real wealth. And wealth is a disguise we put on a person to hide their profound poverty. Those we call the rich are those in whom we choose to see the wealth but are more reluctant to see the deep poverty. Those we call the poor are those in whom we choose to see the hunger but are slower to see the profound riches.

"He has brought down the powerful from their thrones, and lifted up the lowly; he has filled the hungry with good things, and sent the rich away empty." Turns out Mary really *is* talking about us. God takes that in each of us that is rich, and sees through it to our poverty. And God takes our poverty, and sees past it to our deeper riches.

And every day we come before God and enact these words before him. We think of our neighbor, in person, society, and globe, and we think about their wealth. And we call that praise. We think of our neighbor in their poverty, and we call that intercession. We think of ourselves in our poverty, and we call that confession. We think of ourselves in our riches, and we call that thanksgiving. These are the four parts of prayer. Praise, intercession, confession, thanksgiving. The riches of the world, the poverty of the world, the poverty of ourselves, the riches of ourselves. These are the ways we make that courageous intimate conversation a daily act of renewal.

Have that conversation with someone this week. Make it the transforming moment of your Christmas. Make it the time you remember that in Christ God the mighty left his wealth and took on your poverty that he might make you wealthy in the way he is wealthy. Make it the time you discover another's poverty and another's wealth, and redefine your own wealth and your own poverty. Have that sacred conversation with another person this week.

But have that conversation with God every day. For that's what prayer is. Prayer is when we see God's wealth and God's poverty, and bring to God our poverty and wealth, and our neighbor's too. That's a daily conversation, in which our friendships, our lives, and our world are being transformed. And it finishes like this: "Lord, turn me into Mary's song. Through your Holy Spirit, sing a song of joy and hope through me."

Acknowledgments

It was a great honor to be invited to deliver the Currie Lectures at Austin Presbyterian Theological Seminary in February 2014. The shape of this book emerged in preparation for and reflection on those lectures. I am grateful to Ted Wardlaw and all who made my stay in Austin such a fruitful one.

In addition I am grateful to those who first published the following articles for the opportunity to adapt them and rework them into this book.

"Rethinking Service," *The Cresset* 76(4): 6–14 (April 2013); "Bonhoeffer: Theologian, Activist, Educator: Challenges for the Church of the Coming Generations," in *Interpreting Bonhoeffer: Historical Perspectives, Emerging Issues* (Minneapolis: Fortress Press, 2013): 219–234; "Bell and the Voice of the Church in Time of War," *Crucible*: 26–40 (April–June 2010); "Faith Matters: A Different Way to Pray" *Christian Century* 131(9): 51 (April 30, 2014).

A Nazareth Manifesto, Samuel Wells © 2015 John Wiley & Sons, Ltd. Published 2015 by John Wiley & Sons, Ltd.

Afterword

If you never open yourself to surprises and move into new cultures and new conversations, you never find out what you have long taken for granted. This book arose from two moves: in 2005 from the United Kingdom, and more particularly the Church of England, and more especially still ten years living and working in areas of significant social disadvantage, to the United States, and more particularly North Carolina, and more especially still an elite research university with a somewhat unresolved relationship with the city in which it is set; and then, in 2012, back from that exhilarating environment to the intensity and dynamism of Trafalgar Square in London and an institution steeped in a century of concern for and ministry with the destitute and the excluded. From among the striking and jarring impressions of these two moves came the reflections that make up this book.

Three weeks after joining a university community in North Carolina I joined around thirty administrators at an emergency meeting to discuss how most appropriately to respond to Hurricane Katrina, which had hit the Gulf Coast the previous weekend. I was awestruck by the generosity of heart of many who took annual leave and jumped in minivans and headed down to rebuild houses and clear debris. I had never experienced such an energizing can-do attitude in the face of such an enormous disaster. But I was at the same time baffled by the immediate assumption that rebuilding houses and clearing debris was obviously what was required, and that untrained but tremendously willing volunteers were the best people to provide it. I said to the university president, "I thought all this was the government's job. Isn't that why we *have* a government, to protect us from national threats and address disasters?" He said, "Welcome to America."

And on a humbler level it took me back to a moment a month after my ordination in 1991 when my training incumbent had gone on holiday and there was a gas explosion in which several of my new parishioners were

A Nazareth Manifesto, Samuel Wells © 2015 John Wiley & Sons, Ltd. Published 2015 by John Wiley & Sons, Ltd.

involved. I took the bus across town each day to sit by the bedside of those badly hurt. I noticed some in the congregation were greatly energized. Several set about giving the house and garage of the couple most seriously injured a makeover and really getting the place tidy. I wondered how much of this drive to sort out the lives of the hospitalized was really about the needs of those injured, and how much reflected instead the powerlessness and guilt of their friends. The couple, needless to say, had no particular desire to have a tidy house. As a new pastor I had a greater challenge, not being with the injured, but managing the energy of their wider circle.

When I moved to Duke I said that I did not know what church was if it was not in partnership with the poor. Quickly people started to ask what I intended to do "for" the city. When I commissioned a community minister and set up a neighborhood house where recent graduates would live in a disadvantaged community, one influential person took me to one side and said, "I think you ought to know that the problems of this city are greater than you're going to be able to fix on your own." In the silence that ensued – constituting my many layers of bewilderment at this well-meaning and sincerely intended counsel – this book was born. How could he have imagined I intended to "fix" this city? Why would he think the only way to interact with a challenging neighborhood was to fix it? What made him see the city as the repository of the problem and I (or he) as the overburdened source of the solution? What was I truly trying to achieve, in what ways was it so basic to my faith, theology, and notion of ministry that I hardly knew how to begin to explain it, and how could I learn to express it better in a context where it was clearly so novel? These were the questions that helped me work out what I needed to say.

Three developments characterized the kind of book it became. First, I started to teach a course in the Sanford School of Public Policy at Duke University in which I looked at various ways of engaging social disadvantage. Over 150 undergraduates took the course over the next four years and in teaching them I took the subject matter outside the field of theology, refined the arguments, discovered underlying assumptions, encountered countless examples, and pondered many stumbling-blocks. The course reflected the growing culture of "service" in American college settings, and I found myself invited to speak on a number of campuses about the secular religion of service that was becoming so widespread among students and so prized by administrators across the USA. Meanwhile over fifty students lived for shorter or longer periods in the community house in Durham and their experiences shaped the imagination of the course and the ministry as a whole. I am glad to say both the course and the house continue.

Second, I wrote, with Marcia Owen, a book called *Living Without Enemies* (Downers Grove: IVP, 2011) in which I mapped my initial reflections in this field onto Marcia's remarkable ministry among those affected by gun violence in Durham, North Carolina – and we both discovered it was a pretty tidy fit. This small book met the need for a more popular way into these questions and writing it helped me clarify what the theological and pastoral questions really were. That book is different to this one in several respects. It is written in a more accessible style. Its opening chapter remains a succinct summary of the territory of working for, working with, being for, and being with. It is focused around a particular issue – responding to gun violence and, in particular, homicide in one American city. It offers a detailed account of three significant features of being with – silence, touch, and words – and is thus much more a "how-to" book than this one is. It talks about the practice of meeting in small groups to support ex-offenders and congregating in outdoor spaces on the sites of tragic deaths. I think of the two books as a more popular and a more demanding version of the same broad thesis.

Third, I needed to reflect the setting in which I was writing. When I wrote *Improvisation* (Grand Rapids, MI: Brazos, 2004) I was living in an underclass neighborhood in England. Its arguments assumed an upside-down kingdom. One could read this book, in the same spirit, as an attempt not to "block" poverty and adversity but to overaccept them; not to strive with all one's might to overturn and eradicate them but to make them the occasion to renarrate one's story and recast one's location in the scriptural story and to see Christ transfigured through appropriate encounter with them. When I wrote *God's Companions* (Oxford: Blackwell, 2006) I was the priest of a more regular congregation and was seeking to distil the ordinary and the unremarkable. The argument of this book picks up the themes of *God's Companions* by showing a myriad ways in which the church finds abundance in the face of those the world rejects. Being with is an ethic of abundance, because it assumes that God has already saved us – and thus that our fervid and anxious work to secure our salvation is transformed – and that our salvation is encountered in the face of the poor, of which the world seems to experience no shortage. From the setting of Duke University, where I conceived this book, it was appropriate to think about how people with more institutional resources might reflect wisely about mission. I see this book as the third in a series of which *Improvisation* and *God's Companions* are the first and second.

When I used to convene a group of clergy in Norwich we each used to suggest a book the whole group should read. And so it was that my colleague Richard Woodham recommended a book which gave me the vocabulary of working for, working with, and being with. The book was Sarah White and Romy Tiongco, *Doing Theology and Development: Meeting the Challenge of Poverty* (Edinburgh: St. Andrew Press, 1997). The terms are only used in a few pages of the introduction (11–15); neither author has subsequently expanded on these notions. But it is hard for me to imagine how my thinking on these matters would have taken shape without them. I added the notion of being for after reading David Kelsey's absorbing study, *Eccentric Existence: A Theological Anthropology* (2 volumes, Louisville, KY: Westminster John Knox, 2009).

I have many other causes for deep thanks. Rebecca Harkin at Wiley-Blackwell has been an editor without parallel. My gratitude for her partnership on this and many other publications, and especially her enthusiasm for this book, is profound. Rebekah Eklund worked as my research assistant at Duke for several years and we collaborated on many projects: she did a great deal of work on this book, and many chapters bear the marks of her wisdom, grace, and self-effacing insight. To enjoy her challenge, attention to detail, heart for the outcast, and humor has made so many labors a joy. Anna Poulson played a similar role in relation to other parts of the manuscript, and in particular Chapter 10 and Chapter 11, which were greatly enriched by her careful hand and expert judgment. She and her husband Mark brought into the world a gift called Lydia, who lived and, after three years, in January 2010, died in the arms of indescribable love; their witness is everything this book aspires to. Adrienne Koch has been a wise and generous partner on many initiatives; I am grateful for the work she and Jennifer Jaynes have done on the index to this book.

The community that formed around the residential initiative and in particular the public policy course at Duke was a very special one. Keith Daniel and Adam Hollowell played crucial roles in that work, and I am proud to have been alongside them. Lucy Worth, Gaston Warner, Jeff Ensminger, Dorcas Bradley, and Bruce Puckett also shaped the vision. Nathan Bills, Cynthia Curtis, Leigh Edwards, Kori Jones, Craig Kocher, and Mark Storslee provided wonderful teaching assistance and perceptive ministry at different times; I am glad for what I learned from each one of them, and I am especially in debt to Nathan who first introduced me to the work of

John McKnight. Abby Kocher not only shaped the course, but as community minister embarked on a considerable act of trust by putting into practice what this book, as it emerged, was seeking to articulate. I recall in 2007 one neighborhood resident described Abby as having a "beautiful way of just being"; that is as ringing an endorsement of community ministry as anyone could hope for. My thanks to Marcia Owen have been expressed elsewhere – I admired her ministry so much I wrote a book about it; but it would be hard to imagine the experiment in being with that Keith and Abby led so faithfully without an example like Marcia to learn from.

Before, during, and after my time at Duke there have been many conversation partners who have deepened my notion of being with. Among them I owe a debt to David Trelawny-Ross, Neville Black, Colin Marsh, Ray Barfield, Tony Galanos, David Warbrick, Emily Klein, Andrew Grinnell, Robert Pfeiffer, Colin Miller, John Kiess, John Inge, Harriet Panting, and Bob Holman.

At St. Martin-in-the-Fields, where the majority of the book has been written, I am in an institution that has a great reputation for working for and with those on whom the world has turned its back – but which I believe has done its best work when it has sought simply to be with such people. I am grateful to my clergy colleagues Richard Carter, Katherine Hedderly, Clare Herbert, and Will Morris and to a host of lay leaders and good companions who have shown me what being with means, have challenged me to discover more specifically what it means in this context, and have in many cases made space for me to think, read, write, speak, and develop the ideas in this book.

First among those I am called to be with is my family. Anyone engaged on a worthy project may be unnerved by the character Mrs. Jellyby in Charles Dickens' *Bleak House*, who is so devoted to overseas mission that she is incapable of seeing the profound emotional and practical need in her own household. The irony promises to be even greater for a writer whose talking about being with has so often taken him far away. Nonetheless I am blessed beyond measure to have such generous and forgiving companions as Jo, Laurence, and Stephanie to be with me and weigh with me each day the truth of what I am trying to say.

The book is dedicated to Stanley Hauerwas. It is full of things I must have learned somewhere – but I forget where. When I cannot remember where I learned something, the first question to ask is, did I learn it from Stanley? Often I did. More often than I can say. This book is a small token of gratitude.

Scriptural Index

A Nazareth Manifesto, Samuel Wells © 2015 John Wiley & Sons, Ltd. Published 2015 by John Wiley & Sons, Ltd.

Subject Index

Abel *see* Cain and Abel
abundance, 29-30, 116–117, 249,
     253–257, 259, 262, 264
   community, 250, 254, 257, 258, 261,
      264
   gifts, 28, 199
   and heaven, 58
   and Jesus, 165
   joy, 9, 139, 184
   life, 74, 130, 234
   resources, 29, 52, 115, 159
   wonder, 130, 131
abuse(d), 20, 22, 157–158, 173, 175,
     177, 178, 195
academic culture/discourse, 12, 18,
     172, 189, 299
Adam and Eve, 58, 89
addiction, 20, 22, 41, 151, 171, 172,
     256, 285
Agamben, Giorgio, 13, 143, 146
alcohol, 22, 172, 177, 179, 192, 198
Alinsky, Saul, 109, 112–113, 115, 221
Allen, Woody, 233, 234
altruism, 29, 116, 181
Alzheimer's, 293, 296
Americans, 188, 189, 210, 261, 262
Anglicans, 11, 17, 204
Anglicanism *see* Anglicans
anxiety, 5, 57, 79, 106, 126, 130, 141
   and fear, 75, 83
apocalypse, 88, 245

apostles, 79, 202, 216
Aquinas, Thomas, 16
ark of the covenant, the, 72, 234
ascension, 7, 82, 153, 159, 167, 204, 299
Ascension Day, 82, 204
asset-based community development,
     229, 263
atonement, 11, 24, 72, 73, 239–244,
     259, 293, 296
atoning *see* atonement
attention, 126–129, 259
   loving, 162, 222, 263
   pay(ing), 141, 175, 176, 275
   and presence *see* presence
Augustine, 137–140, 143, 148

Babylon, 58, 67, 70–72, 74–75, 88–89,
     151, 234–235
Balthasar, Hans Urs von, 142
Bangladesh(is), 113, 115
baptism, 65, 67, 75, 76, 77, 85, 205
   by John, 78
Basil, 16
beauty, 57, 62, 75, 128, 141, 223, 246,
     249
   of the church, 61
   of creation, 137, 300
   of God, the Lord, 7, 74, 143
   of holiness, 52, 295
   of worship, 272
Beckett, Samuel, 36